Computational Intelligence
in Healthcare

Computational Intelligence in Healthcare

Editors

Giovanna Castellano
Gabriella Casalino

MDPI • Basel • Beijing • Wuhan • Barcelona • Belgrade • Manchester • Tokyo • Cluj • Tianjin

Editors
Giovanna Castellano
University of Bari Aldo Moro
Italy

Gabriella Casalino
University of Bari Aldo Moro
Italy

Editorial Office
MDPI
St. Alban-Anlage 66
4052 Basel, Switzerland

This is a reprint of articles from the Special Issue published online in the open access journal *Electronics* (ISSN 2079-9292) (available at: https://www.mdpi.com/journal/electronics/special_issues/CI_healthcare).

For citation purposes, cite each article independently as indicated on the article page online and as indicated below:

LastName, A.A.; LastName, B.B.; LastName, C.C. Article Title. *Journal Name* **Year**, *Volume Number*, Page Range.

ISBN 978-3-0365-2377-4 (Hbk)
ISBN 978-3-0365-2378-1 (PDF)

© 2021 by the authors. Articles in this book are Open Access and distributed under the Creative Commons Attribution (CC BY) license, which allows users to download, copy and build upon published articles, as long as the author and publisher are properly credited, which ensures maximum dissemination and a wider impact of our publications.

The book as a whole is distributed by MDPI under the terms and conditions of the Creative Commons license CC BY-NC-ND.

Contents

About the Editors vii

Gabriella Casalino and Giovanna Castellano
Special Issue on Computational Intelligence for Healthcare
Reprinted from: *Electronics* **2021**, *10*, 1841, doi:10.3390/electronics10151841 1

Arianna Consiglio, Gabriella Casalino, Giovanna Castellano, Giorgio Grillo, Elda Perlino, Gennaro Vessio and Flavio Licciulli
Explaining Ovarian Cancer Gene Expression Profiles with Fuzzy Rules and Genetic Algorithms
Reprinted from: *Electronics* **2021**, *10*, 375, doi:10.3390/electronics10040375 5

Giovanni Dimauro, Pierpasquale Colagrande, Roberto Carlucci, Mario Ventura, Vitoantonio Bevilacqua and Danilo Caivano
CRISPRLearner: A Deep Learning-Based System to Predict CRISPR/Cas9 sgRNA On-Target Cleavage Efficiency
Reprinted from: *Electronics* **2019**, *8*, 1478, doi:10.3390/electronics8121478 19

Muhammad Ijaz, Gang Li, Huiquan Wang, Ahmed M. El-Sherbeeny, Yussif Moro Awelisah, Ling Lin, Anis Koubaa and Alam Noor
Intelligent Fog-Enabled Smart Healthcare System for Wearable Physiological Parameter Detection
Reprinted from: *Electronics* **2020**, *9*, 2015, doi:10.3390/electronics9122015 29

Giuseppe Coviello, Gianfranco Avitabile and Antonello Florio
A Synchronized Multi-Unit Wireless Platform for Long-Term Activity Monitoring
Reprinted from: *Electronics* **2020**, *9*, 1118, doi:10.3390/electronics9071118 61

Christian Morbidoni, Alessandro Cucchiarelli, Sandro Fioretti and Francesco Di Nardo
A Deep Learning Approach to EMG-Based Classification of Gait Phases during Level Ground Walking
Reprinted from: *Electronics* **2019**, *8*, 894, doi:10.3390/electronics8080894 81

Eufemia Lella, Andrea Pazienza, Domenico Lofù, Roberto Anglani, Felice Vitulano
An Ensemble Learning Approach Based on Diffusion Tensor Imaging Measures for Alzheimer's Disease Classification
Reprinted from: *Electronics* **2021**, *10*, 249, doi:10.3390/electronics10030249 97

Hannah Inbarani H., Ahmad Taher Azar and Jothi G
Leukemia Image Segmentation Using a Hybrid Histogram-Based Soft Covering Rough K-Means Clustering Algorithm
Reprinted from: *Electronics* **2020**, *9*, 188, doi:10.3390/electronics9010188 113

Jyostna Devi Bodapati, N. Veeranjaneyulu, Shaik Nagur Shareef, Saqib Hakak, Muhammad Bilal, Praveen Kumar Reddy Maddikunta. and Ohyun Jo
Blended Multi-Modal Deep ConvNet Features for Diabetic Retinopathy Severity Prediction
Reprinted from: *Electronics* **2020**, *9*, 914, doi:10.3390/electronics9060914 135

Sarah A. Ebiaredoh-Mienye, Ebenezer Esenogho and Theo G. Swart
Integrating Enhanced Sparse Autoencoder-Based Artificial Neural Network Technique and Softmax Regression for Medical Diagnosis
Reprinted from: *Electronics* **2020**, *9*, 1963, doi:10.3390/electronics9111963 153

Vytautas Abromavičius, Firstname Lastname and Firstname Lastname
Two-Stage Monitoring of Patients in Intensive Care Unit for Sepsis Prediction Using Non-Overfitted Machine Learning Models
Reprinted from: *Electronics* **2020**, *9*, 1133, doi:10.3390/electronics9071133 . . . . **167**

Junsheng Yu, Xiangqing Wang, Xiaodong Chen and Jinglin Guo
Searching for Premature Ventricular Contraction from Electrocardiogram by Using One-Dimensional Convolutional Neural Network
Reprinted from: *Electronics* **2020**, *9*, 1790, doi:10.3390/electronics9111790 . . . . **181**

Kathiravan Srinivasan, Nivedhitha Mahendran, Durai Raj Vincent, Chuan-Yu Chang and Shabbir Syed-Abdul
Realizing an Integrated Multistage Support Vector Machine Model for Augmented Recognition of Unipolar Depression
Reprinted from: *Electronics* **2020**, *9*, 647, doi:10.3390/electronics9040647 . . . . **201**

About the Editors

Giovanna Castellano is an Associate Professor at the Department of Computer Science, University of Bari Aldo Moro, Italy, where she is the coordinator of the Computational Intelligence Lab. She is member of IEEE Computational Intelligence Society, the EUSFLAT society and the INDAM-GNCS society. Her research interests are in the area of Computational Intelligence and Computer Vision. She has published more than 200 papers in international journals and conferences. She is Associate Editor of several international journals. She was Co-organizer of the 4th EUSFLAT European Summer School on Fuzzy Logic and Applications (SFLA2018). She was General chair of the IEEE Conference on Evolving and Adaptive Intelligent Systems (IEEE-EAIS2020).

Gabriella Casalino is currently Assistant Professor at the Computational Intelligence LAB of the department of Informatics, University of Bari. Her research activity is focused on Computational Intelligence with a particular interest for data analysis. Three are the main themes she is currently working on: intelligent data analysis, computational intelligence for eHealth, and data stream mining. She is active in the computer science community as a reviewer for international journals and conferences. She is also involved in the organizing committees of international conferences. She is also the Associate Editor of the *Journal of Intelligent and Fuzzy Systems* and she is Guest Co-Editor of several Special Issues on international journals.

Editorial

Special Issue on Computational Intelligence for Healthcare

Gabriella Casalino * and Giovanna Castellano *

Computer Science Department, University of Bari Aldo Moro, 70125 Bari, Italy
* Correspondence: gabriella.casalino@uniba.it (G.C.); giovanna.castellano@uniba.it (G.C.)

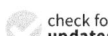

Citation: Casalino, G.; Castellano, G. Special Issue on Computational Intelligence for Healthcare. *Electronics* **2021**, *10*, 1841. https://doi.org/10.3390/electronics10151841

Received: 21 July 2021
Accepted: 27 July 2021
Published: 31 July 2021

Publisher's Note: MDPI stays neutral with regard to jurisdictional claims in published maps and institutional affiliations.

Copyright: © 2021 by the authors. Licensee MDPI, Basel, Switzerland. This article is an open access article distributed under the terms and conditions of the Creative Commons Attribution (CC BY) license (https://creativecommons.org/licenses/by/4.0/).

The number of patient health data has been estimated to have reached 2314 exabytes by 2020. Traditional data analysis techniques are unsuitable to extract useful information from such vast quantity of data. Thus, intelligent data analysis methods combining human expertise and computational models for accurate and in-depth data analysis are necessary. The technological revolution and medical advances made by combining vast quantities of available data, cloud computing services, and AI-based solutions can provide expert insight and analysis on a mass scale and at a relatively low cost. Computational intelligence (CI) methods such as fuzzy models, artificial neural networks, evolutionary algorithms, and probabilistic methods have recently emerged as promising tools for the development and application of intelligent systems in healthcare practice. CI-based systems can learn from data and evolve according to changes in the environments by taking into account the uncertainty characterizing health data, including omics data, clinical data, sensor, and imaging data. The use of CI in healthcare can improve the processing of such data to develop intelligent solutions for prevention, diagnosis, treatment, and follow-up, as well as for analysis of administrative processes.

The present Special Issue on Computational Intelligence for healthcare is intended to show the potential and the practical impacts of CI techniques in challenging healthcare applications. The Special Issue received several submissions, all of which went through a rigorous peer-review process. After the review process, twelve papers were selected on the basis of the review ratings and comments. These selected papers range over main applications of CI in healthcare.

A special case of medical data is the data generated by omics technologies, which enable DNA decoding and genome sequencing. Such data represent the expression of genes or portions thereof in experimental subjects or in cell lines produced in the laboratory. The study of the complex interactions between genes makes it possible to understand their role in the course of a particular disease. In particular, the analysis of the different biological levels allows us to better address the knowledge of pathogenetic mechanisms at the molecular level, allowing the identification of biomarkers that allow us to improve the diagnosis or even to plan personalized therapies However, the complexity of the relationships and the uncertainty present in the data collected and in the phenomena studied make it necessary to use specific methods for the treatment of information with these characteristics. The first paper, entitled, "Explaining Ovarian Cancer Gene Expression Profiles with Fuzzy Rules and Genetic Algorithms" [1], addresses the analysis of gene expression data for approaching the study of expression profiles in ovarian cancer compared to other ovarian diseases. The work combines a feature selection among genes that is guided by the genetic algorithm into the creation of fuzzy if–then rules that explain how classes can be distinguished by observing changes in the expression of selected genes. After testing several parameters, a final model was obtained consisting of 10 genes involved in the molecular pathways of cancer and 10 rules that correctly classify all samples. Omics data of a different kind, namely sgRNA sequences, have been analyzed in the paper "CRISPRLearner: a deep learning-based system to predict CRISPR/Cas9 sgRNA on-target cleavage efficiency" [2]. In particular, ten datasets were considered. After a pre-processing step, including data standardization and augmentation, a convolutional neural network was used to predict sgRNA cleavage efficiency. Experiments on benchmark datasets showed the effectiveness of the proposed method in correctly identifying the disease. Moreover, a comparison with state-of-the-art methods shows the superiority of the proposed deep-learning-based model.

In addition, detection and analysis of physiological data acquired from sensors are an essential process in smart healthcare applications. Indeed, with the advent of low-cost sensors and fast networks, a new discipline called Internet of Medical Things (IoMT) has emerged. It allows a continuous monitoring of patients through intelligent objects. Physiological data analysis can be performed in fog computing to abridge the excess latency introduced by cloud computing. However, the latency for the emergency health status and overloading in fog environment become key challenges for smart healthcare. The paper "Intelligent Fog-Enabled Smart Healthcare System for Wearable Physiological Parameter Detection" [3] presents a novel healthcare architecture for physiological parameter detection that resolves these problems. The overall system is built upon three layers. In the first layer, data from the wearable devices of patients are subjected to fault detection in a personal data assistant (PDA) via a rapid kernel principal component analysis (RK-PCA) algorithm. Then, in the second layer, the faultless data are processed to remove redundancy via a new fuzzy assisted objective optimization by ratio analysis (FaMOORA) algorithm. A two-level health-hidden Markov model (2L-2HMM) finds the user's health status from temporal variations in data collected from wearable devices. Finally, the user's health status is detected in the third layer through a hybrid machine learning algorithm called SpikQ-Net, and according to the user's health status, immediate action is taken. The proposed tri-fog health model is validated by a thorough simulation showing better achievements in latency, execution time, detection accuracy, and system stability.

When different sensors are used for data acquisition, synchronization is a critical factor. In the article "A Synchronized Multi-Unit Wireless Platform for Long-Term Activity Monitoring", a time-synchronized multi-unit, multi-sensor, and multi-rate acquisition system for kinematic and static analysis is proposed [4]. It is a wearable multi-board acquisition system for offline activity monitoring. A master–slave architecture was used to synchronize measures acquired from different sensors. Moreover, a mobile Android application was developed in order to manage the data acquisition. The high modularity of the proposed platform makes it general-purpose. Indeed, experiments on different scenarios have been carried out to validate its performance. In particular, a case study of surface electromyography (sEMG) was used for monitoring muscle activities during walking. sEMG signals are also used in the article "A Deep Learning Approach to EMG-Based Classification of Gait Phases During Level Ground Walking" for gait phase classification [5]. Specifically, an Artificial Neural Network (ANN) was proposed to classify gait events and to predict foot–floor contact. The use of ANN has allowed the automatic selection of relevant features in data, thus avoiding the data engineering phase, which is necessary when using other machine learning algorithms. In vivo experiments have been conducted at the Movement Analysis Laboratory of Università Politecnica delle Marche to acquire gait signals. Raw signals were pre-processed to obtain the final labeled segments of the walking phases. Four different architectures of the multi layer perceptron algorithm (MLP) were proposed by modifying the model structure, and the results have been compared. The aim of the analysis was to detect the transitions between gait phases. Furthermore, a comparison with a feature-based (FB) method has shown that the best MLP model is more accurate in detecting phase changes.

A further essential and crucial task in healthcare is image analysis to support medical diagnosis. In particular, recent advances in neuroimaging techniques, such as diffusion tensor imaging (DTI), represent a crucial resource for brain image analysis in order to detect alterations related to severe neurodegenerative disorders, such as Alzheimer's disease (AD). The paper "An Ensemble Learning Approach Based on Diffusion Tensor Imaging Measures for Alzheimer's Disease Classification" [6] presents an ensemble learning approach for the automatic discrimination between healthy controls and AD patients, using DTI measures as predicting features and a soft-voting ensemble approach for the classification. The proposed approach, efficiently combining single classifiers trained on specific groups of features, is able to improve classification performances with respect to the comprehensive approach of the concatenation of global features and at the same time reducing the dimensionality of the feature space and in turn the computational effort. A different task on images has been implemented in the article "Leukemia Image Segmentation by Using a Hybrid Histogram-Based Soft Covering Rough k-Means Clustering Algorithm" [7]. Image segmentation is the task of partitioning a given image in not-overlapped areas to detect regions of interest. Particularly, authors propose a leukemia diagnosis support system through nucleus segmentation. A soft set together with a rough set were used to represent the uncertainty in nucleus images. A four-step pipeline is proposed. Images are firstly pre-processed, and then a clustering algorithm is applied. A histogram-based method (HSCRKM) is proposed to identify the optimal number of cluster. Then, different features are extracted from the images, and the resulting data are used to predict the areas in the image as belonging to the leukemia tumor class or the healthy class. Several clustering and classification methods have been compared to identify the optimal pair. Results show that the proposed HSCRKM overcomes the compared clustering methods. Moreover, all the classification models increased their performance when trained on groups coming from HSCRKM. However, among all the considered prediction methods, logistic regression and neural network provided the best performance (average accuracy higher than 90%). Diabetic Retinopathy (DR) images are analyzed in the paper "Blended Multi-Modal Deep Convnet Features for Diabetic Retinopathy severity Prediction" for an early recognition of the disease [8]. Both uni-modal and multi-modal approaches, which combine data coming from different sources, were used to predict the severity level of the disease (healthy, mild, moderate, severe, and proliferative). To this aim, Deep Neural Networks (DNN) have been proposed. In particular, in the uni-modal approach, a single pre-trained ConvNet is used to extract the final feature representation. In the multi-modal approach, the final feature representation is obtained by blending deep features extracted from multiple ConvNets.

One main factor that hampers the effectiveness of CI methods in the medical domain is the imbalanced nature of medical data due to non-uniform distribution of the number of instances per class. The paper entitled "Integrating Enhanced Sparse Autoencoder-Based Artificial Neural Network Technique and Softmax Regression for Medical Diagnosis" [9] addresses the problem of unbalancement in medical datasets to create robust models for the prediction of different diseases. The authors propose an approach that integrates an enhanced sparse autoencoder (SAE) for effective feature learning and an optimized Softmax regression for robust classification. When employed for the prediction of three different diseases, namely chronic kidney disease, cervical cancer, and heart disease, the proposed method provides higher test accuracies compared to other machine learning algorithms. In addition, the paper "Two-Stage Monitoring of Patients in Intensive Care Unit for Sepsis Prediction Using Non-Overfitted Machine Learning Models" [10] addresses the problem of unbalanced clinical data. In this case, data concern patients in the Intensive Care Unit (ICU) to face the problem of early detection of sepsis, collected within the PhysioNet/Computing in Cardiology Challenge 2019. The labeled clinical dataset includes only 2% records with the sepsis label, leading to highly unbalanced dataset. To address these issues, the authors propose a method using two separate ensemble models to take into the account the amount of time the patients spent in the ICU. A total of 44 different methods, based on decision trees, naive Gaussian Bayes, SVM, and ensemble learners,are compared. Results show the effectiveness of the proposed method. Moreover, the considered machine learning models return comparable utility score values when the number of features is reduced, suggesting that feature engineering is necessary.

Long-term electrocardiogram (ECG) is used to detect Premature Ventricular Contraction (PVC) in the paper "Searching for Premature Ventricular Contraction from Electrocardiogram by Using One-Dimensional Convolutional Neural Network" [11]. A one-dimensional convolutional neural network (CNN) has been used for the prediction tasks. It allows avoiding pre-processing phases on data, as required by common machine learning algorithms, and it is able to directly analyze raw data while extracting the most relevant features from it. High performance values are returned by the diagnostic system (accuracy of 99.64%).

Finally, a multistage support vector machine model has been proposed for early recognition of Unipolar Depression (UD) disease in the article "Realizing an integrated multistage support vector machine model for augmented recognition of unipolar depression" [12]. A pre-processing phase for feature ranking is implemented in order to reduce the data dimensionality. Comparison with other machine learning algorithms has shown the effectiveness of the proposed approach in correctly identifying the disease, other than overcoming their performance. Moreover, the recursive feature selection method has proved to be able to improve the accuracy of the classifiers.

Acknowledgments: The guest editors Gabriella Casalino and Giovanna Castellano would like to thank the authors for their contributions, the reviewers for their effort in reviewing the manuscripts, and the editorial staff of the MDPI journal *Electronics* for their support in producing this Special Issue. Gabriella Casalino acknowledges funding from the Italian Ministry of Education, University and Research through the European PON project AIM (Attraction and International Mobility), nr. 1852414, activity 2, line 1. This work was partially supported by INdAM GNCS within the research project "Computational Intelligence methods for Digital Health". The guest editors are with the CITEL—Centro Interdipartimentale di Telemedicina, University of Bari Aldo Moro.

Conflicts of Interest: The authors declare no conflict of interest.

References

1. Consiglio, A.; Casalino, G.; Castellano, G.; Grillo, G.; Perlino, E.; Vessio, G.; Licciulli, F. Explaining Ovarian Cancer Gene Expression Profiles with Fuzzy Rules and Genetic Algorithms. *Electronics* **2021**, *10*, 375. [CrossRef]
2. Dimauro, G.; Colagrande, P.; Carlucci, R.; Ventura, M.; Bevilacqua, V.; Caivano, D. CRISPRLearner: A deep learning-based system to predict CRISPR/Cas9 sgRNA on-target cleavage efficiency. *Electronics* **2019**, *8*, 1478. [CrossRef]
3. Ijaz, M.; Li, G.; Wang, H.; El-Sherbeeny, A.M.; Moro Awelisah, Y.; Lin, L.; Koubaa, A.; Noor, A. Intelligent Fog-Enabled Smart Healthcare System for Wearable Physiological Parameter Detection. *Electronics* **2020**, *9*, 2015. [CrossRef]
4. Coviello, G.; Avitabile, G.; Florio, A. A synchronized multi-unit wireless platform for long-term activity monitoring. *Electronics* **2020**, *9*, 1118. [CrossRef]
5. Morbidoni, C.; Cucchiarelli, A.; Fioretti, S.; Di Nardo, F. A deep learning approach to EMG-based classification of gait phases during level ground walking. *Electronics* **2019**, *8*, 894. [CrossRef]
6. Lella, E.; Pazienza, A.; Lofù, D.; Anglani, R.; Vitulano, F. An Ensemble Learning Approach Based on Diffusion Tensor Imaging Measures for Alzheimer's Disease Classification. *Electronics* **2021**, *10*, 249. [CrossRef]
7. Inbarani H, H.; Azar, A.T. Leukemia image segmentation using a hybrid histogram-based soft covering rough k-means clustering algorithm. *Electronics* **2020**, *9*, 188. [CrossRef]
8. Bodapati, J.D.; Naralasetti, V.; Shareef, S.N.; Hakak, S.; Bilal, M.; Maddikunta, P.K.R.; Jo, O. Blended multi-modal deep convnet features for diabetic retinopathy severity prediction. *Electronics* **2020**, *9*, 914. [CrossRef]
9. Ebiaredoh-Mienye, S.A.; Esenogho, E.; Swart, T.G. Integrating Enhanced Sparse Autoencoder-Based Artificial Neural Network Technique and Softmax Regression for Medical Diagnosis. *Electronics* **2020**, *9*, 1963. [CrossRef]
10. Abromavičius, V.; Plonis, D.; Tarasevičius, D.; Serackis, A. Two-Stage Monitoring of Patients in Intensive Care Unit for Sepsis Prediction Using Non-Overfitted Machine Learning Models. *Electronics* **2020**, *9*, 1133. [CrossRef]
11. Yu, J.; Wang, X.; Chen, X.; Guo, J. Searching for Premature Ventricular Contraction from Electrocardiogram by Using One-Dimensional Convolutional Neural Network. *Electronics* **2020**, *9*, 1790. [CrossRef]
12. Srinivasan, K.; Mahendran, N.; Vincent, D.R.; Chang, C.Y.; Syed-Abdul, S. Realizing an integrated multistage support vector machine model for augmented recognition of unipolar depression. *Electronics* **2020**, *9*, 647. [CrossRef]

Article

Explaining Ovarian Cancer Gene Expression Profiles with Fuzzy Rules and Genetic Algorithms

Arianna Consiglio [1,*], Gabriella Casalino [2], Giovanna Castellano [2], Giorgio Grillo [1], Elda Perlino [1], Gennaro Vessio [2] and Flavio Licciulli [1]

[1] Institute for Biomedical Technologies, National Research Council, 70126 Bari, Italy; giorgio.grillo@ba.itb.cnr.it (G.G.); elda.perlino@ba.itb.cnr.it (E.P.); flavio.licciulli@ba.itb.cnr.it (F.L.)
[2] Department of Computer Science, University of Bari Aldo Moro, 70125 Bari, Italy; gabriella.casalino@uniba.it (G.C.); giovanna.castellano@uniba.it (G.C.); gennaro.vessio@uniba.it (G.V.)
* Correspondence: arianna.consiglio@ba.itb.cnr.it

Citation: Consiglio, A.; Casalino, G.; Castellano, G.; Grillo, G.; Perlino, E.; Vessio, G.; Licciulli, F. Explaining Ovarian Cancer Gene Expression Profiles with Fuzzy Rules and Genetic Algorithms. *Electronics* **2021**, *10*, 375. https://doi.org/10.3390/electronics10040375

Academic Editor: Jun Liu
Received: 31 December 2020
Accepted: 30 January 2021
Published: 4 February 2021

Publisher's Note: MDPI stays neutral with regard to jurisdictional claims in published maps and institutional affiliations.

Copyright: © 2021 by the authors. Licensee MDPI, Basel, Switzerland. This article is an open access article distributed under the terms and conditions of the Creative Commons Attribution (CC BY) license (https://creativecommons.org/licenses/by/4.0/).

Abstract: The analysis of gene expression data is a complex task, and many tools and pipelines are available to handle big sequencing datasets for case-control (bivariate) studies. In some cases, such as pilot or exploratory studies, the researcher needs to compare more than two groups of samples consisting of a few replicates. Both standard statistical bioinformatic pipelines and innovative deep learning models are unsuitable for extracting interpretable patterns and information from such datasets. In this work, we apply a combination of fuzzy rule systems and genetic algorithms to analyze a dataset composed of 21 samples and 6 classes, useful for approaching the study of expression profiles in ovarian cancer, compared to other ovarian diseases. The proposed method is capable of performing a feature selection among genes that is guided by the genetic algorithm, and of building a set of *if-then* rules that explain how classes can be distinguished by observing changes in the expression of selected genes. After testing several parameters, the final model consists of 10 genes involved in the molecular pathways of cancer and 10 rules that correctly classify all samples.

Keywords: computational intelligence; classification; fuzzy inference systems; genetic algorithms; next-generation sequencing; ovarian cancer; interpretable models

1. Introduction

Among the most common cancers in women, ovarian cancer is the most lethal, due to its late symptoms and diagnosis, and its onset can be a primary tumor or secondary tumor of the fallopian tube or endometrium [1]. Based on histopathology and molecular genetic alterations, ovarian carcinomas are divided into five main types that can be considered as different diseases: high-grade serous, endometrioid, clear cell, mucinous, and low-grade serous carcinomas [2]. There is currently no reliable test to diagnose asymptomatic ovarian cancer, and any study of the molecular processes that are active in its proliferating cells can contribute to the identification of new molecular biomarkers for efficient diagnosis, prognosis, and therapy.

Next-Generation Sequencing (NGS) technologies provide researchers with experimental datasets that describe the molecular profile of cancerous cells by allowing them to estimate the expression of genes in a tissue sample, which is the number of copies of a gene that are present as Ribonucleic Acid (RNA) fragments and decoded by the sequencer. Standard bioinformatic pipelines are used to compute gene expressions and to compare samples for significant expression differences, with differential expression analysis [3].

However, NGS experiments are quite expensive and require further laboratory validation of the most significant results, as they can present noise in the data that stems from the inherent complexity of the technology. This is why many researchers use NGS with a limited number of samples to extract the most evident molecular activities and validate those results only on a larger number of samples. Moreover, NGS results are highly dependent on the laboratory experimental settings used and the datasets produced with different technical conditions (sequencer type, tissue type, tissue conservation, etc.) are not directly comparable. This is why NGS data are mainly exploited for case-control studies with only two conditions.

Due to the digitalization process, the biomedical domain represents a source of valuable data. A growing amount of this data is generated every day, ranging from vital parameters to omics data and output from imaging devices. Therefore, machine learning techniques have been used extensively in the medical domain, as they can automatically derive useful models for making predictions, and detecting patterns that reveal hidden relationships in the data [4]. Automatic systems have been proposed to support medical experts while avoiding repetitive tasks. Moreover, thanks to the availability of this huge amount of data and the high computational capabilities of modern systems, novel insights, which could not have been discovered through manual analyses, have been returned by automatic techniques.

Machine learning algorithms have been applied to biological data of the most varied diseases such as neurodegenerative diseases [5,6] and cancer [7,8], just to name a few. Computational Intelligence is a research branch dealing with nature-inspired algorithms, such as fuzzy logic, neural networks, and evolutionary algorithms, which can process numerical data to address complex problems that may be difficult to solve with traditional machine learning algorithms [9]. Neural networks have gained a lot of attention in recent years and their "deep" variants have led to Deep Learning (DL), which has redefined the state-of-the-art performance in several domains, including the medical one [10]. In particular, DL algorithms have been successfully applied to omics data for early disease prediction or the extraction of meaningful biomarkers [11,12]. However, DL techniques have two main drawbacks: they are not interpretable, even though research is moving in this direction [13], and they need a huge amount of data to learn a model.

On the contrary, fuzzy logic has been widely used in the medical field due to its ability to represent the uncertainty and vagueness inherent in medical concepts and in the clinician's way of reasoning [14]. It differs from classical Boolean logic as each object partially belongs to a given set. A membership matrix is used to represent the possibility that each object belongs to each set [9]. Moreover, a Fuzzy Inference System (FIS) is a fuzzy logic-based reasoning system that uses linguistic variables and linguistic terms to represent vague and uncertain concepts that are involved in the reasoning, thus leading to natural language-based explanations. In fact, the knowledge base of these systems is composed of fuzzy variables whose values are represented through fuzzy sets and *if-then* rules that represent the reasoning [14]. On the other hand, Genetic Algorithms (GAs) are heuristic methods inspired by natural evolution in which optimal individuals are selected for the reproduction of the next generation of the population [9]. They are commonly used to solve complex problems that cannot be handled with procedural methods due to the high complexity of the task. GAs are typically used in Bioinformatics to select a subset of more informative genes; in fact, omics data usually produce thousands of variables for each single sample in an experimental investigation. This curse of dimensionality affects automatic techniques, so dimensionality reduction techniques are often used to extract the most significant subset of genes for the specific task [15]. Thanks to their ability to gradually refine solutions through natural selection, GAs are not biased by human knowledge of the problem and are effectively used for feature selection [16,17].

In this study, we describe the results of our analyses performed on a set of data presented in previous work [18]. This dataset contains the sequencing of 21 human ovarian tissue samples from 12 cancer and 9 non-cancer samples, grouped into 6 diagnostic classes. Due to the large number of classes and the low number of replicates for each class, this dataset is quite difficult to analyze with standard bioinformatic tools. In this paper, we aim to extract useful information from this dataset. The goal of the research was to characterize ovarian cancer tissues by comparing them with other ovarian and uterine tissues and to find a panel of genes capable of discriminating classes and providing information on the pathologic conditions. The method proposed to analyze this dataset is based on genetic algorithms for the selection of features and fuzzy rule-based systems for the classification task, i.e., the diagnosis of the 6 classes of samples. The proposed method aims to provide experts with an interpretable model that can help them, in further laboratory studies, to clarify still unknown mechanisms behind the pathology.

To the best of our knowledge, this is the first time fuzzy logic and genetic algorithms have been combined for ovarian cancer classification. Furthermore, this is the first time this dataset has been analyzed using automatic techniques. Therefore, both biological analyses and computational intelligence techniques have been applied in this paper to verify the effectiveness of the derived results.

The rest of this paper is organized as follows. Section 2 describes the dataset that has been analyzed through the bioinformatic pipeline, and the computational intelligence techniques employed. Section 3 reports the results obtained with the proposed methodologies. Finally, conclusions are summarized in Section 4.

2. Materials and Methods

In this section, we will present the dataset employed in this work and the techniques used to analyze it and evaluate the results obtained.

2.1. Dataset Description and Bioinformatic Preprocessing

The dataset used in this work was presented in a previous paper [18]. It was produced with the Illumina HiSeq2500 sequencer and consists of approximately 30 million paired-end reads (RNA fragments) per sample.

The sequenced samples were selected from 21 Formalin-Fixed Paraffin-Embedded tissues, belonging to 6 classes that are the target of our investigation:

- 3 endometrioid carcinoma (KE);
- 6 high-grade serous carcinoma (KS);
- 3 low-grade serous carcinoma (KSB);
- 3 serous cystadenofibroma (CS);
- 3 endometriosis (EN);
- 3 healthy tuba (N).

The last three groups are non-cancerous samples. The dataset is represented by raw FASTQ files (text files containing the RNA fragments detected by the sequencer), and the gene expressions (RNA counts) were estimated with the bioinformatic tool STAR [19], combined with RSEM [20] and MultiDEA [21].

After gene expression estimation, the final dataset has 21 samples and over 45 thousand genes (features), but many of them will be filtered out for low intensity as low expressions are not reliable for evaluating significant changes in gene values. By applying the standard filter of gene expressions > 50, the feature space of this dataset is reduced to about 9 thousand genes. The main goal of expression profiling is to identify all the genes that are expressed in the samples under study and to extract the genes that show changes in the expression that may be correlated to the experimental conditions. The gene functions, activities, and interactions are collected in molecular pathways and stored in pathway databases, such as KEGG [22] or BioCarta [23].

2.2. Differential Expression Analysis

Differential expression analysis aims to verify whether an observed change in RNA counts (gene expressions) between two experimental conditions is statistically significant. Changes in expression are correlated to the activation of a series of actions among molecules in the cell (a pathway) that change the state of the cell in response to a stimulus.

Following a standard bioinformatic workflow, differential gene expression analysis was performed with DESeq2 [24]. Significant changes are called overexpressions if the expression of the gene increases and underexpressions if it decreases, and the magnitude of the change is evaluated by fold change computation, which is the logarithmic rate of expression between two conditions. When expression values are estimated from RNA counts, they are proportional to the length of the gene that produced the fragments detected. The fold change metric is independent of gene length, but the significance of its result must be statistically tested. Only mean gene expressions > 50 were considered in the analysis, while the result of at least one halved or doubled expression with a *p*-value < 0.05 was considered statistically significant, after multiple testing adjustments by False Discovery Rate [25].

2.3. Fuzzy Rule-Based System

The classification task was performed on subsets of genes (selected by the genetic algorithm, as will be described in Section 2.4) with a fuzzy rule-based system. A Fuzzy Inference System (FIS) is a popular rule-based method for modeling uncertain and imprecise information. In the medical domain, linguistic terms are used to represent patients' symptoms and suggestions are derived through fuzzy inference mechanisms. The domain knowledge is expressed in the knowledge base in the form of *if-then* fuzzy rules. The strength of these systems is their "interpretability", that is the ability to easily express the reasoning behind the rules in a way that is understandable by humans [26]. This is a critical aspect in medical applications as experts need to understand how certain results are obtained to trust the technology.

The classifier was implemented with the "frbs" R package [27]. As the aim of the work was to analyze the gene expression variations, the input variables are the genes selected through the GA. As variations are usually considered to be high (overexpression) or low (underexpression), we have defined the number of fuzzy terms for each gene domain as three (low, medium, and high expression). The medium expression fuzzy set is centered on the mean expression of the gene. The fuzzy rules are equidistant Gaussian sets, and the extreme sets have their center defined by the most extreme values of their gene domain. As domain experts are interested in observing the fold change rate, to linearly represent the increase and decrease of expression (for example, a halving or doubling of expression), we have defined the fuzzy sets on a logarithmic transformation of the estimated expressions, as shown in Figure 1.

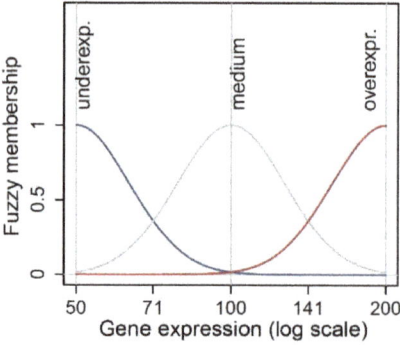

Figure 1. Three fuzzy sets cover the domain of gene expression, thus describing underexpression for low values, medium for the mean expression of the gene, overexpression for high values.

The output of the model is a set of *if-then* rules in which the input fuzzy variables and their values (fuzzy terms) are concatenated in the premise. The consequent contains the output variable and its value, which in our case is discrete and corresponds to the 6 diagnoses of the samples (KE, KS, KSB, CS, EN, N). Table 1 shows an example of fuzzy rule where the selected genes assume Medium/Overexpressed/Underexpressed values, and the target class is KE: endometrioid carcinoma.

Table 1. Example of a fuzzy rule for the classification of samples based on gene expression.

Premise (If)	Consequent (Then)
Gene$_1$ is *medium* and Gene$_2$ is *overexpressed* and ... Gene$_n$ is *underexpressed*	class is *KE*

Due to the low number of samples, the leave-one-out cross-validation method was used to assess the accuracy of the fuzzy classifier.

2.4. Genetic Algorithm

To preserve the interpretability of the fuzzy rule output, only a small number of genes should be included in the rules. The selection of these genes has been implemented with a genetic algorithm.

The evaluation of the most important and influential genes is a complex task because this feature selection task should take into account two important characteristics of NGS data: (1) gene expressions and their magnitude depend on gene length; (2) genes influence each other. These factors undermine the use of feature selection methods based on statistical assumptions such as variance evaluation. Our genetic algorithm can select the features considering multiple factors, suitably tuned by the fitness function.

These are the main parameters of the genetic algorithm:

- Individuals—An individual is an array of integers, each element representing a feature in the feature space (the names of expressed genes).
- Initial population—The initial population is generated randomly.
- Crossing—A new individual is obtained by randomly selecting elements from two parents.
- Selection—A parent is selected for crossing with roulette extraction. Each individual has a probability of being selected that is proportional to its fitness.
- Mutation—Each new individual obtained from crossing can be randomly selected for a mutation event. If the mutation occurs (with a probability of 0.5), one of the elements of the individual is increased by 1 (or decreased if it represents the last feature).
- Elitism—In each generation, a subset of individuals is reintroduced into the next generation.
- Immigration—In each generation, a subset of new individuals is generated randomly.
- Fitness function—Each individual is evaluated with the following fitness function:

$$\text{Fitness} = \text{Accur} \times 0.5 + \text{Simpl} \times 0.3 + \text{Inter} \times 0.2 \qquad (1)$$

where Accur is the accuracy of the model (number of correctly classified samples/total samples), Simpl is a value in [0,1] inversely proportional to the number of rules generated by the model (1 if the number of rules is equal to the number of classes), so that individuals with fewer rules are preferred, Inter is a value in [0,1] that evaluates how many selected genes are relevant for the biomedical task under analysis: if the gene is already known to be involved in cancer molecular pathways (as defined by KEGG [22,28]), the model is rewarded with additional fitness. Initially, only the accuracy (Accur) of the model was considered, but the final individuals showed a large number of fuzzy rules; in fact, the number of fuzzy rules is strictly dependent on the selection of variables returned by the GA. Then we introduced a factor that increases as the number of rules decreases (Simpl), which helped us to select the final individuals with a minimum number of fuzzy rules. However, repeatedly running the genetic algorithm with a different initial random seed produced very different final individuals (only a few genes were present in all results), so we decided to inject biological information into the model. This was performed by selecting the genes involved in cancer (by extracting KEGG's cancer pathway from GSEA) and by adding another factor into the fitness function that increases when the individual contains those genes (Inter). The three parameters are weighted and summed, to obtain a total fitness in [0,1] and to give different (decreasing) importance to each element of the sum. We tested multiple weights and chose the final three shown in the formula to give slightly more importance to the classification accuracy and decreasing importance to the last two addends. This fitness function has been proposed to suit the classification task at hand.

- Stop criteria: the genetic algorithm stops after a predefined number of generations, chosen empirically by observing the diversity of the population over the generations, or when the elite population contains less than 3 different individuals.
- Final individuals: the final individuals will be selected based on the best accuracy and minimum number of final rules.

The fitness evaluation is the most time-consuming operation as it must be performed on all individuals of each generation. As its processing is independent for each individual, parallel computing could be used to speed up the execution time of each generation. Indeed, we compared the execution times required to compute 100 generations of 400 individuals by using both serial and parallel processing (with a 64 cores architecture). While the first took more than 4 h to stop, the second one ended after about 10 min, thus with a saving of over 20 times. The genetic algorithm was implemented with an R script and the R "parallel" package was adopted for parallel computing.

3. Results

In this section, we present the results of the elaboration performed on the ovarian cancer dataset. The data were analyzed with both a standard pipeline used by bioinformaticians and the model proposed in this paper. The analysis aims to extract information on changes in gene expression that can be useful for discriminating between different tissues, and thus to study the molecular mechanisms that differ in the samples.

As the dataset consists of only 3 samples for each class (6 samples in one case), the main objective is to highlight only the most important expression changes in an interpretable system that also takes into account the interactions among genes. The results obtained will also be discussed from a biomedical point of view.

3.1. Differential Expression Analysis

To give an idea of how complex and difficult it is to interpret an expression analysis with more than 2 classes, here we report some results of a standard differential expression analysis workflow we have applied (described in Section 2). This type of analysis allows one to highlight those changes of expression that show statistical significance in the comparison between two conditions. We have performed this analysis in two steps.

In the first step, we have compared each group with the complete set of samples not belonging to the selected group, to search for those expression variations that are typical of the selected group. This analysis describes how specific a class tissue is, and is useful for the researcher who needs to study the singular events that occur in a tissue class and not in all the other classes analyzed, but it hides the events that occur in two or more classes and not in the other. The results are summarized in Table 2. The "Specific genes" column contains the number of genes that are differentially expressed only in that specific group.

Table 2. Results of the differential expression analysis performed on each group against all other data, considered together.

Group	Differentially Expressed Genes (Overexpressed + Underexpressed)	Specific Genes
KE	630 (12 + 501)	591
KS	534 (25 + 281)	459
KSB	549 (47 + 73)	485
CS	75 (5 + 70)	51
EN	350 (87 + 263)	291
N	124 (47 + 77)	99

In the second step, we have compared each possible pair of groups to each other, to compute the differences of each tissue relative to another (Table 3). This analysis is more useful for the researcher who needs to select a set of biomarkers, i.e., a minimal set of genes that allows one to distinguish all the tissues of a study.

Table 3. Results of the differential expression analysis performed on each group versus each other data group, considered separately. Each cell contains the total of genes that are significantly differentially expressed and the partial counts of overexpressed and underexpressed).

	KS	KSB	CS	EN	N
KE	825	196	1439	2041	1160
	(298 + 527)	(42 + 154)	(721 + 718)	(975 + 1066)	(588 + 572)
KS	-	777	668	1133	502
		(272 + 505)	(365 + 303)	(541 + 592)	(236 + 266)
KSB	-	-	489	956	621
			(395 + 94)	(605 + 351)	(459 + 162)
CS	-	-	-	237	213
				(131 + 106)	(139 + 74)
EN	-	-	-	-	725
					(374 + 351)

From this analysis, we can extract the information in Table 4. As we can see, these results are quite difficult to interpret and do not take into account the interactions among genes. Usually, at this stage, researchers analyze the molecular pathways of the differentially expressed genes and select a subset of genes to further study and validation; however, in this multiclass case this step is very complex. In Section 3.2, we will present the results obtained with our proposed model based on fuzzy rules and genetic algorithms.

Table 4. Number of differentially expressed genes present in grouped comparisons (1 = only one comparison, 2 = gene DE in 2 comparisons, etc.).

Number of Comparison Groups & Number of DE Genes									
1	2	3	4	5	6	7	8	9	10
1491	1026	783	533	319	173	95	53	24	2

3.2. Fuzzy Rule-Based System & Genetic Algorithm

In this section, we describe the results obtained with the combination of genetic algorithms and fuzzy rules on the same dataset.

Table 5 summarizes the parameters tested for the execution of the genetic algorithm. Several values have been tested to speed up the execution of each generation, to avoid local minima, and to obtain final individuals with the highest fitness. In particular, the number of total individuals was increased to speed up the best individual's selection (because the number of preserved and brand new individuals also increased), and the mutation was inserted to avoid local minima. The number of generations, initially set at 1000, was increased to 2000, because only a minority of executions stopped for a small elite population (see stop criteria in Section 2.4). We also analyzed the composition of the population and observed that each feature appears at least once in the population after about 50 generations.

The number of features to be selected was based on the trade-off between the choice of a set of features capable of discriminating the 6 sample classes and the need to maintain the cardinality of the set rather low, to preserve the interpretability of the fuzzy rules and define a small number of genes to be selected for further biological study and laboratory validation. In addition, the domain experts wished to obtain a panel of genes capable of distinguishing samples of around 10–15 genes.

Table 5. All parameters tested for the Genetic Algorithm. The final parameters are presented in bold.

Parameter	Values Tested
Features	{**10**, 15, 20}
Individuals	{100, 200, 300, **400**}
Mutation	no mutation, **1 mutation with probability 0.5**
Elitism	1/4 of individuals
Immigration	1/4 of individuals
Fitness function	Accur + Simpl + Inter, Accur $\times$ w1 + Simpl $\times$ w2 + Inter $\times$ w3 (with different combinations of weights), **Accur $\times$ 0.5 + Simpl $\times$ 0.3 + Inter $\times$ 0.2**
Number of generations	1000, **2000**
Repetitions	50 different seeds

Several experiments were performed for the fitness function, as already detailed in Section 2.4, near Equation (1). Different fitness functions were compared and—based on the empirical analyses made—the one including accuracy, the number of rules obtained, and involvement of cancer-associated genes were found to be the most suitable for our genetic algorithm. Moreover, a weighting mechanism has been used to give to each addend a different importance. Indeed, we give slightly more importance to the classification accuracy and decreasing importance to the last two addends. The final parameters are shown in bold in Table 5.

The final individuals were selected based on accuracy only (100%), computed with leave-one-out cross-validation, then sorted by fitness. After repeating the genetic algorithm with different random seeds, we selected 72 best individuals. The final individuals are similar to each other for 78% of the selected features and differ on the remaining genes, and each individual is a subset of 10 out of the same 14 genes, listed in Table 6. The parameter that encouraged the model definition with respect to genes already known to be strongly involved in cancer pathways (as collected in KEGG) influenced the selection of 6 cancer-related genes in each individual. The remaining four genes (the first 4 in the table) are the most important in the classification task; in fact, they are present in each of the 72 individuals. The number of fuzzy rules automatically extracted for each best individual is always equal to 10.

Table 6. The genes selected by the genetic algorithm, sorted by frequency of occurrence in the final 72 individuals with the best accuracy and fitness. The genes known to be correlated to cancer are marked with (*).

Gene Symbol	Gene Description
XPNPEP1	X-prolyl aminopeptidase 1
GATA4	GATA binding protein 4
DTX3L	deltex E3 ubiquitin ligase 3L
NPIPB12	nuclear pore complex interacting protein family member B12
CREB1 (*)	cAMP-responsive element-binding protein 1
EGFR (*)	epidermal growth factor receptor
CREB5 (*)	cAMP-responsive element-binding protein 5
SMAD4 (*)	SMAD family member 4
CKS1B (*)	CDC28 protein kinase regulatory subunit 1B
MAPK1 (*)	mitogen-activated protein kinase 1
KRAS (*)	KRAS proto-oncogene, GTPase
CUL2 (*)	cullin 2
MAPK9 (*)	mitogen-activated protein kinase 9
CBL (*)	proto-oncogene

Table 7 lists the molecular pathways collected in the KEGG database and the genes involved. Moreover, MAPK9, MAPK1, KRAS, CBL, and EGFR are also involved in other molecular mechanisms active in cancer, such as choline metabolism, proteoglycan, and central carbon metabolism.

Table 7. The genes known to be involved in cancer, from the KEGG database of molecular.

KEGG Pathway	Count	Gene Symbols
Endometrial cancer	3	MAPK1, KRAS, EGFR
Pancreatic cancer	6	MAPK9, SMAD4, MAPK1, KRAS, EGFR, CBL
Prostate cancer	5	CREB1, MAPK1, KRAS, EGFR, CREB5
Colorectal cancer	4	MAPK9, SMAD4, MAPK1, KRAS
Bladder cancer	4	MAPK1, KRAS, EGFR, CBL
Small cell lung cancer	2	CKS1B, CBL
Non-small cell lung cancer	3	MAPK1, KRAS, EGFR
Thyroid cancer	2	MAPK1, KRAS
Renal cell carcinoma	1	CUL2

From a literature search, XPNPEP1, GATA4, DTX3L, and NPIPB12 also show some correlation with cancer. In particular: XPNPEP1 was found overexpressed in clear cell renal cell carcinoma [29]; multiple studies have shown that GATA4 is closely associated with tumorigenesis [30]; DTX3L is involved in cell proliferation, differentiation, and survival [31]; NPIPB12 has also been correlated to cancer [32].

Figure 2 shows an example of a set of rules defined by one of the final 72 individuals. As mentioned above, the final individuals all contain XPNPEP1, GATA4, DTX3L, and NPIPB12 and a different combination of the other genes. Moreover, all the final individuals exhibit a similar structure to the final rules. In particular:

1. The class that needs more rules to be described is always KS (high-grade serous carcinoma). This may be due to the complex and multifactorial nature of this cancer. Two rules capture the overexpression of DTX3L, and one rule also includes the overexpression of MAPK9 and the underexpression of NPIPB12.
2. The medium fuzzy set is very common in the rules, both in cancer and non-cancer rules. We expected non-cancer rules to be most represented by the "medium" membership functions, but as the dataset is mostly represented by cancer (12) or diseased (6) samples, and normal data are represented only by 3 samples, it is straightforward that the central data in the expression domains are mostly present in the rules.
3. For the genes that are selected in these final rules, we observed that underexpression is significantly present in non-cancer class rules and overexpression is present only in cancer class rules. We also noticed that in this set there is one rule for the KSB class (low grade of KS) that is significantly different from the others. This result requires deeper biological insights.
4. The KE, CS, and EN classes need only one rule to be described. In particular, the KE class is identified directly by the overexpression of XPNPEP1 and NPIPB12. This result underlines that the KS-KSB disease is the most difficult to describe.
5. The class N needs two rules to be described that differ only in the expression of NPIPB12, which can be medium or underexpressed. Moreover, GATA4 seems to be crucial for normal tissue identification, as it is underexpressed only in class N, in both rules.

Figure 3 shows two examples of fuzzy sets defined on MAPK9 and DTX3L, for KS data only. The MAPK9 gene (known to be strongly involved in cancer pathways) shows a tendency to overexpression, while the DTX3L gene shows an evident overexpression in KS data. This trend is correctly described by the fuzzy sets defined over the expression domain.

IF **MAPK9** (*) is medium and **MAPK1** (*) is medium and **XPNPEP1** is overexp. and **CREB1** (*) is medium and **KRAS** (*) is medium and **GATA4** is medium and **SMAD4** (*) is medium and **EGFR** (*) is medium and **DTX3L** is medium and **NPIPB12** is overexp. THEN class is **KE**

IF **MAPK9** (*) is medium and **MAPK1** (*) is medium and **XPNPEP1** is medium and **CREB1** (*) is medium and **KRAS** (*) is medium and **GATA4** is medium and **SMAD4** (*) is medium and **EGFR** (*) is medium and **DTX3L** is overexp. and **NPIPB12** is medium THEN class is **KS**

IF **MAPK9** (*) is medium and **MAPK1** (*) is medium and **XPNPEP1** is medium and **CREB1** (*) is medium and **KRAS** (*) is medium and **GATA4** is medium and **SMAD4** (*) is medium and **EGFR** (*) is medium and **DTX3L** is medium and **NPIPB12** is medium THEN class is **KS**

IF **MAPK9** (*) is overexp. and **MAPK1** (*) is medium and **XPNPEP1** is medium and **CREB1** (*) is medium and **KRAS** (*) is medium and **GATA4** is medium and **SMAD4** (*) is medium and **EGFR** (*) is medium and **DTX3L** is overexp. and **NPIPB12** is underexp. THEN class is **KS**

IF **MAPK9** (*) is medium and **MAPK1** (*) is medium and **XPNPEP1** is medium and **CREB1** (*) is medium and **KRAS** (*) is medium and **GATA4** is medium and **SMAD4** (*) is medium and **EGFR** (*) is medium and **DTX3L** is medium and **NPIPB12** is overexp. THEN class is **KSB**

IF **MAPK9** (*) is underexp. and **MAPK1** (*) is underexp. and **XPNPEP1** is underexp. and **CREB1** (*) is underexp. and **KRAS** (*) is underexp. and **GATA4** is overexp. and **SMAD4** (*) is underexp. and **EGFR** (*) is underexp. and **DTX3L** is underexp. and **NPIPB12** is overexp. THEN class is **KSB**

IF **MAPK9** (*) is medium and **MAPK1** (*) is medium and **XPNPEP1** is medium and **CREB1** (*) is medium and **KRAS** (*) is medium and **GATA4** is medium and **SMAD4** (*) is medium and **EGFR** (*) is medium and **DTX3L** is underexp. and **NPIPB12** is medium THEN class is **CS**

IF **MAPK9** (*) is medium and **MAPK1** (*) is medium and **XPNPEP1** is medium and **CREB1** (*) is medium and **KRAS** (*) is medium and **GATA4** is medium and **SMAD4** (*) is medium and **EGFR** (*) is medium and **DTX3L** is medium and **NPIPB12** is underexp. THEN class is **EN**

IF **MAPK9** (*) is medium and **MAPK1** (*) is medium and **XPNPEP1** is medium and **CREB1** (*) is medium and **KRAS** (*) is medium and **GATA4** is underexp. and **SMAD4** (*) is medium and **EGFR** (*) is medium and **DTX3L** is medium and **NPIPB12** is medium THEN class is **N**

IF **MAPK9** (*) is medium and **MAPK1** (*) is medium and **XPNPEP1** is medium and **CREB1** (*) is medium and **KRAS** (*) is medium and **GATA4** is underexp. and **SMAD4** (*) is medium and **EGFR** (*) is medium and **DTX3L** is medium and **NPIPB12** is underexp. THEN class is **N**

Figure 2. A set of fuzzy rules with accuracy = 100%, able to classify and describe the samples correctly.

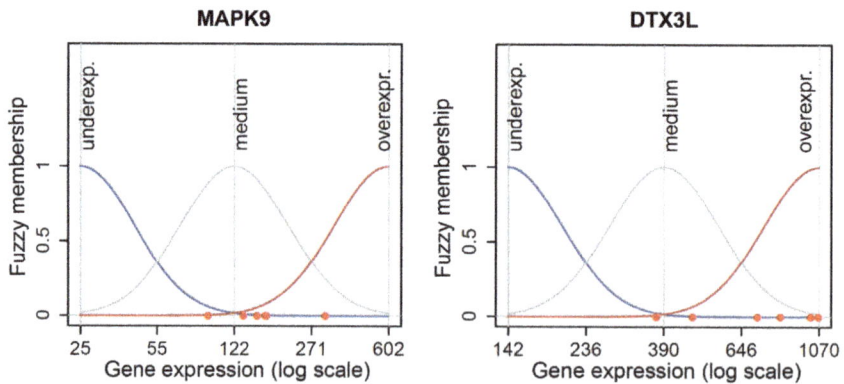

Figure 3. The fuzzy sets defined over the gene expression of MAPK9 and DTX3L for the KS samples.

As can be seen, fuzzy rules are easily understood by users who are not technicians. Fuzzy systems can describe complex behaviors with a transparent description in terms of linguistic knowledge that is interpretable, i.e., easy to read and understand by human users [26]. If we observe the rules generated by the FIS, they clearly explain which are the genes and their expressions involved in the activation of each rule. They are written by using terms coming from natural language, such as the names of the genes, the terms medium, under, and overexpression, that are commonly used by the domain experts, and the derived classes refer to different diseases, as classified by experts. This is a very desirable result as biologists have to analyze these outcomes. Indeed, all the results and comments that we were able to extract with this model based on the combination of fuzzy rule-based systems and genetic algorithms will be subject to further examinations and assessments by biologists and clinicians. Further laboratory validation of the expression of the 14 selected genes on a larger cohort of patients will allow the selection of the final set of genes useful for the definition of a final panel of biomarkers for ovarian cancer characterization.

4. Discussion and Conclusions

Ovarian cancer is a complex multifactorial disease characterized by complex gene interactions. Different types of ovarian cancer are essentially distinct diseases, as indicated by differences in epidemiological and genetic risk factors, precursor lesions, patterns of spread, and molecular events during oncogenesis, response to chemotherapy, and prognosis. A previous study attempted to address this disease by producing NGS datasets of 6 different classes of samples from surgical ovarian tissues, but classical bioinformatic workflows are unable to extract easily interpretable information for studying the expression profiles of the genes involved in the disease. The low number of replicates for each group does not allow the application of algorithms for automatic pattern extraction such as Artificial Neural Networks, and their limitations in result interpretation do not make them suitable for studying the genes involved in the disease mechanisms.

In this paper, we have tried to extract a set of genes that can be used to distinguish the 6 classes of samples and also to provide an explanation of how their expression changes in the data. We have compared the results of the most used bioinformatic pipeline with our model, based on the extraction of fuzzy rules on a set of genes selected by a genetic algorithm. The bioinformatic pipeline is designed for binary classes of case-control studies, and it allows the selection of statistically significant differentially expressed genes, but the results obtained on our 6 groups are difficult to interpret and to use for the extraction of biological markers. Moreover, it does not take into account the correlation and interactions among genes. Our proposal extracts a set of fuzzy rules that are indeed easier to interpret and selects genes both considering their ability to distinguish samples and their known involvement in cancer pathways. We have chosen to exploit fuzzy sets for our model because they represent well the concept of overexpression and underexpression, and we have applied genetic algorithms for gene selection because they allow us to select the features through a random search in the feature space, guided by some factors that are not based on variance evaluation and statistical testing. The perfect accuracy achieved by our classification model can be justified considering the very small size of the dataset we have adopted, which limits the generalizability of our results. Unfortunately, collecting a large sample of data in this particular domain is an extremely difficult task. However, we believe that the results obtained on our experimental data are still very promising and pave the way for a working system capable of supporting domain experts in ovarian cancer evaluation.

The result of our work is that with our method it is possible to select a small subset of genes able to distinguish the 6 classes of samples and to define an interpretable set of rules that can be used by domain experts to further study the selected genes, their involvement in cancer and the possibility of using them as early biomarkers for ovarian cancer diagnosis. Another important achievement of our proposal is that it allows us to elaborate meaningful results even with a reduced number of replicates for each class. As an extension of this work, in the near future, we will apply our model to other NGS datasets and define a more flexible function for pathway information in the fitness function.

Author Contributions: Conceptualization, A.C., E.P. and F.L.; data curation, A.C. and E.P.; formal analysis, A.C., G.C. (Gabriella Casalino), G.G. and G.V.; software, A.C.; validation, G.C. (Gabriella Casalino), G.C. (Giovanna Castellano), G.G. and G.V.; supervision, F.L.; writing—original draft, A.C.; writing—review and editing, A.C., G.C. (Gabriella Casalino), G.C. (Giovanna Castellano), G.G., E.P., G.V. and F.L. All authors have read and agreed to the published version of the manuscript.

Funding: This work was partially supported by INdAM GNCS within the research project "Computational Intelligence methods for Digital Health". G.C. (Gabriella Casalino), G.C. (Giovanna Castellano), A.C., and G.V. are members of the INdAM GNCS research group.

Data Availability Statement: The FASTQ files used in this work are available upon request from the authors of the paper that first described the dataset [18].

Acknowledgments: The authors thank E. Maiorano and L. Resta (Department of Emergency and Organ Transplantation, Operating Unit of Pathological Anatomy, University of Bari Aldo Moro, Bari, Italy) for their essential contribution of tissue samples without which no study would have been possible. G.C. (Gabriella Casalino), G.C. (Giovanna Castellano), and G.V. are members of the "CITEL-Centro Interdipartimentale di Telemedicina" research center of the University of Bari Aldo Moro.

Conflicts of Interest: The authors declare no conflict of interest.

References

1. Prat, J. Ovarian Carcinomas: Five Distinct Diseases with Different Origins, Genetic Alterations, and Clinicopathological Features. *Virchows Arch.* **2012**, *460*, 237–249. [CrossRef]
2. Prat, J.; D'Angelo, E.; Espinosa, I. Ovarian Carcinomas: At Least Five Different Diseases with Distinct Histological Features and Molecular Genetics. *Hum. Pathol.* **2018**, *80*, 11–27. [CrossRef]
3. Zhang, Z.H.; Jhaveri, D.J.; Marshall, V.M.; Bauer, D.C.; Edson, J.; Narayanan, R.K.; Robinson, G.J.; Lundberg, A.E.; Bartlett, P.F.; Wray, N.R.; et al. A Comparative Study of Techniques for Differential Expression Analysis on RNA-Seq data. *PLoS ONE* **2014**, *9*, e103207. [CrossRef]
4. El Houby, E.M.F. A Survey on Applying Machine Learning Techniques for Management of Diseases. *J. Appl. Biomed.* **2018**, *16*, 165–174. [CrossRef]
5. Casalino, G.; Castellano, G.; Consiglio, A.; Nuzziello, N.; Vessio, G. MicroRNA Expression Classification for Pediatric Multiple Sclerosis Identification. *J. Ambient Intell. Humaniz. Comput.* **2021**, in press.
6. Lella, E.; Vessio, G. Ensembling Complex Network 'perspectives' for Mild Cognitive Impairment Detection with Artificial Neural Networks. *Pattern Recognit. Lett.* **2020**, *136*, 168–174. [CrossRef]
7. Tabares-Soto, R.; Orozco-Arias, S.; Romero-Cano, V.; Bucheli, V.S.; Rodríguez-Sotelo, J.L.; Jiménez-Varón, C.F. A Comparative Study of Machine Learning and Deep Learning Algorithms to Classify Cancer Types based on Microarray Gene Expression Data. *PeerJ Comput. Sci.* **2020**, *6*, e270. [CrossRef]
8. Esposito, F.; Boccarelli, A.; Del Buono, N. An NMF-Based Methodology for Selecting Biomarkers in the Landscape of Genes of Heterogeneous Cancer-Associated Fibroblast Populations. *Bioinform. Biol. Insights* **2020**, *14*, 112–121. [CrossRef] [PubMed]
9. Pedrycz, W. *Computational Intelligence: An Introduction*; CRC Press: Boca Raton, FL, USA, 1997.
10. Zhao, R.; Yan, R.; Chen, Z.; Mao, K.; Wang, P.; Gao, R.X. Deep Learning and Its Applications to Machine Health Monitoring: A Survey. *IEEE Trans. Neural Netw. Learn Syst.* **2016**, *14*, 319–333. [CrossRef]
11. Sathe, S.; Aggarwal, S.; Tang, J. Gene Expression and Protein Function: A Survey of Deep Learning Methods. *ACM SIGKDD Explor. Newsl.* **2019**, *21*, 23–38. [CrossRef]
12. Dimauro, G.; Colagrande, P.; Carlucci, R.; Ventura, M.; Bevilacqua, V.; Caivano, D. CRISPRLearner: A deep learning-based system to predict CRISPR/Cas9 sgRNA on-target cleavage efficiency. *Electronics* **2019**, *8*, 1478. [CrossRef]
13. Tjoa, E.; Guan, C. A Survey on Explainable Artificial Intelligence (XAI): Towards medical XAI. *IEEE Trans. Neural Netw. Learn Syst.* **2019**, 402–417.
14. Casalino, G.; Castellano, G.; Castiello, C.; Pasquadibisceglie, V.; Zaza, G. A fuzzy rule-based decision support system for cardiovascular risk assessment. In *International Workshop on Fuzzy Logic and Applications*; Springer: Cham, Switzerland, 2018; pp. 97–108.
15. Casalino, G.; Coluccia, M.; Pati, M.L.; Pannunzio, A.; Vacca, A.; Scilimati, A.; Perrone, M.G. Intelligent Microarray Data Analysis through Non-negative Matrix Factorization to Study Human Multiple Myeloma Cell Lines. *Appl. Sci.* **2019**, *9*, 5552. [CrossRef]
16. Piserchia, Zachary. Applications of Genetic Algorithms in Bioinformatics. Master's Thesis, University of California Riverside, Riverside, CA, USA, May 2018.
17. Senesi, G.S.; Manzari, P.; Consiglio, A.; De Pascale, O. Identification and Classification of Meteorites using a Handheld LIBS Instrument Coupled with a Fuzzy Logic-based Method. *J. Anal. At. Spectrom.* **2018**, *33*, 1664–1675. [CrossRef]
18. Brandini, S.; Consiglio, A.; Licciulli, F.; Liuni, S.; Napoli, A.; Maiorano, E.; Resta, L.; Perlino, E. NGS approach for new Ovarian Cancer Biomarker Discovery. *Biomed. Res. Rev.* **2018**, *10*, 421–438.

19. Dobin, A.; Davis, C.A.; Schlesinger, F.; Drenkow, J.; Zaleski, C.; Jha, S.; Gingeras, T.R. STAR: Ultrafast universal RNA-seq aligner. *Bioinformatics* **2013**, *29*, 15–21. [CrossRef]
20. Li, B.; Dewey, C.N. RSEM: Accurate transcript quantification from RNA-Seq data with or without a reference genome. *BMC Bioinform.* **2011**, *12*, 323. [CrossRef]
21. Consiglio, A.; Mencar, C.; Grillo, G.; Marzano, F.; Caratozzolo, M.F.; Liuni, S. A fuzzy method for RNA-Seq differential expression analysis in presence of multireads. *BMC Bioinform.* **2016**, *17*, 345. [CrossRef]
22. Ogata, H.; Goto, S.; Fujibuchi, W.; Kanehisa, M. Computation with the KEGG pathway database. *Biosystems* **1998**, *47*, 119–128. [CrossRef]
23. Nishimura, D. BioCarta. *Biotech Softw. Internet Rep.* **2004**, *2*, 117–120. [CrossRef]
24. Love, M.I.; Huber, W.; Anders, S. Moderated Estimation of Fold Change and Dispersion for RNA-seq Data with DESeq2. *Genome Biol.* **2014**, *15*, 550. [CrossRef]
25. Benjamini, Y.; Hochberg, Y. Controlling the False Discovery Rate: A Practical and Powerful Approach to Multiple Testing. *J. R. Stat. Soc. Ser. B Stat. Methodol.* **1995**, *57*, 289–300. [CrossRef]
26. Mencar, C.; Castellano, G.; Fanelli, A.M. On the Role of Interpretability in Fuzzy Data Mining. *Int. J. Uncertain. Fuzz.* **2007**, *15*, 521–537. [CrossRef]
27. Riza, L.S.; Bergmeir, C.; Herrera, F.; Benitez, J.M. frbs: Fuzzy Rule-Based Systems for Classification and Regression in R. *J. Stat. Softw.* **2015**, *65*, 1–30. [CrossRef]
28. Liberzon, A. A description of the molecular signatures database (MSigDB) web site. In *Stem Cell Transcriptional Networks*; Humana Press: New York, NY, USA, 2014; pp. 153–160.
29. Drendel, V.; Heckelmann, B.; Chen, C.Y.; Weisser, J.; Espadas, G.; Schell, C.; Sabido, E.; Werner, M.; Jilg, C.A.; Schilling, O. Proteome Profiling of Clear Cell Renal Cell Carcinoma in Von Hippel-Lindau Patients Highlights Upregulation of Xaa-Pro aminopeptidase-1, an Anti-proliferative and Anti-migratory Exoprotease. *Oncotarget* **2017**, *8*, 100066. [CrossRef]
30. Zhou, Y.; Chang, H.; Yang, B. GATA4 is upregulated in Nasopharyngeal Cancer and Facilitates Epithelial-mesenchymal Transition and Metastasis through Regulation of SLUG. *Exp. Ther. Med.* **2018**, *16*, 5318–5326. [CrossRef]
31. Bachmann, S.B.; Frommel, S.C.; Camicia, R.; Winkler, H.C.; Santoro, R.; Hassa, P.O. DTX3L and ARTD9 inhibit IRF1 Expression and Mediate in Cooperation with ARTD8 survival and Proliferation of Metastatic Prostate Cancer Cells. *Mol. Cancer.* **2014**, *13*, 125. [CrossRef]
32. Xu, S.; Powers, M.A. Nuclear Pore Proteins and Cancer. *Semin. Cell Dev. Biol.* **2009**, *20*, 620–630. [CrossRef] [PubMed]

Article

CRISPRLearner: A Deep Learning-Based System to Predict CRISPR/Cas9 sgRNA On-Target Cleavage Efficiency

Giovanni Dimauro [1,*], Pierpasquale Colagrande [1], Roberto Carlucci [2], Mario Ventura [2], Vitoantonio Bevilacqua [3] and Danilo Caivano [1]

1. Department of Computer Science, University of Bari, 70125 Bari, Italy; p.colagrande@studenti.uniba.it (P.C.); danilo.caivano@uniba.it (D.C.)
2. Department of Biology, University of Bari, 70125 Bari, Italy; roberto.carlucci@uniba.it (R.C.); mario.ventura@uniba.it (M.V.)
3. Department of Electrical and Information Engineering, Polytechnic University of Bari, 70125 Bari, Italy; vitoantonio.bevilacqua@poliba.it
* Correspondence: giovanni.dimauro@uniba.it

Received: 3 November 2019; Accepted: 30 November 2019; Published: 4 December 2019

Abstract: CRISPRLearner, the system presented in this paper, makes it possible to predict the on-target cleavage efficiency (also called on-target knockout efficiency) of a given sgRNA sequence, specifying the target genome that this sequence is designed for. After efficiency prediction, the researcher can evaluate its sequence and design a new one if the predicted efficiency is low. CRISPRLearner uses a deep convolutional neural network to automatically learn sequence determinants and predict the efficiency, using pre-trained models or using a model trained on a custom dataset. The convolutional neural network uses linear regression to predict efficiency based on efficiencies used to train the model. Ten different models were trained using ten different gene datasets. The efficiency prediction task attained an average Spearman correlation higher than 0.40. This result was obtained using a data augmentation technique that generates mutations of a sgRNA sequence, maintaining the efficiency value. CRISPRLearner supports researchers in sgRNA design task, predicting a sgRNA on-target knockout efficiency.

Keywords: convolutional neural network; CRISPR; deep learning

1. Introduction

1.1. Background

Genetic engineering in different living beings has always been used for various tasks, such as treating particular diseases or creating species with particular genetic features. Editing and modifying these features can be accomplished with various biotechnology techniques, which, most of the time, are quite complex.

However, things started to get easier with the discovery of CRISPR, an acronym that stands for Clustered Regularly Interspaced Short Palindromic Repeats. CRISPR was originally discovered in bacteria and archaea in late 1990s and early 2000s as a family of DNA segments containing short repeated sequences. These sequences separate fragments of DNA acquired from viruses that previously attacked the cell, forming an adaptive immunity system. In fact, after a virus attack, new viral DNA is incorporated into the CRISPR locus in form of spacers. Researchers also found that this repeated cluster was accompanied by a set of genes, called CRISPR associated system (Cas) genes, used to generate Cas proteins. Once a virus attacks again, a portion of the CRISPR region is transcribed into CRISPR RNA, or crRNA, that gets joined to a trans-activating crRNA (tracrRNA). These sequences, forming a unique one, are then bound to a Cas9 protein, guiding it to the target site of the virus DNA. The Cas9 protein then unwinds the DNA and performs a double stranded cut, knocking out the virus. The sequence targeted by Cas9 is followed by a 2-6 base pair (bp) sequence called protospacer adjacent motif (PAM), which is part of the invading virus DNA, but not part of the CRISPR region, to prevent Cas9 from cutting the CRISPR locus itself. In fact, Cas9 will not bind to a target sequence if it is not followed by PAM.

Jennifer Doudna and Emmanuelle Charpentier re-engineered the Cas9 endonuclease fusing crRNA and tracrCRNA into a single RNA sequence called sgRNA (single guide RNA). This sequence, when bound with Cas9, can find and cut a target DNA specified by the sequence itself. By manipulating the sgRNA sequence, the artificial Cas9 system can recognize and cut any DNA sequence. CRISPR then becomes a powerful genome editing tool, called CRISPR/Cas9 [1,2]. Recognition and knockout occur via a 23-bp sequence composed by a 20-bp sequence followed by a 3-bp sequence, PAM.

Designing and developing this sequence is an important task because not all the sgRNAs designed to cut a target DNA are equally effective. The efficiency of CRISPR/Cas9 sgRNA depends on the features like the target site, the properties of the endonuclease, and the design of the sequence [3]. Additionally, when DNA gets cut, the cell tends to repair this cut, leading to more or less serious mutations. Predicting efficiency in cutting DNAs (on-target cleavage efficiency or on-target knockout efficiency) and its side effects and mutations (off-target profile or off-target effects) has an important role in sgRNA design task. Also, researchers will be able to obtain these sequence parameters without performing a physical genetic modification, saving time and resources for the actual experimentation. To refine sgRNA design task, various efficiency prediction systems have been developed, using various approaches. For example, locating PAM sequence (CasFinder [4]), scoring efficiencies empirically based on sequence key features (CHOPCHOP [5]), or predicting them with training models (sgRNA designer [6], sgRNA scorer [7,8], SSC [9], CRISPRscan [10]). However, prediction systems based on deep learning principles have surpassed their competitors in both predicting on-target and off-target efficiencies.

The repetitions in a CRISPR locus have variable size: they usually range from 28 to 37 bp. Much shorter repetitions (23 bp) have been discovered and we focused on these ones. Other authors focused on these lengths too, in these preliminary experiments. This paper is presenting CRISPRLearner, a system that uses a deep convolutional neural network (CNN) to extract and automatically learn sequence features and determinants and predict on-target cleavage efficiency of an up to 23-bp sgRNA.

1.2. Related Works

Deep learning for sequencing data has been used [11–13]; it has also been used in some works to predict sgRNA on-target and off-target efficiency. For example, a deep learning approach to predict off-target effects is described by Lin in [14]. Another work that used deep learning to predict both off-target and on-target efficiencies is described in [15]. In this system, called DeepCRISPR, the sequence is encoded into a one-hot matrix, composed of 4 rows, one for each nucleobase, and 23 columns, one for each nucleobase in the 23-bp sgRNA sequence. The matrix gets augmented with additional rows corresponding to epigenetic features, to build a generalized model. This matrix then gets passed as input to a CNN, which is able to use both linear regression and classification to predict efficiencies. In the first case, the predicted value is a real value, while in second case a class is predicted (0 low efficiency, 1 high efficiency).

The system developed by Xue [16], called DeepCas9, uses a CNN too. A sequence up to 30-bp is encoded into a one-hot matrix using the same one-hot encoding scheme used in [15], but without adding additional rows for epigenetic features. The obtained matrix gets passed as input to the CNN that uses linear regression to predict efficiency represented by a real value.

All these three studies use similar encoding mechanism to transform each sgRNA sequence into a data format suitable for the CNN. In fact, CNNs take as input a matrix of values, corresponding to the pixel matrix of an image. Each cell of this matrix contains a value representing the color in the corresponding cell of the pixel matrix. For grey-level pictures, matrix cells only contain real values from 0 to 1, where 0 represents white, 1 represents black, and values in between them represent the shades of grey. In [14–16], the sgRNAs get encoded into matrices where cells assume only 0 and 1 values. Each of them is then served as input to the CNN that makes predictions. Other techniques for comparing images can be found in [17] and an interesting application of NN-based sequencing system is in [18].

The system presented in this paper uses a CNN to predict a score for on-target knockout efficiency: 10 models regarding different type of organisms and cells have been trained using 10 different datasets. The efficiency of a sequence is calculated using one of these 10 models, depending on the organism the sequence has been designed for. In DeepCas9, the efficiency score is calculated with a weighted sum between the scores predicted by three trained models. Moreover, in DeepCas9, the sequence accepted are 30-bp sequence, which we found out was an uncommon type. In DeepCRISPR, different models are used to predict efficiency, some based on a binary classification (1 efficient, 0 not efficient) and some on regression. The system here presented system uses regression, and aims to output a more useful grade of efficiency instead of knowing just if a sequence is efficient or not.

In our work, the sgRNA sequence is encoded into a 4 × 23 one-hot matrix that is served as input to the CNN. We also implemented a particular technique to encode sequences with a length less than 23-bp. In addition, datasets are augmented with a particular technique. These details will be described further.

2. Materials and Methods

2.1. Datasets

To train and develop the system here presented, the datasets used by Xue in [16] were used, consisting in 10 sgRNA efficiency datasets covering several cell types of five species, which were collected by Haeussler in [19]. These ten datasets were:

- Chari dataset [7], consisting in 1234 guides targeting Human 293T cells
- Wang/Xu dataset [9,20], consisting in 2076 guides targeting 221 genes in Human HL-60 cells
- From Doench dataset [21], 951 guides targeting various mouse-EL4 cells were kept (as said in [16], the sequences that were kept targeted Cd5, Cd28, H2-K, Cd45, Thy1, and Cd43 genes)
- A new version of Doench et al. dataset [6], consisting in 2333 guides targeting CCDC101, MED12, TADA2B, TADA1, HPRT, CUL3, NF1, and NF2 genes from Human A375 cells
- Hart dataset [22], consisting in 4239 guides targeting 829 genes in Human Hct116 cells
- Moreno-Mateos dataset [10], consisting in 1020 guides targeting 128 genes in Zebrafish genome
- Gandhi dataset, consisting in 72 guides targeting different genes in Ciona genome
- Farboud dataset [23], consisting in 50 guides targeting different genes in Caenorhabditis elegans genome
- Varshney dataset [24], consisting in 102 guides targeting different genes in Zebrafish genome
- Gagnon dataset [25], consisting in 111 guides targeting different genes in Zebrafish genome

These datasets were aggregated with others in [19], creating a dataset of 31625 sgRNAs with their relative knockout efficiencies. Unfortunately, we were not able to merge datasets from the same organisms (e.g., Human, Zebrafish datasets). In fact, human datasets were referring to different cell types while for zebrafish dataset were left separated since it was not possible to extract information about cell types or tissues. Each dataset had its own measurement scale for knockout efficiencies, producing a dataset with non-standardized knockout efficiency measurements. Moreover, some datasets presented sequences with a length less than 23-bp, meaning that these sequences were not in form of a 20-bp sequence followed by a 3-bp PAM sequence, leading to non-standardized sequences too. To solve these problems, we adopted some strategies that will be described later.

2.2. Software

The system was developed using Python language, because of its simplicity and popularity compared to other programming languages. The integrated development environment used to develop CRISPLearner was Pycharm, in combination with VSCode for minor modifications. Also, Git version control system was used, in combination with GitHub.

To develop the core of the system, the convolutional neural network behind the prediction task, Tensorflow has been used, including Keras. Keras uses a data structure called model to represent the way which network layers are organized. In this project, the sequential model has been used. Other libraries used are Scipy, an open library dedicated to scientific computing, NumPy, a library for scientific calculation that provides many functions for operations between matrices, Scikit-learn, a library for machine learning supporting algorithms and Python default libraries, like os, re, and shutil for various purposes.

3. System Description

This section will describe the techniques used to extract datasets from Haeussler [19] dataset, the strategies adopted to standardize sequences and efficiencies, along with the sequence representation technique used. In addition, the dataset augmentation technique adopted, the CNN architecture and the CLI (Command-Line Interface) implemented will be described.

3.1. Dataset Creation

This section will describe the procedure adopted to extract and prepare data.

3.1.1. Data extraction

As said before, the datasets used to train the CNN are ten, which were collected with others in the Haeussler dataset [19]. Each row of this last dataset contained data regarding a single sgRNA sequence. The columns used to extract each dataset were four:

- dataset column, containing the name of the dataset where the sequence was extracted from
- seq column, containing the actual sgRNA sequence
- modFreq column, containing the efficiency value
- longSeq100Bp column, the extended 100-bp sequence

For each of the ten datasets, a file containing only a 23-bp sequence and its efficiency was created. To identify only the sequences from the datasets needed, the dataset column was used, which contained the dataset name. Using these names, ten files corresponding to the ten datasets were created. Each extracted dataset contained only two columns, a column containing the 23-bp sgRNA sequence and a column containing cleavage efficiency.

3.1.2. Standardizing sgRNA Sequences

Some datasets include sequences with a length less than 23-bp. For example, Gandhi dataset had sequences of 22-bp, composed of a 19-bp sequence followed by a 3-bp PAM sequence. Instead, Doench A375 and Hart datasets had sequences of 20-bp not followed by a 3-bp PAM, as it should be.

Therefore, before extracting the datasets, 23-bp sgRNA sequences in form of 20-bp sequences followed by a 3-bp PAM sequence had to be extracted. In fact, in Doench A375 and Hart datasets, the missing PAM sequence was instead in the 3 nucleobases immediately following the seq sequence in longSeq100Bp extended sequence. So, the seq sequence was first found in longSeq100Bp sequence and then extracted along with the 3 immediately following nucleobases (the PAM sequence), obtaining a 23-bp sequence composed of a 20-bp sequence followed the 3-bp PAM sequence.

Instead, for Ghandi dataset, the seq sequence was first found in longSeq100Bp sequence and then extracted along with the first immediately preceding nucleobase.

After this operation, the ten files corresponding to the extracted datasets were created.

3.1.3. Standardizing Efficiency Measurement

Each dataset used a different scale to measure cleavage efficiency, based on the technique used to measure these values. In order to train a regression model, it was necessary to rescale each of these values to a standard measurement scale.

To do this, the same solution described by Xue in [16] was adopted. Each extracted dataset was rescaled using a min–max scaler mapping a value in the range [0, 1]. This function was defined as $f_{nk} = \frac{f_k - f_{min}}{f_{max} - f_{min}}$, where f_{max} and f_{min} are, respectively, the maximum and minimum efficiency value of the dataset, f_k is the original efficiency value to rescale and f_{nk} is the rescaled value. This rescaling function was applied on each sequence of the ten extracted datasets. For each extracted dataset, a rescaled dataset file was created, containing a column with the 23-bp sequence and a column with its rescaled efficiency, rescaled using the minmax function described above. Efficiency was standardized in order to have a general measuring of the it, even if the datasets are not merged, so even if the original efficiency is in a different scale than [0, 1], the system will always output an efficiency included in this interval, no matter what the trained model is.

3.1.4. Data augmentation Technique

During the experimentation, data from different cell types has been used to train the CNN model. Initially, only the rescaled datasets were used, but the results obtained were unsatisfactory, leading to an overfitted and less performing model. Modifying the CNN architecture or changing some of its hyperparameters did not improve model performances.

For this reason, a data augmentation technique was adopted. In particular, the data augmentation technique used by Chuai in [15] was adopted. In fact, it seems that mismatches in the PAM distal region, which is the 5' end of a 23-bp sgRNA, have no influence on the sequence efficiency [6,15,20], giving us the possibility to generate new sequences, starting from a single sgRNA, with the same efficiency value of the original one. The rescaled sets were then augmented, generating two mismatches in the first two nucleobases of the extracted sequences, obtaining sixteen new sequences for each original sgRNA sequence (one of them was the original sgRNA sequence), each of them having the same identical efficiency value.

Augmenting data has proved to be a key step in improving the CNN performances, as the problem of low performances and high losses seemed to reside in the data itself rather than in the CNN architecture. Table 1 resumes the number of sequences for each dataset before and after augmentation procedure (training on 80% of the sequences, see Section 4).

Table 1. Number of sequences in the original and augmented datasets.

Dataset	Original Sequences	Augmented Sequences
Chari	1234	19,744
Wang/Xu	2076	33,216
Doench mouse-EL4	951	15,216
Doench A375	2333	37,328
Hart	4239	67,824
Moreno-Mateos	1020	16,320
Gandhi	72	1152
Farboud	50	800
Varshney	102	1632
Gagnon	111	1776

3.2. Data Representation for Training

To make the sequences usable for the CNN, each sequence was encoded in a one-hot matrix with 23 columns, corresponding to the nucleobases of the sequence, and 4 rows, corresponding to A, C,

G, and T bases channels. CRISPRLearner supports sequence up to a maximum of 23 nucleobases. For sequences with less than 23 nucleobases, a different approach has been adopted. Since an sgRNA gets encoded into a one-hot manner, if a sequence as a length less than 23, some columns of zeros have been added at the beginning of the real one-hot matrix. So, for example, a sequence of 19-bp will be encoded into a 4 × 19 one-hot matrix and 4 (23 minus length of sequence) columns of zeros have been added at the start of the matrix, creating a matrix of 4 × 23 and making the matrix usable for the CNN. All the dataset that we used for these experiments contains only sequences of 23-bp, so this problem should never appear, since the system is designed to work efficiently with 23-bp sequences. However, we have left the possibility to experiment on shorter sequences if the PAM sequence cannot be extracted, retrieved or is omitted or if a researcher wants to experiment using simply shorter sequences. Figure 1 shows an example of one-hot encoding of a sequence that has a length less than 23-bp.

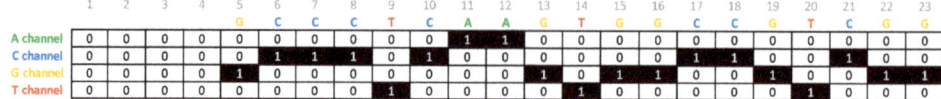

Figure 1. One-hot encoding of a 19-base pair (bp) sequence.

3.3. Description of the Convolutional Neural Network Architecture

The core of the system is a convolutional neural network that performs regression to predict sgRNA cleavage efficiency. Differently from Chuai et al. [15], this model is focused on a regression task instead of a classification task. This system uses only real value labels since it's based on regression instead of using class label. In regression, the labels are real values, indicating precisely the efficiency of the sgRNA on a range of real values between 0 and 1. In classification, labels are class labels, indicating only a binary efficiency, i.e., 0 if a sgRNA is not effective and 1 if it is effective.

The first layer is an input layer that takes as input a 4 × 23 × 1 one-hot matrix. Then, a convolution layer performs 50 convolutions with 4x4 kernel on the input matrix, producing 50 feature maps of size 1 × 20. After convolution, a ReLU activation layer removes outputs below 0, transforming them into zeros. After ReLU activation layer, a max pooling layer performs 1 × 2 max pooling of the feature maps produced by the convolution layer, producing 50 feature maps of size 1 × 10. After pooling, a flatten layer combines the pooling results in a vector with size of 500. Then, two fully connected layers are added, each with 128 nodes. Each fully connected layer is followed by a ReLU activation layer. Between the fully connected layers, a dropout layer is added, with a dropout rate of 0.3, to reduce overfitting. Then, a fully connected (or dense) layer serves as output layer followed by a linear regression activation layer. Table 2 resumes the CNN architecture.

Specifically, after being converted into a one-hot matrix with 4 rows and 23 columns, the sequence is passed to the CNN. The input layer reads the matrix as if it is a 4 × 23 black and white image. The first convolutional layer performs 50 convolutions with a 4 × 4 filter and a stride of 1, generating 50 feature maps of dimension 1 × 20. After convolution, the ReLU layer outputs results above threshold. The next pooling layer performs a 1 × 2 max pooling of each feature map using a stride of 1, producing 50 feature maps of size 1 × 10. All the pooling results are combined into a single vector by a flatten layer, resulting in a vector of 500 elements. The vector is then passed to two fully connected layers, each composed of 128 nodes, which have a ReLU layer and a dropout layer in between them, with a dropout rate of 0.3, to avoid overfitting. After the fully connected layers, the output layer outputs the prediction for on-target efficiency using linear regression.

Table 2. Layers of the convolutional neural network.

N	Layer
1	Input: $4 \times 23 \times 1$
2	Convolution: 4×4 size, 50 filters, 1 stride
3	ReLU
4	Max pooling: 1×2 size, 1 stride
5	Flatten
6	Fully connected: 128 units
7	ReLU
8	Dropout: 0.3 dropout rate
9	Fully connected: 128 units
10	ReLU
11	Fully connected (output): 1 unit
12	Linear regression

For each dataset, a model was trained on 250 epochs with a batch size of 32 and a learning rate of 0.001. An early stopping was also added to detect automatically the minimum validation loss, with a patience of 100 epochs. The models were also optimized with Adam algorithm, trained using 80% of each dataset and validated on the remaining 20% [26,27]. Each dataset was also randomly shuffled before training.

To evaluate each model, the loss function used was Mean Squared Error, while the metric used was Spearman correlation coefficient from Scipy library. The Spearman score of each model was calculated between the predicted efficiencies (on the 20% validation set) and the respective real efficiencies from the datasets. After each model training procedure, the model weights were saved.

4. Results

The efficiency prediction of the system CRISPRLearner was evaluated using Spearman correlation coefficient and using Mean Squared Error loss. The system was trained on 80% of each dataset and tested on the 20% left, generating ten different models. Few evaluations made before adding the data augmentation technique previously described, pointed out low performances, with an average Spearman correlation coefficient of about 0.2 and a high loss. The models trained also showed overfitting and high validation losses. Adding data augmentation improved both losses and Spearman scores, avoiding overfitting and making the system more effective. In Table 3 it is reported a Spearman score comparison between this system and DeepCas9. The results are interesting, but it is clear that we cannot speak of a decisive improvement in performance in comparison with DeepCas9, which however in some datasets achieves better results. It is also interesting to compare the results with other competitors by analyzing Figure 2 in [16].

Table 3. Performance comparison of CRISPRLearner with DeepCas9.

Dataset	CRISPRLearner	DeepCas9
Chari	0.49	0.49
Wang/Xu	0.69	0.61
Doench mouse-EL4	0.51	0.59
Doench A375	0.23	0.38
Hart	0.55	0.41
Moreno-Mateos	0.19	0.23
Gandhi	0.36	0.32
Farboud	0.60	0.57
Varshney	0.35	0.3
Gagnon	0.35	0.25

5. Conclusion and Future Work

As indicated in the Table 3, CNN-based systems perform better that other system on some of the datasets. This means that deep-learning based systems are generally performing better than machine-learning based systems and systems based on other techniques. There are some exceptions, like Doench mEl4, Doench A375, and Ghandi datasets, indicating that some other approaches still may perform better on some kind of data.

The system presented in this paper shows good performances, paying a lower generalization. However, allowing the user to train his own models based on the datasets he provides, leads to a generalization of the system, even if the model itself is not generalized. In fact, a single model was not trained for all the datasets, but for each dataset a model was trained and training more models on new datasets will allow the system to predict more and more sgRNA efficiencies of different genomes, cell types, and genes.

To support multiple cell identification, the user is free to train its own model using a different dataset, expanding the system and allowing it to predict sgRNA efficiencies regarding new cell types, gene, or genome types. This approach will allow researchers to contribute in the overall expansion and improvement of the system, adding new trained models to perform predictions on new types of cells.

A question could be why performance results were not better than the DeepCas9 in some datasets, but the answer could not be definitive. Performances can depend on type of data augmentation, on the number of original sequences, on the similarity between some sequences and obviously on the design details of each system. It is not easy to describe the behavior of the internal layers of the CNN, but we will deepen this argument in a further study.

The system here presented will be expanded, as just said, with more cell and genome types. Also, the ability to predict off-target efficiencies will be added to the system, transforming CRISPRLearner in a complete system for CRISPR/Cas9 sgRNA design. Also, deploying the system online will permit it to be expanded with new trained models more easily.

Author Contributions: Conceptualization, G.D. and P.C.; methodology, R.C., M.V. and G.D.; software, P.C. and D.C.; validation, V.B.; formal analysis, V.B.; investigation, P.C. and R.C.; resources, D.C.; data curation, P.C.; writing—original draft preparation, G.D. and P.C.; writing—review and editing, P.C., R.C., and M.V.; project administration, G.D.

Funding: This research received no external funding.

Conflicts of Interest: The authors declare no conflict of interest.

References

1. Jinek, M.; Chylinski, K.; Fonfara, I.; Hauer, M.; Doudna, J.A.; Charpentier, E. A programmable dual-RNA-guided DNA endonuclease in adaptive bacterial immunity. *Science* **2012**, *337*, 816–821. [CrossRef] [PubMed]
2. Doudna, J.A.; Charpentier, E. The new frontier of genome engineering with CRISPR-Cas9. *Science* **2014**, *346*, 1258096. [CrossRef] [PubMed]
3. Zahra, H.; Ali, M.; Hui, W.; Dawei, L.; Yasin, O.; Honghua, R.; Qiang, Z. Strategies to Increase On-Target and Reduce Off-Target Effects of the CRISPR/Cas9 System in Plants. *Int. J. Mol. Sci.* **2019**, *20*, 3718. [CrossRef]
4. Aach, J.; Mali, P.; Church, G.M. CasFinder: Flexible algorithm for identifying specific Cas9 targets in genomes. *bioRxiv* **2014**, 005074. [CrossRef]
5. Labun, K.; Montague, T.G.; Gagnon, J.A.; Thyme, S.B.; Valen, E. CHOPCHOP v2: A web tool for the next generation of CRISPR genome engineering. *Nucleic Acids Res.* **2016**, *44*, W272–W276. [CrossRef]
6. Doench, J.G.; Fusi, N.; Sullender, M.; Hegde, M.; Vaimberg, E.W.; Donovan, K.F.; Smith, I.; Tothova, Z.; Wilen, C.; Orchard, R.; et al. Optimized sgRNA design to maximize activity and minimize off-target effects of CRISPR-Cas9. *Nat. Biotechnol.* **2016**, *34*, 184–191. [CrossRef]
7. Chari, R.; Mali, P.; Moosburner, M.; Church, G.M. Unraveling CRISPR-Cas9 genome engineering parameters via a library-on-library approach. *Nat. Methods* **2015**, *12*, 823–826. [CrossRef]
8. Chari, R.; Yeo, N.C.; Chavez, A.; Church, G.M. sgRNA Scorer 2.0: A Species-Independent Model To Predict CRISPR/Cas9 Activity. *ACS Synth. Biol.* **2017**, *6*, 902–904. [CrossRef]

9. Xu, H.; Xiao, T.; Chen, C.-H.; Li, W.; Meyer, C.A.; Wu, Q.; Wu, D.; Cong, L.; Zhang, F.; Liu, J.S.; et al. Sequence determinants of improved CRISPR sgRNA design. *Genome Res.* **2015**, *25*, 1147–1157. [CrossRef]
10. Moreno-Mateos, M.A.; Vejnar, C.E.; Beaudoin, J.-D.; Fernandez, J.P.; Mis, E.K.; Khokha, M.K.; Giraldez, A.J. CRISPRscan: Designing highly efficient sgRNAs for CRISPR-Cas9 targeting in vivo. *Nat. Methods* **2015**, *12*, 982–988. [CrossRef]
11. Zhang, S.W.; Wang, Y.; Zhang, X.X.; Wang, J.Q. Prediction of the RBP binding sites on lncRNAs using the high-order nucleotide encoding convolutional neural network. *Anal. Biochem.* **2019**, *583*, 113364. [CrossRef] [PubMed]
12. Ding, W.; Mao, W.; Shao, D.; Zhang, W.; Gong, H. DeepConPred2: An Improved Method for the Prediction of Protein Residue Contacts. *Comput. Struct. Biotechnol. J.* **2018**, *16*, 503–510. [CrossRef] [PubMed]
13. Le, N.Q.K.; Ho, Q.T.; Ou, Y.Y. Incorporating deep learning with convolutional neural networks and position specific scoring matrices for identifying electron transport proteins. *Comput. Chem.* **2017**, *38*. [CrossRef] [PubMed]
14. Lin, J.; Wong, K.-C. Off-target predictions in CRISPR-Cas9 gene editing using deep learning. *Oxf. Acad. Bioinform.* **2018**, *34*, i656–i663. [CrossRef] [PubMed]
15. Chuai, G.; Ma, H.; Yan, J.; Chen, M.; Hong, N.; Xue, D.; Zhou, C.; Zhu, C.; Chen, K.; Duan, B.; et al. DeepCRISPR: Optimized CRISPR guide RNA design by deep learning. *Genome Biol.* **2018**, *19*, 80. [CrossRef]
16. Xue, L.; Tang, B.; Chen, W.; Luo, J. Prediction of CRISPR sgRNA activity using a deep convolutional neural network. *J. Chem. Inf. Modeling* **2019**, *59*, 615–624. [CrossRef]
17. Dimauro, G. A new image quality metric based on human visual system. In Proceedings of the 2012 IEEE International Conf. on Virtual Environments Human-Computer Interfaces and Measurement Systems, Tianjin, China, 2–4 July 2012; pp. 69–73. [CrossRef]
18. Casalino, G.; Castellano, G.; Consiglio, A.; Liguori, M.; Nuzziello, N.; Primiceri, e.D. Analysis of microRNA expressions for pediatric multiple sclerosis detection. In *Modeling Decisions for Artificial Intelligence. MDAI2019*; Lecture Notes in Computer Science. LNAI 11676; Springer: Cham, Switzerland, 2019; pp. 177–188. [CrossRef]
19. Haeussler, M.; Schonig, K.; Eckert, H.; Eschstruth, A.; Mianne, J.; Renaud, J.-B.; Schneider-Maunoury, S.; Shkumatava, A.; Teboul, L.; Kent, J.; et al. Evaluation of off- target and on-target scoring algorithms and integration into the guide RNA selection tool CRISPOR. *Genome Biol.* **2016**, *17*, 148. [CrossRef]
20. Wang, T.; Wei, J.J.; Sabatini, D.M.; Lander, E.S. Genetic Screens in Human Cells Using the CRISPR-Cas9 System. *Science* **2014**, *343*, 80–84. [CrossRef]
21. Doench, J.G.; Hartenian, E.; Graham, D.B.; Tothova, Z.; Hegde, M.; Smith, I.; Sullender, M.; Ebert, B.L.; Xavier, R.J.; Root, D.E. Rational design of highly active sgRNAs for CRISPR-Cas9-mediated gene inactivation. *Nat. Biotechnol.* **2014**, *32*, 1262–1267. [CrossRef]
22. Hart, T.; Chandrashekhar, M.; Aregger, M.; Steinhart, Z.; Brown, K.R.; MacLeod, G.; Mis, M.; Zimmermann, M.; Fradet-Turcotte, A.; Sun, S.; et al. High-Resolution CRISPR Screens Reveal Fitness Genes and Genotype-Specific Cancer Liabilities. *Cell* **2015**, *163*, 1515–1526. [CrossRef]
23. Farboud, B.; Meyer, B.J. Dramatic Enhancement of Genome Editing by CRISPR/Cas9 Through Improved Guide RNA Design. *Genetics* **2015**, *199*, 959–971. [CrossRef] [PubMed]
24. Varshney, G.K.; Pei, W.; LaFave, M.C.; Idol, J.; Xu, L.; Gallardo, V.; Carrington, B.; Bishop, K.; Jones, M.; Li, M.; et al. High-throughput gene targeting and phenotyping in zebrafish using CRISPR/Cas9. *Genome Res.* **2015**, *25*, 1030–1042. [CrossRef] [PubMed]
25. Gagnon, J.A.; Valen, E.; Thyme, S.B.; Huang, P.; Ahkmetova, L.; Pauli, A.; Montague, T.G.; Zimmerman, S.; Richter, C.; Schier, A.F. Efficient Mutagenesis by Cas9 Protein-Mediated Oligonucleotide Insertion and Large-Scale Assessment of Single-Guide RNAs. *PLoS ONE* **2014**, *9*, e98186. [CrossRef] [PubMed]
26. Hussain, W.; Khan, Y.D.; Rasool, N.; Khan, S.A.; Chou, K.C. SPalmitoylC-PseAAC: A sequence-based model developed via Chou's 5-steps rule and general PseAAC for identifying S-palmitoylation sites in proteins. *Anal. Biochem.* **2019**, *568*, 14–23. [CrossRef]
27. Le, N.Q.K.; Fertility, G.R.U. Identifying Fertility-Related Proteins by Incorporating Deep-Gated Recurrent Units and Original Position-Specific Scoring Matrix Profiles. *J. Proteome Res.* **2019**, *18*, 3503–3511. [CrossRef]

© 2019 by the authors. Licensee MDPI, Basel, Switzerland. This article is an open access article distributed under the terms and conditions of the Creative Commons Attribution (CC BY) license (http://creativecommons.org/licenses/by/4.0/).

Article

Intelligent Fog-Enabled Smart Healthcare System for Wearable Physiological Parameter Detection

Muhammad Ijaz [1,2], Gang Li [1,2], Huiquan Wang [3], Ahmed M. El-Sherbeeny [4], Yussif Moro Awelisah [1,2], Ling Lin [1,2,*], Anis Koubaa [5,6] and Alam Noor [5,*]

1. State Key Laboratory of Precision Measurement Technology and Instrument, Tianjin University, Tianjin 300072, China; ijazm09@gmail.com (M.I.); ligang59@tju.edu.cn (G.L.); yussif@tju.edu.cn (Y.M.A.)
2. China and Tianjin Key Laboratory of Biomedical Detecting Techniques and Instruments, Tianjin University, Tianjin 300072, China
3. School of life sciences, Tiangong University, Tianjin 300387, China; huiquan@tiangong.edu.cn
4. Industrial Engineering Department, College of Engineering, King Saud University, PO Box 800, Riyadh 11421, Saudi Arabia; aelsherbeeny@ksu.edu.sa
5. Robotics and Internet-of-Things Lab, Prince Sultan University, Riyadh 11586, Saudi Arabia; akoubaa@psu.edu.sa
6. CISTER, INESC-TEC, ISEP, Polytechnic Institute of Porto, 4249-015 Porto, Portugal
* Correspondence: linling@tju.edu.cn (L.L.); eng.alamnoor@gmail.com (A.N.)

Received: 26 October 2020; Accepted: 24 November 2020; Published: 28 November 2020

Abstract: Wearable technology plays a key role in smart healthcare applications. Detection and analysis of the physiological data from wearable devices is an essential process in smart healthcare. Physiological data analysis is performed in fog computing to abridge the excess latency introduced by cloud computing. However, the latency for the emergency health status and overloading in fog environment becomes key challenges for smart healthcare. This paper resolves these problems by presenting a novel tri-fog health architecture for physiological parameter detection. The overall system is built upon three layers as wearable layer, intelligent fog layer, and cloud layer. In the first layer, data from the wearable of patients are subjected to fault detection at personal data assistant (PDA). To eliminate fault data, we present the rapid kernel principal component analysis (RK-PCA) algorithm. Then, the faultless data is validated, whether it is duplicate or not, by the data on-looker node in the second layer. To remove data redundancy, we propose a new fuzzy assisted objective optimization by ratio analysis (FaMOORA) algorithm. To timely predict the user's health status, we enable the two-level health hidden Markov model (2L-2HMM) that finds the user's health status from temporal variations in data collected from wearable devices. Finally, the user's health status is detected in the fog layer with the assist of a hybrid machine learning algorithm, namely SpikQ-Net, based on the three major categories of attributes such as behavioral, biomedical, and environment. Upon the user's health status, the immediate action is taken by both cloud and fog layers. To ensure lower response time and timely service, we also present an optimal health off procedure with the aid of the multi-objective spotted hyena optimization (MoSHO) algorithm. The health off method allows offloading between overloaded and underloaded fog nodes. The proposed tri-fog health model is validated by a thorough simulation performed in the iFogSim tool. It shows better achievements in latency (reduced up to 3 ms), execution time (reduced up to 1.7 ms), detection accuracy (improved up to 97%), and system stability (improved up to 96%).

Keywords: Tri-Fog Health System; fault data elimination; health status prediction; health status detection; health off

1. Introduction

In recent times, smart healthcare becomes an emerging application of the internet of things (IoT). A smart healthcare system consists of wearable sensors used to monitor the specific health status of the users or patients [1,2]. Most importantly, wearable technology has become a vital part of not only remote patient monitoring but also for user health monitoring regularly. The introduction of wearable devices minimizes the frequent involvement of doctors in health monitoring. It also assists in the early detection of diseases, drug research, smart hospital development, and safety provisioning [3,4]. Two major technologies have to be investigated to develop a smart healthcare system. Firstly, through biomedical sensors like temperature, motion, blood pressure, and how the wearable devices are appended on the user's body to acquire, their health status is studied [5]. Secondly, the useful fog computing technology that enables real-time and delay minimized health services [6,7] should be examined. As a result of the fog enabled healthcare system, the data acquired from the wearable devices are analyzed by the fog layer, which further minimizes the latency for healthcare services.

In the wearable based physiological monitoring, fault data detection from biosensors is one of the main issues [8]. Analyzing the fault data sensed by the wearable leads to inaccurate decision making. As the health data must be more reliable, the adaptive neuro-fuzzy inference system (ANFIS) is presented to diagnose health data [9]. A distributed similarity test has been introduced to detect the sensor data fault [10]. Based on the sensor reading variations, the sensor fault is detected. Thus, in a smart healthcare system, fault data diagnosis and elimination are the first and foremost process. In recent times, deep learning is addressed as one of the effective solutions for classification and prediction problems [11,12]. Deep learning algorithms are capable of handling and analyzing the massive amount of data without minimum prediction errors [13,14]. When it comes to fog-enabled smart healthcare, the faultless data need to be analyzed by the fog nodes. In most fog-based smart healthcare systems, a deep learning approach is incorporated to detect the abnormalities in the user's health status [15,16]. The deep learning approaches analyze the user's physiological data aggregated from the wearable devices. The multi-classifier system works based on data fused from different kinds of wearable sensors [17]. Both data fusion and multi-classifier methods offer better performance. A transfer learning model is proposed to detect Parkinson's disease from the wearable data [18].

In conventional healthcare systems, the data are analyzed in the cloud layer, which means the latency is high. Thus, fog computing becomes an essential part of the smart healthcare system [19]. Although the smart healthcare system has potentiality worked in many applications; still, the fault data detection has not yet been addressed. Firstly, while all works focus on the data analysis in the fog layer, the major issue of fog computing (i.e., fog overloading) is not yet concentrated for the healthcare environment. With the increase in users or patients in the healthcare system, there are relatively increasing concerns about the overloading issue [20]. Secondly, most research works utilized only biosensors or body sensors or wearable data to monitor the user's health status. However, environmental factors are also equally important to detect the user's health status accurately [21]. Environmental data like environment temperature, noise level, pollution level have a direct impact on the user's health data generated by wearable devices [22]. Both of the issues, including fog offloading and environmental data analysis, are not thoroughly analyzed in the prior research works from the perspective of healthcare systems. Apart from these issues, another challenge is that the duplicate data processing in fog or cloud layer leads to unnecessary resource consumption [23]. For example, the sensors report the data for each fraction of seconds. But the temperature data may be the same for a while. Thus, redundant data elimination will speed up the analysis process and also preserve the resources of fog and cloud computing.

1.1. Motivation and Inspiration

This research work is motivated by the existing problems in the smart healthcare system, such as high latency for emergency health status, fault and duplicate data analysis, and fog overloading. The brief summarization on research issues in our smart healthcare is provided here:

- Latency—High latency is introduced due to data processing in the cloud layer. In general, healthcare services need on-time data transmission. Latency in healthcare applications directly affects the patient's or user's health.
- Fault Data—Most wearable or biosensors are deployed in the open or mobile (on the human) environment. It makes the sensors to generate erroneous data. Analyzing the inaccurate data ultimately leads to incorrect prediction.
- Low Accuracy—Health status prediction accuracy is down due to improper algorithms and attributes. All research works considered only wearable sensor data, which are unable to provide accurate results. However, environmental data are also crucial for accurate prediction. As the wearable data consists of duplicate data, it also affects the data processing accuracy.
- Fog Overloading—One of the best solutions for minimizing latency is to use fog computing. However, when more users are connected in the same region, the fog will become overloaded. This overloading problem is the major research issue in smart healthcare.

These research issues motivate us to design a novel smart healthcare system. This paper concentrates on all these aspects to design an efficient smart healthcare system. For those, we formulate the following research objectives:

- Design a family healthcare system by using wearable for monitoring physiological parameters.
- Accurately predict the user state through physiological parameters.
- Minimize latency and detect the user state promptly.

To achieve these objectives, we designed a novel tripartite fog-enabled healthcare (Tri-FogHealth) architecture to monitor the health status of users through wearable physiological parameters. Apart from this, we made the following contributions in Tri-FogHealth architecture:

- Erroneous data from the wearable is diagnosed by using a rapid kernel principal component analysis (RK-PCA) algorithm. The RK-PCA algorithm is incorporated in a personal data assistant (PDA) (i.e.,) the faulty data is detected and eliminated in the wearable layer.
- From the faultless data, the data deduplication process is carried by the data on-looker node. To detect and eliminate duplicate data, we present a fuzzy assisted objective optimization by ratio analysis (FaMOORA) algorithm. If no duplicate data is found, then the fog node predicts the user's health status through temporal features using the two-level health hidden Markov model (2L-2HMM). The 2L-2HMM appends the severity level of the user's health status and provides apt action for severe cases.
- To prevent the fog layer from overloading the issue, we enable the health off procedure. The health of works upon two states. In the first stage, the offloading decision is made based on two rules. Then, an optimal node is selected for offloading by using the multi-objective spotted hyena optimization (MoSHO) algorithm.
- Then, the user's current health status is detected in the cloud layer based on behavioral, biomedical, and environmental attributes. All these attributes are fed into the spiking quantum neural network (SpikQ-Net) that accurately classifies the user's health status into normal action required, no action required, and immediate action required classes.

1.2. Paper Layout

The rest of this paper is organized as follows: Section 2 surveys existing research works held on smart healthcare systems. In Section 3, we highlight the problem statement and the background of the problems considered in this work. Section 4 clearly explains the overall proposed work with all algorithms. In Section 5, we describe the experimentation detail of the proposed work with experimental setup and comparative analysis. Section 6 concludes the overall contributions of this work.

2. Related Work

In this section, we present existing important research works proposed in the smart healthcare system.

2.1. Research Works on Cloud-Based Smart Healthcare System

A smart healthcare system is designed to monitor elderly peoples and optimal access control [24]. For providing access control, the Pearson correlation coefficient (PCC) algorithm is presented with the Manhattan distance measure. Firstly, algorithms work in parallel to identify older people. Then, the PCA algorithm is applied to reduce the dimensionality reduction for the collected elderly data. Lately, the normalization cross-correlation (NCC) algorithm is utilized for final results. However, the PCA and NCC algorithms are insufficient to process the large amount of data collected from elderly peoples. In a smart healthcare system designed with multiple heterogeneous wearable sensors [25], the proposed approach uses an analytical hierarchy process (AHP) with the VIseKriterijumska Optimizacija I Kompromisno Resenje (VIKOR) method to make a proper decision on hospital selection based on two steps. Firstly, the data from the wearable device was collected and analyzed. Then, the hospital is selected by considering the user's health status and multiple criteria. In this work, the processing algorithm is only applied to determine the optimal hospital; however, a more intelligent mechanism will make decisions based on the health data.

For reliable medical monitoring, fault data detection was performed by the threshold tuning method [26]. The medical data is collected from wearable devices. As it could be corrupted from the environmental factors and sensor faults, the fault detection using Bayesian neural network was performed initially. Although fault data detection improves data reliability, health status monitoring performance is still inefficient. The Bayesian neural network increases the complexity of the personal devices of the patient.

As a result, a statistical approach was presented for patient monitoring [27]. The vital signs are acquired from the wearable, and the data is processed to predict the patient's health status. First, gaussian process (GP) models are built for interpretive signs with varying complexity. For this purpose, the covariance kernels and the fixed parameters are utilized. Then, the Bayesian model is proposed to find the health status of the user based on two main hypotheses, such as (i) use of patient-specific model and (ii) use of optimal hyperparameter values. Here, the selection of hyperparameters increases the complexity of the system.

A new cloud digital twins (CloudDTH) framework was introduced for smart healthcare monitoring [28]. The concept of digital twins is integrated multi-physics, multi-scale and probabilistic simulation of a system. In CloudDTH, a virtual object is created for all users in the cloud environment. The virtual object data was used for modelling, simulating, and evaluating the user data. From the analysis of the virtual object, the healthcare status of the user was predicted. In general, digital twins are hard to deploy and manage. In addition, to create a digital twin for each user is not scalable.

To further enhance the prediction accuracy, a complement naïve Bayesian (CNB) classifier was deployed in the cloud environment to classify the user's health data [29]. Firstly, the medical data was acquired from the wearable and biosensors. Before classification, the preprocessing mechanism was applied to handle the noisy data. The CNB classifier uses double learning processes to improve classification accuracy. First, the naïve Bayes classifier was trained with the dataset. Then, the classifier was tested by using the same dataset. It is known as double learning. Here the misclassified data was used for original test data classification.

2.2. Research Works on Fog-Enabled Healthcare System

The concept of edge computing is introduced to mitigate latency in healthcare applications [30]. The proposed system computed the criticality measure index (CMI) from the gathered wearable data. Then the alert message was triggered in emergencies. Here, the CMI value is calculated for each data without considering temporal and environmental data. It tends to inaccurate health status prediction.

The fog computing-based gateway design explores a geo-distributed intermediary layer of intelligence [31]. This layer was introduced between the sensors and the cloud. In the fog enabled healthcare systems, the fog node takes the responsibility of the sensors such as severity detection. The highlight is that the use of the fog layer in the e-healthcare system improves energy efficiency, scalability, and reliability problems and also supports user mobility. Therefore, fog computing plays a pivotal role in e-healthcare applications.

However, the data analysis accuracy is low since there no intelligence algorithm is applied to the collected health data. Therefore, a smart treatment for personalized healthcare (STPH) model was presented with edge computing [32]. The STPH model provides the optimal treatment solution to minimize the cost of the intelligent agent. This approach uses an intelligent agent (IA), which assists in constructing a personalized treatment plan. Furthermore, the edge servers were introduced to help the cloud server in the data processing. Here the treatment plan is optimally selected for emergencies. However, optimal treatment plan selection without detecting the user's current health status results in low accuracy.

An edge of thins (EoT) driven ambient assisted living framework was proposed for e-healthcare applications [33]. This framework uses a hybrid classifier to predict the health status of the user. The hybrid classifier is made up of the hybrid ambient assisted living with naïve bayes classifier and the firefly algorithm (HAAL-NBFA). The firefly algorithm is employed to select the optimal features for classification. Upon optimal features chosen by the firefly algorithm, the naïve Bayes classifier detects the state of the user. Before the imbalanced dataset is balanced by the synthetic minority over-sampling technique (SMOTE), the naïve Bayes classifier has less accuracy due to the class dependencies. This work fails when the incoming data has faulty reading.

A HealthFog framework was developed to monitor the heart diseases in the IoT environment to minimize the latency and response time for personalized healthcare [34]. The HealthFog integrates the ensemble deep learning algorithm with edge computing. Further, the fog-enabled framework is defined as FogBus, which efficiently detects the health status of heart patients. At the same time, real-time medical data is collected from the sensors of the wearable. The FogBus is designed using the broker node, the worker node, and the cloud data center. The same data is analyzed in different worker nodes, and the results are ensemble for final classification. Here the deep learning model is trained in each worker node of each fog node; this increases the time consumption.

As fog overloading increases the latency for the emergency data, an ubiquitous cloud edge enabled healthcare (UbeHealth) system was aimed to improve the quality of service (QoS) in the healthcare system [35]. The healthcare data was processed in both the cloudlet and network layer. In the cloudlet layer, the deep learning-based data prediction approach was applied, and in the network layer, data classification by deep learning approach was proposed. Both deep learning approaches use a recurrent neural network (RNN) for classification. In the cloudlet layer, the flow clustering and analysis (FCA) process was employed with the density-based spatial clustring of application with noise (DBSCAN) clustering algorithm. Consequently, using two deep learning algorithms increases the time consumption.

2.3. Research Works on Fog Offloading

Load balancing in fog-based healthcare applications was focused on improving service quality [36]. The fog computing resources were consolidated in this work to balance the load among foglets. Only critical resources were redirected to cloud computing, and the rest requests were scheduled to fog nodes locally. Although this work utilizes fog nodes to prevent overloading, a random selection of fog nodes leads to that the fog nodes to become overloaded.

Multiple agents are deployed in the smart healthcare system to maintain load balancing among fog nodes [37]. The primary aim of the multi-agent fog computing model was to serve critical tasks within the given time. For this, optimal scheduling was enabled by the multiple agents to access the fog resources. Here, the most suitable fog node was selected based on resource availability information. However, numerous criteria are required to process critical and emergency tasks.

A novel four-tier fog architecture was presented to balance load among fog nodes [38]. A dual fuzzy logic algorithm classified the tasks received from the IoT devices to assign priority levels for the tasks. Then the tasks were scheduled based on an artificial neural network. Herein, the single objective is considered for fog node selection, where the energy utility is inefficient.

An energy-efficient offloading strategy was presented for IoT applications [39]. The objective was to achieve better QoS and energy efficiency. For this, a firefly algorithm based offloading scheme was proposed. The firefly algorithm uses a weighted-sum method to determine fitness function. The firefly algorithm is inefficient in local search as it is not suitable for optimal fog node selection.

Comment on Literature: In Table 1, we summarize the literature works with limitations. The analyzes show a massive research gap that needed to be addressed while designing a smart healthcare system.

Table 1. Summarization of literature survey.

Category	Presented Works	Research Issues
Cloud-Smart Healthcare	• PCC and NCC [24] • AHP-VIKOR Model [25] • Fault Monitoring [26] • Statistical Approach [27] • CloudDTH [28] • CNB-Cloud [29]	• Health status detection time is high • Unable to process a large amount of data • Involvement of inefficient algorithms
Fog-Smart Healthcare	• CMI-Fog [30] • Fog-Gateway [31] • STPH [32] • EoT-Hybrid Classifier [33] • HealthFog [34] • UbeHealth [35]	• Low accuracy due to ineffective algorithms • Not able to support a large number of users • High processing time due to the presence of redundant data
Fog Offloading	• Health Load Balancing [36] • Multi-Agent Fog Model [37] • Four-Tier Fog Architecture [38] • QoS Offloading [39]	• Nonoptimal fog selection degrades the offloading performance • single objective is insufficient to select optimum fog node

3. Problem Overview

In this section, we present the problem statement of this work with the background of the problems.

3.1. Overall Problem Statement

In wearable-based smart healthcare, more research works have been presented in the view of a clinical study, and non-clinical home-based health monitoring is concentrated less. The biomedical sensors have been used only for health monitoring, but environmental factors play a pivotal role in healthcare monitoring. Furthermore, fault and duplicate data processing often results in inaccurate outcomes and increases time consumption. Although fog-enabled IoT healthcare systems minimize the latency, this depreciation is not sufficient for emergency events. Because the regional fog node where the number of users is high or the environmental status is worst will become overloaded, it drastically increases the latency for the particular region.

3.2. Background of the Problem

A cognitive dynamics (CDS) concept is presented for smart healthcare and disease diagnosis, along with decision tree-based classification [40]. Here, the decision tree is unstable, i.e., a small change in the data results in a massive change in the structure, which leads to wrong decisions. Further, it is not suitable to handle streaming data like smart healthcare. The overall analysis is performed here in the cloudlet layer, which will increase latency drastically. A structured Gaussian process is proposed for patient-specific physiological monitoring based on its health trajectory [41]. The Gaussian method is a highly parametric approach that considers all parameters known in prior while increasing the complexity. This work finds a single vital sign for determining the health level of the patients.

Furthermore, this work is not suitable to handle mobile users since the cluster formation become complex. Mobile-based physiological sensor system (MoPS) uses a smart shirt and wearable technology [42]. Analysis of the massive data from wearable demands highly efficient algorithms and methodologies. Here the data analysis is performed in a cloud server without using proper algorithms and based on the conventional threshold. It leads to inaccurate classification and also increases the time consumption.

Further, the user status is detected based on the current physiological sign only. But in general, the health status of a user depends upon the time series data. The overall analysis considers a single physiological sign which is insufficient for health status detection.

In a fog-assisted patient health monitoring, Bayesian belief network (BBN) was introduced in the fog layer for health status prediction [43]. In the cloud layer, the temporal information is used to compute the temporal health index (THI) for the patients. In this work, both fog and cloud layers work upon the same attributes (environmental, medical, and behavior). This time consumption increasing makes it not suitable for healthcare monitoring. Processing in the cloud layer increases the latency of emergency events. This work is not appropriate to handle large-scale systems and also unable to support mobile users. However, patients with chronic disease will have mobile nature instead of static. This system is not suitable for real-time analysis. In addition, the BBN classifier is hard to construct and also has low classification accuracy. A hierarchical data fusion method uses the complex event processing (CPE) method for clinical patient monitoring [44]. In each level (sensor, fog, and cloud), data fusion is performed based on a threshold value. All three levels consider biosensor reading only for the patient's health status monitoring. However, environmental factors also play a pivotal role in healthcare monitoring. CPE, which is used in all three levels, uses some pre-defined rules to detect the patient status. However, this is not suitable in the practical scenario since each user has different signs and parameters. Thus, the CPE based analysis is not suitable for real-time analysis. In the fog-cloud smart office healthcare system, the severity index is computed based on environmental, behavior, and posture data [45]. The Bayesian classifier is complex and has less accuracy. Thus, data classification by Bayesian classifiers often results in inaccurate outcomes. The final decision on the user's health status is determined at the cloud layer. It increases the latency considerably for emergency events. Poor load management in the fog layer affects the overall processing ability of the fog layer.

4. Proposed Tri-Fog Health System

In this section, we discuss the proposed tri-fog healthcare system in detail. Each proposed methodology is explained in each subsection.

4.1. System Overview

The proposed tri-foghealth system is designed with three primary layers, such as the wearable layer, the intelligent fog layer, and the cloud layer, as shown in Figure 1. The main intention of the system is to enable remote health monitoring for wellbeing lifestyle. It also supports mobile users. The first layer consists of n users ($u_1, u_2, .; u_n$) with wearable sensors (we consider a smart shirt with biosensors) and a single PDA device and environmental sensors. The next layer comprises m Data On-Looker nodes ($Ol_1, Ol_2, .; Ol_m$) and k fog nodes ($F_1, F_2, .; F_k$). The first layer is responsible for collecting health data from the patients. The second layer involves two different entities, such as data on-lookers and fog nodes. The data on-looker nodes are responsible for redundant data elimination and health status prediction. The health status prediction is the process of the forecasting health status of the user in the next time frame based on the collected time-series data. The result will be added with the current data to increase the accuracy of classification. The fog nodes are responsible for classifying the user's current health status based on the wearable data and predicted report. The final cloud layer consists of a cloud server. The detail of the three layers is provided in the Table 2.

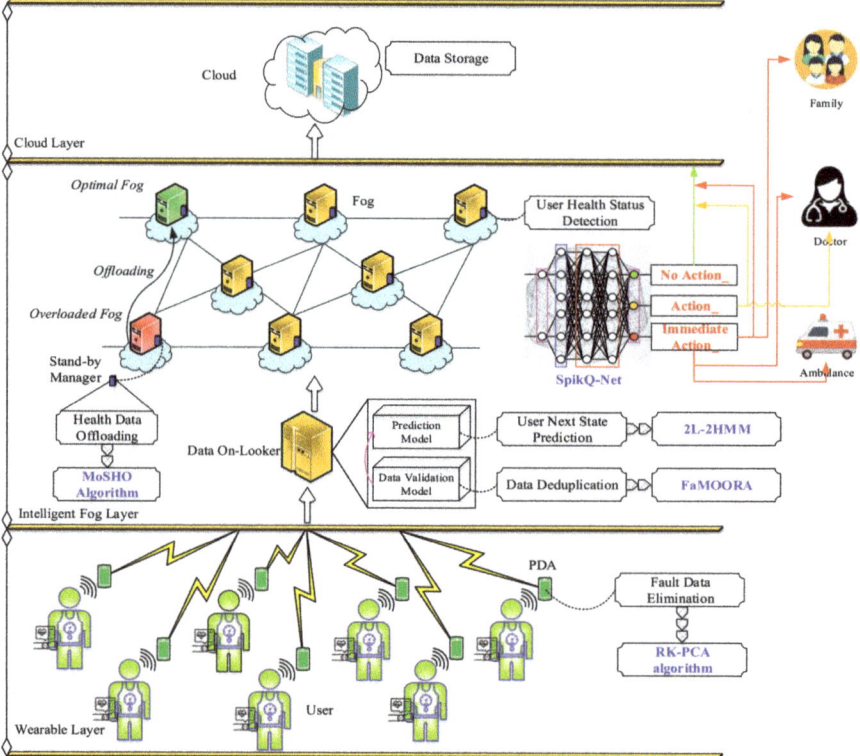

Figure 1. Tri-FogHealth System Architecture.

Table 2. Description of Three Layers in Tri-FogHealth.

Layer	Entities Involved	Functions Incorporated
Wearable Layer	• Users with smart shirts • Wearable Devices with biosensors • PDA	• Data Generation and Aggregation • Fault Data Detection and Elimination by RK-PCA
Intelligent Fog Layer	• Data On-Looker Nodes • Intelligent Fog Nodes	• Redundant Data Elimination by FaMOORA • Health Status Prediction by Temporal Analysis (2L-2HMM) • Health Status Detection by SpikQ-Net • Alert Generation on Emergency Cases
• Cloud Layer	• Cloud Servers	• Data Storage and Retrieval

As shown in the table, each layer works upon different algorithms. Each algorithm is intended for a different process. Each process contributes to improving the quality and accuracy of the healthcare system. On the proposed healthcare system, we make the following assumptions,

- All users have the same number of wearable devices to sense and generate health data;
- The number of fog nodes always equal or higher than the number of data on-looker nodes (i.e.,) $k \geq m$;

By considering the above two assumptions, we designed the tri-foghealth system. Functions carried in each layer of the proposed system are explained in the consecutive subsections.

4.2. Fault Data Elimination in the Wearable Layer

In the device layer, the health data and environmental data are aggregated. The wearable smart shirt is the primary source of health data for each user. Further, the environmental data is collected in every region to detect the user's health status accurately. As the main issue in wearable sensors is fault data generation, the first layer designed in a way such that the fault data problem will be overwhelmed. The fault data is detected and eliminated at the device layer for each user. For that, we present the RK-PCA algorithm in PDA. A fault data in the healthcare system can be detected based on the deviation with the normal data model and the variation with the other sensor data. For instance, the heart rate is generally proportional to the respiratory rate. When there is conflict occurs, then any one of those sensors reported fault data. Thus, the consideration of multiple sensor data models should much support the fault data detection and elimination.

To improve accuracy and processing speed, we present the RK-PCA algorithm. Let u_i wears a smart shirt with w biosensors as $S_1, S_2, \ldots, S_w$. Each biosensor senses the data and reports the data to PDA in a regular time interval. RK-PCA has to find fault data by comparing the current data with the normal data model. To this end, the normal data model is built for the sensor data received from the wearable sensors. The sensor data can be denoted as $\{X = X_1, X_2, .; X_t\}$. The data is captured in d dimensions in t time instances. The data model is represented as the Eigenvector. The Eigenvalue equation is defined as $\sum_\varphi e_i = \alpha_i e_i$. In this, e_i is estimated as;

$$e_i = \sum_{j=1}^{t} \alpha_i(j) \varphi(X_i(z)) \tag{1}$$

Here, X_i is the chosen data from the normal data model. Similarly, the eigenvalue is computed for all normal data values. From the normal data model, the fault data is detected, as shown in Figure 2.

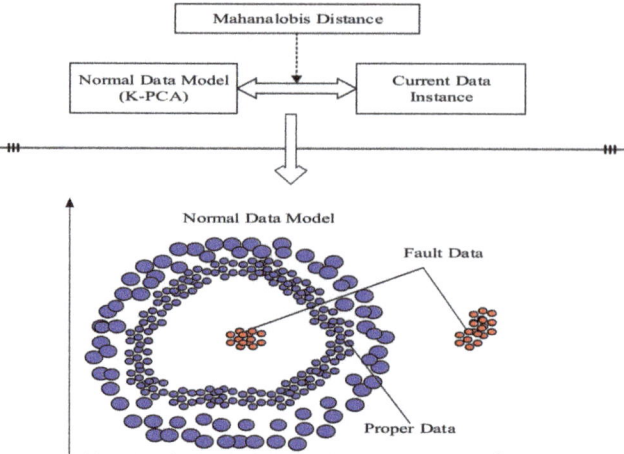

Figure 2. Fault Data Detection by Rapid Kernel Principal Component Analysis (RK-PCA).

As in the figure, the first step is to model the normal data by the RK-PCA algorithm. Here, kernel selection is carried as follows,

$$Ker(X_i, X_j) = \exp\left(\frac{1}{2\sigma^2}(X_i - X_j)^T Q^{-1}(X_i - X_j)\right) \quad (2)$$

The considered kernel is Mahalanobis Kernel (MK) since it supports the non-linear transformations of the data points.

The next step is to compute the similarity between current data instance (S_C) and normal data model (S_{nor}). The similarity is computed as Mahalanobis distance as follows,

$$dis(S_c, S_{nor}) = \sqrt{(S_C - S_{nor})^T CM^{-1}(S_C - S_{nor})} \quad (3)$$

Here, CM defines the covariance matrix defined by the eigenvalues of the normal data model. If the distance is low, then the data is normal. Otherwise, the data is a fault. The PDA carries this process, and the fault data is suppressed in the PDA. In Algorithm 1, we provided a detailed algorithm for RK-PCA algorithm-based fault data detection. The information with no fault is then transmitted to the next layer (i.e.,) intelligent fog layer.

Algorithm 1: RK-PCA for Fault Data Detection.

    Initialize X_i
    For all $u \in Layer\ 1$
      Get $\{X_i\}$ from u_i
      Set RK-PCA Dimension
      Select Ker function   //Equation (2)
      Build e_i //Normal Data Model
      Construct CM //From e_i
      Compute (dis) //Mahanalobis Function
      If X_i to Fault
        Drop X_i
      Else
        Send X_i to Layer 2

      End If
    End For
    End

4.3. Redundant Data Elimination by Data Validation

In the fog layer, two primary functions are performed by the data on-looker nodes. The first process is redundant data elimination, and the next process is the user's health status prediction. The faultless data from PDA is received by the data on-looker nodes in the region. The data on-looker nodes are the special nodes that maintain the previous data records from the wearable devices and environmental sensors. The data on-looker nodes are designed with data validation model and prediction model. The data validation model is responsible for redundant data elimination by comparing the current data with previous data instances. Then, the redundant free data is fed into the prediction model to perform first-level health status prediction. The conceptual structure of the data on-looker node is illustrated in Figure 3.

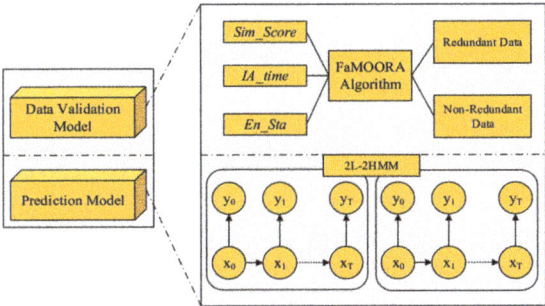

Figure 3. Structure of Data On-Looker Node.

4.3.1. Redundant Data Elimination

In this work, we intend to eliminate redundant data without affecting emergency data. In general, the redundant data elimination is performed if any one of the instances in prior records is matched with the current data. However, in the healthcare system, a redundant may also be emergency data. In this case, the data analysis will be affected. Thus, the problem of redundant data elimination is formulated as a decision-making problem and resolved by a hybrid multi-criteria decision-making algorithm.

We present the FaMOORA algorithm that works upon three major criteria, such as similarity score (Sim_Score), inter arrival time (IA_Time) and environmental status (En_Sta). Each criterion can be defined as follows,

Sim_Score—The current data instance D1 is verified with prior data records from the same user. D1 is the current data instance from the ith user. A data instance is made up of sensor readings sensed by the biosensors incorporated on the user. Thus, D1={Sd1, Sd2, ; Sdw}. Then D1 is compared with succeeding data D2, D3, ..., Dq of the same sensor of the same user:

$$Sim\_Score(D_1, D_j) = \sqrt{(x_1 - x_2)^2 + (y_1 - y_j)^2} \quad (4)$$

The score is computed between all prior data instances.

IA_Time—The inter-arrival time is considered to find whether D_1 is needed to be eliminated or not. If the time between two similar data is relatively less, then the data is duplicate. If the time difference is high, then the data is new, and it is essential for data analysis.

En_Sta—The difference in environmental status also plays a vital role in redundant data elimination. It is because the biosensor data may be the same, but the environmental data may be different. In the worst environmental scenario, the biosensor data will be necessary. In this scenario, data must be preserved.

All three criteria are considered in the FaMOORA algorithm for making decisions on the current data instance. The procedure of the FaMOORA algorithm is detailed below.

Firstly, the decision matrix (DM) is constructed with data upon three criteria as follows,

$$DM = \begin{bmatrix} SS(1,2) & SS(1,3) & SS(1,q) \\ IA(1,2) & IA(1,3) & IA(1,q) \\ EN(1,2) & EN(1,3) & EN(1,q) \end{bmatrix} \quad (5)$$

Then DM is normalized, taking the square root of the sum of all the squares of each alternative per attribute. This ratio can be given as,

$$SS(1,q)^* = \frac{SS(1,q)}{\sqrt{\left[\sum_{q=2}^{q} SS(1,q)^*\right]}} \quad (6)$$

From the normalized DM, the attributes are weighted by using the fuzzy approach. In conventional MOORA [46], the weight value is given for the characteristics based on the analytic hierarchy process (AHP). However, it consumes a significant amount of time. Thus, we present a fuzzy weighting scheme for the FaMOORA algorithm. The weight value of the attribute SS is given as,

$$nSS_q = \sum_{q=1}^{g} w_q SS(1,q)^* - \sum_{q=g+1}^{h} w_q SS(1,q)^* \quad (7)$$

Here, g denotes the number of attributes that need to be maximized (beneficial attributes), and h indicates the number of attributes to be minimized (non-beneficial attributes). Further, nSS_q is the normalized attribute value. Then the fuzzy weight value is computed within the range of [0, 1]. The weight value calculated above will be in [r_1, r_2]. Then it can be mapped into fuzzy values as,

$$FW(nSS_q) = \frac{|nSS_q - r_1|}{|r_1 - r_2|} \quad (8)$$

For each attribute value, the weight value is computed as above. Thus, the normalized DM becomes the fuzzy weighted DM (FWDM) with the values of [0, 1]. From the FWDM, the decision on the current data instance is made based on the following if-then rule,

If (SS(1, q) to (> 0.5) &IA(1, q)&&EN(1, q) to (< 0.5)
Then, D_1 = Duplicate

By following the above rule, the data duplication decision is made, and the data on-looker nodes suppress the duplicate data. Then, the redundant free data is fed into the nearby fog node for health status prediction.

4.3.2. User Health Status Prediction by Temporal Analysis

The prediction model receives the user's health data from the data on-looker node then analysis the data based on temporal information. The prediction module carries the process of health status prediction. In this section, we introduce the 2L-2HMM model that predicts the users' health status. In this stage, the data instance from biosensors is analyzed with time series. The proposed 2L-2HMM works upon two levels. In the first level, the biosensor data is interpreted as in the HMM model. Let D_i be the data instance of u_j. The fog node first extracts the time series data u_j of the u_j. The next status of u_j upon biosensor data is characterized by $\delta_i(t+1)$ of $\{\pi, \mathbb{A}, \mathbb{B}\}$. Here, A denotes the transition probability matrix, and B is the observation probability matrix. The observation matrix is composed of the data instances gathered by the biosensors. The initial state distribution is denoted as,

$$\pi_i = P(H_1 = 1), \quad 1 \leq i \geq p \tag{9}$$

where, P is the number of probability distributions, and H denotes the hidden state. The state transition probability of transition from state x to state y is computed as,

$$a_{x,y} = P(H_t = y | H_{t-1}), \quad 1 \leq y \geq p, 1 \leq k \geq w \tag{10}$$

The observation probability distribution defines the probability of state transition for the observation lk as,

$$b_k = P(l_k | H_t = y), \quad 1 \leq y \geq p, 1 \leq k \geq w \tag{11}$$

In general, the observation variable lk depends on the hidden state H_k while the hidden state depends on the previous hidden state H_{t-1}. The prediction of the next state of u_i is performed based on the Bayes assumption on observation distribution as follows,

$$P(l_k | H_t = y) = \prod_{w=1}^{|L_k|} P(l_k | H_t = y) \tag{12}$$

The user's health status is determined as normal or emergency based on the time-series data.

In the second level, the location variations of the users are considered. For instance, the set of locations of the user denotes $= \{L_1, L_2, \ldots, L_t\}$. As the tri-foghealth works upon remote monitoring, the user location may cover home, home surroundings, home long-distance. In this level, the user's current location is verified, whether it is frequent or non-frequent. Upon this information and the status predicted from the first level, 2L-2HMM uses the following rules,

- When the user's next status is emergency, and the location is not-frequent of the user, then the user is in a critical situation (C_1).
- When the user's next status is emergency, and the location is a frequent location of the user, then the user is in a near-critical situation (C_2).
- When the user's next status is normal, then the user is in the non-critical situation (C_3).

41

The user's next health status is appended with the data to increase the accuracy in the fog nodes. In addition, the health status prediction process assists in timely data analysis. In Algorithm 2, we detailed the process carried by data on-looker nodes, including redundant data elimination and user's health status prediction. At the end of this algorithm, the data instance is appended with the user's next state to make health status detection accurate.

Algorithm 2: Process in Data On-Looker.

Initialize $D_1, D_2, ..., D_i, ...$
//Start Validation Model→ FaMOORA
For D_i do
   Compute *Sim_Score*
   Compute *IA_Time*
   Compute *EN_Sta*
   Construct *DM*
   Normalize *DM*
   Update weights by *FW*
   Apply IF-THEN Rules
   If D_i to Duplicate
     Drop D_i
   Else
     Fed D_i to 2L – 2HMM
   End if
End for
//Start Prediction Model →2L-2HMM
   For Di do
     Extract μ_i
     Compute $a_{x,y}, b_k$ //Equations (10) and (11)
     Predict Next State
     Extract $\theta = \{L_1, L_2, ..., L_t\}$
     Fuse Two Levels
     Append User's Next Status
   End for
End

4.3.3. User's Health Status Detection by Fog Nodes

After predicting the user's health status by data on-looker, the health data is delivered to the fog nodes. In fog nodes, health status detection is performed based on three categories of attributes by using SpikQ-Net. The proposed SpikQ-Net combines a spiking neural network that mimics the natural neural network [47] and a quantum neural network that works upon quantum mechanics [48]. The fusion of both neural networks results in better accuracy of the user's health status detection process. First, we clearly described the attributes detail in the Table 3.

Table 3. Attributes Description.

Category	Attributes	Description
Behavior	• Cholesterol • Smoke • Cig/Day • Height • Weight • Activity • Chronic_Disease • Location	Attributes are related to the user's normal behavior. We consider the static information like smoke or not and dynamic information like location to monitor the user's health status
Biomedical	• Blood_Pressure • Glucose_Level • Heart_Rate • Respiratory_Rate • Temperature	We consider the data from wearable devices. All data related to the biomedical data that shows the user's current health status
Environmental	• Room_Temperature • Noise_Level • Air_Quality	These data are collected from the regional environmental sensors.

The SpikQ-Net gets the input of these three categories of attributes, such as behavioral, biomedical, and environmental. Generally, the user's health status is detected based on the biomedical data. The reason for considering behavioral and environmental attributes is that both attributes have a high impact on the biomedical sensor data. For example, the heart rate is increased when the user is doing exercise and also in a noisy environment. In this case, the abnormal heart rate is reported by the biomedical sensors due to the tenancy of environmental and behavioral attributes. Thus, we considered all three categories of attributes in the user's health status detection. All three types of attributes are fed into the SpikQ-Net from the current data instance, as shown in Figure 4.

Let the current data instance be $D_i(t)=\{(BD_i)(BMD_i)(EN_i)\}$. The data instance at time t is composed of behavior (BD_i) biomedical (BM_i), and environmental (EN_i) attributes at time instance t. For each user, SpikQ-Net first extracts these attributes by learning the data received. Then, the weight value is adjusted based on the fusion of these attributes to detect health status. Similarly, the instances from various users are fed as input to the SpikQ-Net. The proposed SpikQ-Networks as follows,

1. The set of input functions ($D_1(t)$, $D_2(t)$, .; $D_i(t)$, ..., $D_n(t)$) is fed into the input layer;
2. Each neuron learns the input to produce output vectors in the hidden layers;
3. The initial weight values (W_i) are initialized as the random numbers;
4. Then the weight values are updated according to the update rule of quantum mechanics;

$$W_i(t+1) = W_i(t) + \eta(|o\rangle - |y(t)\rangle)\langle D_j| \qquad (13)$$

5. Here o is the desired output provided for the training stage, η is step size, and it is set as $0 < \eta < 1$;
6. At last, the out layer learns the output based on the weights learned from hidden layers. The output of the quantum perceptron at the time t is,

$$|y(t)\rangle = \sum_{j=1}^{n} W_i(t)|D_i\rangle \qquad (14)$$

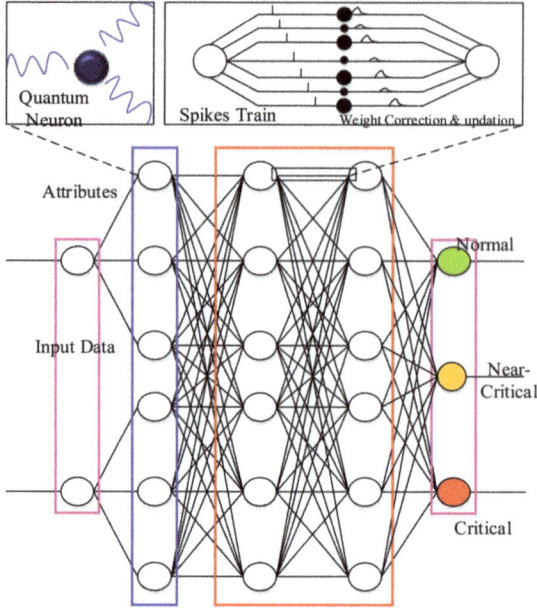

Figure 4. SpikQ-Network for Health Status Detection.

In this procedure, we introduce spikes between quantum neurons. The current activation function value is considered the neuron's state, and the spikes increase its value to achieve better accuracy. The introduction of spikes alters the weight update expression as follows,

$$W_i(t+1) = W_i(t) + \eta \delta_i(t) + v \Delta W_i(t-1) \tag{15}$$

Here, v is the momentum parameter and $\Delta W_i(t-1)$ is the weight correction in the previous iteration. In this manner, the weight values of each neuron are updated for each parameter, and the output layer detects the user's health status.

The main aim of this process is to detect the user's health status as normal, critical, and non-critical classes. As per the class, the necessary action is taken. The fog nodes take all the steps. That is, the latency is relatively low for the users. In addition, emergency actions assist in the timely detection of abnormalities as the process is performed in the fog layer.

4.3.4. Health Data Offloading

The data on-looker node assigns the data for analysis to random fog nodes. Thus, the fog nodes become overloading. To overcome this issue, we present the health off procedure. Although data processing in the fog layer minimizes latency, there has been a huge issue that is fog overloading. Users within the same region often access the same fog node. In such a case, when user density is high in a particular area, the fog node will become overloaded. Besides, if the environmental condition of a specific region becomes worst, then many users in that region will require immediate action. Thus, we present a fog offloading scheme in healthcare services. Each fog node has the stand-by manager who monitors the load of the fog node regularly and makes a decision on fog overloading. The health off decision is made in the following two cases,

Case 1: When the fog node becomes overloaded

Case 2: When the environmental condition becomes worst

If the health off decision is made, the stand-by manager selects an optimal fog node for health data offloading. For optimal fog node selection, we propose the MoSHO algorithm. Consider, f_{ol} becomes overloaded, then it selects the optimal fog node (fopt) from the set of fog nodes. The spotted hyena optimization algorithm is a bio-inspired optimization algorithm that works upon the social behavior of spotted hyenas [49]. As single objective-based offloading is inefficient to maintain the load among fog nodes, we formulate multiple objective functions in the MoSHO algorithm. The proposed MoSHO algorithm works in three steps: searching prey, encircling, and attacking the target. The overall process of the MoSHO algorithm is summarized below.

Fitness Evaluation—Initialize the spotted hyenas' population. The initial population list consists of a set of candidate fog nodes as $IP \in \{F_1, F_2, .; F_k\}$. Then, the fitness value is computed for each node in the IP set. In the MoSHO algorithm, multiple criteria are considered for the computation of the fitness function of jth candidate search agent $Fn(F_j)$. The considered multiple criteria are load value β, distance τ, and energy required ρ. The first objective function computes the current load value of the candidate fog nodes in terms of the number of processing tasks and available resources. The second objective function computes the distance between the current and candidate fog nodes. Thus, the offloading is performed between two nearby fog nodes, which minimizes the offloading time. The third objective function is formulated based on the energy required for offloading the current load from the current fog node to the optimal fog node. Thus, the fitness value is expressed as follows,

$$Fn(F_j) = \frac{1}{\sum(\beta_j, \tau_j, \rho_j)} \qquad (16)$$

The fitness function is computed for all fog nodes in the candidate set.

Hunting—From the candidate solutions, the search agent who has the highest fitness value is selected to explore solutions in the given search space. The best search agent has the location of the prey. Thus, the other search agents form a cluster to move towards the best search agent. The cluster and the movement are expressed mathematically as follows,

$$D_h = |B.\omega_{h_1} - \omega_{h_2}| \qquad (17)$$

$$\omega_{h_2} = \omega_{h_1} - E.D_h \qquad (18)$$

$$C_{h1} = \omega_{h_2} + \omega_{h_2+1} + \ldots + \omega_{h_2+V} \qquad (19)$$

Here, ω_{h_2} defines the position of the first best-spotted hyena, ω_{h_1} represents the position of other spotted hyenas. In addition, V denotes the number of spotted hyenas, and it is computed as follows,

$$V = Count_{nos}(\omega_{h_2} + \omega_{h_2+1} + \ldots + (\omega_{h2} + Ran)) \qquad (20)$$

where Ran defines the random vector [0.5, 1], nos represents several solutions and count all candidate solutions.

Attacking Prey (Exploitation)—In this phase, the solutions are updated towards the best search agent. This phase is known as attacking the prey. It can be mathematically formulated as,

$$\omega(b+1) = \frac{C_h}{V} \qquad (21)$$

The $\omega(b+1)$ saves the best solution and updates the positions of other search agents. The position updation is performed according to the best search agent. Next, the search agent fitness value is updated towards the ideal solution. This process is iterated until the optimal fog node is selected.

In Algorithm 3, the procedure of MoSHO based health off is proposed. Then, the data is offloaded to the optimal fog node selected by the MoSHO algorithm. The process of emptying prevents the fog nodes from overloading the problem. As offloading is performed between closest fog nodes, the latency is minimized. All three functions are performed in the fog layer to achieve better performance.

Algorithm 3: Procedure of Health Off by MoSHO.

Initialize population $F_1, F_2, .. F_k \in IP$
For all $F_j \in IP$
  Compute $F_n(F_i)$ using Equation (16)
  Find best search agent
  Moves clusters   //Equations (17)–(19)
  Find number of hyenas   //Equation (20)
  Update solutions   //Equation (21)
  Find F_{opt}
  Offload data
End for
End

---

5. Experimental Evaluation

In this section, we present the experimental setup and comparative analysis of the proposed smart healthcare system.

5.1. Experimental Setup

In this section, we illustrate the experimental model of the tri-foghealth system. The proposed tri-foghealth is modelled in the iFogSim simulation tool. The iFogSim tool is best to model fog based environments with the functionalities of CoreCloudSim on the top of the cloud layer. For the proposed system, the code is written in Java language. All necessary packages and tools are installed on the PC to make experiments on the proposed tri-foghealth system. The proper software and hardware parameters are provided in the Table 4.

Table 4. Software and Hardware Description.

Software/Hardware	Description
Simulation Tool	iFogSim
Simulator Version	3.0.3
Operating System	Windows 7 Ultimate
Programming Language	Java
Development Kit	JDK 1.8
IDE	NetBeans 8.2
Database	MySQL-5.1.36 (Wamp Server 2.0)

The MySQL database is used to store the healthcare data of users. The other simulation parameters set in the experimentation is provided in the Table 5.

The proposed tri-foghealth system is built up based on the above simulation settings. At first, the users are needed to register with the proposed method by reporting their behaviors in the initial form. Then, the user data is stored in the cloud layer. Data from the same user is stored in a separate database after analysis by the fog nodes. The proposed experimental setup and flow are illustrated in Figure 5. As in Figure 5, we construct our fog topology for the smart healthcare system. The users and the fog nodes are deployed in different regions. The proposed tri-foghealth system analyzes the data from another region.

Table 5. Experimental Settings.

Parameter		Value
Number of users		≅ 50
Number of biosensors in each user		5
Number of data on-lookers		10
Number of fog nodes		10
Fog Node Configuration	Storage	1 GB
	Bandwidth	1000 KBs
	Resource Cost	3.0
	Memory Cost	0.5
Cloud Configuration	MIPS	1000
	Memory	10 MB
	Bandwidth	1000 KBs
SpikQ-Net	Number of neurons	10
	Number of hidden layers	3
	Activation Function	Sigmoid
	Step Size	0.2
MoSHO	Initial Population	100
	Ran	0.3
	Iteration	100

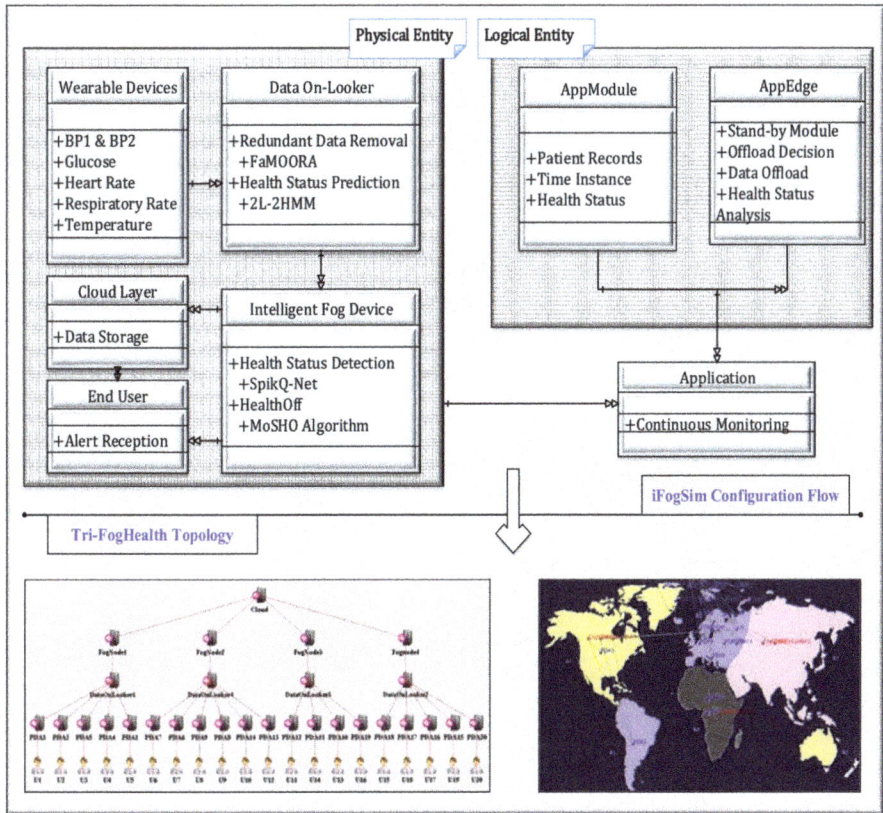

Figure 5. Experimental Setup of Tri-FogHealth System.

Data generation and analysis: in this work, we present a framework for monitoring the user's regular health status. Thus, we generate health data from the sensors. For each user, we create health data as per the considered attributes. The sample data generated for the users in a given time instance in a synchronized manner, as shown in the Figure 6b. In this way, we create nearly 1000 sample data with biomedical, behavior, and environmental attributes (i.e.,) each sample represents the biomedical, behavior and ecological data. The data is generated from 50 users registered in the system. The generated samples are sufficient to train the SpikeQ-Net neural network. Then, we use this data to train our healthcare system. Figure 6c shows the data points classified by the 2L-2HMM algorithm. Then, these data points are fed into SpikQ-Net, which is shown in the Figure 6d. Here, we set the binary values for specific attributes. For instance, we set Activities as Sit_(0), Sleep_(1), and Work_(2). Thus, the data contains either 0 or 1 or 2 at a given time instance. The proposed system also supports a particular disease diagnosis if the proper dataset is used.

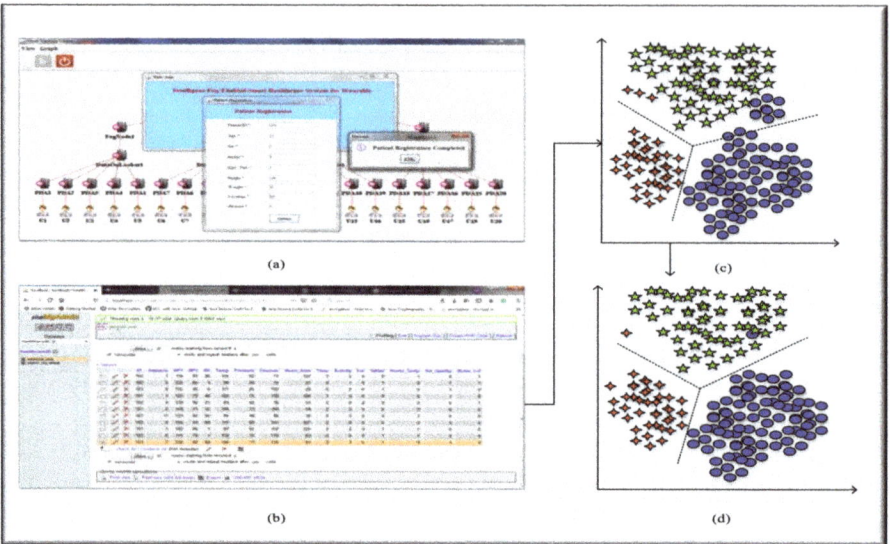

Figure 6. (a) User Registration in Tri-FogHealth, (b) Sample Data Generated, (c) Health Status Prediction (2L-2HMM), (d) Health Status Detection (SpikQ-Net).

5.2. Application Scenario: Remote Quarantine Monitoring for Covid-19 Outbreak

The novel corona virus (Covid-19) outbreaks are the significant and severe outbreak that healthcare systems handle. In Covid-19, it is impossible to treat all patients in the hospitals since the count is increasing rapidly. In such cases, remote patient monitoring will be a practical solution [46]. It can be achieved by our proposed tri-fog heath system, which focuses on remote monitoring. In Covid-19, most of the affected peoples have mild external symptoms like fever, cough and throat pain but have severe internal symptoms such as oxygen level reduction. As a result of these symptoms, the patient suffers from respiratory problems. We can apply the proposed tri-fog health for monitoring the patients who are in self-quarantine. The application setup is demonstrated in Figure 7.

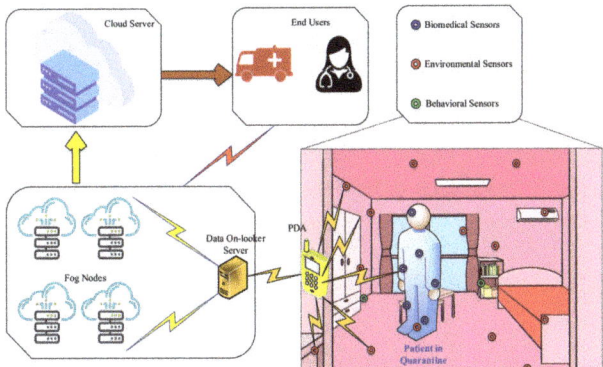

Figure 7. Covid-19 Remote Monitoring by Tri-FogHealth.

As shown in the setup, the patient who is quarantined in a room is equipped with biomedical sensors such as BP, glucose, respiratory rate, and temperature. Additionally, the place is equipped with environmental sensors to measure environmental changes. Before quarantine, the patient must be registered in the system by providing health history, which is further helpful in analyzing health status. The data collected from the quarantine room is sent to the data on-looker node through wireless communication. There, the data is cleaned, and the health status is predicted. Then, the information is fed into the fog nodes, which detect the health status by SpikQ-Net upon all three sets of attributes. It is worth to mention that tri-fog health generates an immediate alert to hospitals and doctors if any abnormality is detected in data. Corresponding government authorities can handle the fog and cloud servers. Thus, patient monitoring will be easy and accurate. Above all, the patients will get timely health services, which prevent early deaths due to Covid-19. In addition, the involvement of the health off procedure assists in offloading data among regions if any one of the regions become more congested. This prototype can be implemented by deploying wearable devices for quarantined patients. Nowadays, the usage of wearable (smart watches) becomes interesting among many users same as smartphones (can be used as PDA). Thus, data collection and analysis is easy in the proposed prototype.

5.3. Comparative Analysis

After setting up all necessary parameters, we generate data in the system to compare the efficiency of the proposed method. The proposed tri-foghealth system is compared with prior healthcare systems. For comparison, we consider fog based healthcare systems such as Fog-BBN [43], Fog-CPE [44], Fog-Smart Office [45] and also cloud-based healthcare systems such as Cloud-CDS [40], Cloud-Gaussian [41], and Cloud-MoPS [42]. We have summarized comparison between all these works in the Table 6. In the considered results, attributes are also varying. Fog-BBN and Fog-Smart Office works have considered all three sets of attributes, including biomedical, behavior, and environmental attributes. The rest of the current research works consider a single set of attributes (i.e.,) biomedical attributes. Besides, none of the existing healthcare works has concentrated on the offloading procedure in fog computing. Thus, the health load among fog nodes is imbalanced, which affects the overall performance.

Table 6. Comparison of Prior Works.

Work	Architecture	Concept	Attributes Considered	Cons		Common Issues
Cloud-CDS [40]	Cloud-based Smart Healthcare System	CDS based Healthcare System Decision Tree-based classification	Biomedical	1	The involvement of decision tree increases latency and also it is not stable	Latency is high since the data processing is performed in the cloud layer
				2	The CDS system is unable to handle streaming data for healthcare services	
Cloud-Gaussian [41]	Cloud-based Physiological Sign Monitoring	Gaussian Model detects health level Patient's Health Trajectory is extracted	Biomedical	1	The high Gaussian parametric approach increases the complexity	Processing redundant data in the cloud layer improves execution too Not suitable for emergency services
				2	Single physiological sign consideration limits the accuracy of abnormality detection	
				3	Not able to support mobile users	
Cloud-MoPS [42]	Cloud-based Mobile Healthcare System	A smart shirt and Wearable Technology is used for health monitoring	Biomedical	1	Massive data analysis by threshold technique is inefficient	
				2	Classification accuracy is low, but the latency is high	
Fog-BBN [43]	Cloud-Fog based Patient Health Monitoring	BBN Classifier is used in Fog Layer THI is computed in Cloud Layer	Biomedical Behavior Environmental	1	Processing the same attributes in fog & cloud layer increases latency	Imbalanced load among fog nodes affects the system stability
				2	BBN classifier is hard to complex and analyze	
				3	Only supports static users	
Fog-CPE [44]	Hierarchical Data Fusion Model with Sensor, Fog and Cloud Model	Biosensor Readings are Classified in each Level	Biomedical		Biosensor data alone is insufficient to analyze the health data accurately CPE works upon pre-defined rules which are not efficient for dynamic health data	Execution time is high due to the presence of a fault and redundant data from wearable devices
Fog-Smart Office [45]	Fog-Cloud Healthcare System for Smart Office	Severity Index is constructed to monitor the health status	Biomedical Behavior Environmental		Bayesian classifier which is used here is complex and has less accuracy Final health status is detected and a decision made in the cloud layer which increases latency	

The proposed tri-foghealth system resolves the major issues encountered in the prior research works. Thus, the proposed work achieves better results. The comparisons are made based on latency, execution time, detection accuracy, and system stability.

5.3.1. Analysis of Latency

Latency is defined as the overall time taken by the system to respond to the user's received data. The latency includes propagation and processing time. Latency (α) is computed as follows,

$$\alpha = \alpha_p + \beta \qquad (22)$$

Here, α_p denotes the propagation time taken by the data to reach the fog layer and β indicates execution time (i.e.,) processing time. In Figure 8, we compare the latency achieved by proposed and prior works concerning the number of users.

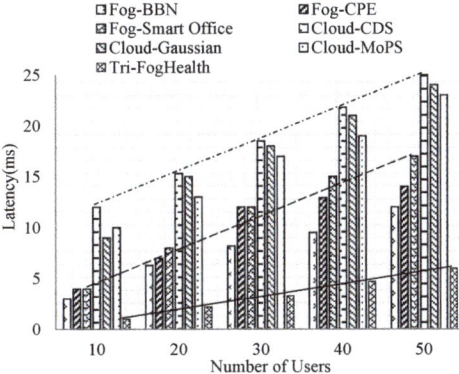

Figure 8. 7 Comparison on Latency upon Number of Users.

The analysis shows that the proposed tri-foghealth system has minimum latency than other cloud-based and fog-based systems. The cloud-based approaches like CDS, Gaussian, and MoPS methods have latency up to 20 ms, which is twice the time higher than the fog-based systems. Among the fog based systems, the proposed Tri-FogHealth system attains latency 6 ms even for 50 users. In the CDS system, a decision tree is used for classification. In general, the decision tree has higher time consumption, which increases the latency for users.

Similarly, the Gaussian approach has high complexity, and the MoPS algorithm works upon a static threshold, which can't handle the massive amount of data. Besides, the cloud-based systems relatively introduce high latency for users. Although BBN, Smart Office, and CPE methods decrease latency better than the cloud systems, still latency is high due to inefficient algorithms.

In Figure 9, we compare the latency achieved by fog-based approaches based on the number of fog nodes. Latency in fog-BBN is high since the second level THI computation is performed in the cloud layer. Thus, the latency is high in fog-BBN. In fog-CPE, rule-based health status detection increases the latency in the presence of a small number of fog nodes. In the fog-smart office, the Bayesian classifier has higher time consumption. Each fog-based approach has some limitations, such as increasing the latency and decreasing the efficiency of fog nodes. In proposed tri-foghealth, the system minimizes the latency with the efficient algorithm. The tri-foghealth system has only 5 ms of latency, even with two fog nodes. The main reason behind this high efficiency is that the tri-foghealth system follows the health off procedure in cases of fog overloading. Therefore, the issue of fog overloading has been overwhelmed. Thus, the proposed tri-foghealth system achieves much better efficiency.

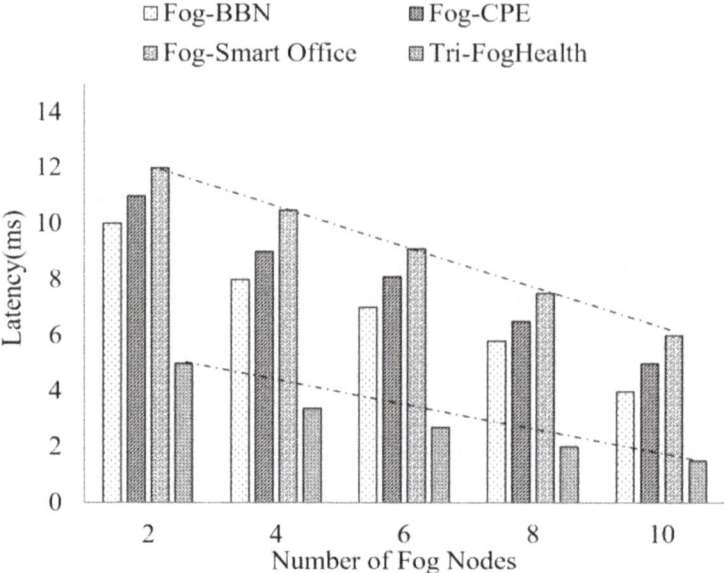

Figure 9. Comparison of Latency upon Number of Fog Nodes.

5.3.2. Analysis of Execution Time

Execution time is defined as the time taken by the healthcare system to predict the users' health status. The execution time measures the health status prediction and detection time.

In Figure 10, we compare the execution time achieved by the proposed tri-foghealth system. And the analysis shows that the execution time performed by the proposed tri-health system is lower. In comparison, the main reason for high execution time is the inefficiency of the algorithm. In fog-BBN, the Bayesian classification and THI computation are performed based on the same attributes (i.e.,) processing the same attributes increases the execution time. In the fog-CPE and smart office, the conventional rule-based algorithms are incorporated. Thus, the execution time is high in all these works. To mention that the Cloud-MoPS method takes 19 ms to process data from 50 users. As MoPS incorporates no algorithm for data analysis, it takes much time, which is nearly thrice time higher than the tri-foghealth system. In Figure 11, we analyzed execution time based on the number of fog nodes.

The comparative analysis shows that all of the fog based approaches suffer from higher execution time. Another leading cause for excessive execution time is that all works analyze fault and duplicate data from wearable devices. This analysis increases the execution time for the user's health data up to 15 ms. In addition, the curve shows that fog-smart office work has 8 ms of execution time, even in 10 fog nodes. The increase in the number of fog nodes alone is ineffective in achieving better efficiency.

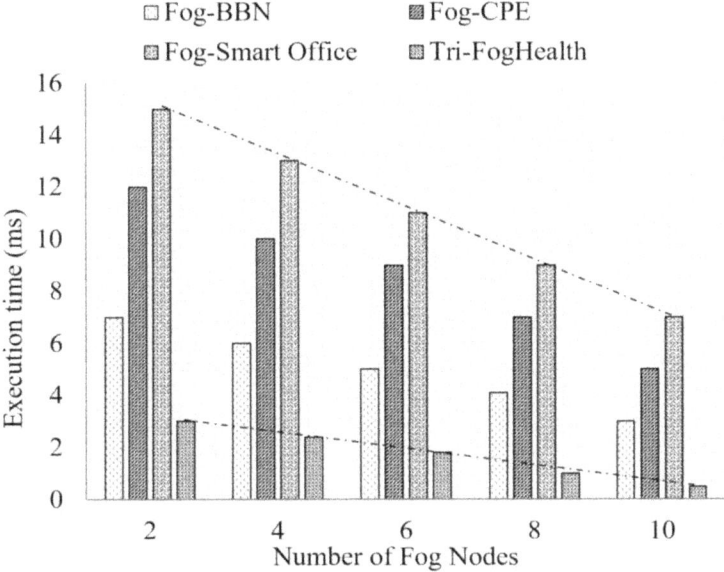

Figure 10. Comparison on Execution Time upon Number of Fog Nodes.

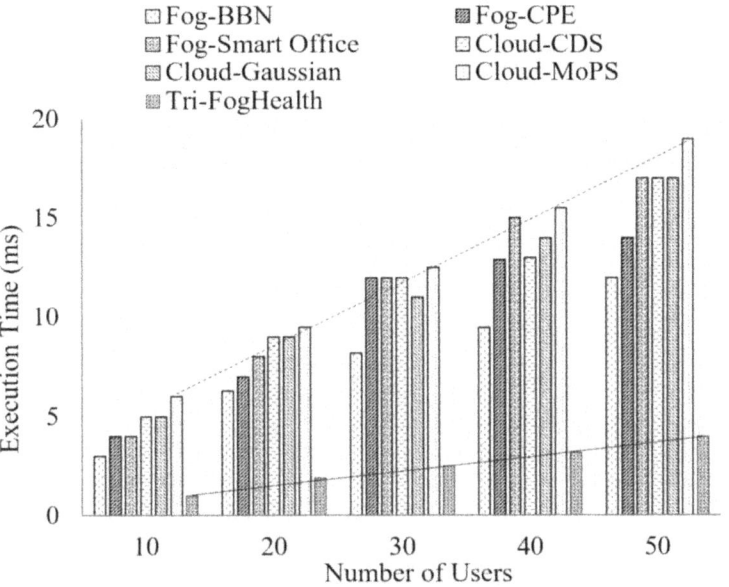

Figure 11. Comparison of Execution Time.

On the other hand, the proposed tri-foghealth system has only 3 ms of execution, even with two fog nodes. And the execution time is 0.5 ms in the presence of 10 fog nodes. This analysis shows that the fault data and redundant data elimination phases play a pivotal role in analyzing health data. With both approaches, we achieve timely detection on the user's health status.

5.3.3. Analysis of Detection Accuracy

Detection accuracy is defined as the number of corrective actions taken by the fog layer after analyzing the user's health status. Accurate detection is the ultimate goal of any smart healthcare system.

In Figure 12, the detection accuracy achieved by tri-foghealth work is compared with all prior research works concerning the number of users. In Figure 13, the detection accuracy is compared with fog based approach based on the number of fog nodes. In both analyzes, we can see that the tri-foghealth system has only slight variations. It maintains the accuracy curve more significantly than 95%.

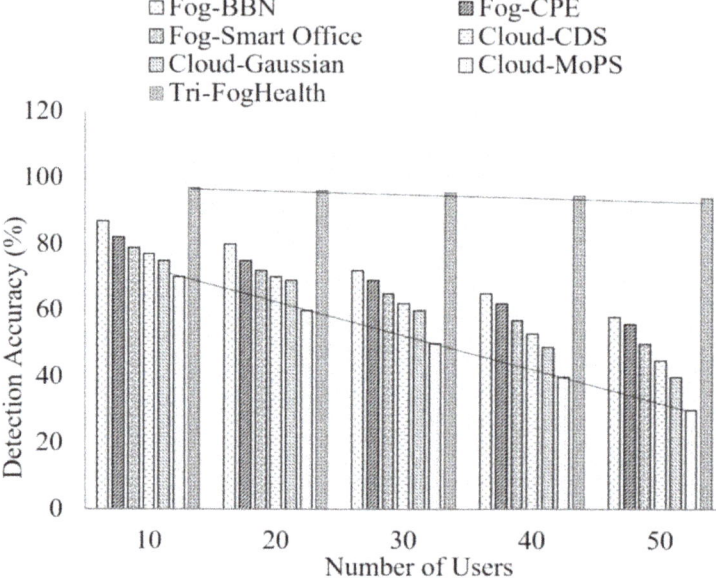

Figure 12. Comparison of Detection Accuracy.

The other methods have lower detection accuracy when the number of users increases. The existing accuracy curve shows that accuracy is decreased linearly. The main reason behind this much accuracy degradation is the algorithms used by the existing works are inefficient. In most cases, the Bayesian classifier is proposed, which has limitations in constructing the classifier model. Besides, most of the current works use the biosensor data for the user's health status detection. For accurate detection, behavior and environmental data are required. Thus, the lack of these data in existing works traps the detection accuracy to 30%. Even for 50 users, the tri-foghealth system achieves 94% in detection accuracy.

On the other hand, accuracy concerning the number of fog nodes shows that the proposed work achieves better accuracy even with two fog nodes. As we suppressed fault data and redundant data in the wearable layer, we make better accuracy greater than 90%, while other fog-based methods acquire lower accuracy, lower than 60%. In addition, the data overloading of fog nodes is a major problem in fog-based ways. Analyzing a massive amount of data in a single fog node makes the fog node inefficient. The presence of the health off procedure in proposed work supports at a high accuracy level.

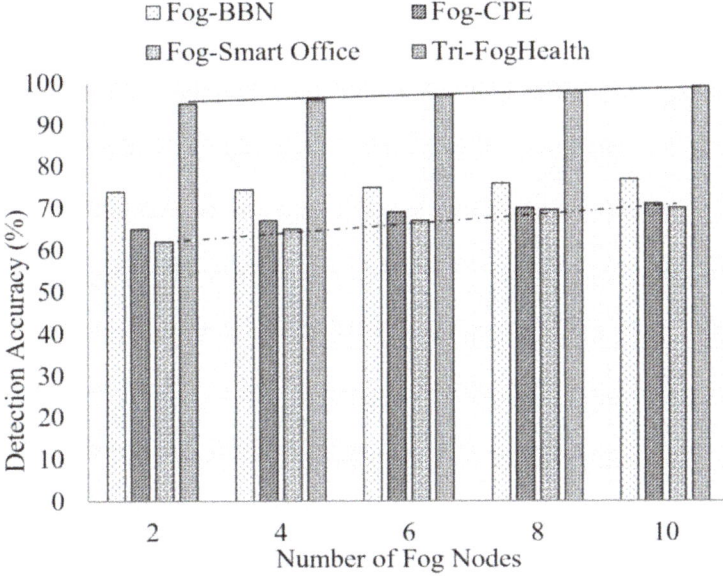

Figure 13. Comparison of Detection Accuracy.

5.3.4. System Stability

System stability is defined as the ability of the healthcare system to support a large number of users without a reduction in its efficiency and accuracy. In precise terms, it validates the scalability of the proposed healthcare system.

The comparative analysis of system stability is shown in Figure 14. Comparison is made for fog-based systems since the cloud-based systems can support a more significant number of users due to resource availability. The main drawback of cloud-based systems is high latency. Although fog-based systems resolve these problems, the stability of the system is still a concern. Since the fog nodes generally have resources lower than the cloud server and most of the users in the same region access the same fog nodes. In this analysis, we consider 50 users in the system.

In the presence of two fog nodes, most of the works have nearly 75% of stability. The stability is then increased linearly concerning the number of fog nodes. However, the highest stability achieved by the existing works is lower than 80% because all these works have an imbalanced load among fog nodes. As a result, the overloading fog nodes become unable to process data requests. On the other hand, the proposed tri-foghealth system achieves 96% for users, even with two fog nodes. The main reason behind these results is (i) fault data elimination by PDA, (ii) redundant data elimination by data on-looker, and (iii) health off by using the MoSHO algorithm. Altogether, tri-foghealth achieves system stability up to 98%. Form the comparison; we can conclude that the proposed tri-foghealth system has much better efficiency.

In Figure 15, system stability is compared between fog based and cloud-based approaches concerning the number of users. For a smart healthcare system, it is necessary to process many users without compromising accuracy. The analysis shows that the proposed foghealth approach achieves better stability regardless of the number of users (i.e.,) it reaches 96% and above strength for a varying number of users. An increase in the number of users and amount of data does not affect the stability of the proposed system. In this case, different fog based and cloud-based approaches achieve the same level of stability, which lies between 65% to 80%.

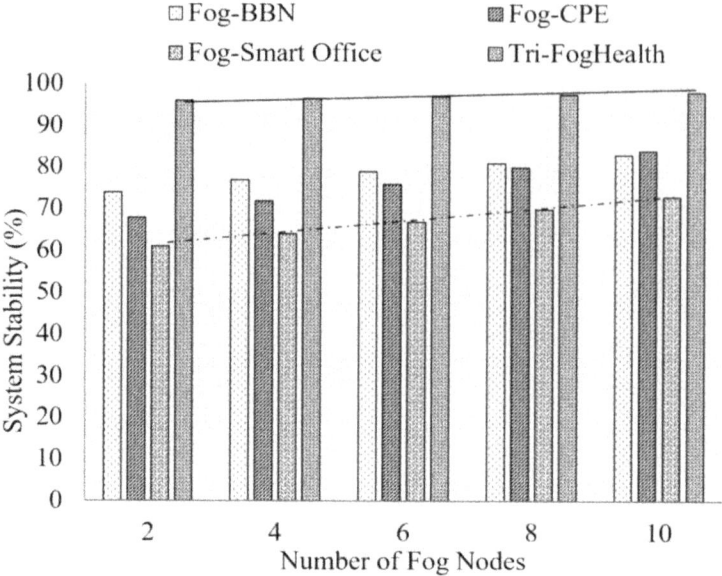

Figure 14. Comparison of System Stability.

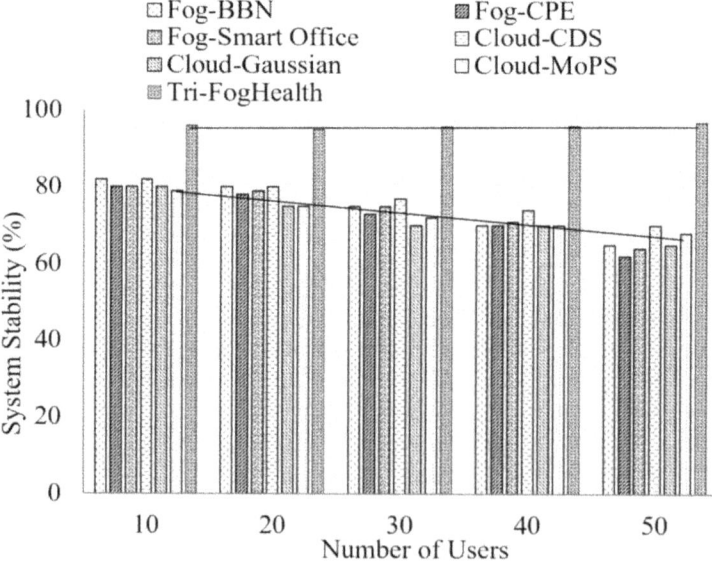

Figure 15. Comparison of System Stability based on Number of Users.

Further, there is a gradual decrease in stability with an increase in the number of users. An increase in the number of users increases the amount of data to be processed in fog and cloud layers. Although the cloud is more scalable than fog nodes, algorithm design also matters in achieving system stability. This analysis shows that the proposed tri-foghealth approach and the algorithms involved are effectual in analyzing the user's health status.

5.3.5. Discussion on Results

In this subsection, we discuss our proposed system. First, we summarize the average results of the proposed tri-foghealth system in Table 7. In this table, we have compared the proposed and existing works based on the average values obtained for each metric. The comparison shows that the proposed work achieves much better performance compared to existing research works. Mainly, the latency and execution time is relatively low in the proposed system without loss in detection accuracy. It shows that the proposed tri-foghealth system is suitable for real-time healthcare analysis.

Table 7. Numerical Comparison on Obtained Results.

Parameter	Cloud-CDS [36]	Cloud-Gaussian [37]	Cloud-MoPS [38]	Fog-BBN [39]		Fog-CPE [40]		Fog-Smart Office [41]		Tri-FogHealth	
				WRT n	WRT m	WRT n	WRT m	WRT n	WRT m	WRT n	WRT m
Latency (ms)	18.52	17.4	16.4	7.8	6.96	9.98	7.92	11.2	9.02	3.44	2.9
Execution Time (ms)	11.2	11.2	12.5	7.8	5.02	9.98	8.6	11.2	11	2.52	1.74
Detection Accuracy (%)	61.6	58.6	50	72.4	75.3	68.8	68.4	64.6	66.7	95.44	97
System Stability (%)	76.6	72	72.8	78.8	74.4	76	72.6	67	73	97	96

In this subsection, we discuss our proposed system. First, we summarize the average results of the proposed tri-foghealth system in Table 7. The comparison shows that the proposed work achieves much better performance compared to existing research works. Mainly, the latency and execution time is relatively low in the proposed system without loss in detection accuracy. It shows that the proposed tri-foghealth system is suitable for real-time healthcare analysis.

In Table 8, we summarize the overall contribution made in this work and its impact on results. We can see that the proposed algorithm supports the system to achieve better results in terms of latency, execution time, detection accuracy, and system stability. Although the proposed approach performs better efficiency, it also achieves tolerable complexity.

Table 8. Summarization of Proposed System.

The Methodology Used in Tri-FogHealth	Contribution in Results
RK-PCA Fault Detection	Eliminates fault data generated by wearable devices Increases detection accuracy since it allows only proper data for analysis Minimizes execution time since a large amount of fault data is suppressed
FaMOORA Redundant Data Elimination	Eliminates redundant data generated by wearable devices Minimizes execution time since the repeated data has been removed
2L-2HMM Health Status Prediction	Predicts user's health status based on temporal variations Increases detection accuracy since it predicts the user's next state Minimizes latency
SpikQ-Net Health Status Detection	Detect user's current health status Minimizes latency since the response is generated in the fog layer Detection accuracy is high since it considers there categories of attributes Execution time is low as the SpikQ-Net which is a machine learning technique that works faster than statistical approaches
MoSHO Health Off	Enable offloading procedure when the fog becomes overloaded Minimizes latency by offloading data to optimal fog nodes Increases system stability by maintaining a balanced load among the fog

The complexity analysis of the proposed system is summarized as follows,

$$Complexity = nT + (n - FD)T + 2T + T$$

As in the above, the complexity is also low in the proposed system. Here, n represents the number of data instances, and FD defines fault data. When compared to Gaussian and BBN classifiers, the complexity is low in the tri-foghealth system.

6. Conclusions

In this paper, we propose a novel tri-foghealth system for the smart healthcare system. The tri-foghealth system has worked upon three main layers by using wearable technology. The biomedical data generated from the wearable layer is processed in PDA to eliminate fault data using the RK-PCA algorithm. Then, the faultless data is fed into the data on-looker node in the intelligent fog layer; the data on-looker node is responsible for predicting the user's health status. For this, it uses temporal data in the 2L-2HMM algorithm. Before prediction, the current data instance is subjected to redundant data elimination process by the FaMOORA algorithm. After health status prediction, the data is processed by the fog nodes using SpikQ-Net, which works upon behavior, biomedical, and environmental attributes. Based on the emergency level of data, the immediate action is taken in the fog layer. Simultaneously, the health off procedure followed with the MOSHO algorithm to prevent the intelligent fog layer from overloading. The experimental results show that the proposed tri-foghealth system outperforms the current research works. In the future, we have planned to test the tri-foghealth system for specific disease diagnosis as the present system is designed to find general abnormalities. In addition, we intend to extend this healthcare system with trusted services as the health data is relatively sensitive. Thus, security provisioning is also a better research direction to extend the tri-foghealth system.

Author Contributions: Conceptualization, M.I. and L.L.; methodology, M.I.; software, M.I.; validation, M.I.; L.L. and A.N.; formal analysis, M.I.; L.L. and A.K.; investigation, L.L.; resources, G.L. and L.L.; data curation, G.L. and H.W.; writing—original draft preparation, M.I.; writing—review and editing, M.I.; A.N. and A.K.; visualization, M.I and Y.M.A.; supervision, L.L.; project administration, L.L.; funding acquisition, A.M.E.-S. All authors have read and agreed to the published version of the manuscript.

Funding: This research supported by King Saud University with grand of Researchers Supporting Project number (RSP-2020/133).

Acknowledgments: The authors extend their appreciation to King Saud University for funding this work through Researchers Supporting Project number (RSP-2020/133), King Saud University, Riyadh, Saudi Arabia.

Conflicts of Interest: The authors declare no conflict of interest.

References

1. Mohapatra, S.; Mohanty, S.; Mohanty, S. Smart healthcare: An approach for ubiquitous healthcare management using IoT. In *Advances in Ubiquitous Sensing Applications for Healthcare*; Academic Press: Cambridge, MA, USA, 2019.
2. Ahad, A.; Tahir, M.A.; Yau, K.A. 5G-based smart healthcare network: Architecture, taxonomy, challenges, and future research directions. *IEEE Access* **2019**, *7*, 100747–100762. [CrossRef]
3. Tian, S.; Yang, W.; Grange, J.M.; Wang, P.; Huang, W.; Ye, Z. Smart healthcare: Making medical care more intelligent. *Glob. Health J.* **2019**, *3*, 62–65. [CrossRef]
4. Muzny, M.; Henriksen, A.; Giordanengo, A.; Mužík, J.; Grøttland, A.; Blixgård, H.; Hartvigsen, G.; Årsand, E. Wearable sensors with possibilities for data exchange: Analyzing status and needs of different actors in mobile health monitoring systems. *Int. J. Med. Inform.* **2019**, *133*, 104017. [CrossRef] [PubMed]
5. Papa, A.; Mital, M.; Pisano, P.; Giudice, M.D. E-health and wellbeing monitoring using smart healthcare devices: An empirical investigation. *Technol. Forecast. Soc. Chang.* **2020**, *153*, 119226. [CrossRef]
6. Mutlag, A.A.; Ghani, M.K.; Arunkumar, N.; Mohammed, M.A.; Mohd, O. Enabling technologies for fog computing in healthcare IoT systems. *Future Gener. Comput. Syst.* **2019**, *90*, 62–78. [CrossRef]
7. Mahmud, R.; Ramamohanarao, K.; Buyya, R. Application management in fog computing environments: A taxonomy, review, and future directions. *ACM Comput. Surv.* **2020**. [CrossRef]
8. Zhao, R.; Yan, R.; Chen, Z.; Mao, K.; Wang, P.; Gao, R.X. Deep Learning and Its Applications to Machine Health Monitoring: A Survey. *arXiv* **2016**, arXiv:abs/1612.07640. [CrossRef]

9. Soualhi, M.; Nguyen, K.T.; Soualhi, A.; Medjaher, K.; Hemsas, K.E. Health monitoring of bearing and gear faults by using a new health indicator extracted from current signals. *Measurement* **2019**, *141*, 37–51. [CrossRef]
10. Fu, Y.; Peng, C.; Gomez, F.; Narazaki, Y.; Spencer, B.F. Sensor fault management techniques for wireless smart sensor networks in structural health monitoring. *Struct. Control Health Monit.* **2019**. [CrossRef]
11. Petrovska, B.; Zdravevski, E.; Lameski, P.; Corizzo, R.; Štajduhar, I.; Lerga, J. Deep learning for feature extraction in remote sensing: A case-study of aerial scene classification. *Sensors* **2020**, *20*, 3906. [CrossRef]
12. Munir, M.; Siddiqui, S.A.; Chattha, M.A.; Dengel, A.; Ahmed, S. FuseAD: Unsupervised anomaly detection in streaming sensors data by fusing statistical and deep learning models. *Sensors* **2019**, *19*, 2451. [CrossRef]
13. Merrill, N.; Eskandarian, A. Modified autoencoder training and scoring for robust unsupervised anomaly detection in deep learning. *IEEE Access* **2020**, *8*, 101824–101833. [CrossRef]
14. Ceci, M.; Corizzo, R.; Japkowicz, N.; Mignone, P.; Pio, G. ECHAD: Embedding-based change detection from multivariate time series in smart grids. *IEEE Access* **2020**, *8*, 156053–156066. [CrossRef]
15. Hu, J.; Wu, K.; Liang, W. An IPv6-based framework for fog-assisted healthcare monitoring. *Adv. Mech. Eng.* **2019**, *11*. [CrossRef]
16. Jeyaraj, P.R.; Rajan, S.E.; Martis, R.J.; Panigrahi, B.K. Fog computing employed computer aided cancer classification system using deep neural network in internet of things based healthcare system. *J. Med. Syst.* **2019**, *44*, 34.
17. Nweke, H.F.; Wah, T.Y.; Mujtaba, G.; Al-garadi, M.A. Data fusion and multiple classifier systems for human activity detection and health monitoring: Review and open research directions. *Inf. Fusion* **2019**, *46*, 147–170. [CrossRef]
18. Goschenhofer, J.; Pfister, F.M.; Yuksel, K.A.; Bischl, B.; Fietzek, U.; Thomas, J. Wearable-based Parkinson's Disease Severity Monitoring using Deep Learning. *arXiv* **2019**, arXiv:1904.10829.
19. Mani, N.; Singh, A.; Nimmagadda, S.L. An IoT guided healthcare monitoring system for managing real-time notifications by fog computing services. *Procedia Comput. Sci.* **2020**, *167*, 850–859. [CrossRef]
20. Zheng, H.; Xiong, K.; Fan, P.; Zhong, Z.; Letaief, K.B. Fog-assisted multiuser swipt networks: Local computing or offloading. *IEEE Internet Things J.* **2019**, *6*, 5246–5264. [CrossRef]
21. Runkle, J.; Sugg, M.; Boase, D.; Galvin, S.L.; Coulson, C.C. Use of wearable sensors for pregnancy health and environmental monitoring: Descriptive findings from the perspective of patients and providers. *Digit. Health* **2019**, *5*. [CrossRef]
22. Sangeetha, A.; Thangavel, A. Pervasive healthcare system based on environmental monitoring. *Intell. Pervasive Comput. Syst. Smarter Healthc.* **2019**. [CrossRef]
23. Aboudi, N.E.; Benhlima, L. Big data management for healthcare systems: Architecture, requirements, and implementation. *Adv. Bioinform.* **2018**. [CrossRef]
24. Sun, F.; Zang, W.; Gravina, R.; Fortino, G.; Li, Y. Gait-based identification for elderly users in wearable healthcare systems. *Inf. Fusion* **2020**, *53*, 134–144. [CrossRef]
25. Albahri, A.S.; Albahri, O.S.; Zaidan, A.A.; Zaidan, B.B.; Hashim, M.; Alsalem, M.A.; Mohsin, A.H.; Mohammed, K.I.; Alamoodi, A.H.; Enaizan, O.; et al. Based on multiple heterogeneous wearable sensors: A smart real-time health monitoring structured for hospitals distributor. *IEEE Access* **2019**, *7*, 37269–37323. [CrossRef]
26. Zhang, H.; Liu, J.; Kato, N. Threshold tuning-based wearable sensor fault detection for reliable medical monitoring using bayesian network model. *IEEE Syst. J.* **2018**, *12*, 1886–1896. [CrossRef]
27. Colopy, G.W.; Roberts, S.J.; Clifton, D.A. Bayesian optimization of personalized models for patient vital-sign monitoring. *IEEE J. Biomed. Health Inform.* **2018**, *22*, 301–310. [CrossRef]
28. Liu, Y.; Zhang, L.; Yang, Y.; Zhou, L.; Ren, L.; Wang, F.; Liu, R.; Pang, Z.; Deen, M.J. A novel cloud-based framework for the elderly healthcare services using digital twin. *IEEE Access* **2019**, *7*, 49088–49101. [CrossRef]
29. Anagaw, A.; Chang, Y. A new complement naïve Bayesian approach for biomedical data classification. *J. Ambient Intell. Humaniz. Comput.* **2019**, *10*, 3889–3897. [CrossRef]
30. Pathinarupothi, R.K.; Durga, P.; Rangan, E. IoT-based smart edge for global health: Remote monitoring with severity detection and alerts transmission. *IEEE Internet Things J.* **2018**, *6*, 2449–2462. [CrossRef]
31. Rahmani, A.M.; Gia, T.N.; Negash, B.; Anzanpour, A.; Azimi, I.; Jiang, M.; Liljeberg, P. Exploiting smart e-Health gateways at the edge of healthcare Internet-of-Things: A fog computing approach. *Future Gener. Comput. Syst.* **2018**, *78*, 641–658. [CrossRef]

32. Gai, K.; Lu, Z.; Qiu, M.; Zhu, L. Toward smart treatment management for personalized healthcare. *IEEE Netw.* **2019**, *33*, 30–36. [CrossRef]
33. Hassan, M.K.; El-Desouky, A.I.; Badawy, M.M.; Sarhan, A.M.; Elhoseny, M.; Manogaran, G. EoT-driven hybrid ambient assisted living framework with naïve Bayes–firefly algorithm. *Neural Comput. Appl.* **2018**, *31*, 1275–1300. [CrossRef]
34. Tuli, S.; Basumatary, N.; Gill, S.S.; Kahani, M.; Arya, R.C.; Wander, G.S.; Buyya, R. HealthFog: An ensemble deep learning based smart healthcare system for automatic diagnosis of heart diseases in integrated IoT and fog computing environments. *Future Gener. Comput. Syst.* **2020**, *104*, 187–200. [CrossRef]
35. Muhammed, T.; Mehmood, R.; Albeshri, A.A.; Katib, I.A. UbeHealth: A personalized ubiquitous cloud and edge-enabled networked healthcare system for smart cities. *IEEE Access* **2018**, *6*, 32258–32285. [CrossRef]
36. Khattak, H.A.; Arshad, H.; Islam, S.U.; Ahmed, G.; Jabbar, S.; Sharif, A.M.; Khalid, S. Utilization and load balancing in fog servers for health applications. *Eurasip J. Wirel. Commun. Netw.* **2019**, *2019*, 1–12. [CrossRef]
37. Mutlag, A.A.; Ghani, M.K.; Mohammed, M.A.; Maashi, M.S.; Mohd, O.; Mostafa, S.A.; Abdulkareem, K.H.; Marques, G.; Díez, I.D. MAFC: Multi-Agent fog computing model for healthcare critical tasks management. *Sensors* **2020**, *20*, 1853. [CrossRef]
38. Sharma, S.; Saini, H. A novel four-tier architecture for delay aware scheduling and load balancing in fog environment. *Sustain. Comput. Inform. Syst.* **2019**, *24*, 100355. [CrossRef]
39. Adhikari, M.; Gianey, H.K. Energy efficient offloading strategy in fog-cloud environment for IoT applications. *Internet Things* **2019**, *6*, 100053. [CrossRef]
40. Naghshvarianjahromi, M.; Kumar, S.; Deen, M.J. Brain-inspired intelligence for real-time health situation understanding in smart e-health home applications. *IEEE Access* **2019**, *7*, 180106–180126. [CrossRef]
41. Zhu, T.; Colopy, G.W.; MacEwen, C.; Niehaus, K.E.; Yang, Y.; Pugh, C.W.; Clifton, D.A. Patient-specific physiological monitoring and prediction using structured gaussian processes. *IEEE Access* **2019**, *7*, 58094–58103. [CrossRef]
42. Leu, F.; Ko, C.; You, I.; Choo, K.R.; Ho, C. A smartphone-based wearable sensors for monitoring real-time physiological data. *Comput. Electr. Eng.* **2018**, *65*, 376–392.
43. Verma, P.; Sood, S.K. Fog assisted-IoT enabled patient health monitoring in smart homes. *IEEE Internet Things J.* **2018**, *5*, 1789–1796. [CrossRef]
44. Dautov, R.; Distefano, S.; Buyya, R. Hierarchical data fusion for smart healthcare. *J. Big Data* **2019**, *6*, 1–23. [CrossRef]
45. Bhatia, M.; Sood, S.K. Exploring temporal analytics in fog-cloud architecture for smart office healthcare. *Mob. Netw. Appl.* **2019**, *24*, 1392–1410. [CrossRef]
46. Brauers, W.K.; Zavadskas, E.K. The MOORA method and its application to privatization in a transition economy. *Control Cybern.* **2006**, *35*, 445–469.
47. Xiang, S.; Zhang, Y.; Gong, J.; Guo, X.; Lin, L.; Hao, Y. STDP-based unsupervised spike pattern learning in a photonic spiking neural network With VCSELs and VCSOAs. *IEEE J. Sel. Top. Quantum Electron.* **2019**, *25*, 1–9. [CrossRef]
48. Salahshour, E.; Malekzadeh, M.; Gholipour, R.; Khorashadizadeh, S. Designing multi-layer quantum neural network controller for chaos control of rod-type plasma torch system using improved particle swarm optimization. *Evol. Syst.* **2019**, 1–15. [CrossRef]
49. Dhiman, G.; Kumar, V. Spotted hyena optimizer: A novel bio-inspired based metaheuristic technique for engineering applications. *Adv. Eng. Softw.* **2017**, *114*, 48–70. [CrossRef]

Publisher's Note: MDPI stays neutral with regard to jurisdictional claims in published maps and institutional affiliations.

© 2020 by the authors. Licensee MDPI, Basel, Switzerland. This article is an open access article distributed under the terms and conditions of the Creative Commons Attribution (CC BY) license (http://creativecommons.org/licenses/by/4.0/).

Article

A Synchronized Multi-Unit Wireless Platform for Long-Term Activity Monitoring

Giuseppe Coviello *, Gianfranco Avitabile and Antonello Florio

Department of Electrical and Information Engineering, Polytechnic University of Bari, 70126 Bari, Italy; gianfranco.avitabile@poliba.it (G.A.); antonello.florio@poliba.it (A.F.)
* Correspondence: giuseppe.coviello@poliba.it

Received: 4 May 2020; Accepted: 8 July 2020; Published: 10 July 2020

Abstract: One of the objectives of the medicine is to modify patients' ways of living. In this context, a key role is played by the diagnosis. When dealing with acquisition systems consisting of multiple wireless devices located in different parts of the body, it becomes fundamental to ensure synchronization between the individual units. This task is truly a challenge, so one aims to limit the complexity of the calculation and ensure long periods of operation. In fact, in the absence of synchronization, it is impossible to relate all the measurements coming from the different subsystems on a single time scale for the extraction of complex characteristics. In this paper, we first analyze in detail all the possible causes that lead to have a system that is not synchronous and therefore not usable. Then, we propose a firmware implementation strategy and a simple but effective protocol that guarantees perfect synchrony between the devices while keeping computational complexity low. The employed network has a star topology with a master/slave architecture. In this paper a new approach to the synchronization problem is introduced to guarantee a precise but not necessarily accurate synchronization between the units. In order to demonstrate the effectiveness of the proposed solution, a platform consisting of two different types of units has been designed and built. In particular, a nine Degrees of Freedom (DoF) Inertial Measurement Unit (IMU) is used in one unit while a nine-DoF IMU and all circuits for the analysis of the superficial Electromyography (sEMG) are present on the other unit. The system is completed by an Android app that acts as a user interface for starting and stopping the logging operations. The paper experimentally demonstrates that the proposed solution overcomes all the limits set out and it guarantees perfect synchronization of the single measurement, even during long-duration acquisitions. In fact, a less than 30 µs time mismatch has been registered for a 24 h test, and the possibility to perform complex post-processing on the acquired data with a simple and effective system has been proven.

Keywords: IMU; gait analysis; sEMG; long-term monitoring; multi-unit; multi-sensor; time synchronization; Internet of Medical Things; body area network; MIMU

1. Introduction

In many areas of research, medicine, and sport it is important to collect data on particular parameters concerning a subject to obtain information on his/her health condition. Normally, detailed measurements are performed for short periods and in a controlled laboratory environment. With the advent of micro-electro-mechanical system (MEMS) technology and thanks to the non-invasiveness of the equipment available today, a great step forward has been made, allowing acquisitions for long time intervals, during individual procedures in normal daily life. An important task to perform in order to make the procedural steps effective is to check whether the patient is correctly following the doctor's treatment instructions. Nowadays, Information and Communication Technologies' (ICT) progress allows the doctors to remotely follow their patients. Furthermore, thanks to the availability of new

ICT tools, it is possible to study the long-term evolution of particular symptoms related to specific diseases, without affecting patients' everyday lives. They are real on-body laboratories that belong to the field of the Internet of Medical Things (IoMT). For example, considering specific units equipped with heartbeat sensors, it is possible to analyze a patient's heart health in different time slots during the day, monitoring for the presence or insurgence of anomalies [1].

Complex systems are usually needed when monitoring the symptoms of a disease requires verification of several parameters and requires flow algorithms capable of taking into account the evolution of data for recognizing changes in them [2,3], or efficiency optimization algorithms [4] or systems that improve wireless communications [5]. A possible field of application of such a complex system, for instance, could be the study of patients with precocious diagnoses of Parkinson's Disease (PD) [6,7]. Its main symptoms induce motor issues, such as tremor, rigidity, and instability. Thus, a gait analysis or posture monitoring could be helpful to identify those symptoms' progression or regression. Gait analysis can be conducted in several ways [8]—for example, with video frame analysis. The case of kinematic gait analysis is brought out using multiple sensor units. Thanks to information coming from accelerometers and gyroscopes, it is possible to identify an object's motion in the space; in our case those pieces of information are related to an arm or a leg movement.

Advanced forms of PD involve the possibility for the patient to alternate phases in which motor muscles are operative (ON) to phases in which they stop to work (OFF) [9]. This can be related to an ineffective or changed drug therapy and only platforms for long-term monitoring of the patient can be helpful for identifying these types of issues. Those platforms usually match the already mentioned set of gyroscopes and accelerometers for gait characterization with sensors for the sEMG.

Many implementations rely on multiple units with a single sensor as an alternative to a single unit equipped with the whole sensors set. Additionally, especially for sEMG, it is important to monitor points that may be distant in space, so two or more units may be needed. We introduce, in this way, the concept of the multi-unit acquisition system.

From the networking point of view, for a multi-board acquisition system, we talk about Body Area Networks (BANs) [10], which are networks usually with a star topology and connected by wireless protocols, whose coverage is of the order of 1–2 m [11] (that is, the necessary area to cover the entire body).

The length of the time interval used to perform the analysis should be carefully considered. In some cases, it is necessary to do real-time (online) monitoring while in other cases *a posteriori* (offline) monitoring is required. In the first case, the central node (BAN coordinator) is in charge of collecting, processing, and matching the data, before exposing them to the external network to the BAN—the Internet. It is important to have a persistent connection between the BAN coordinator and the Internet. According to [12], this may lead to a significant power consumption associated with the RF portion of the sensing device. Since we are considering wearable motes, it is unfeasible for the devices to use expensive batteries or overly heavy batteries. Additionally, it may be useless to expose very frequently data on the Internet during long-term monitoring.

A better solution seems to be represented by offline processing, in which every mote saves the results of its surveys on a persistent memory and after gathering the data from the whole set of units the data collection is processed. This final step calls for the BAN coordinator to be in charge of strict time synchronization between all motes. In this scenario, the timestamp of each measure is crucial, since the possibility of correctly analyzing the measures by referring them to the same instant depends on it. Some off-the-shelf solutions give the opportunity to store the measured data in a memory. They usually require some extra non-portable and complex hardware, and either their specified accuracy is too low [13] or no details are given regarding the accuracy itself [14].

The paper aims to present a time-synchronized multi-unit, multi-sensor, and multi-rate acquisition system for kinematic and static analysis. The data are collected from different sensors, even using different data rates, over a long time interval of observation during normal daily activities of the patient. The system can be employed for many specific applications, depending on the virtually unlimited number of boards used, the sensors they are equipped with, and their positioning on the body. Because of this, the experiments validating the proposed platform will aim to prove the effectiveness of the approach, generalizing and not specifying a precise operating scenario.

The organization of this paper is as follows: Section 2 reviews related works, while Section 3 formulates the operating problems. Section 4 describes the platform developed, and in Section 5 some experimental results, validating the system, are reported. Finally, conclusions are given in Section 6.

2. Related Work

2.1. Gait Analysis through sEMG

The EMG is the measurement of the electrical activity of a muscle. EMG actually gives only minor information about the contraction of individual muscles, but it provides a visible indication of the muscle activity. The information provided can be extremely interesting when considering the time instance in which a muscle activates [8].

Many methods are available for EMG. The least invasive one, but also one of the most subject to interference, is the surface EMG (sEMG). In fact, first of all, it is not always possible to distinguish one muscle's activity from that of the adjacent ones (the so-called "cross-talk" phenomenon [8]). Moreover, since there is a thick layer of skin covering the muscle, the voltage signal arrives at the electrodes with a significant attenuation that must be compensated with specific preamplification techniques.

However, the sEMG is the preferable way of performing gait activity monitoring over a long time period as it only requires the patient to have some surface electrodes on specific parts of its body.

In the literature, it is possible to find some examples of gait characterization through sEMG-based systems. For example, in [15], the authors propose a gait cadence analysis performed through sEMG. The system is in charge of acquiring electrode signals and processes them according to a first-order statistic, in order to characterize the periodicity of gait in healthy patients.

In [16], a more complicated analysis involving deep learning is presented. In fact, still employing sEMG, the author provides a method to identify and classify two sub-phases of gait (proper stance and swing phases) based on an artificial neural network approach.

In [17], another gait sub-phase recognition system is proposed, with an inferential algorithm for studying and characterizing the sub-phases. The great advantage of this latter approach is its reduced cost, since it is based on Arduino Mega 2560 for signal processing, and it is wearable, thereby allowing one to perform non-invasive remote analysis of gait.

2.2. Multi-Board Acquisition Systems

This work presents a wearable multi-board acquisition system for offline activity monitoring. In the literature, other systems with the same purpose are present, with similar characteristics but with some issues that our design aims to mitigate.

In [9], a wearable system for long-term monitoring of gait is presented. The board has the advantage of being an "add-on" to the patient, unlike others described in the literature that require the patient to wear specific shoes or other specifically designed clothes. Salarian et al.'s work, instead, allows one to equip the patient with the system and remove it when the monitoring is over. The board employed for testing is equipped only by gyroscopes. Nevertheless, the authors claim to have reached interesting results. Note that the proposed system works for offline monitoring, thanks to the fact that the motes store their revelations on 8 MB memory cards.

Laerhoven et al. [18] focused their attention on how to reduce the power consumption for wearable devices of this type. Toward that purpose, they first check for the presence of motion using a set of tilt switches, and then activate an accelerometer to track the motion itself. This latter sensor, indeed, drains far more current than a tilt switch. Moreover, since tilt switches furnish a binary output, it is possible to reduce the computational power required to reveal the presence of motion. Actually, due to the nature of the tilt switches, this system does not guarantee a reduced number of false positive or false negative events of motion, thereby preventing the achievement of high levels of accuracy.

In 2011, Cancela et al. [19] presented a distributed wearable system for online gait analysis in PD made with five 3-axial accelerometers put on limbs and a gyroscope with accelerometer put on the belt. Zigbee protocol is used as the telecommunications standard between the motes and to communicate with a personal computer (PC) that receives and stores the data. The main issues of the approach arise from the fact that online monitoring can be power hungry, as already discussed. Nevertheless, it is useless to collect and process data immediately in long-term monitoring. Moreover, the proposed system requires a PC that must be specifically equipped with algorithms and telecommunication standards transceivers in order to work and collect data, and this may be an obstacle for doctors and patients.

Finally, Oniga et al. [20] developed a solution for studying motion activity/inactivity for a subject in the long term. Wearable motes equipped with only gyroscopes and 3-axis accelerometers are considered and coordinated by a smartphone, in charge of receiving and processing data, before storing them in a persistent online database. The proposed solution is an online monitoring system. It is still capable of reducing some sources of power consumption, thanks to intelligent (triggered) activation of the motes by the smartphone. Nevertheless, the patients must have a smartphone equipped with a specific application and a persistent internet connection to store data on the remote database, accessible to the doctor.

The system presented in this paper allows a more complete analysis of systems of the type previously described in terms of completeness of the measurements that can be made thanks to the variety of sensors used, and by the simplicity and versatility of use. The approach ensures a longer battery life as it minimizes the computational complexity of the synchronization process. Moreover, it allows an easy reconfiguration and expansion of the group of units without any change in the settings, as the synchronization protocol is quite simple and does not involve any bidirectional communication.

2.3. Time Synchronization Protocols

The main issue when analyzing multi-unit (i.e., distributed) systems consists of the physical clocks synchronization. The sub-elements themselves of a multi-board system are not synchronized. It is mandatory that each and every subsystem has the same vision of the time domain, as the units are meant to capture events that later must be cross-correlated. Even assuming the theoretical possibility that every device turns on at at the same time, it is well known that the natural clock drift due to environmental changes may lead to time mismatches in the run-time phase. As a consequence, the need for a time synchronization algorithm arises.

Time synchronization protocols belong either to the distributed protocols (DPs) (consensus-based) or to the centralized protocols (CPs) classes. In the DPs, the decision on the global system time is made by specific algorithms aiming to solve the problem of consensus. The latter, in distributed systems, calls to the single nodes to "agree" on a given property, decision, or quantity [21] (in our case, time). A consensus algorithm has the following properties:

- Termination: after ending, every node makes a decision;
- Agreement: every couple of nodes agrees on the same decision;
- Validity: every decided value is a proposed one;
- Integrity: every node makes a decision at least once.

Obviously, a time synchronization algorithm based on consensus guarantees a high level of accuracy, at the cost of long computation time needed to reach the consensus itself. As a consequence, a DP could be unacceptably heavy in time-critical systems and in fast-changing-events observing systems.

In CPs, the decision is made by a single node, called the leader, that we will identify as the BAN coordinator in our context. Note that backup-leaders can be considered to implement fault tolerance. Some algorithmic solutions are directly inheritable from classical distributed systems theory, while other techniques are specially designed for BANs and other kinds of ad-hoc networks.

The simplest example is constituted by the algorithm proposed by Cristian in [22]. This algorithm operates in two stages: first, the peer node N asks the coordinator C to be time-synchronized; then, after, the coordinator sends a message containing its local time (that will become the network global time) T_C. Once the peer has received this message, it sets its local time to be:

$$T_N = T_C + \tilde{\tau} \qquad (1)$$

with $\tilde{\tau}$ an estimation of the actual communication delay detailed in Section 3.2.2. The algorithm furnishes a good approximation when the random components of τ are negligible when compared to the deterministic ones.

Another solution is presented in [23], the so-called Berkeley algorithm, adopted in Unix 4.3 BSD. Here, the coordinator observes message exchange containing local clock values T_N^i still to estimate τ_i for each node i, as in the previous case. Then, it averages the clock values. Instead of sending the decided time, the coordinator sends to each node how much it should increase or decrease its clock according to the global decided time.

The presented algorithms are more suitable than the consensus-based synchronization algorithms, but still, they face a time latency in which the event cannot be located in a precise global time instant, that is, until the whole network agrees on a specific timestamp. This issue suggests the need for a new class of algorithms, specifically designed for BANs, that is, more time bound. In fact, since BANs for event sensing must cope with physical quantity measurements which can vary very rapidly, or have to deal with strict energy constraints [24], it is necessary to introduce new strategies.

Let us consider the class of broadcast-based time synchronization algorithms. In this case, the BAN coordinator periodically sends the same message to all the BAN nodes (i.e., a broadcast message). Once each node has received the message, they adjust their internal time according to the specific algorithm procedures.

The reference broadcast synchronization (RBS) algorithm proposed in [24] offers a solution in which the leader sends a broadcast message to all the nodes. These latter register the time in which they received the message as a function of their local clock and inform the other nodes about their local time computation. A global time consensus is reached in a way similar to Berkeley algorithm—that is, once the relative time difference computation in each node is known. Unfortunately, a simpler approach with faster convergence would be needed in some applications.

A lightweight solution is represented by the Flooding Time Synchronization Protocol (FTSP) [25,26]. FTSP sends the MAC layer timestamp to all the nodes in the flooding mode. Each node that received the message computes the local drift as a function of the global time and aligns its local time to it. Linear regression is used for compensating clock skewing and drifting. The main con of the approach is the large amount of exchanged information [26].

In this scenario, our algorithm is a simplified version of the fusion of RBS and FTSP protocols. In fact, we eliminated the clock skewing and drifting compensations needed in FTSP. Furthermore, the message sent in the broadcast will contain the value of the real-time clock (RTC) as payload, instead of taking the time value from the MAC layer, as in the RBS protocol.

3. Problem Formulation

In this section the most important error sources for the time synchronization mismatch will be discussed. They can be divided into two main categories: errors related to the hardware implementation and errors related to other sources that we will call non-hardware implementation.

3.1. Hardware Implementation

3.1.1. RTC Mismatch

In most of the low-cost/low-power systems, the RTC accuracy is guaranteed by using a 32.768 kHz crystal oscillator. Several aspects must be considered when choosing this component for the project;

one of them is the frequency tolerance declared by the manufacturer. Low-cost 32.768 kHz crystals usually have a frequency tolerance of about ±20 parts per million (ppm) that introduces an intrinsic delay of ±10 min/year at its maximum.

Another source of frequency drift is the crystal capacitive loading mismatch. The effective load of a PCB mounted crystal depends on the external loading capacitance tolerance, the PCB parasitics, and the oscillator circuit parasitics. The difference from the load capacitance specified by the manufacturer can lead to an error up to ±200 ppm [27], which introduces a further delay of ±100 min/year at its maximum. Probably, this is the most important error source, so the design phase is very crucial; a typical characteristic is shown in Figure 1.

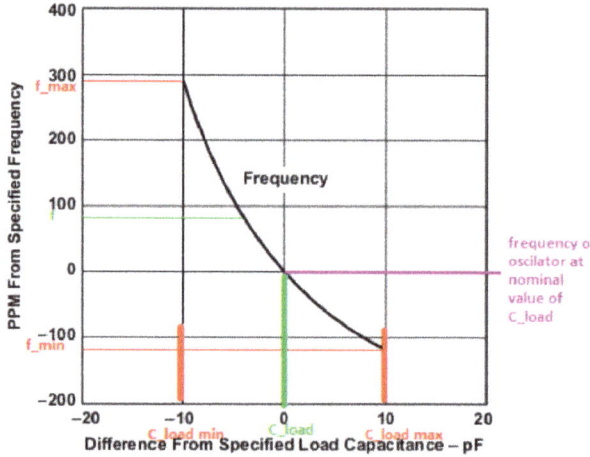

Figure 1. Crystal frequency drift with load capacitance.

It is common for crystal manufacturers to specify the drift due to aging in the first year without specifying the trend for subsequent years because it is unpredictable. This value is around ±3 ppm which means about ±90 s/year at its maximum.

The last source of inaccuracy is represented by the temperature changes that, for quartz, have a trend represented by a parabola whose vertex is the so-called turnover temperature (TOT). Figure 2 shows the graph for crystal ABS07-32.768KHZ-9-T [28] from Abracon (Spicewood, TX, USA) used in the project. In this case, the turnover temperature is around 25 °C. The effect is that the oscillator slows down when the temperature changes around the TOT. It is important to underline that the drift could be significant. Let us consider a 55 °C temperature; the frequency drift is about ±26 ppm which means a delay of about ±13 min/year.

All these aspects lead to the consideration that a calibration or synchronization technique is mandatory. Many calibration techniques are present in literature [29] and producers' data sheets [30,31]. Even though those techniques compensate the clock drift with very little battery power drain, they still require the presence of an external temperature sensor, and most of all, the final accuracy is around ±3.5 ppm which means a delay of about ±0.2 ms/min.

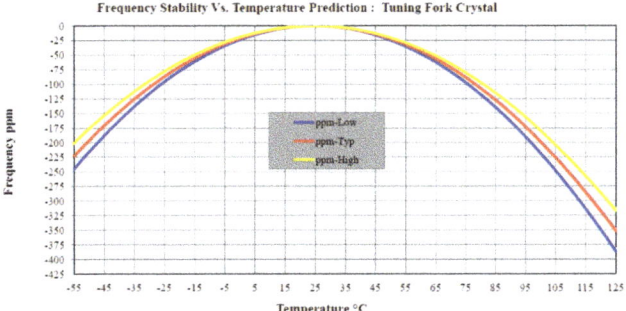

Figure 2. Crystal frequency drift with temperature.

We compared the performances of the RTCs of two identical boards for a 14 h log at a constant temperature of 30 °C. As expected, the mismatch grows linearly and at the end of the observation interval it is around 12 k milliseconds, as shown in Figure 3. That means a total mismatch between the boards of about 238 ppm; that is a delay of about 119 min/year.

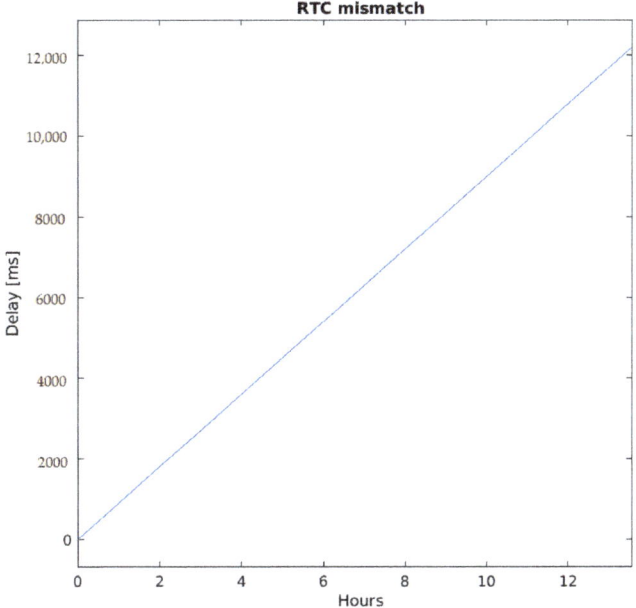

Figure 3. Real-time clock (RTC) difference between two identical boards.

3.1.2. IMUs Sampling Frequency Differences

IMUs with analog-to-digital converters (ADCs) for digitizing the gyroscope, accelerometer, and magnetometer outputs, have several interesting features, such as the selection of the sampling rate, the interrupt feature to alert the processor that a value is exceeding a user-programmable threshold or that a new data are available to read. The sampling frequency of a typical low-cost unit is in the range of a few Hz up to a few kHz. The right sampling frequency could be chosen as a function of the application requirements [32]. Usually, for gait analysis, postural monitoring, or activity monitoring, the frequency of 100 Hz is the right choice [33]. Even in this case, the clock accuracy is important since timing errors directly affect the distance and angle calculations performed by the processor.

In order to show this clock diversity, we use two identical units with a sampling frequency of 100 Hz and the interrupt feature enabled. The output pin is active low and is triggered as soon as the processor reads the data. In Figure 4 it can be noticed that the mismatch is about 57 mHz, while the time needed for the processor to read the data is about 80 µs. This means that the measured frequency differences should be attributed only to the frequency clock tolerance, which is about ±2% for the IMU used [34], and to the internal delays.

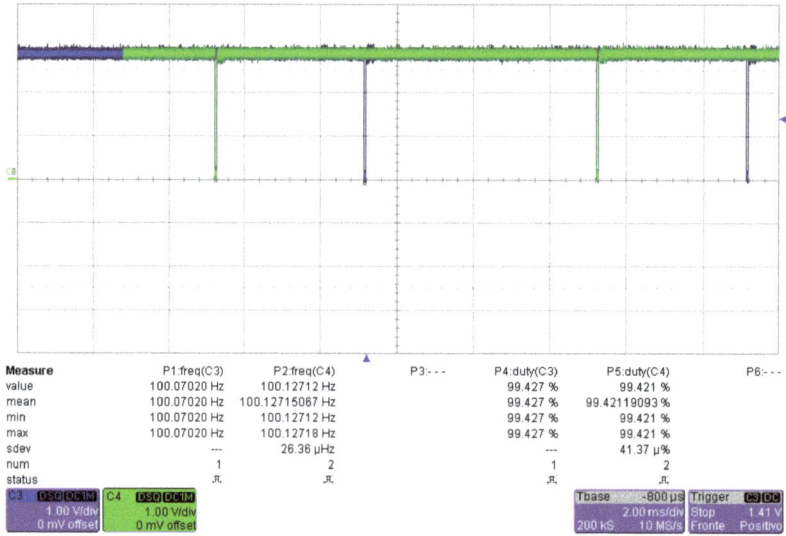

Figure 4. inertial measurement unit (IMU) clock misalignment for two different boards.

As a consequence, it cannot be used as a reference time generator, creating a serious problem. In fact, let us consider the measured IMU clock of 100.12712 Hz as in Figure 4 and an ideal system clock with a resolution of 10ms. In such a situation, every sample from the IMU is associated with a system timestamp. Nevertheless every 7.88 s there is ambiguity and two samples are associated with the same timestamp. The situation is shown in Figure 5. Instead, if the measured clock is smaller than the ideal system clock, we have sampling events without a sample.

This issue can be overcome simply by imposing an oversampling at the IMUs, as discussed in the next section.

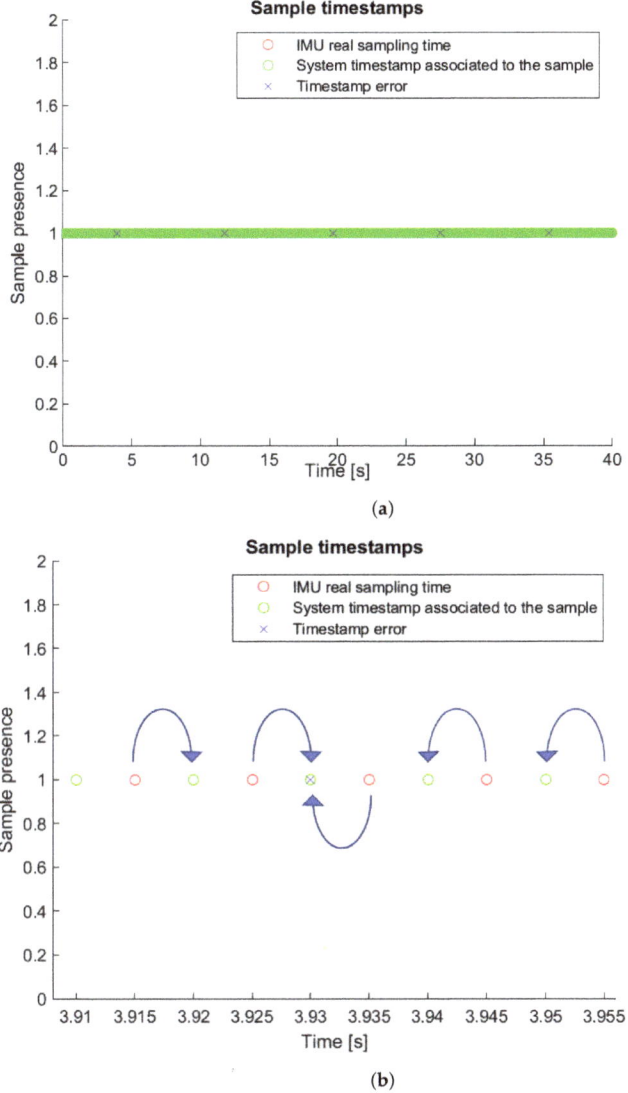

Figure 5. IMU timestamp error: (**a**) global view and (**b**) zoom.

3.2. Non-Hardware Implementation

This section will describe the problems that are not related to the hardware realization, but, rather, to the firmware implementation or the network topology choice and so on.

3.2.1. Micro SD Card Speed Classes

In applications of the type described in this paper, it is necessary to provide a local data storage system. The use of micro SD card memories represents the simplest and most economical solution, due to their reduced cost and dimensions. In order to simplify the data analysis on a PC, the FAT32 file system has been chosen. The drawback is that the writing process is slower than raw writing without a file system. For example, in our tests, closing a file and opening a new one may require several tens of seconds and it depends on the micro SD card speed class. The goal is not to miss any measurement coming from the IMU but at the same time to guarantee the right timestamp for each measurement. Two simple actions allow one to reach the goal: the first, to put the writing on micro SD card at a low priority, favoring the RTC and the communication with the IMU; the second, to prefer burst writing, correctly sizing the vectors to store in the RAM for the temporary storage of the values coming from the IMU or sensors in general while writing on the micro SD card.

3.2.2. Network Topology

The majority of time synchronization algorithms deal with message exchange. In particular, since we are coping with a wireless connected system, along with the non-determinism coming with clock drift, other sources of synchronization noise must be taken into account, directly depending on the random nature of the radio medium.

In general, the time interval required for the synchronization message to be received from the time instance in which it leaves its source (denoted as τ) can be decomposed into five parts [25]:

- Send time (t_S): the time from the instant the message is composed to that in which it arrives to the network interface;
- Access time (t_A): waiting time for the shared communication channel to be free;
- Transmission time (t_{TX}): time needed for the sender to put the message on the communication channel;
- Propagation time (t_P): traveling time of the electromagnetic signal from the sender to the receiver.
- Reception time (t_R): the dual time of t_S

The overall delay can be expressed as in (2):

$$\tau = t_S + t_A + t_{TX} + t_P + t_R \qquad (2)$$

Recalling that in a BAN we are dealing with very short distances (in 1–2 m range), the propagation time difference between two nodes can be neglected. Hence:

$$\tau \approx t_S + t_A + t_{TX} + t_R \qquad (3)$$

In this paper, we consider the class of broadcast-based time synchronization algorithms. For these algorithms, the BAN coordinator sends, under some conditions, a message for triggering the correct time setting. In this way, some terms of τ can be neglected. In fact, since we have only one access to the channel, i.e., the one for sending the broadcast message, t_A can be neglected. Additionally, the message is equal for each node, so also t_S can be neglected. Then, the expression (3) further reduces in:

$$\tau \approx t_{TX} + t_R \qquad (4)$$

Under these hypotheses, the greatest non-deterministic synchronization artefact is represented by t_R; it should be reduced as much as possible.

4. Platform Presentation

In this section, the synchronized multi-board wireless platform for long-term activity monitoring is discussed. The general idea is to build a flexible and expandable system composed by a wireless network of sensor nodes simultaneously providing multiple measures of different physiological and environmental signals. The organization of the used units will be discussed at a block diagram level as these were designed using standard commercial components configured according to the producers' recommendations. The core system is the synchronization mechanism which makes possible the correlation of the offline post-processed measurements made by different units that are fused for more complex analysis.

It is important to underline that this solution does not necessarily guarantee an absolute timestamp but guarantees an identical timestamp for all slaves. The accuracy of the entire system depends on the accuracy of the RTC implemented on the master. This is because in many cases it is not important to have an accurate absolute RTC system, but it is very important that for each sample of each unit there is a common synchronized timestamp that allows an *a posteriori* perfect alignment of the samples. For example, if we consider a 24 h long posture or step monitoring, an absolute delay of tens of seconds is absolutely not a problem if and only if this delay is present on all the units that compose the system. However, it is possible to change the precision of the system simply by acting on the master hardware implementation, keeping the complexity and cost of the slaves low.

In the next subsections a complete description of the system is presented, starting from the two different units used in this paper, through the architecture used for protocol implementation and the Android app used for managing the execution of the measurements.

4.1. Hardware of IMU Board

The custom designed IMUboard-HW-1-0-0 allocates a nine degrees of freedom (DoF) MPU-9250 nine-axis MEMS MotionTracking™ device from TDK-InveSense (San Jose, CA, USA). The MPU-9250 integrates on the same chip, the TDK-INV 6-axis IMU MPU-6500 and the AKM magnetometer AKM-8963 mutually connected using the AUX-I2C of the MPU-6500 [34]. The angular velocity ranges from ± 250 (deg/s) to ± 2000 (deg/s), while the measurement range of the acceleration is from ± 2 (g) to ± 16 (g). The measurement range of the magnetometer is about ± 4800 (uT), the sampling rate is up to 8 kHz, and the communication clock frequency is up to 20 MHz for the Serial Peripheral Interface (SPI) reading protocol. The system core is the Nordic Semiconductor (Trondheim, Norway) SoC nRF52832 that integrates a 64 MHz ARM®Cortex™-M4 CPU with 512 kB Flash memory and 64 kB RAM. The SoC manages a multiprotocol Bluetooth 5, ANT/ANT+, and proprietary 2.4 GHz. The processor uses a micro SD card for data logging and it communicates with it in SPI bus mode using the FAT32 file system to allow direct download of the data onto a PC. The user interface uses a couple of LEDs (green and red), two push-button switches for user interaction, and one main power switch. Finally, the power is supplied to the entire system either with a CR2450 coin cell battery, using a proper battery holder on the board, or with an external battery, using the JST connector on the board. The IMUboard-HW-1-0-0 unit is depicted in Figure 6 and the block diagram shown in Figure 7 depicts its structure.

Figure 6. Top and bottom view of IMUboard-HW-1-0-0 unit.

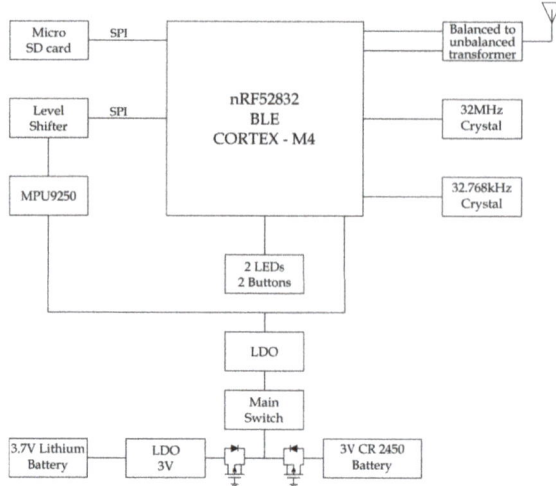

Figure 7. IMUboard-HW-1-0-0 unit block diagram.

4.2. Hardware of sEMG Board

The custom designed sEMG-HW-1-0-0 is an extension of the IMUboard-HW-1-0-0 previously described. It has onboard the circuital part for detecting and conditioning the muscle activity signal. The sEMG-HW-1-0-0 unit is depicted in Figure 8 and the block diagram is shown in Figure 9.

Figure 10 shows the circuit block schematic of the sEMG. The first stage is a differential instrumentation amplifier with a gain of about 300 V/V. Its output can be routed to the ADC of a processor to analyze the raw data. The second stage is a rectifier block. The signal, then, is fed to a low-pass filter (LPF) with a cut-off frequency at 3 Hz to suppress the rapid muscle contraction. The fourth stage is an amplifier with a variable gain controlled by the processor to equalize the signal amplitude coming from different quality electrodes or different muscles. The final stage is a comparator whose digital output is sampled at 50 Hz by the microprocessor and indicates that there is muscle activity. The sampling frequency used for the sEMG is independent of the IMU sampling frequency. In fact, two different threads are used for acquisitions and writing takes place on two different files. It is important to underline that each measurement is referenced over time, thereby allowing the correct temporal location of the stored measurements.

Figure 8. Top and bottom view of sEMG-HW-1-0-0 unit.

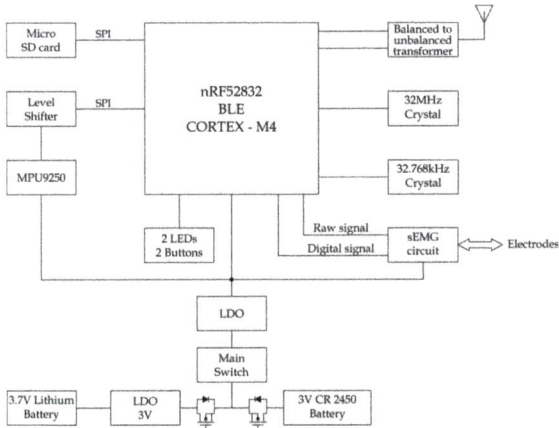

Figure 9. sEMG-HW-1-0-0 unit block diagram.

The circuital simulation performed in Keysight Advanced Design System (ADS) is reported in Figure 11. This circuit allows one to monitor the muscle activity and trigger a specific action without using the microprocessor resources.

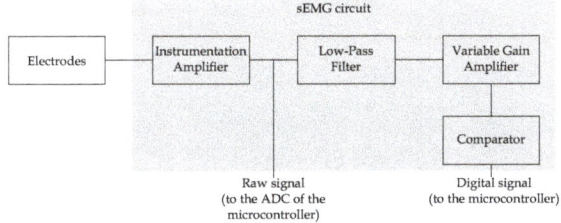

Figure 10. Superficial electromyography (sEMG) circuit block diagram.

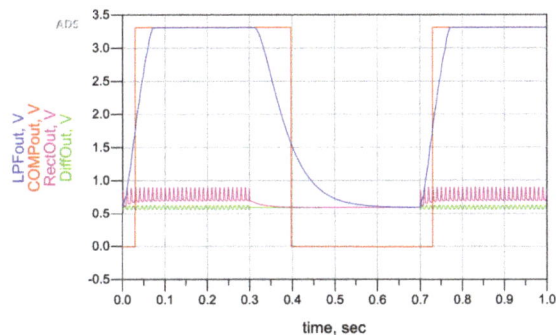

Figure 11. sEMG Advanced Design System (ADS) simulation.

4.3. Master–Slave Architecture

The protocol proposed in this work can be described as a simplified version of the fusion of RBS and FTSP protocols described in Section 2.3. The architecture used is a master–slave architecture, sketched in Figure 12, where the single master node acts as the BAN coordinator. Each BAN has a unique two-byte network ID included in the packets and used for packet filtering. Two types of messages are possible: broadcast messages with no acknowledgment feature which are used when the master needs to communicate with all the slaves in its sub-network and slaveID-oriented messages with an acknowledgment feature for any other communication. The master uses a broadcast message to send its own RTC value at predefined intervals depending on the actual hardware implementation, as it will be discussed in the preceding sections. The slaves refresh their own RTC values according to the values received by the master.

The advantage shared with the RBS protocol is that it eliminates any non-deterministic behavior introduced by the transmitter t_{TX}. The only critical issue is represented by the reception time t_R, defined in [25] as the time interval from the message reception up to the end of its processing. Differently from FTSP protocol, a simple update of the RTC register is the only task to perform during the receiving interval. Therefore, the firmware organization is quite critical because it must guarantee that computational delays are reduced to the minimum possible value.

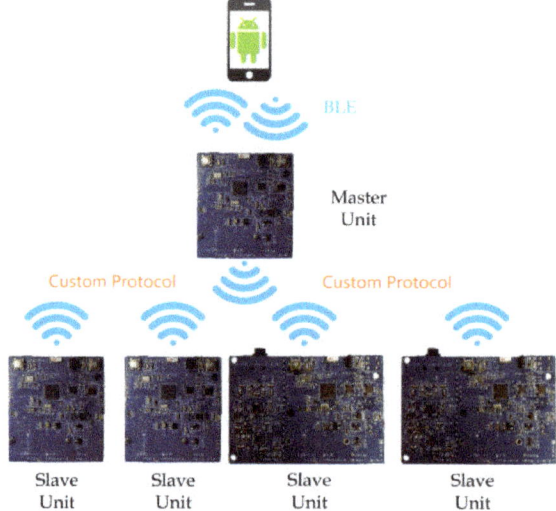

Figure 12. Master–slave architecture.

4.4. Android App

The Android app communicates with the master through Bluetooth Low Energy (BLE) protocol. It represents the user interface for starting, pausing, and stopping the local data logging for the entire system. Finally, it gives the actual RTC value at the start-up, as the units have no backup battery for keeping track of the time when switched off.

4.5. Firmware Considerations

As stated in previous sections, the greatest non-deterministic synchronization artifact is represented by t_R. The firmware should be organized while striving to reduce the elaboration time of the synchronization packet received by the slaves. The flowchart of the packet reception routine is illustrated in Figure 13 where it can be noticed that the synchronization packet is immediately processed.

Further, the micro SD card R/W interrupt level is lower than the one of the RTC module.

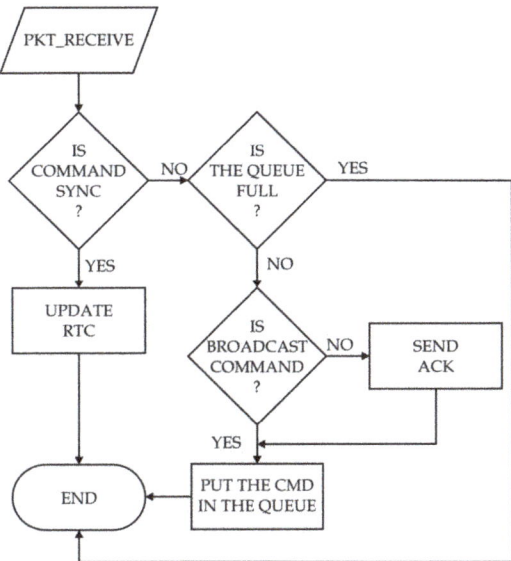

Figure 13. Flowchart of the packet reception routine.

Finally, in order to overcome the issue explained in the Section 3.1.2, the sampling frequency imposed at the IMU is about 200 Hz.

5. Experimental Results

In order to validate the platform performance, different tests were carried out in several application contexts. The hardware settings were: 200 Hz IMU sampling frequency; ≈5 ms RTC resolution; 10 ms IMU sample interval storage in the micro SD card (100 Hz equivalent sampling frequency); 20 s synchronization packet rate; ±250 dps gyroscope sensitivity; ±2 g accelerometer sensitivity.

5.1. Rotating Platform

The first setup is shown in Figure 14 where a total of four slaves, two IMUs, and two sEMGs, were mounted on a rotating platform. A microcontroller drives a stepper motor that rotates the disc according to very specific routines quasi-randomly alternating movements and pauses.

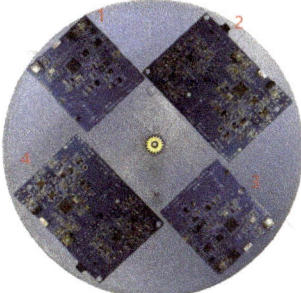

Figure 14. Experimental arrangement on a rotating platform.

Figure 15 reports the analysis of the variance (ANOVA) of the delays for each slave. To that end, the firmware has been modified, lowering the RTC resolution to 10 μs and introducing a routine for memorizing the time difference between the local and the received timestamp. The test lasted 24 h. The figure evidences that the error distribution is comparable for the four slaves used, its mean value being around 25–30 µs, and the 25th and 75th percentiles are about 15 µs and 40 µs, respectively. The reported results demonstrate that the proposed system can be used in applications with much more stringent synchronization requirements.

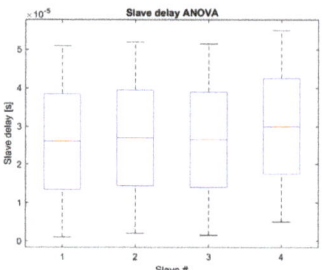

Figure 15. Analysis of the variance (ANOVA) test.

Figure 16 shows the raw values along the z-axis for each unit after about 2.5 h. Each waveform is shifted along the y-axis to improve visibility. Perfect synchronization was noticed along the x-axis, as expected. Even in this case the synchronization was perfect, and duplicate samples were not generated, nor was any missing sample reported, demonstrating the effectiveness of the proposed strategy.

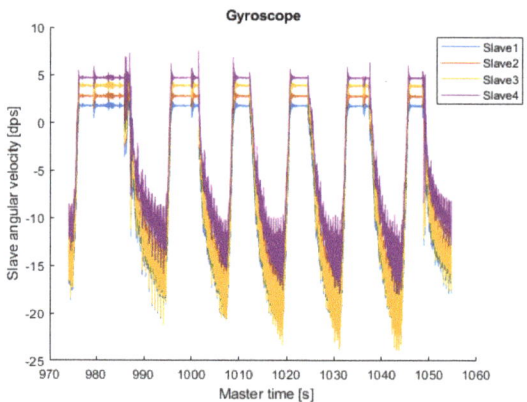

Figure 16. Gyroscope raw data.

5.2. Walking

As stated in the introduction, the proposed system gives the main advantage of cross-relating not only the signals coming from different similar units but even signals coming from units equipped with different sensors, allowing one, thus, to correlate heterogeneous signals and perform more complex processing.

In this configuration, one sEMG unit (slave 1) was placed on the tibia of the right leg and one IMU unit (slave 2) on the tibia of the left leg; the IMU orientation for both legs is shown in Figure 17. The electrodes were positioned, as an exercise, as in Figure 17 to analyze the relationship between muscle activity in the area of the Achilles tendon rather than that of a single muscle. Finally, the master is worn by the user in his pocket. For sake of clarity, an extract of the elaborations made on the data of a walk of a healthy individual during a 24 h logging of his daily activities will be reported and discussed below.

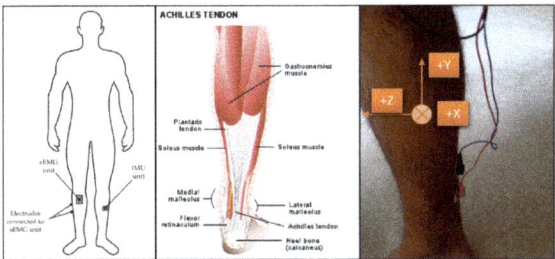

Figure 17. Units placement, achilles tendon area detail, electrode placement, and IMU orientation.

Figure 18 reports the data coming from the gyroscopes, filtered with a bandpass filter with the upper and lower cut-off frequencies of 100 Hz and 2 Hz respectively, along with the electromyography. The figure evidences both the symmetry in the movements of the two lower limbs and the presence of a periodicity in the muscles' activity in the examined region. In particular, the symmetry can be noticed in the regular zero-crossing moment distribution and in the maximum/minimum values of the measured angular speed. The sEMG ON curve has been normalized to the maximum absolute value of the other waveforms reported in the figure to better visualize it.

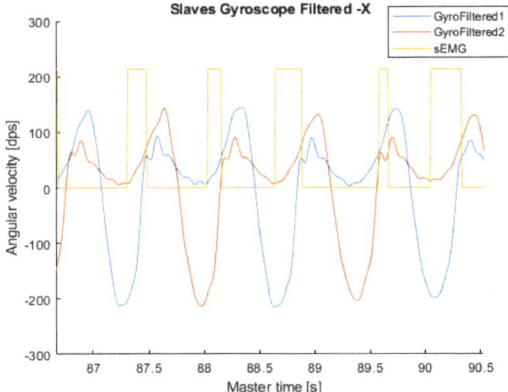

Figure 18. Gyroscope x-axis filtered data for slaves 1 and 2.

The analysis of the angles formed by the tibia in relation to electromyographic data is more relevant. In Figure 19 it is evident that in the analyzed area there is brief muscle activity both in the heel strike and midstance. In this representation the almost-perfect symmetry of the movements of the two limbs is more evident; meanwhile, the measured muscular activity is slightly variable, as it is associated with the walk of a healthy individual during his/her normal day-life, and thus not necessarily following a straight path. This implies that several distinct muscles are involved in the movements. The figure reports the overall activity in the Achille's tendon area.

Finally, as a last example, Figure 20 shows the raw data of the z-axes of the accelerometers with muscle activity. As in the previous case, the figure evidences the symmetry in the two limbs' movements. Much more interesting is the difference in the waveform reporting the accelerations along the z-axis that implies a different intensity of the two foot rests.

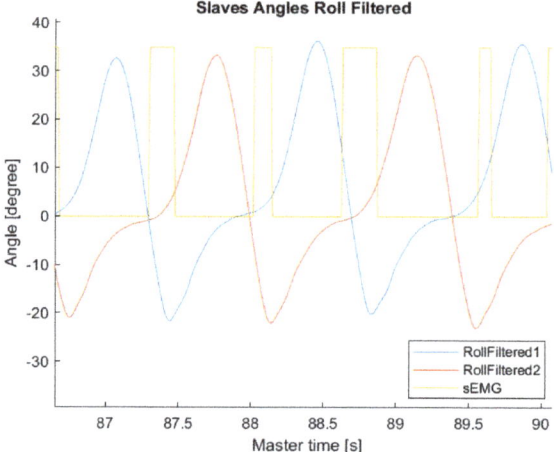

Figure 19. Roll angles for slaves 1 and 2.

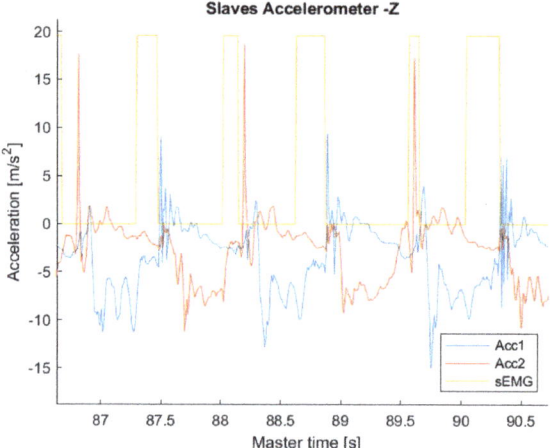

Figure 20. Accelerometer z-axis raw data for slaves 1 and 2.

6. Conclusions

The paper described a platform composed by different units and sensors to be used for long duration monitoring of daily activities. The currently installed and tested sensors are an IMU with nine DoF and a unit for sEMG capable of storing raw data or ON/OFF muscle activation information. The system uses an extremely simple synchronization protocol based on a master–slave architecture, in which the master regularly transmits the reference timestamp. Each slave of the same subnet uses the reference timestamp to avoid time-mismatches.

The reported results aim to demonstrate that all the error sources due to the time synchronization mismatch presented in Section 3 are resolved and overcome. In fact, the synchrony error is below 30 μs, a value that is far beyond the real needs in this type of application related to human activities.

It is important to underline that the measured time mismatch quantifies the slaves' ability to align with the master timestamp. We reiterate once again that it is not necessary that the master timestamp has absolute accuracy, but as demonstrated by the reported experiments, it can itself be affected by all the errors exposed in the Section 3.

The reported results demonstrated the effectiveness of the proposed approach, and most of all, its enormous potential, as it allows one to obtain even more complex processing by correlating apparently unrelated measurements by inserting different sensor types.

As a matter of fact, different in-depth analyses are possible by varying the unit number, the sensor types, the positions, and the post-processing of the measurements, allowing one to correlate apparently uncorrelated parameters. The proposed approach allows the use of non-invasive wearable units for long time periods that could evidence any possible anomaly. Usually, it is quite difficult to observe them in a regular laboratory visit where such anomalies are not detected both due to their their sporadic insurgency and the unconscious attitude to correct them while the patient focuses his/her attention on them.

An important evolution of the platform currently under analysis elects the master unit to decision hub rank, appointing him a real-time analysis of a subset of data arriving from the sensor nodes. In this scenario, the master acts as a time coordinator and decision hub. The evolution does not greatly affect the slave units moving the computational complexity to the master.

Author Contributions: Conceptualization, G.C.; Investigation, G.C.; Resources: A.F.; Validation, G.C.; Writing—original draft: G.C. and A.F.; Writing—review & editing: G.C., G.A. and A.F.; Supervision, G.A. All authors have read and agreed to the published version of the manuscript.

Funding: This research received no external funding.

Conflicts of Interest: The authors declare no conflict of interest.

References

1. Giorgio, A.; Guaragnella, C. ECG Signal Denoising using Wavelet for the VLP effective detection on FPGA. In Proceedings of the 2018 AEIT International Annual Conference, Bari, Italy, 3–5 October 2018; pp. 1–5.
2. Casalino, G.; Castellano, G.; Mencar, C. Data Stream Classification by Dynamic Incremental Semi-Supervised Fuzzy Clustering. *Int. J. Artif. Intell. Tools* **2019**, *28*, 1960009. [CrossRef]
3. Ahmed, M.U.; Brickman, S.; Dengg, A.; Fasth, N.; Mihajlovic, M.; Norman, J. A machine learning approach to classify pedestrians' events based on IMU and GPS. *Int. J. Artif. Intell.* **2019**, *17*, 154–167.
4. Carli, R.; Dotoli, M.; Pellegrino, R.; Ranieri, L. Using multi-objective optimization for the integrated energy efficiency improvement of a smart city public buildings' portfolio. In Proceedings of the 2015 IEEE International Conference on Automation Science and Engineering (CASE), Gothenburg, Sweden, 24–28 August 2015; pp. 21–26.
5. Bianchi, A.; Pizzutilo, S.; Vessio, G. CoreASM-based evaluation of the N-AODV protocol for mobile ad-hoc networks. *J. Mob. Multimed.* **2016**, *12*, 31–51.
6. Parkinson, J. An essay on the shaking palsy. *J. Neuropsychiatry Clin. Neurosci.* **2002**, *14*, 223–236. [CrossRef]
7. Margiotta, N.; Avitabile, G.; Coviello, G. A wearable wireless system for gait analysis for early diagnosis of Alzheimer and Parkinson disease. In Proceedings of the 2016 5th International Conference on Electronic Devices, Systems and Applications (ICEDSA), Ras Al Khaimah, UAE, 6–8 December 2016; pp. 1–4.
8. Whittle, M.W. Chapter 4—Methods of gait analysis. In *Gait Analysis*, 4th ed.; Butterworth-Heinemann: Oxford, UK, 2007; pp. 137–175.
9. Salarian, A.; Russmann, H.; Vingerhoets, F.J.; Dehollain, C.; Blanc, Y.; Burkhard, P.R.; Aminian, K. Gait assessment in Parkinson's disease: Toward an ambulatory system for long-term monitoring. *IEEE Trans. Biomed. Eng.* **2004**, *51*, 1434–1443. [CrossRef]
10. Coviello, G.; Avitabile, G. Multiple Synchronized Inertial Measurement Unit Sensor Boards Platform for Activity Monitoring. *IEEE Sens. J.* **2020**, *20*, 8771–8777. [CrossRef]
11. Chen, M.; Gonzalez, S.; Vasilakos, A.; Cao, H.; Leung, V.C. Body area networks: A survey. *Mob. Netw. Appl.* **2011**, *16*, 171–193. [CrossRef]
12. Martinez, B.; Monton, M.; Vilajosana, I.; Prades, J.D. The power of models: Modeling power consumption for IoT devices. *IEEE Sens. J.* **2015**, *15*, 5777–5789. [CrossRef]
13. Wearable IMU Sensor | Motion Sensor | 9DOF-Shimmer3 IMU Unit. Available online: http://www.shimmersensing.com/products/shimmer3-imu-sensor (accessed on 28 May 2020).
14. NGIMU x-io Technologies. Available online: https://x-io.co.uk/ngimu/ (accessed on 28 May 2020).

15. Sun, Q.; Zhou, Z.; Jiang, J.; Hu, D. Gait cadence detection based on surface electromyography (sEMG) of lower limb muscles. In Proceedings of the 2014 International Conference on Multisensor Fusion and Information Integration for Intelligent Systems (MFI), Beijing, China, 28–29 September 2014; pp. 1–4.
16. Morbidoni, C.; Cucchiarelli, A.; Fioretti, S.; Di Nardo, F. A Deep Learning Approach to EMG-Based Classification of Gait Phases during Level Ground Walking. *Electronics* **2019**, *8*, 894. [CrossRef]
17. Luo, R.; Sun, S.; Zhang, X.; Tang, Z.; Wang, W. A Low-Cost End-to-End sEMG-Based Gait Sub-Phase Recognition System. *IEEE Trans. Neural Syst. Rehabil. Eng.* **2020**, *28*, 267–276. [CrossRef] [PubMed]
18. Laerhoven, K.V.; Gellersen, H.W.; Malliaris, Y.G. Long term activity monitoring with a wearable sensor node. In Proceedings of the International Workshop on Wearable and Implantable Body Sensor Networks (BSN'06), Cambridge, MA, USA, 3–5 April 2006; pp. 4–174.
19. Cancela, J.; Pastorino, M.; Arredondo, M.T.; Pansera, M.; Pastor-Sanz, L.; Villagra, F.; Pastor, M.A.; Gonzalez, A.P. Gait assessment in Parkinson's disease patients through a network of wearable accelerometers in unsupervised environments. In Proceedings of the 2011 Annual International Conference of the IEEE Engineering in Medicine and Biology Society, Boston, MA, USA, 30 August–3 September 2011; pp. 2233–2236.
20. Oniga, S.; Tisan, A.; Bólyi, R. Activity and health status monitoring system. In Proceedings of the 2017 IEEE 26th International Symposium on Industrial Electronics (ISIE), Edinburgh, UK, 8 August 2017; pp. 2027–2031.
21. Fischer, M.J. The consensus problem in unreliable distributed systems (a brief survey). In *Foundations of Computation Theory*; Karpinski, M., Ed.; Springer: Berlin/Heidelberg, Germany, 1983; pp. 127–140.
22. Cristian, F. Probabilistic clock synchronization. *Distrib. comput.* **1989**, *3*, 146–158. [CrossRef]
23. Gusella, R.; Zatti, S. The accuracy of the clock synchronization achieved by TEMPO in Berkeley UNIX 4.3BSD. *IEEE Trans. Softw. Eng.* **1989**, *15*, 847–853. [CrossRef]
24. Elson, J.; Girod, L.; Estrin, D. Fine-grained network time synchronization using reference broadcasts. *ACM SIGOPS Oper. Syst. Rev.* **2002**, *36*, 147–163. [CrossRef]
25. Maróti, M.; Kusy, B.; Simon, G.; Ledeczi, A. The Flooding Time Synchronization Protocol. 2004; pp. 39–49. Available online: https://dl.acm.org/doi/abs/10.1145/1031495.1031501 (accessed on 28 May 2020).
26. Wang, S.; Shi, M.; Li, D.; Du, T. A Survey of Time Synchronization Algorithms for Wireless Sensor Networks. In Proceedings of the 2019 Chinese Control Conference (CCC), Guangzhou, China, 27–30 July 2019; pp. 6392–6397.
27. AT03155: Real-Time-Clock Calibration and Compensation. Available online: http://ww1.microchip.com/downloads/en/appnotes/atmel-42251-rtc-calibration-and-compensation_ap-note_at03155.pdf (accessed on 23 March 2020).
28. Abracon 32.768 kHz Low Profile Crystal. Available online: http://abracon.com/Resonators/ABS07.pdf (accessed on 28 November 2019).
29. Blazinsek, I.; Chowdhury, A. Enhancing the accuracy of standard embedded RTC module with random synchronization events and dynamic calibration. *Przeglad Elektrotechniczny* **2016**, *92*, 248–251. [CrossRef]
30. ISL12022 RTC Accuracy Optimization Calibration Procedure—Application Note. Available online: https://www.renesas.com/us/en/www/doc/application-note/an1400.pdf (accessed on 28 November 2019).
31. Underwood, S. Implementing a Temperature Compensated RTC—Application Note. Available online: http://www.ti.com/lit/ml/slap107/slap107.pdf (accessed on 28 November 2019).
32. Munoz Diaz, E.; Heirich, O.; Khider, M.; Robertson, P. Optimal sampling frequency and bias error modeling for foot-mounted IMUs. In Proceedings of the International Conference on Indoor Positioning and Indoor Navigation, Montbeliard-Belfort, France, 28–31 October 2013; pp. 1–9.
33. Provot, T.; Chiementin, X.; Oudin, E.; Bolaers, F.; Murer, S. Validation of a High Sampling Rate Inertial Measurement Unit for Acceleration During Running. *Sensors* **2017**, *17*, 1958. [CrossRef] [PubMed]
34. TDK MPU-9250 Datasheet. Available online: https://invensense.tdk.com/wp-content/uploads/2015/02/PS-MPU-9250A-01-v1.1.pdf (accessed on 28 November 2019).

© 2020 by the authors. Licensee MDPI, Basel, Switzerland. This article is an open access article distributed under the terms and conditions of the Creative Commons Attribution (CC BY) license (http://creativecommons.org/licenses/by/4.0/).

Article

A Deep Learning Approach to EMG-Based Classification of Gait Phases during Level Ground Walking

Christian Morbidoni *, Alessandro Cucchiarelli, Sandro Fioretti and Francesco Di Nardo *

Department of Information Engineering, Università Politecnica delle Marche, 60100 Ancona, Italy
* Correspondence: c.morbidoni@univpm.it (C.M.); f.dinardo@staff.univpm.it (F.D.N.);
  Tel.: +39-071-220-4830 (C.M.); +39-071-220-4838 (F.D.N.)

Received: 30 July 2019; Accepted: 9 August 2019; Published: 14 August 2019

Abstract: Correctly identifying gait phases is a prerequisite to achieve a spatial/temporal characterization of muscular recruitment during walking. Recent approaches have addressed this issue by applying machine learning techniques to treadmill-walking data. We propose a deep learning approach for surface electromyographic (sEMG)-based classification of stance/swing phases and prediction of the foot–floor-contact signal in more natural walking conditions (similar to everyday walking ones), overcoming constraints of a controlled environment, such as treadmill walking. To this aim, sEMG signals were acquired from eight lower-limb muscles in about 10.000 strides from 23 healthy adults during level ground walking, following an eight-shaped path including natural deceleration, reversing, curve, and acceleration. By means of an extensive evaluation, we show that using a multi layer perceptron to learn hidden features provides state of the art performances while avoiding features engineering. Results, indeed, showed an average classification accuracy of 94.9 for learned subjects and 93.4 for unlearned ones, while mean absolute difference ($\pm SD$) between phase transitions timing predictions and footswitch data was 21.6 ms and 38.1 ms for heel-strike and toe off, respectively. The suitable performance achieved by the proposed method suggests that it could be successfully used to automatically classify gait phases and predict foot–floor-contact signal from sEMG signals during level ground walking.

Keywords: sEMG; deep learning; neural networks; gait phase; classification; everyday walking

---

1. Introduction

Electromyography is a widely-accepted tool able to provide an essential and original contribution to the characterization of the neuromuscular system [1]. In particular, surface electromyography (sEMG) is acknowledged as a non-invasive approach, specifically suitable to monitor muscle activity during dynamic tasks, such as walking [2–4]. In order to achieve a spatial/temporal characterization of muscular recruitment during walking, gait events, such as the instant of foot-floor contact and ground clearance, need to be assessed. This process starts from the identification of the two main gait phases, stance and swing. The stance phase designates the entire period during which the foot is on the ground, while the swing phase is characterized by the time the foot is in the air for limb advancement. The transitions between a swing and the subsequent stance phase is commonly referred to as heel-strike (HS), while the transition between a stance and the subsequent swing phases is referred to as toe-off (TO). Stance and swing identify the functional subdivisions of total limb activity within the gait cycle [2], thus precisely identifying HS and TO events is important to analyze the gait activity. For this reason, sEMG signals are typically coupled with signals able to provide the synchronization of the gait cycle, such as signals from foot-switch sensors [5], pressure mats [6], stereo-photogrammetric systems [7], and inertial measurements units (accelerometers and gyroscopes) [8].

Stereo–photogrammetric systems and pressure mats are affected by different relevant issues: high costs of the instrumentation, limited number of cycles observed, and/or invasiveness of experimental set-up. The use of wearable sensors seems to mitigate the impact of the costs and to allow the identification of gait events in a suitable number of cycles. Even so, the problems of encumbrance and time-consuming experimental set-up are still relevant, especially for applications in pathology. Moreover, wearable sensors can require particular care for the correct placement and the need of specific calibration procedures, not consistent with the timing of clinical practice. Thus, the idea of overcoming all these limitations developing novel techniques able to detect and classify gait events from sEMG signal alone is indeed starting to catch on. This kind of approach may involve machine learning and deep learning techniques.

1.1. Aim of the Study

Classifying gait events is a typical task which could be addressed by machine learning and deep learning techniques. Many examples were reported in literature [9–12]. However, only few reports addressed the issue of gait-phase classification from sEMG signal only [13–15]. These very recent approaches were based on hand-crafted features extracted from sEMG signals during treadmill walking and were evaluated on a relatively small number of subjects (up to eight). Walking on a treadmill is known to affect gait performance, resulting in increased number of steps and cadence, decreased preferred walking speed, stride and stance-phase length, slightly decreased joint range of motion, and changes in EMG activation with respect to level ground walking [16–19]. Thus, the reliability of the above mentioned EMG-based classifiers of stance and swing phases [13–15] is limited to treadmill data and is not tested on ground-walking data. In addition, treadmill walking occurs in very controlled conditions, characterized by a high repeatability of spatial/temporal parameters (including stance and swing duration). In contrast, everyday walking is characterized by a wider variability of spatial/temporal parameters and sEMG signals introduced by deceleration, reversing, curves and acceleration [16–19]. This variability is expected to affect the performance of a possible stance/swing classification and the consequent prediction of temporal parameters, such as heel-strike and toe-off timing.

Therefore, the aim of the present study is to propose an artificial neural network (ANN)-based approach to classify gait events (proper stance and swing phases) and to predict foot-floor-contact signal from sEMG signals, in conditions similar to everyday walking. With "conditions similar to everyday walking" we mean that, differently from previous study where gait phases were classified in the very controlled conditions of treadmill walking [13–15], in the present study each subject walked on level ground following an eight-shaped path (Figure 1) which includes natural deceleration, reversing, curve, and acceleration.

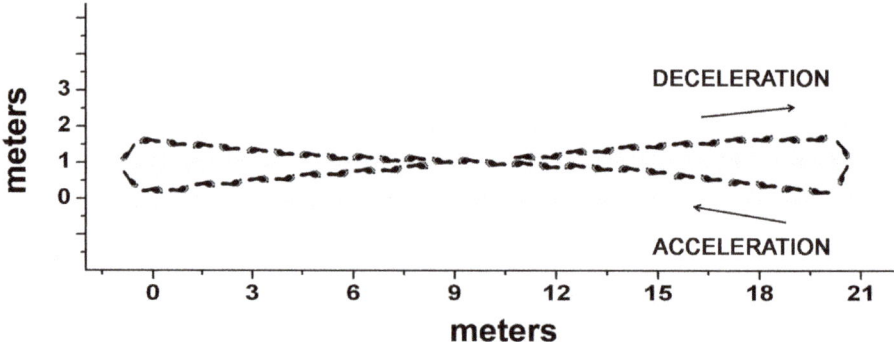

Figure 1. Illustration of the eight-shaped path used in our experiments.

1.2. Contributions

The main contributions of the present study are three:

- first, providing a classification of stance and swing phases and the prediction of foot-floor-contact signal in more natural walking conditions (similar to everyday walking), overcoming the limitations and the constraints of a controlled environment, such as treadmill walking;
- second, proposing a different approach to process the sEMG signal used to train deep neural networks: while previous studies [13–15] processed sEMG signals to extract time/frequency domain features which were used to feed the neural networks, the present study directly used the envelopes of the EMG signal to train the networks, attempting to automatically learn relevant higher level (hidden) features;
- third, improving the reliability of the prediction of gait events (HS and TO) in unseen subjects reported in literature [13], despite the challenging condition of everyday walking. This has been achieved by both enlarging the testing data (four-minute ground walking of 23 different subjects) and decreasing the average error in the prediction of HS and TO timing.

The remainder of this paper is organized as follows. Section 2 reports a brief review of the related works. Section 3 describes the dataset, the acquisition and the pre-processing of the signals, and the gait- phase classification by deep learning. Section 4 reports and discusses the results. Section 5 concludes the present study.

2. Related Works

Machine learning techniques, such as ANNs, are typically used for analyzing and classifying large amount of data and complex signals. Many applications of machine learning approaches in health care were reported [20–22]. Similar approaches were proven to be reliable also in classifying EMG signals during different tasks. Wavelet neural network and multi-layer perceptrons were used to handle EMG signals in order to identify neuromuscular disorders [23,24]. Learning vector quantization, support vector machine, and Levenberg–Marquardt-based networks were applied to EMG signals for classifying hand-motion patterns [25–27]. EMG-based unsupervised competitive learning techniques were employed for the identification of the muscle activity during pregnancy [28]. Efforts have been made to adapt these techniques for walking-task characterization: different machine learning approaches were applied to gait analysis data by Joyseeree et al. for disease identification [9]. Kaczmarczyk et al. [11] applied ANNs for gait classification in post stroke patients. Wang and Zieliska [12] designed an EMG-based method for detecting the variability in gait features depending on footwear, by applying vector quantization classifying networks and clustering competitive networks. Zou et al. [10] performed gait recognition analyzing inertial sensor data by means of deep convolutional neural network (and deep recurrent neural network approaches

In particular, literature reports only few attempts to provide a machine learning approach which used the sEMG signal only for the classification of stance and swing phases [13–15]. In [15] a set of time-domain features is extracted from EMG signal segments and hidden Markov models are used to individuate stance and swing phases. Evaluation is performed on a single subject walking on a treadmill, reporting a maximum classification accuracy of 91.08%. In [14] a novel bilateral feature is extracted from the EMG signal and is used to classify stance and swing phases by training a support vector classifier. The method is evaluated on two subjects walking on a treadmill at different speeds. The best reported accuracy (96%) corresponds to the case where a subset of the gait cycles from a subject are used to classify the entire walk of the same subject. In [13] a set of time-domain features are extracted from EMG signals and fed to a single hidden layer neural network to classify gait phases. This study is the most similar to ours, as it explicitly targets unlearned subjects, i.e., subjects not used as inputs during the training phase and attempts to predict timing of phase transitions. However, the data used is derived from 8 subjects walking on a treadmill and the evaluation of phase transition detection is performed on only 5 s of the walking of a single unlearned subject, reporting a mean average error of 35 ± 25 ms for HS and 49 ± 15 ms for TO. All these recent approaches were based on hand-crafted features extracted from sEMG signals during treadmill walking and were evaluated on relatively small populations of subjects (up to eight).

3. Materials and Methods

3.1. Dataset

The dataset included signals recorded from 23 healthy adults (12 females and 11 males), acquired in the Movement Analysis Laboratory of Università Politecnica delle Marche, Ancona, Italy. Mean (±SD) characteristics were: age = 23.8 ± 1.9 years; height = 173 ± 10 cm; mass = 63.3 ± 12.4 kg; body mass index (BMI) = 20.8 ± 2.1 kg/m^2. None of the subjects presented any pathological condition or had undergone orthopedic surgery that might have affected lower limb mechanics. Therefore, subjects with joint pain, neurological pathologies, orthopedic surgery, abnormal gait or a body mass index (BMI) higher than 25 (overweight and obese) were not recruited. The research was undertaken in compliance with the ethical principles of the Helsinki Declaration and was approved by an institutional expert committee. Participants signed informed consent prior to the beginning of the test.

3.2. Signal Acquisition

The multichannel recording system, Step 32 (Medical Technology, Italy, Version PCI-32 ch2.0.1. DV, resolution: 12 bit; sampling rate: 2 kHz) was used to acquire surface electromyographic (sEMG) and basographic signals (i.e., the signals from footswitches). Each lower limb was instrumented with three foot-switches and four sEMG probes. Foot-switches (surface: 1.21 cm^2, activation force: 3 N), were pasted beneath the heel, the first and the fifth metatarsal heads of the foot. Single differential sEMG probes with fixed geometry (Ag/Ag-Cl disk; electrode diameter: 0.4 cm; inter-electrode distance: 0.8 cm; gain: 1000; high-pass filter: 10 Hz; input impedance: 1.5 G; CMRR > 126 dB; input referred noise: 1 Vrms) and with variable geometry (Ag/Ag-Cl disks; minimum inter-electrode distance: 12 mm, gain: 1000, high-pass filter: 10 Hz, input impedance >1.5 G, CMRR >126 dB, input referred noise 200 nVrms) were placed on the belly muscle to detect the sEMG signals. Skin was shaved, cleansed with abrasive paste and wet with a damp cloth. Probes were placed over tibialis anterior, gastrocnemius lateralis, hamstrings, and vastus lateralis, following the recommendations provided by the European concerted action SENIAM (surface EMG for a non-invasive assessment of muscles) for electrodes location with respect to tendons, motor points and fiber orientation [29]. Each volunteer walked barefoot on the floor at her/his own chosen pace for about 5 min, following an eight-shaped path [30], which includes natural deceleration, reversing, curve and acceleration (Figure 1).

3.3. Pre-Processing

Footswitch signals were converted and processed so as to identify the different gait cycles and phases (stance and swing), according to the approach discussed in details in [31].

Electromyographic signals were processed by a high-pass, linear-phase FIR filter (cut-off frequency: 20 Hz), in order to avoid phase distortion effects and by a low-pass, linear-phase FIR filter (cut-off frequency: 450 Hz). Then, sEMG signals were full-wave rectified and the envelope was extracted (second-order Butterworth low-pass filter, cut-off frequency: 5 Hz). Figures 2 and 3 showed, respectively, the raw EMG signals recorded for the right leg and the envelope obtained as a result of the pre-processing step.

The sEMG and basographic data analyzed in the present study are going to be published in a public dataset, and are currently available for research purposes by contacting the authors.

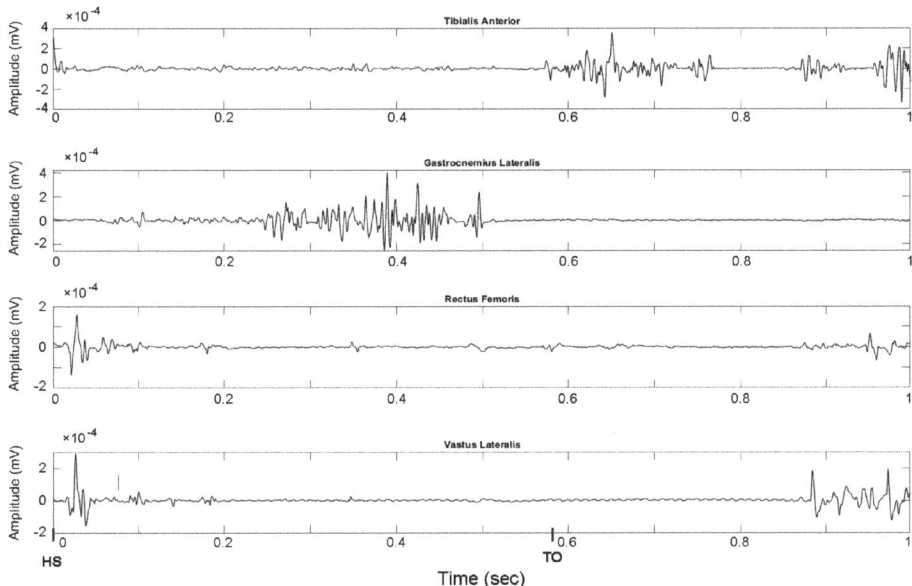

Figure 2. Raw electromyographic (EMG) signals recorded from the four muscles of the right leg. Corresponding heel-strike (HS) and toe-off (TO) timing are highlighted.

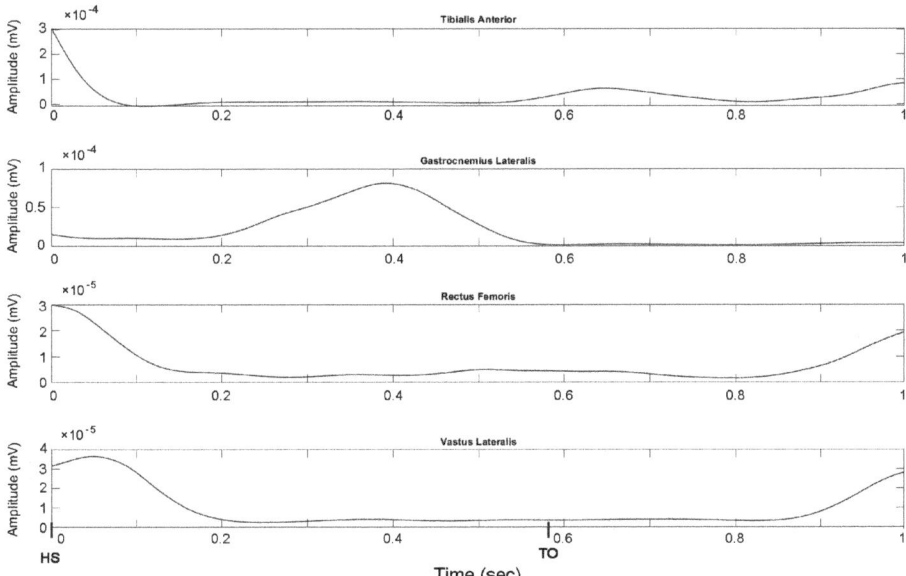

Figure 3. The envelope resulting from the pre-processing of the raw EMG signals recorded from the four muscles of the right leg. Corresponding HS and TO timing are highlighted.

3.4. Gait Phase Classification

3.4.1. Data Preparation

Before feeding data into the classifier, a min-max normalization of each muscle signal was performed within each subject, thus mapping the values in the [0–1] interval. In order to train the classifier, we split the signals into 20 data samples windows (corresponding to 10 milliseconds) for both stance and swing phases.

We then aggregated the synchronized EMG-signal segments corresponding to the eight muscles (four for each leg) into a single vector of 160 elements. Each EMG vector was composed of 20 sequences of eight elements. Each element represents the EMG-signal values of the eight muscles in that single time-sample. Thus, the first eight elements of the vector were the EMG signal values of the eight muscles computed in the first sample of the segment. The following eight elements of the vector are the EMG signal values of the eight muscles computed in the second sample of the segment, and so on up to the twentieth sample. The structure of the input vector is illustrated in Figure 4. $L1_i$, $L2_i$, $L3_i$, and $L4_i$ were the values of EMG signals in the sample i corresponding to the muscles of the left leg, respectively: tibialis anterior, gastrocnemius lateralis, hamstring, vastus lateralis. $R1_i$, $R2_i$, $R3_i$, and $R4_i$ represented the correspondent for the right leg. Each input vector was assigned to the label 0 if the corresponding signals belong to a stance phase, and to 1 if the corresponding signals belong to a swing phase. After removing the segments before the first swing phase, to avoid considering muscle activation recorded in non-walking conditions, we obtained 522.936 labelled segments from the 23 subjects.

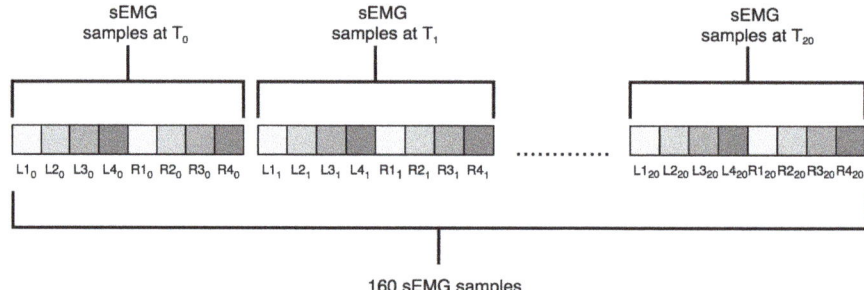

Figure 4. The structure of EMG vectors fed as input to the artificial neural networks (ANNs).

In our study we attempted to classify gait phases and to detect the timing of phase transitions (HS and TO events). In particular we are targeting previously unseen subjects, i.e., subjects whose gait recordings were not used in the training phase.

Accordingly, we performed a cross-validation using 23 folds, each of which uses data from 22 subjects (LS set) in training and 1 in test (US set). At each fold, a different subject is used as the test subject (unseen). In order to measure the phase classification performances also for learned subjects, we further split the LS set into training set (LS-train) and test set (LS-test). More precisely, LS-train includes the first 90% of the each subject strands (approximately 3 min and 30 s, 180 gait cycles) and LS-test the remaining 10% (approximately 30 s, 20 gait cycles).

3.4.2. Neural Networks

We experimented with different multi layer perceptron (MLP) architectures. In Table 1 we summarize the different architectures for which we report the results in the following section. The first model (MLP_1) was a shallow network with one single hidden layer composed of 128 units (neurons) and had a one-dimensional output. The output was fed to a sigmoid function and a 0.5 threshold is used to obtain a binary output: when the output of the sigmoid was >0.5 we assigned the label

1, otherwise we assigned the label 0. We then experimented with deeper networks, composed of 2–5 hidden layers (Table 1). In all the architectures we used rectified linear units (ReLU) to provide non-linearity between hidden layers. As an example, in Figure 5 we illustrate the structure of the MLP_4 architecture.

In our experiments, we used stochastic gradient descent (SGD) as the optimization algorithm and binary cross entropy as the loss function (BCE).

The value 0.1 was experimentally identified as the optimal learning rate for all the tested models and thus adopted in all the experiments. Finally, all ANN models were trained using an early stop technique, according to the following procedure. The networks were trained for a maximum of 100 epochs, stopping when the accuracy on the validation set did not increase for 10 consecutive epochs. The best-performing learned parameters were adopted to evaluate the model performances over LS-test and US sets and the basographic signal was used as ground truth.

Table 1. Overview of the multi layer perceptron (MLP) architectures.

Model Name	Model Structure
MLP_1	mlp(128)
MLP_2	mlp(256, 128)
MLP_3	mlp(512, 256, 128)
MLP_4	mlp(1024, 512, 256 ,128)
MLP_5	mlp(1024, 1024, 512, 256 ,128)

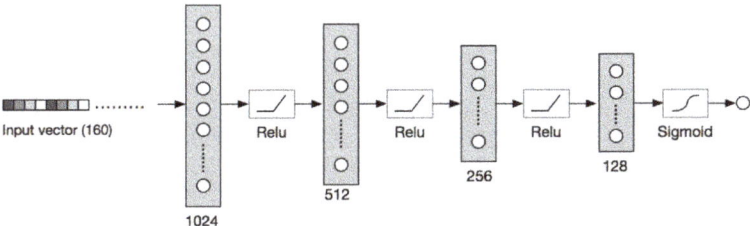

Figure 5. The architecture of multi layer perceptron (MLP)$_4$.

3.5. Gait Events Timing Detection

The predicted foot–floor-contact signal was reconstructed by chronologically arranging the binary output of the network. Thus, a vector was obtained, composed of sequences of 0 (stance phase) alternating with sequences of 1 (swing phase). This vector was chronologically scanned in order to detect the transitions between gait phases: from swing to stance phase (HS) and from stance to swing phase (TO). HS was identified as the sample where the transition from 1 to 0 occurred. TO was identified as the sample where the transition from 0 to 1 occurred.

Then, the predicted signal was cleaned by removing those phases that were too short according to physiological constraints, probably due to classification errors. We adopted the following procedure. Starting from the first HS, the following 500 samples (250 ms) were scanned to find out and remove those having a value of 1. Then, the following HS was identified, the process was repeated and so on. In the same way, starting from the first TO, the following 500 samples were scanned to find out and remove the samples which assumed the value of 0. Then, the following TO was identified, the process was repeated and so on. Eventually, the cleaned vector was chronologically scanned again in order to detect the transitions between gait phases (from 0 to 1 and from 1 to 0) and thus the timing of the gait events.

3.6. Evaluation Measures

In this work, a EMG signal's segment classifier is ultimately used to predict a biographic signal, that is predicting the precise timing of gait phase transition. We first evaluate the performance of the classifier in assigning the correct label (0 for stance and 1 for swing) to single EMG segments. This is done using standard classification metrics, by calculating accuracy, precision, recall and F_1 score, as the harmonic average of the precision and recall. However, this measure does not provide enough information to evaluate the performances of the basographic signal prediction. In fact, even a high accuracy, if errors are concentrated in proximity of transitions, may lead to unsatisfactory results in terms of time error of transition instants. Furthermore, we apply a post processing to the classifier output, to remove false prediction and improve performances, thus we need to explicitly evaluate the predicted basographic.

For that purpose, we adopt the following procedure, used in literature to evaluate gait events prediction, e.g., in [32,33]. We first chose a temporal tolerance T, which we set to 600 milliseconds. Then we consider as true positive each predicted TO or HS event at time tp if an event of the same type exists in the ground truth signal at time tg such that $|tg - tp| < T$. Otherwise we consider the predicted event a False Positive. We then measure the precision, recall and F_1 score and, for all the true positives, we calculate the mean average error (MAE) as the average time distance between the predicted event and the one, of the same type, in the ground truth signal.

We adopted this evaluation strategy to measure the performances of our approach and comparing it with a feature-based one.

4. Results and Discussion

To the best of our knowledge, this study is the first attempt to provide a reliable binary classification of level ground walking into stance and swing phases, by means of the application of deep learning techniques to sEMG signal. Starting from gait-phase classification, the study achieves also a prediction of foot-floor-contact signal and a consequent identification of heel-strike and toe-off timing.

4.1. Gait-Phase Classification

Mean classification accuracy (±SD) obtained over the 23 folds with different MLP architectures for both learned subjects (LS-test set) and unlearned ones (US set) is shown in Table 2, where the best results are in bold. The same convention is used in all the tables.

Table 2. Gait phase classification accuracy (± standard deviation (SD)) averaged over the 23 folds for each considered network.

	Accuracy on US	Accuracy on LS-Test
MLP_1	92.62 ± 2.3	93.83 ± 0.28
MLP_2	93.01 ± 2.1	94.41 ± 0.23
MLP_3	**93.41 ± 2.3**	94.83 ± 0.2
MLP_4	93.25 ± 2.9	**94.94 ± 0.3**
MLP_5	93.03 ± 2.8	94.93 ± 0.2

As expected, classification accuracy for learned subjects was higher than for unseen ones. However, the limited gap (around 1–2 percent) suggests that all the networks succeed in learning signal patterns that generalize well to unseen subjects. The best accuracy on unlearned subjects was obtained with MLP_3. By looking at the standard deviation reported in Table 2, one can notice that, while for learned subjects the accuracy was uniform across the different folders, there was a higher variability when considering unseen subjects. This is partially due to the fact that there were 22 unlearned subjects in the LS-test in each folder, while the US set was composed of a single subject. Such a variability also suggests that walking patterns might be very different from subject to subject, especially in everyday walking conditions, making the classification harder if a subject had never been seen before. However, looking at results on US sets over the 23 folds, as shown in Figure 6, the accuracy does not fall below 87.6% (subject 13) and reaches the highest value of 97.3% (subject 20). Such results are, in our opinion, promising and suggest that the variability could be reduced, and mean accuracy increased, by considering a larger number of subjects to learn from. Tables 3 and 4 report precision, recall and F_1 score of the classification of Stance and Swing phases for, respectively, unlearned (US set) and learned (LS-test set) subjects. Results are averaged over the 23 folds. It is worth noticing that, in line with what was reported in literature [2], the segments belonging to a stance phase were more frequent (around 60%) than those belonging to a swing phase. This is because in normal walking the stance phase duration was 60% of the gait cycle (while the swing phase duration was the remaining 40%) on average. Despite this, results obtained for swing labelled segments are better than those obtained for stance labeled ones, both in unlearned and learned data.

Table 3. Gait phase classification performances for stance and swing phases in unlearned subjects (set US). Precision, recall and F_1 scores are averaged over the 23 folds.

	Stance Phase		
	Precision	Recall	F_1 Score
MLP_1	92.99 ± 4.5	90.50 ± 5.9	91.49 ± 2.9
MLP_2	93.15 ± 4.4	91.22 ± 4.9	91.99 ± 2.4
MLP_3	**93.68 ± 3.9**	91.57 ± 5.0	**92.46 ± 2.7**
MLP_4	93.29 ± 2.9	**91.78 ± 5.3**	92.35 ± 3.2
MLP_5	92.89 ± 4.7	91.53 ± 5.2	92.04 ± 3.4
	Swing Phase		
	Precision	Recall	F_1 Score
MLP_1	92.49 ± 4.8	94.74 ± 3.2	93.45 ± 2.0
MLP_2	92.97 ± 4.3	94.84 ± 3.1	93.77 ± 1.9
MLP_3	93.24 ± 4.3	**95.21 ± 2.9**	**94.11 ± 2.1**
MLP_4	**93.32 ± 4.7**	94.80 ± 3.6	93.93 ± 2.7
MLP_5	93.29 ± 4.0	94.47 ± 3.7	93.77 ± 2.5

Table 4. Gait phase classification performances for stance and swing phases in learned subjects (set LS-test). Precision, recall and F_1 scores are averaged over the 23 folds.

	Stance Phase		
	Precision	Recall	F_1 Score
MLP_1	94.15 ± 0.3	91.72 ± 0.8	92.92 ± 0.3
MLP_2	94.48 ± 0.6	92.75 ± 0.8	93.60 ± 0.3
MLP_3	94.63 ± 0.5	93.59 ± 0.5	94.11 ± 0.2
MLP_4	**94.80 ± 0.5**	93.67 ± 0.9	94.22 ± 0.4
MLP_5	94.50 ± 0.5	**93.99 ± 0.6**	**94.24 ± 0.3**
	Swing phase		
	Precision	Recall	F_1 Score
MLP_1	93.60 ± 0.5	95.50 ± 0.3	94.54 ± 0.2
MLP_2	94.37 ± 0.5	95.72 ± 0.6	95.04 ± 0.2
MLP_3	94.99 ± 0.3	95.81 ± 0.4	95.40 ± 0.2
MLP_4	95.06 ± 0.7	**95.94 ± 0.4**	**95.50 ± 0.2**
MLP_5	**95.28 ± 0.5**	95.68 ± 0.4	95.48 ± 0.2

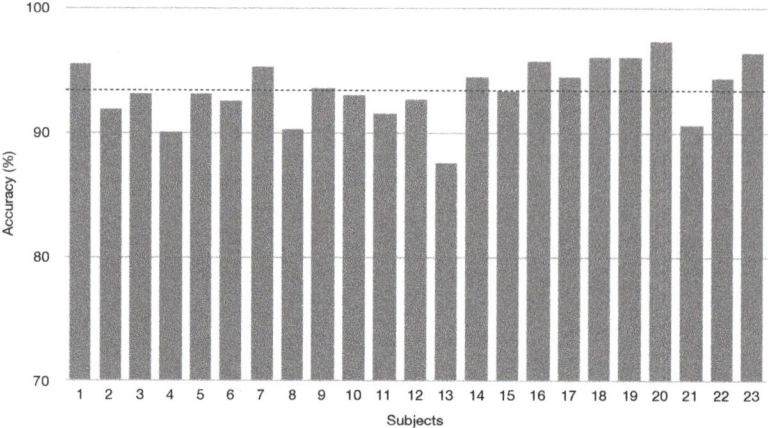

Figure 6. Classification accuracy over the 23 folds for the unlearned subjects (US set).

4.2. Comparison with Feature-Based Approach

Classification of EMG signals from lower-limb muscles is usually based on time/frequency domain features extraction [34]. In order to provide a comparison with a feature-based method, we implemented a classifier following the approach described in [13]. We used a window size of 200 samples and for each sEMG signal we calculated the following features: standard deviation (SD), root mean square (RMS), mean absolute value (MAV), integrated EMG (IEMG) and waveform length (WL). They correspond to the group 2 features used in [13], which provide the best classification accuracy. We then concatenated the features obtaining a 40 length input vector (five features for each of the eight muscles). This was fed into a multi layer perceptron to train a gait phase classifier. A single hidden layer with 10 units is used in [13], where the input vector length was 10. We ran classification experiments over the 23 folds training a single layer network with 10 units, a single layer network with 40 units (corresponding to the size of our input vector) and all the networks in Table 1. The best average classification accuracy of 87.69 ± 5.9 for unlearned subjects was achieved with MLP_3, while accuracy for LS was 88.03 ± 2.7, thus we used MLP_3 for predicting HS an TO timing, adopting the same procedure applied to our approach and described in Section 3.5. In the following sections we refer to such a feature based method as FB.

4.3. Gait Events Detection

The analysis of the results identified MLP_3 as the best model for the classification of unlearned data, obtaining an accuracy of 93.41% (Table 2), a F_1 score of 92.46% for stance phases and of 94.11% for swing phases (Tables 3 and 4). Thus, MLP_3 has been adopted to predict foot-floor-contact signal and identify HS and TO timing in unlearned subjects, following the procedure described in Section 3.5. The prediction was tested by comparing HS and TO timing provided by the present approach vs. heel-strike and toe-off timing measured from the basographic signal. Examples of prediction of foot–floor-contact signal provided by the present approach in US subjects (blue line) vs. the ground truth (red line) are depicted in Figure 7. As one can see, our method provides good predictions also in the presence of an irregular walking activity, i.e., non uniform gait phases duration, due to the everyday walking conditions addressed in this study.

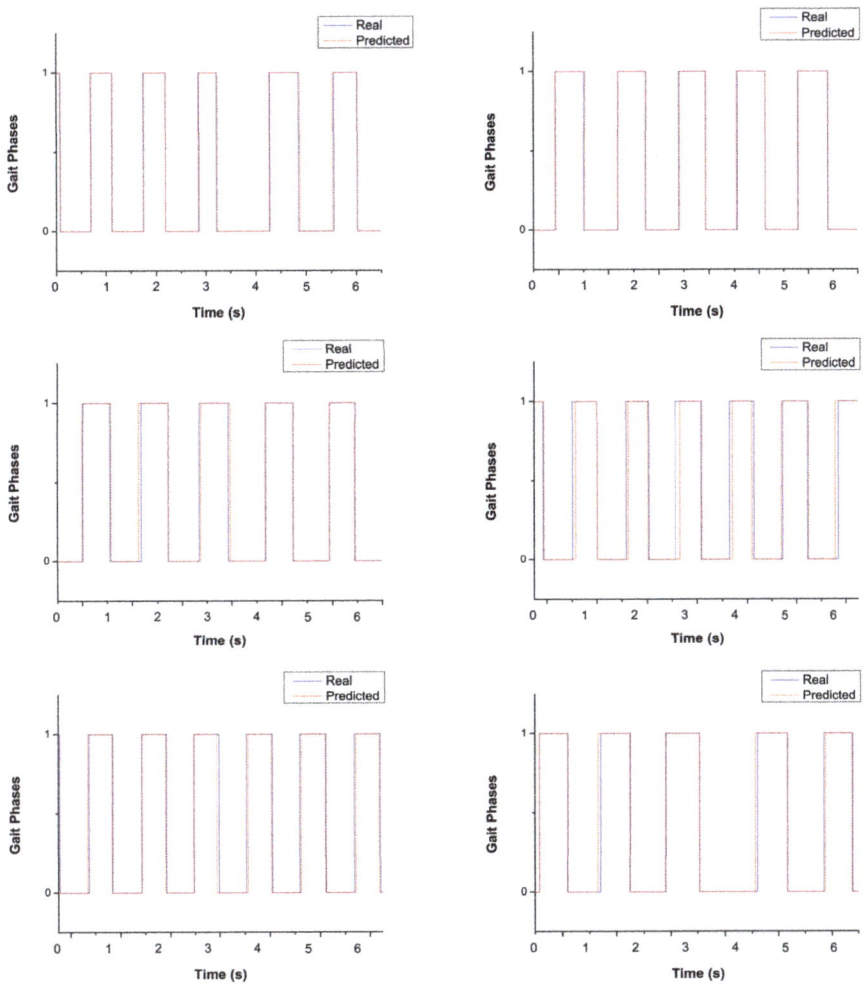

Figure 7. Examples of TO and HS predictions on six random subjects.

Purely data-driven approaches for gait-phase identification have been shown to achieve lower performance in less controlled scenarios, such as conditions similar to everyday walking [32]. Adapting to the larger variability of sEMG signals collected from dynamic environments and activities is more challenging for the classifiers. This could be due to the reported differences [16–19] between treadmill and straight ground walking (i.e., increased number of steps and cadence, decreased preferred walking speed, stride and stance-phase length and changes in sEMG activation) and to the further variability of spatial and temporal parameters and sEMG signals introduced by deceleration, reversing, curve and acceleration typical of everyday walking [16]. Despite this, the accuracy of MLP_3 classification is good for both LS-test subjects and US subjects (93.41%). The high classification accuracy and the effective post-processing of model output allowed to achieve an average absolute prediction error over unlearned subjects of 21.42 ± 7.0 ms for HS and 38.1 ± 15.2 ms for TO (Table 5). Both HS and TO predictions may be considered reasonably suitable, since they show an average absolute error <1% and <2% of a gait cycle duration, respectively. The present approach shows better performance in detecting heel-strikes rather than toe-offs. This result matches previous EMG-based and accelerometer-based reports [13,32].

Table 5. Performance of toe-off (TO) and heel-strike (HS) detection for unlearend subjects over 23 folds.

	HS			
	MAE	Precision	Recall	F_1
MLP_3	**21.6 ± 7.0**	**99.67 ± 0.5**	**99.50 ± 2.9**	**99.04 ± 2.6**
FB	56.7 ± 31.9	99.19 ± 1.5	96.40 ± 9.4	97.56 ± 2.6
	TO			
	MAE	Precision	Recall	F_1
MLP_3	**38.1 ± 15.2**	**99.07 ± 1.5**	**97.90 ± 3.5**	**98.40 ± 2.4**
FB	64.4 ± 42.7	98.45 ± 2.6	95.67 ± 9.9	96.84 ± 6.9

To test the reliability of HS and TO prediction, results provided by our approach have been compared with the results achieved by feature-based (FB) approach. Comparison is reported in Table 5. Our approach outperformed the FB one, suggesting that the neural network succeeded in learning latent features that are better suited for the task at hand if compared to the ones used in previous studies [13]. Besides the above reported direct comparison with the FB approach in the same population, an idea of the quality of the present results could be given also through the analysis of the results reported in [13] in their own population, during treadmill walking. The classification accuracy reported in [13] was 87.5% on learned subjects and 77% for unlearned ones. The associated average prediction error computed in unlearned subjects was 35 ± 25 ms for HS and 49 ± 15 ms for TO. Compared with those performances, results provided by the present study are encouraging, despite the challenging conditions of everyday walking. Besides the different approach (different neural network and different processing of the input signal), the elevated classification-accuracy values and the satisfactory HS/TO-prediction achieved here are supposed to be due also to the characteristics of the experimental set-up: high number of strides acquired per subject (about 500) associated with quite a large number of subjects (23); four different muscles per leg for every subject involved in training process. Moreover, foot-switches [31,35] represent the gold standard in gait segmentation since each gait phase can be associated with a specific value of the sensor output [36]. Finally, in the present study, data from three foot-switches was considered, in line with what reported in literature [31]. Using three foot-switches, instead of the two used in [13], probably improved the reliability of basographic signals as ground truth as well as the reliability of performance evaluation.

5. Conclusions

The present study proposed a suitable approach for classifying stance vs. swing and predicting the occurrence of the transition between phases, such as heel strike and toe off. The main contribution of the study is to provide reliable performances in gait-phase classification and gait-event prediction in natural walking conditions (similar to everyday walking), overcoming the constraints associated to the controlled environment (such as treadmill walking) used by previous studies to address this kind of task. A further methodological contribution consists of proposing a different pre-processing of sEMG-signal in order to better train the neural networks; the direct use of linear envelopes proposed here allows the network to automatically learn relevant higher level (hidden) features, avoiding hand crafting ad-hoc features and contributing to improve the performances.

From the clinical point of view, a relevant contribution is the fact that the present approach is based on sEMG signals only. This could considerably help reduce the number of sensors necessary for a complete gait protocol, limiting the clinical encumbrance, time-consumption, and cost. Thus, one of the main application domains of the present methodology should be in the field of neuromuscular diseases, such as spastic cerebral palsy, where the acquisition and then the analysis of sEMG signals are essential and special care should be exercised in the treatment of the patients.

Moreover, the present classifier may also support the process of gait phase detection in EMG-driven assistive devices [37], such as hip–knee, ankle–foot, and knee–ankle–foot orthoses and exoskeletons, as the identification of gait events is a continuing concern in the use of these devices. Evaluating the performance of the classifier after reducing the complexity of experimental protocol (i.e., the number of monitored muscles) could also be valuable. At the time of writing, all these applications are beyond the goals of the present work. However, future efforts will point in that direction.

Author Contributions: conceptualization, F.D.N., C.M., S.F. and A.C.; methodology, F.D.N. and C.M.; software, C.M.; investigation, C.M. and F.D.N.; validation, C.M.; resources, F.D.N. and S.F. ; data curation, F.D.N. and C.M.; writing—original draft preparation, F.D.N. and C.M.; writing—review and editing, A.C. and S.F.; visualization, F.D.N. and C.M.; supervision, A.C. and S.F.

Funding: This research received no external funding.

Acknowledgments: Thanks to Guido Mascia and Lorenzo Principi for the support provided in preparing the experiments.

Conflicts of Interest: The authors declare no conflict of interest.

References

1. Loeb, G.E.; Gans, C. *Electromyography for Experimentalists*; University of Chicago Press: Chicago, IL, USA, 1986.
2. Perry, J. *Gait Analysis: Normal and Pathological Function*; Slack Inc.: Thorofare, NJ, USA, 1992.
3. Špulák, D.; Čmejla, R.; Bačáková, R.; Kračmar, B.; Satrapová, L.; Novotný, P. Muscle activity detection in electromyograms recorded during periodic movements. *Comput. Biol. Med.* **2014**, *47*, 93–103. [CrossRef] [PubMed]
4. Wang, W.; Stefano, A.; Allen, R. A simulation model of the surface EMG signal for analysis of muscle activity during the gait cycle. *Comput. Biol. Med.* **2006**, *36*, 601–618. [CrossRef] [PubMed]
5. Mengarelli, A.; Maranesi, E.; Burattini, L.; Fioretti, S.; Di Nardo, F. Co-contraction activity of ankle muscles during walking: A gender comparison. *Biomed. Signal Process. Control* **2017**, *33*, 1–9. [CrossRef]
6. Gurney, J.; Kersting, U.; Rosenbaum, D. Between-day reliability of repeated plantar pressure distribution measurements in a normal population. *Gait Posture* **2008**, *27*, 706–709. [CrossRef] [PubMed]
7. Bovi, G.; Rabuffetti, M.; Mazzoleni, P.; Ferrarin, M. A multiple-task gait analysis approach: Kinematic, kinetic and EMG reference data for healthy young and adult subjects. *Gait Posture* **2011**, *33*, 6–13. [CrossRef] [PubMed]
8. Caldas, R.; Mundt, M.; Potthast, W.; Buarque de Lima Neto, F.; Markert, B. A systematic review of gait analysis methods based on inertial sensors and adaptive algorithms. *Gait Posture* **2017**, *57*, 204–210. [CrossRef] [PubMed]
9. Joyseeree, R.; Abou Sabha, R.; Mueller, H. Applying Machine Learning to Gait Analysis Data for Disease Identification. *Stud. Health Technol. Inf.* **2015**, *210*, 850–854. [CrossRef]
10. Zou, Q.; Wang, Y.; Zhao, Y.; Wang, Q.; Shen, C.; Li, Q. Deep Learning Based Gait Recognition Using Smartphones in the Wild. *arXiv* **2018**, arXiv:1811.00338.
11. Kaczmarczyk, K.; Wit, A.; Krawczyk, M.; Zaborski, J.; Piłsudskii, J. Artificial Neural Networks (ANN) Applied for Gait Classification and Physiotherapy Monitoring in Post Stroke Patients. In *Artificial Neural Networks*; IntechOpen: Rijeka, Croatia, 2011; Chapter 16.
12. Wang, J.; Zielińska, T. Gait features analysis using artificial neural networks—Testing the footwear effect. *Acta Bioeng. Biomech.* **2017**, *19*, 17–32.
13. Nazmi, N.; Abdul Rahman, M.; Yamamoto, S.I.; Ahmad, S. Walking gait event detection based on electromyography signals using artificial neural network. *Biomed. Signal Process. Control* **2019**, *47*, 334–343. [CrossRef]
14. Ziegier, J.; Gattringer, H.; Mueller, A. Classification of Gait Phases Based on Bilateral EMG Data Using Support Vector Machines. In Proceedings of the IEEE RAS and EMBS International Conference on Biomedical Robotics and Biomechatronics, Enschede, The Netherlands, 26–29 August 2018; Volume 2018, pp. 978–983. [CrossRef]

15. Meng, M.; She, Q.; Gao, Y.; Luo, Z. EMG signals based gait phases recognition using hidden Markov models. In Proceedings of the 2010 IEEE International Conference on Information and Automation, ICIA 2010, Harbin, China, 20–23 June 2010; pp. 852–856. [CrossRef]
16. Stolze, H.; Kuhtz-Buschbeck, J.; Mondwurf, C.; Boczek-Funcke, A.; Jöhnk, K.; Deuschl, G.; Illert, M. Gait analysis during treadmill and overground locomotion in children and adults. *Electroencephalogr. Clin. Neurophysiol. Electromyogr. Mot. Control* **1997**, *105*, 490–497. [CrossRef]
17. Batlkham, B.; Oyunaa, C.; Odongua, N. A Kinematic Comparison of Overground and Treadmill Walking. *Value Health* **2014**, *17*, A774. [CrossRef] [PubMed]
18. Riley, P.O.; Paolini, G.; Della Croce, U.; Paylo, K.W.; Kerrigan, D.C. A kinematic and kinetic comparison of overground and treadmill walking in healthy subjects. *Gait Posture* **2007**, *26*, 17–24. [CrossRef] [PubMed]
19. Song, J.; Hidler, J. Biomechanics of overground vs. treadmill walking in healthy individuals. *J. Appl. Physiol.* **2008**, *104*, 747–755. [CrossRef]
20. Alanazi, H.; Abdullah, A.; Qureshi, K. A Critical Review for Developing Accurate and Dynamic Predictive Models Using Machine Learning Methods in Medicine and Health Care. *J. Med. Syst.* **2017**, *41*, 69. [CrossRef] [PubMed]
21. Abbas, R.; Hussain, A.; Al-Jumeily, D.; Baker, T.; Khattak, A. Classification of Foetal Distress and Hypoxia Using Machine Learning Approaches. *Lect. Notes Comput. Sci.* **2018**, *10956*, 767–776._81. [CrossRef]
22. Aljaaf, A.; Al-Jumeily, D.; Haglan, H.; Alloghani, M.; Baker, T.; Hussain, A.; Mustafina, J. Early Prediction of Chronic Kidney Disease Using Machine Learning Supported by Predictive Analytics. In Proceedings of the 2018 IEEE Congress on Evolutionary Computation (CEC), Rio de Janeiro, Brazil, 8–13 July 2018.
23. Subasi, A.; Yilmaz, M.; Ozcalik, H.R. Classification of EMG signals using wavelet neural network. *J. Neurosci. Methods* **2006**, *156*, 360–367. [CrossRef]
24. Elamvazuthi, I.; Duy, N.; Ali, Z.; Su, S.; Khan, M.; Parasuraman, S. Electromyography (EMG) based Classification of Neuromuscular Disorders using Multi-Layer Perceptron. In Proceedings of the 2015 IEEE International Symposium on Robotics and Intelligent Sensors (IEEE IRIS2015), Langkawi, Malaysia, 18–20 October 2015; Volume 76, pp. 223–228. [CrossRef]
25. Ibrahimy, M.; Ahsan, M.; Khalifa, O. Design and optimization of levenberg-marquardt based neural network classifier for EMG signals to identify hand motions. *Meas. Sci. Rev.* **2013**, *13*, 142–151. [CrossRef]
26. Liu, Z.; Luo, Z. Hand motion pattern classifier based on EMG using wavelet packet transform and LVQ neural networks. In Proceedings of the 2008 IEEE International Symposium on IT in Medicine and Education, ITME 2008, Xiamen, China, 12–14 December 2008; pp. 28–32. [CrossRef]
27. Oskoei, M.; Hu, H. Support vector machine-based classification scheme for myoelectric control applied to upper limb. *IEEE Trans. Biomed. Eng.* **2008**, *55*, 1956–1965. [CrossRef]
28. Moslem, B.; Diab, M.; Khalil, M.; Marque, C. Classification of multichannel uterine EMG signals by using unsupervised competitive learning. In Proceedings of the 2011 IEEE Workshop on Signal Processing Systems, SiPS 2011, Beirut, Lebanon, 4–7 October 2011; pp. 267–272. [CrossRef]
29. Hermens, H.; Freriks, B.; Disselhorst-Klug, C.; Rau, G. Development of recommendations for SEMG sensors and sensor placement procedures. *J. Electromyogr. Kinesiol.* **2000**, *10*, 361–374. [CrossRef]
30. Di Nardo, F.; Mengarelli, A.; Maranesi, E.; Burattini, L.; Fioretti, S. Gender differences in the myoelectric activity of lower limb muscles in young healthy subjects during walking. *Biomed. Signal Process. Control* **2015**, *19*, 14–22. [CrossRef]
31. Agostini, V.; Balestra, G.; Knaflitz, M. Segmentation and classification of gait cycles. *IEEE Trans. Neural Syst. Rehabil. Eng.* **2014**, *22*, 946–952. [CrossRef]
32. Khandelwal, S.; Wickstrasm, N. Evaluation of the performance of accelerometer-based gait event detection algorithms in different real-world scenarios using the MAREA gait database. *Gait Posture* **2017**, *51*, 84–90. [CrossRef]
33. Trojaniello, D.; Cereatti, A.; Della Croce, U. Accuracy, sensitivity and robustness of five different methods for the estimation of gait temporal parameters using a single inertial sensor mounted on the lower trunk. *Gait Posture* **2014**, *40*, 487–492. [CrossRef]
34. Toledo-Pérez, D.; Martínez-Prado, M.; Gómez-Loenzo, R.; Paredes-García, W.; Rodríguez-Reséndiz, J. A study of movement classification of the lower limb based on up to 4-EMG channels. *Electronics* **2019**, *8*, 259. [CrossRef]

35. Taborri, J.; Palermo, E.; Rossi, S.; Cappa, P. Gait partitioning methods: A systematic review. *Sensors* **2016**, *16*, 66. [CrossRef]
36. Winiarski, S.; Rutkowska-Kucharska, A. Estimated ground reaction force in normal and pathological gait. *Acta Bioeng. Biomech.* **2009**, *11*, 53–60.
37. Ma, Y.; Xie, S.; Zhang, Y. A patient-specific EMG-driven neuromuscular model for the potential use of human-inspired gait rehabilitation robots. *Comput. Biol. Med.* **2016**, *70*, 88–98. [CrossRef]

© 2019 by the authors. Licensee MDPI, Basel, Switzerland. This article is an open access article distributed under the terms and conditions of the Creative Commons Attribution (CC BY) license (http://creativecommons.org/licenses/by/4.0/).

Article

An Ensemble Learning Approach Based on Diffusion Tensor Imaging Measures for Alzheimer's Disease Classification

Eufemia Lella [1], Andrea Pazienza [1,*], Domenico Lofù [1,2], Roberto Anglani [1,†] and Felice Vitulano [1,†]

1. Innovation Lab, Exprivia S.p.A., Via A. Olivetti 11, I-70056 Molfetta, Italy; eufemia.lella@exprivia.com (E.L.); domenico.lofu@poliba.it (D.L.); roberto.anglani@exprivia.com (R.A.); felice.vitulano@exprivia.com (F.V.)
2. Department of Electrical and Information Engineering (DEI), Politecnico di Bari, Via E. Orabona 4, I-70125 Bari, Italy
* Correspondence: andrea.pazienza@exprivia.com
† These authors contributed equally to this work.

Abstract: Recent advances in neuroimaging techniques, such as diffusion tensor imaging (DTI), represent a crucial resource for structural brain analysis and allow the identification of alterations related to severe neurodegenerative disorders, such as Alzheimer's disease (AD). At the same time, machine-learning-based computational tools for early diagnosis and decision support systems are adopted to uncover hidden patterns in data for phenotype stratification and to identify pathological scenarios. In this landscape, ensemble learning approaches, conceived to simulate human behavior in making decisions, are suitable methods in healthcare prediction tasks, generally improving classification performances. In this work, we propose a novel technique for the automatic discrimination between healthy controls and AD patients, using DTI measures as predicting features and a soft-voting ensemble approach for the classification. We show that this approach, efficiently combining single classifiers trained on specific groups of features, is able to improve classification performances with respect to the comprehensive approach of the concatenation of global features (with an increase of up to 9% on average) and the use of individual groups of features (with a notable enhancement in sensitivity of up to 11%). Ultimately, the feature selection phase in similar classification tasks can take advantage of this kind of strategy, allowing one to exploit the information content of data and at the same time reducing the dimensionality of the feature space, and in turn the computational effort.

Keywords: diffusion tensor imaging; ensemble learning; decision support systems; healthcare; machine learning; computational intelligence; Alzheimer's disease

Citation: Lella, E.; Pazienza, A.; Lofù, D.; Anglani, R.; Vitulano, F. An Ensemble Learning Approach Based on Diffusion Tensor Imaging Measures for Alzheimer's Disease Classification. *Electronics* **2021**, *10*, 249. https://doi.org/10.3390/electronics10030249

Academic Editor: Heung-Il Suk
Received: 30 December 2020
Accepted: 19 January 2021
Published: 22 January 2021

Publisher's Note: MDPI stays neutral with regard to jurisdictional claims in published maps and institutional affiliations.

Copyright: © 2021 by the authors. Licensee MDPI, Basel, Switzerland. This article is an open access article distributed under the terms and conditions of the Creative Commons Attribution (CC BY) license (https://creativecommons.org/licenses/by/4.0/).

1. Introduction

Alzheimer's disease (AD) is the most common type of neurodegenerative disorder causing dementia, generally characterized by loss of memory and a progressive decline of cognitive functions. AD affects millions of people worldwide, and according to the World Alzheimer's report 2015 [1], people affected by dementia will reach 131.5 million in 2050. The in vivo diagnosis of AD is still a hard task because of the diversity of symptoms manifested by patients. In this context, a very challenging goal is the development of innovative computational-intelligence-based diagnostic tools that can support physicians and specialists in the early identification of the pathology and in therapeutic plan decisions. Advances in neuroimaging techniques have been fundamental for structural and functional brain analysis allowing the identification of AD-related brain alterations [2–4]. Due to the difficulty of integrating data on a large scale, machine learning methods (ML) allowing patient classification driven by large amounts of data are gaining increasing interest in recent years in the field of digital healthcare [5,6]. ML algorithms are a collection of computational and statistical models that can learn through experience and make predictions based on new data [7]. Machine learning approaches are able to uncover patterns in the data for differentiating diagnostic groups and identifying pathological scenarios [8,9]. Several recent studies have analyzed the potential of applying ML-based analytical frameworks to MRI data for the characterization and the automatic diagnosis of AD [10–13]. Indeed, the biological hypothesis that the cognitive decline due to AD is related to a connectivity disruption between brain regions caused by white matter degeneration (WM) has been widely investigated in literature [14,15]. In this context, diffusion tensor imaging (DTI) has emerged in the last fifteen years as a promising technique that measures the diffusion of water along WM fibers, providing information on their integrity [16]. The trajectory and the integrity of the main WM fiber bundles in the brain can be evaluated by tracing the highly anisotropic diffusion of water along axons [17]. Since DTI is a neuroimaging technique capable of characterizing white matter fiber trajectories and of highlighting microscopic WM lesions in these bundles, it can be exploited to uncover signs of connectivity impairment not detectable by means of standard anatomical MRI. Among the different measures that can be calculated from the diffusion tensor [17], fractional anisotropy (FA) and mean diffusivity (MD) have played major roles as AD biomarkers [18]. As a matter of fact, in a healthy axon water diffusion is highly anisotropic, because it is almost completely bound in one direction; consequently, large values of FA paired to small MD measures usually describe non-pathological scenarios. From this perspective, DTI allows to investigate microstructural disease-related changes complementary to the information on brain atrophy highlighted by anatomical MRI.

Recent applications of DTI techniques, together with ML algorithms for the classification of AD, use three possible methods for feature extraction: region of interest (ROI)-based, voxel-based and tractography-based approaches. In a ROI-based approach, the brain is parceled into regions of interest, and the mean of the DTI measures is then calculated for each ROI. The DTI scalar indexes averaged over each ROI are then used as features for feeding ML algorithms to classify AD subjects also at early stages of the disease and for investigating WM integrity alterations [19,20]. Several studies based on this approach have been conducted with multimodal analysis [21]. In tractography-based approaches, DTI fiber tracking algorithms together with a parcelation scheme are used to model the brain as a network and to study its connectivity through graph theory. Network measures turned out to be effective variables to characterize the connectivity alterations due to AD [22–24], and valid features from which to build classification models [25–27]. In voxel-based approaches, starting from fractional anisotropy maps and using the tract-based spatial statistics, a white matter "skeleton" is obtained, containing WM tracts common to all subjects. The diffusion maps of each subject are projected onto the average fractional anisotropy skeleton; hence, all diffusivity measures of the voxels belonging to that skeleton can be exploited for feeding classification algorithms and for performing voxel-wise statistical analyses aimed at localizing brain changes related to the onset and development of the pathology.

Machine learning methods for the identification of AD phenotypes are typically based on individual classifiers [28–30] or ensembles of different classifiers trained on the same set of features [25,31]. Ensemble learning is a ML approach—generally improving classification performances [32,33]—that integrates multiple classifiers fed with the same group of features or with several vectors of variables describing different representations of the same physical phenomenon [34]. Ensemble learning was conceived to simulate human behavior in making decisions, and for this reason it can be a suitable approach in the medical diagnosis context, where humans usually ask the opinions of various doctors to increase the reliability of a diagnosis.

In this paper, we propose a novel classification framework based on ensemble learning for the automatic discrimination between healthy controls (HC) and AD cases, relying on DTI measures as predicting variables. This kind of ensemble method is able to conveniently exploit the informative contents of individual maps, associated with specific aspects of microstructural fiber integrity, and to enhance the generalization ability, taking into account the peculiarities of different classifiers related to each set of features. Moreover, this methodology is aimed at enhancing computational efficiency, focusing in particular on combinations of single groups of variables instead of considering the usual approach of global feature concatenation. The paper is organized as follows. Section 2 introduces the diffusion tensor imaging (DTI) techniques able to investigate white matter fiber integrity through measurement of anisotropy of WM tracts and water diffusion along them. In Section 3 after a brief description of feature extraction procedures and classification models adopted in the present work, a learning experiment is detailed. Finally, Section 4 reports the results of the experiment and Section 5 discusses the main findings together with future research directions.

2. Diffusion Tensor Imaging

Diffusion, also known as Brownian motion, is the process of the random constant microscopic molecular motion caused by heat. In an anisotropic mean, like WM, diffusion is characterized by a tensor, called the effective diffusion tensor D_{eff}, which fully describes the molecular mobility along the three spatial directions and the correlations between these directions. In the framework of MRI-based neuroimaging, diffusion tensor imaging (DTI) is a technique which evaluates the location, orientation and anisotropy of the brain's WM tracts, providing the estimation of the diffusion tensor for each voxel of the 3D image.

From a geometric point of view, the diffusion tensor completely characterizes the shape of an ellipsoid by means of six variables describing the diffusion coefficient of water molecules at a specific time in each direction. In the case of isotropic diffusion, the diffusion coefficient is equal in every direction and the ellipsoid turns into a sphere. Instead, in the case of anisotropic diffusion the greater mean diffusion along the longest axis of the ellipsoid is described by an elongated ellipsoid. The tensor matrix is symmetric according to a property describing the antipodal symmetry of Brownian motion that is called "conjugate symmetry". The diagonal terms of the diffusion tensor quantify the intensity of diffusivity in each of three orthogonal directions. The off-diagonal terms (vanishing in case of isotropy) indicate the magnitude of diffusion along one direction arising from a concentration gradient in an orthogonal direction.

Therefore, diffusion data are crucial in order to gain information on tissue microstructure and architecture for each voxel [16,17]. In particular, the three eigenvectors and the eigenvalues λ_1, λ_2 and λ_3 of D_{eff} describe the directions and lengths of the three diffusion ellipsoid axes, respectively, in descending order of magnitude. The largest (primary) eigenvector and the related eigenvalue λ_1 represent the direction and magnitude of greatest water diffusion, respectively. The primary eigenvector provides an important contribution to the fiber tractography algorithms, since it indicates the orientation of axonal fiber bundles. Eigenvalue λ_1, called "longitudinal diffusivity" (LD), indicates the diffusion rate along the fibers' orientation. Eigenvalues λ_2 and λ_3, associated with second and third eigenvectors orthogonal to the primary one, represent the magnitude of diffusion in the plane transverse to the axonal bundles. The mean value,

$$RD = \frac{\lambda_2 + \lambda_3}{2}, \quad (1)$$

is called "radial diffusivity" (RD). The mean diffusivity (MD) indicates the mean displacement of molecules (average ellipsoid size) and describes the directionally averaged diffusivity of water within a voxel. It is defined as the mean of the three eigenvalues:

$$MD = \frac{\lambda_1 + \lambda_2 + \lambda_3}{3} \quad (2)$$

The fractional anisotropy (FA) measures the degree of directionality of intravoxel diffusivity, i.e., the fraction of the diffusion that is anisotropic:

$$FA = \sqrt{\frac{1}{2} \frac{(\lambda_1 - \lambda_2)^2 + (\lambda_2 - \lambda_3)^2 + (\lambda_3 - \lambda_1)^2}{\lambda_1^2 + \lambda_2^2 + \lambda_3^2}} \quad (3)$$

This measure basically represents a distance between the tensor ellipsoidal shape from a perfect sphere. Values of the fractional anisotropy range from zero, meaning an isotropic diffusion, to 1, in case of a linear diffusion occurring only along the primary eigenvector. When $\lambda_1 \gg \lambda_2, \lambda_3$, the fractional anisotropy measure is close to 1, indicating a preferred direction of diffusion.

3. Materials and Methods

3.1. Data Collection

Real-world data have been gathered from the Alzheimer's Disease Neuroimaging Initiative (ADNI) which has the primary goal of testing whether serial magnetic resonance imaging (MRI), positron emission tomography (PET), other biological markers, and clinical and neuropsychological assessments can be combined to measure the progression of mild cognitive impairment (MCI) and early Alzheimer's disease (AD) (for up-to-date information, see www.adni-info.org) [35].

The dataset is made of diffusion-weighted scans from a cohort of 92 subjects of both genders, with age ranging from 55 to 90, from the ADNI-GO and ADNI-2 phases. According to their diagnoses, the subjects were grouped into 49 HC and 43 AD patients. Pre-processed FA, MD, RD and LD maps, available in ADNI databases, were randomly selected from baseline and follow-up study visits. It is worth mentioning that healthy subjects did not report symptoms of mild cognitive impairment, dementia, or depression; subjects with AD were those who met the NINCDS/ADRDA criteria for probable AD. The acquisition of diffusion-weighted scans was carried out through a 3-T GE Medical Systems scanner. In particular, for each subject 46 distinct images were collected articulated in 41 diffusion-weighted images ($b = 1000$ s/mm^2) and 5 scans with negligible diffusion effects (b_0 images).

3.2. Image Processing and Feature Extraction

The first step of the image processing is a double registration step. It consists of aligning the maps of all subjects so that the same microstructural areas of the anatomical regions correspond to the same voxels in the images. Then the maps are transformed into an existing standard space template image (in this case the MNI152 standard space [36] is used). After the registration, the voxels belonging to the white matter main fiber tracts are extracted from each map.

Following the acquisition of general diffusivity maps (including FA, MD, RD and LD), for each subject, all image processing steps were performed with FMRIB Software Library (*FSL*) [37], and in particular its diffusion toolkit *FDT*. In order to carefully align FA, MD, RD and LD maps to a group-wise space and to focus the analysis only on voxels that belong to the WM fiber bundles, a tract-based spatial statistics (*TBSS*) [38] standard procedure, included in *FSL*, was performed according to the following steps:

1. Application of a nonlinear registration for the alignment of all fractional anisotropy maps to a common registration template: in the present analysis, we used the mean FMRIB58_FA standard target, available with the software, obtained as the average of 58 FA images in the MNI152 standard space. This step was performed for MD, RD and LD maps too.
2. Affine transformation of the entire aligned dataset to a $1 \times 1 \times 1$ mm^3 standard space: the aligned maps were transformed into the standard space template MNI152.
3. Extraction of the white matter skeleton: by averaging all the FA maps of the dataset, a mean FA image was obtained, and this result was used to create a mean FA skeleton of WM fiber tracts that were common to all subjects (see Figure 1). A threshold was applied to the mean FA skeleton in order to exclude gray matter and cerebrospinal fluid voxels, and the voxels of the zones characterized by greater inter-subject variability belonging to the outermost part of the cortex.

4. Projection of all FA maps onto the mean FA skeleton: this allowed us to achieve an alignment among all subjects in the direction orthogonal to the fiber bundle orientation. The same elaboration steps were applied to RD, MD and LD maps.

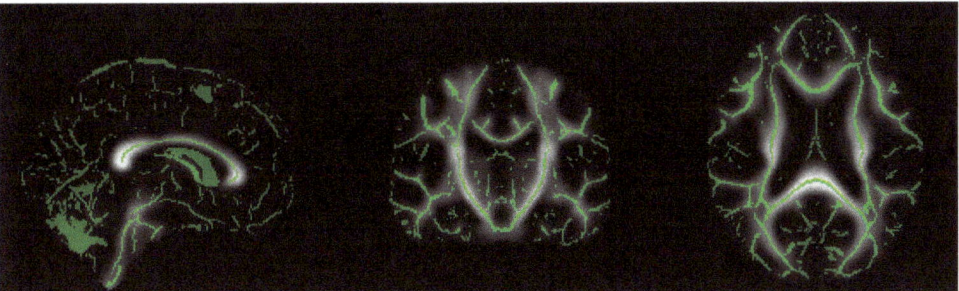

Figure 1. Coronal, sagittal and axial views of the brain obtained in the FSLeyes image viewer: the mean fractional anisotropy (FA) skeleton (green) is overlaid with the mean FA map. For the following analysis all maps were projected onto the white matter skeleton.

The *TBSS* procedure generates, for each subject and for each diffusivity metric (FA, MD, RD, LD), approximately 9×10^4 voxels, belonging to the WM skeleton and representing the features of our classification task.

3.3. Classification Methods

Supervised learning methods are statistical learning techniques aimed to the classification of instances based on labeled training data. In the present paper, in order to build the ensemble approach, we investigate the most commonly used ML algorithms for medical classification tasks: support vector machine, random forest and multi-layer perceptron.

Support vector machine (SVM) [39] is a supervised learning algorithm based on the concept of an optimal hyper-plane that separates observations belonging to two different classes. In the case of a linear classification problem, given n data points belonging to two linearly separable sets in a $p-$dimensional space, the task is to find a $(p-1)-$dimensional hyper-plane that can classify two classes with the largest margins, i.e., the largest distance to the boundary from the closest points in each set. In cases when data are not linearly separable, a possible solution is to map the original data onto a higher-dimensional feature space in order to favor a more effective separation. Support vector classifiers are then generalizations of the linear classifier approach to an "augmented" feature space with significantly high dimensionality (see left panel in Figure 2). Assuming that the transformed feature vectors are given by the function $h(\mathbf{x})$, the optimization problem can be conveniently recast as a quadratic programming problem using Lagrange multipliers in which the transformed vectors $h(\mathbf{x})$ are involved in the form of scalar products. Thanks to this trick, it is not important to know the transformation, but only the type of the kernel function $K(x, x') = \langle h(\mathbf{x}), h(\mathbf{x}') \rangle$. Consequently, the configuration of a SVM classifier is completely characterized by the regularization parameter C and the choice of kernel function. In the present work, for the hyper-parameter tuning phase, the chosen functions are: (1) $d-$degree polynomial: $K(\mathbf{x}, \mathbf{x}') = (1 + \langle \mathbf{x}, \mathbf{x}' \rangle)^d$; (2) radial basis function (RBF): $K(\mathbf{x}, \mathbf{x}') = \exp(-\gamma ||\mathbf{x} - \mathbf{x}'||^2)$, where values of parameters d, γ, κ_1 and κ_2 span specific ranges.

Random forest (RF) is a supervised learning algorithm based on the construction of a collection of decision trees, known to be one of the best classifiers in terms of prediction accuracy and efficiency for high-dimensional datasets [40,41]. RF models operate by constructing a multitude of decision trees in the training phase and returning as a prediction the class predicted most frequently by each tree composing the forest, with the aim of reducing the variance of the final result. The RF training algorithm is based on the general technique of bootstrap aggregating to the trees under training. Let (X, Y) be the pair of training set X and target vector Y where $X = \{x_1, \ldots, x_n\}$ and $Y = y_1, \ldots, y_n$. The strategy applies repeated (B times) extraction with the replacement of a random sample from X and a fit of the trees to this sample. In particular, for $b = 1, \ldots, B$, the procedure is the following: (1) Random sampling with replacement of n observation from training set X obtaining the subsets (X_b, Y_b). Generally, for a classification problem with p features, the cardinality of the subset is of order $\sqrt{p}$ in order to reduce the correlation between trees originated by bagging. (2) Training of the b-th tree f_b on (X_b, Y_b). (3) Out-of-sample prediction on unseen dataset x^* is the response outcome obtained from the majority of the results generated by each single tree. The number of trees B in a forest is the free parameter of the model, usually set at an order of magnitude of at least 10^2.

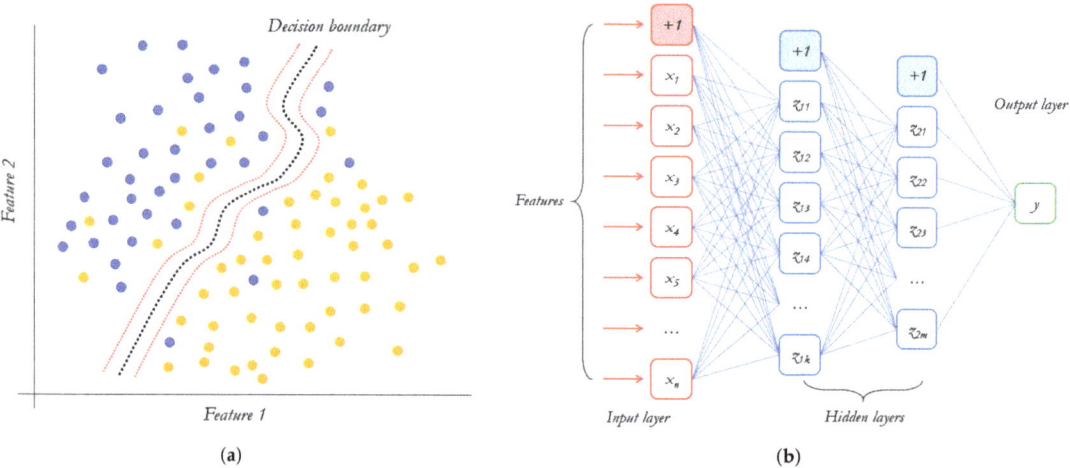

Figure 2. (a) Cartoon picture of a SVM classifier with nonlinear kernel: dots of different colors represent instances of two different classes; dotted lines represent the decision boundaries. (b) Example of a multi-layer perceptron with two hidden layers.

Multi-layer perceptron (MLP) [42] is a supervised learning algorithm using a feed-forward neural network technique. An MLP is composed of an input layer, one or more hidden layers of threshold logic units (TLUs) and an output layer. Each hidden layer is fully connected with the next one, and each TLU computes a weighted sum of its inputs then applies an activation function to provide a result that will be used as input for the next layer (see right panel in Figure 2). The activation function is in general nonlinear and is selected to be C^1-differentiable. The learning process is based on the back-propagation algorithm that can be summarized as follows [43]: for each training instance, the algorithm generates a prediction and measures the performance (error). Consequently, each layer in reverse is analyzed in order to evaluate the contribution to the error from each connection; then edge weights are tuned in order to improve the performance. In this study, the hyper-parameter tuning phase of MLP is driven by the choice of an activation function and the number of hidden layers. Classification algorithms and performance metrics analyzed refer to the Python scikit-learn library [44].

3.4. Learning Experiment

Once the image processing and feature extraction procedure was completed, each subject was represented by different feature groups associated with diffusivity metrics (FA, MD, RD and LD) each with dimensions in the order of 10^5. These groups can be used separately or combined in a single high-dimensional feature vector to feed a learning algorithm for the classification of patients with AD. The learning experiment proposed in the present work consists of comparing these two procedures with an ensemble learning approach in which each feature group is used to feed a classification algorithm and all the models are then combined through a voting scheme (see Figure 3). The idea is that different models trained independently can take into account different aspects of the data, and consequently a combination of algorithms can improve the predictions obtained with the single models in the ensemble. The ensemble configurations analyzed in this work are listed in Table 1.

Table 1. List of all ensemble configurations.

Label	Configuration	Label	Configuration
1-1	$\mathcal{E}(M_{FA})$	2-5	$\mathcal{E}(M_{LD}, M_{RD})$
1-2	$\mathcal{E}(M_{MD})$	2-6	$\mathcal{E}(M_{MD}, M_{RD})$
1-3	$\mathcal{E}(M_{RD})$	3-1	$\mathcal{E}(M_{FA}, M_{LD}, M_{MD})$
1-4	$\mathcal{E}(M_{LD})$	3-2	$\mathcal{E}(M_{FA}, M_{LD}, M_{RD})$
2-1	$\mathcal{E}(M_{FA}, M_{LD})$	3-3	$\mathcal{E}(M_{FA}, M_{MD}, M_{RD})$
2-2	$\mathcal{E}(M_{FA}, M_{MD})$	3-4	$\mathcal{E}(M_{LD}, M_{MD}, M_{RD})$
2-3	$\mathcal{E}(M_{FA}, M_{RD})$	4-1	$\mathcal{E}(M_{FA}, M_{MD}, M_{RD}, M_{LD})$
2-4	$\mathcal{E}(M_{LD}, M_{MD})$	5-1	$\mathcal{E}(M_{FA,MD,RD,LD})$

M_i is the best classification method associated with the i-th feature group and $\mathcal{E}(M_1, M_2, \ldots, M_j)$ is the ensemble learning method based on the combination of best classifiers $M_1, M_2, \ldots, M_j$. The ensemble of a singleton corresponds to the best classifier, i.e., $\mathcal{E}(M_i) \equiv M_i$. Finally, configuration 5-1 refers to the best classifier trained on a single high-dimensional vector concatenating all feature groups.

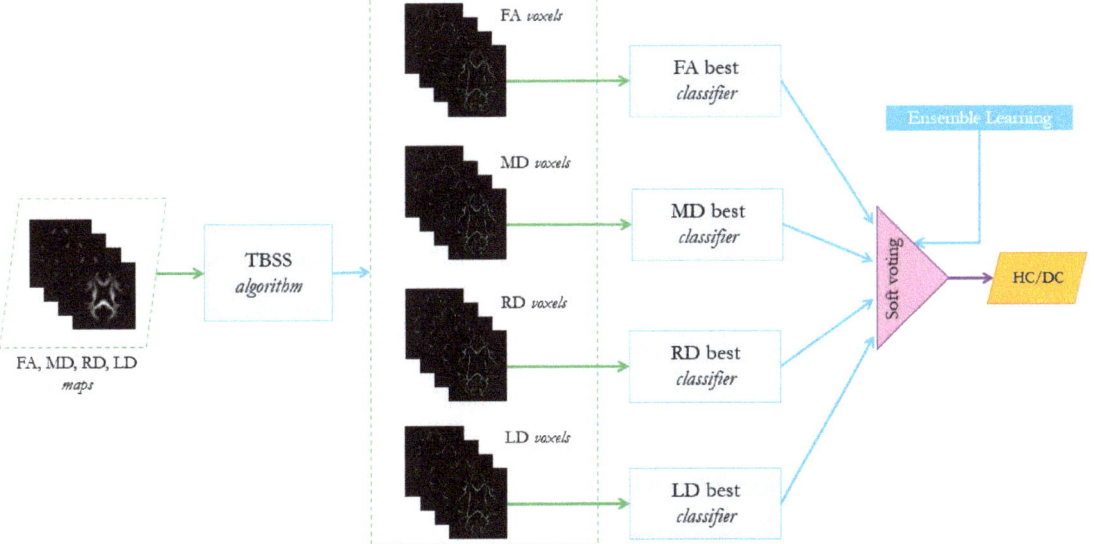

Figure 3. Classification framework based on ensemble learning with a soft-voting strategy.

The learning experiment consists of three steps.

1. For each group of features in (FA, MD, RD, LD) and their combined feature vector, find the best associated classifier among the three algorithms SVM, RF and MLP, as described in Section 3.3. A 5-fold cross validation grid search procedure should be performed to tune the hyperparameters and evaluate the best performer for each configuration, as shown in Table 2.

Table 2. Best model selection procedure.

	1-1	1-2	1-3	1-4	5-1
5-fold SVM best	$SVM_b^{1\text{-}1}$	$SVM_b^{1\text{-}2}$	$SVM_b^{1\text{-}3}$	$SVM_b^{1\text{-}4}$	$SVM_b^{5\text{-}1}$
5-fold RF best	$RF_b^{1\text{-}1}$	$RF_b^{1\text{-}2}$	$RF_b^{1\text{-}3}$	$RF_b^{1\text{-}4}$	$RF_b^{5\text{-}1}$
5-fold MLP best	$MLP_b^{1\text{-}1}$	$MLP_b^{1\text{-}2}$	$MLP_b^{1\text{-}3}$	$MLP_b^{1\text{-}4}$	$MLP_b^{5\text{-}1}$
Best Classifier	M_{FA}	M_{MD}	M_{RD}	M_{LD}	$M_{5\text{-}1}$

For instance, for configuration 1-1 the model M_{FA} is chosen among $SVM_b^{1\text{-}1}$, $RF_b^{1\text{-}1}$ and $MLP_b^{1\text{-}1}$.

2. For each possible configuration listed in Table 1, evaluate the performance of the ensemble learning algorithm, based on the combination of the best classifier selected in step 1. The voting scheme is a soft-voting procedure which is based on averaging the probability scores given by the individual classifiers according to the following equation:

$$\hat{y} = \underset{i}{\mathrm{argmax}} \sum_{j=1}^{n} w_j p_{ij} \qquad (4)$$

where $\hat{y}$ is the ensemble predicted label, n is the number of classifiers, w_j is the weight that can be assigned to the jth classifier (in the present analysis we consider uniform weights) and p_{ij} is the probability score assigned to the ith class from the jth classifier. In the case of binary classification $i \in \{0,1\}$. The ensemble algorithm analyzed in the present work refers to the ensemble.VotingClassifier method of Python scikit-learn library [44]. The choice of this scheme is due to the fact that it is more flexible than the hard one, since it takes into account the classifiers' uncertainty about the final decision, which is more informative than the simple binary prediction.

3. Repeat steps 1 and 2 on a balanced dataset obtained from the original one (43 AD vs. 49 HC), removing 6 healthy controls using the instance hardness threshold method (IHT) of Smith et al. [45]. IHT is an under-sampling method for reducing class imbalance based on the removal of the "hard" instances (where instance hardness is the likelihood of being misclassified), while focusing on the majority class samples that overlap the minority class sample space. The balanced dataset is then composed of 43 diseased cases and 43 healthy controls.

The classification performances in step 2 are evaluated through a 10-fold stratified cross-validation (CV) such that each fold is composed of approximately the same number of patients associated with each diagnostic group. This CV procedure was repeated ten times with different permutations of the training and test samples, in order to make the performance evaluation more robust and generalized. The metrics used for the performance assessment were accuracy, precision, recall and area under the ROC curve (AUC). For the comparison among ensemble combinations, statistically significant differences between the performances of classification configurations were assessed through non-parametric one-tailed Mann–Whitney U-test (MWU) [46]. Given F as the distribution function corresponding to population A and G as the distribution function corresponding to population B, MWU tested the null hypothesis $H_0 : F(t) = G(t)$, for every t (i.e., X and Y random variables have the same probability distribution) against the alternative hypothesis that Y is larger (or smaller) than X [47]. In order to address the problem of multiple comparison, p-values were corrected for multiple testing using the Benjamini–Hockberg (BH) procedure, summarized as follows: (1) Let $H_1, H_2, \ldots, H_N$ be the sequence of the null hypotheses to test with $p_1, p_2, \ldots, p_N$ as the associated p-values. (2) Rank p-values such that $p^{(1)} \leq p^{(2)} \leq p^{(3)} \leq \cdots \leq p^{(N)}$. (3) Given the level q^*, find the largest k such that $p^{(k)} \leq k \cdot q^*/N$. (4) Reject all the null hypotheses $H^{(j)}$ with $j = 1, 2, \ldots, k$. The theorem of Benjamini–Hochberg states that the above procedure controls the false discovery rate with level q^* [48].

4. Results

In this section, we outline the results of the experiment. Firstly, we discuss the effects of ensemble learning in terms of performances on the original imbalanced dataset; then we show the results for the balanced dataset obtained via instance hardness threshold method. Finally, we discuss the outcomes of nonparametric statistical tests carried out to compare the different configurations and to obtain an overview of the efficacy of the ensemble approach.

The results associated with the imbalanced case (49 HC, 43 AD) are reported in Figure 4. In panel (a), the performance average values are plotted as a function of the possible configurations. Each point in the plot represents the average over the 100 estimates of the performance metrics, obtained from the 10-times repeated, 10-fold stratified cross validations. The best configuration, according to the overall metrics, is the configuration 3-3 corresponding to the ensemble $\mathcal{E}(M_{FA}, M_{MD}, M_{RD})$. In terms of accuracy, precision and AUC, the singleton $\mathcal{E}(M_{FA})$ outperformed the other individual configurations 1-2, 1-3, 1-4 and all other ensembles that did not contain fractional anisotropy as a feature group. On the other hand, in the case of recall, the ensemble strategy is crucial for enhancing the performances: almost all the ensemble configurations outperformed the single feature set configurations, and the best recall value was obtained for the most complex ensemble $\mathcal{E}(M_{FA}, M_{MD}, M_{RD}, M_{LD})$ (configuration 4-1). The performance comparisons among all possible configurations were performed through a Mann–Whitney (MWU) test. The outcomes of MWU tests, for each performance measure, are reported in Panel (b-c-d-e). Each square of the heatmap represents the one-tailed MWU test between samples Y and X, where Y and X are given by 100 performance measures of the configurations on the y-axis and x-axis, respectively. The null hypothesis is that X and Y have the same probability distribution against the alternative hypothesis that Y is larger than X. The colors of heatmaps are related to the p-values of the test ranging from 0 (red) to 1 (blue). Levels shown in the maps refer to p-values corrected for multiple testing using the Benjamini–Hockberg procedure. Panel (b) shows that recall is generally enhanced by ensemble learning approaches and that ensemble configuration with n groups of features has higher sensitivity that those with $n-1$ groups. This behavior occurs in the other performance comparisons, with the exception that ensemble methods without fractional anisotropy are not affected by significant improvement. Finally, in order to test whether the balancing effects on the dataset can impact the performances of ensemble methods, due to the instance hardness threshold procedure, we performed the same comparisons of the imbalanced case on a fair ground of 43 diseased cases versus 43 healthy controls. The results associated with the balanced case are reported in Figure 5. As expected, we notice in panel (a) that the average performance values as a function of configurations are generally shifted upwards. Indeed, as shown by Wei et al. in [49] the use of balanced training data can provide the highest balanced performances in classifiers based on support vector machines, neural networks and decision trees. Conversely, the balancing procedure attenuates the ensemble effects in the enhancement of recall and predicting accuracy. From panels (b-c-d-e), the ensemble $\mathcal{E}(M_{FA}, M_{MD})$ emerges as the best configuration over all performance measures, and all the methods that contain fractional anisotropy and mean diffusivity outperformed the $\mathcal{E}(M_{FA,MD,RD,LD})$ method that concatenates all features in a high-dimensional single vector.

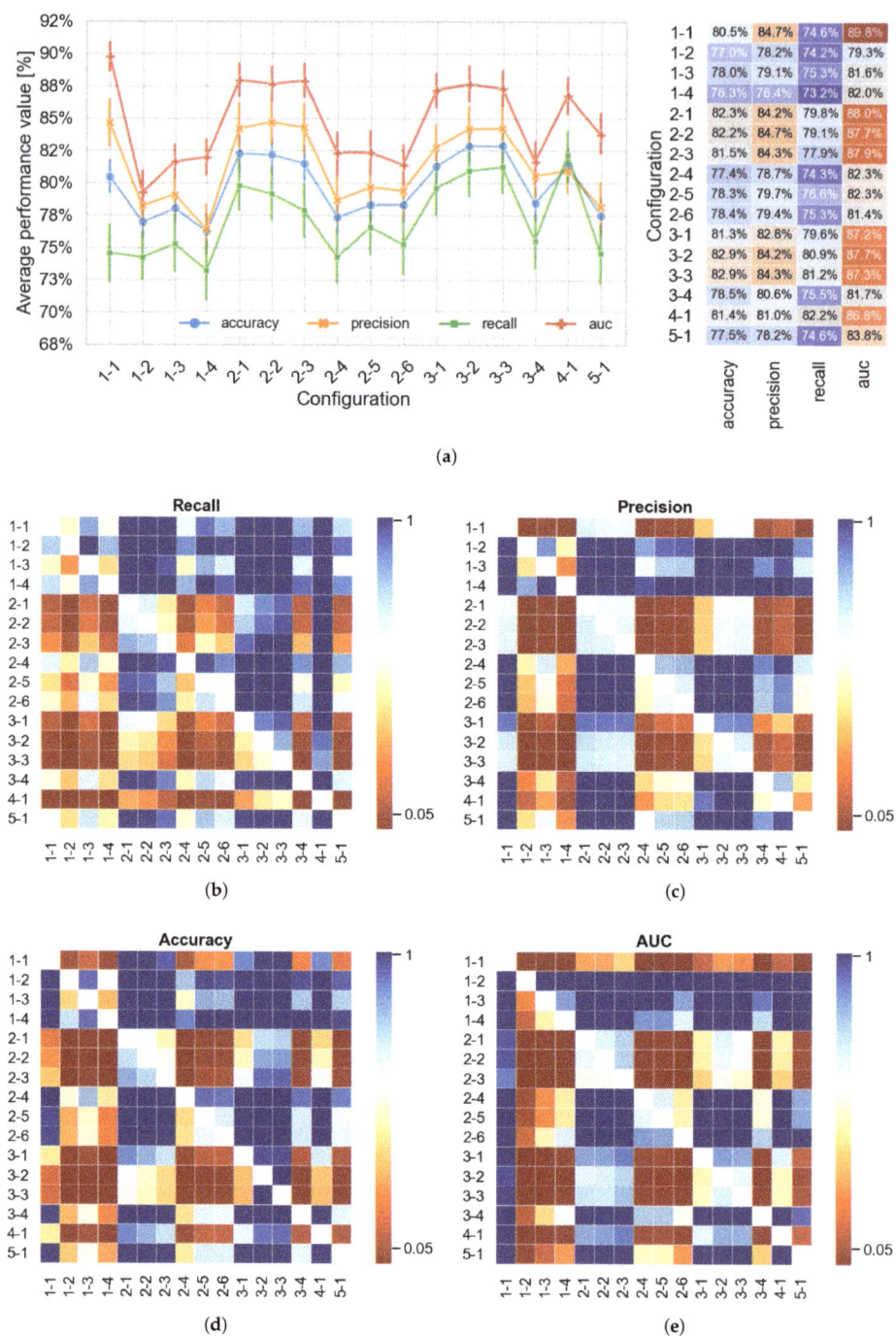

Figure 4. The case of an imbalanced dataset. (**a**) Average performance values for each configuration. (**b**–**e**) Heatmaps of Mann–Whitney tests. Each square represents the p-value outcome of a one-tail Mann–Whitney test between a configuration on the y-axis and the other on the x-axis. Each p-value in the heatmap was corrected for multiple tests using the Benjamini–Hochberg procedure.

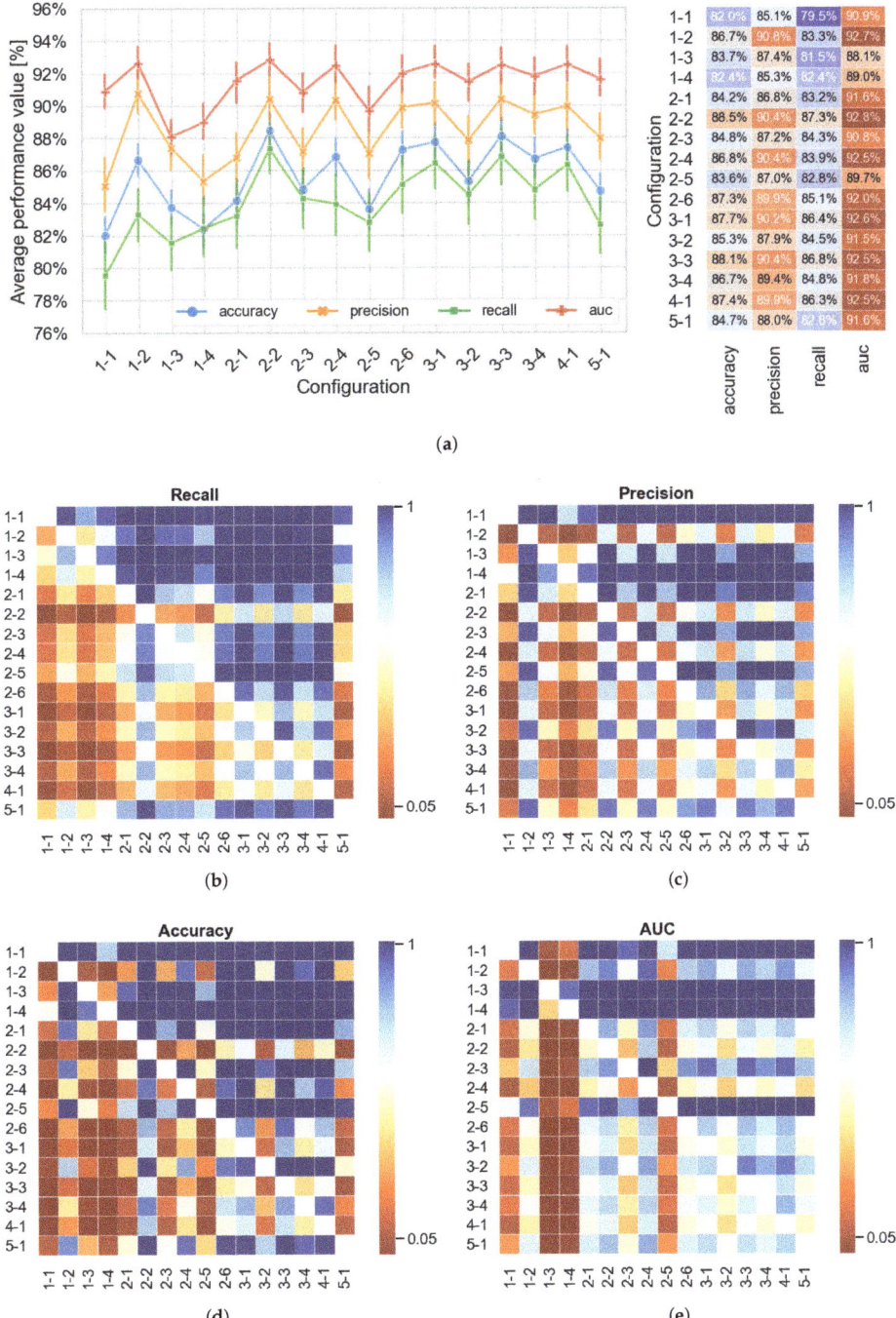

Figure 5. The case of a balanced dataset. (**a**) Average performance values for each configuration. (**b**–**e**) Heatmaps of Mann–Whitney tests. Each square represents the *p*-value outcome of a one-tail Mann–Whitney test between a configuration on the y-axis and the other on the x-axis. Each p-value in a heatmap has been corrected for multiple tests using the Benjamini–Hochberg procedure.

5. Discussion and Conclusions

Computational systems aimed at the automatic classification of Alzheimer's disease patients through voxel-based diffusivity measures have been widely investigated but mainly focused on the exploitation of individual learning methods. The authors of [18,50] used anisotropy and diffusivity voxels values of WM main tracts as features for HC/MCI discrimination with a single support vector machine, showing very high classification performances. However, as pointed out in [28], the key shortcoming of these approaches is given by a bias due to a non-nested feature selection method affecting the learning procedure. On the other hand, a recent study [30] based on an individual SVM classifier with Fisher score feature selection has reported valid performances focusing only on anisotropy measures of specific brain areas with well known AD-related connectivity abnormalities. Consequently, the idea of this work is to circumvent the problem of restricting the procedure to a single classifier or to an a priori selected group of features by exploiting all the information power of diffusion imaging techniques, through a computationally efficient learning strategy based on combinations of several feature groups and different classifiers. As a matter of fact, the simple concatenation of all feature groups (FA, MD, RD, LD) in a single high-dimensional vector would not be convenient in terms of time complexity and machinery efforts. Therefore, this approach addresses the problem of handling and selecting variables in the conditions where the feature dimensions are much larger than sample sizes typically available in medical classification tasks. In this framework, we presented a novel approach based on an ensemble learning strategy which combines classifiers that take into account different perspectives of the microstructural white matter integrity associated with each feature group. The work in [51] applied a similar ensemble methodology, feeding an a priori specified classifier with different tractography network measures describing specific aspects of brain connectivity.

We have investigated the validity of this ensemble learning procedure in the classification of HC vs. AD patients, in both cases of the original imbalanced dataset and a balanced dataset obtained by the instance hardness threshold under-sampling method. In particular, in the imbalanced case we found that all the ensemble combinations, including FA invariants, outperformed the singletons $\mathcal{E}(M_{MD})$, $\mathcal{E}(M_{RD})$ and $\mathcal{E}(M_{LD})$, and also the single vector containing all the feature groups. These results show the crucial contribution of fractional anisotropy in the correct classification of diseased subjects. In fact, fractional anisotropy, defined from diffusion tensor fitting as the degree of directionality of intravoxel diffusivity, has a behavior heavily related to variations in fiber density, axonal diameter and myelination in white matter in the presence of the onset of neurodegenerative diseases. According to Pierpaoli et al. [52], a hallmark of damage in white matter is the generalized loss of fiber tract integrity. Interestingly, further studies have shown that FA-associated voxel values have been able to uncover voxel microstructural alterations in the brains of AD patients at early stages too [18,28,53,54]. Moreover, while for AUC, accuracy and precision, the ensemble method did not significantly improve the performances of the single FA, the ensemble strategy was crucial for enhancing the recall of the classification framework. Furthermore, it is worth mentioning that, in terms of accuracy and sensitivity, the use of ensembles of classifiers associated with the diffusion measures not only turned out to be better than considering all measures concatenated in a single feature vector, but also provided higher performances as the combinations' dimensions increased. In the balanced scenario, mean diffusivity emerged as the second most informative measure for pathology discrimination. This evidence is supported by the fact that MD represents the overall mean squared displacement of molecules in the non-collinear directions of free diffusion. Consequently, a variation of mean diffusivity is a signal of an increase in free water diffusion and in turn of a loss of anisotropy of molecular mobility [52]. In literature there is evidence supporting the hypothesis that the microstructural alterations in molecular diffusivity along white matter fiber bundles, described by MD, may be of higher predictive value compared to FA microstructural changes [55,56]. In the balanced case, the effects on the improvement of accuracy and recall of the ensemble procedure were attenuated. However, ensemble combinations that included FA and MD performed better than other variable sets considered individually and than the feature vector concatenating all groups together.

Based on results emerging in the present analysis, we can conclude that our ensemble classification framework, based on DTI features, is effective to improve HC/AD classification performances, and that ensembles including FA and MD are the best performing, confirming their role in the literature as most effective DTI measures for AD detection [57–60]. Moreover, although artificial data balancing attenuates the benefits of ensemble learning, the ensemble-based strategy generates significant improvements in the classification sensitivity and accuracy with respect to the general concatenation of all features into a high-dimensional vector. For this reason, the feature selection phase in similar classification tasks can take advantage of this kind of strategy, allowing one to exploit as much information as possible, but at the same time reducing the dimensionality of the feature space, and in turn the computational effort. Hence, the ensemble learning can be a promising approach to combining different types of features derived for DTI data, extending the application to DTI tractography network measures and diffusion voxel-based features.

Future advancements of the present work will consider firstly an extension of dataset size in order to ensure more robust procedures of algorithms calibration and validation. In this scenario, one would be enabled to analyze feature selection methods together with several families of classifiers in more extensive ensemble strategies. Indeed, the possibility of comparisons on a wider base between pairs of feature selectors and classifiers could lead to the identification of efficient methods for discriminating between diseased cases and healthy controls (for a thorough review of this kind of approach, see the large comparative study performed by Parmar et al. in [61]). Moreover, the availability of a larger number of observations would allow the application of state-of-the-art deep learning methods that could give important contributions in the uncovering of signatures and biomarkers of neurodegenerative disorders for highlighting hidden patterns. The key advantage of deep learning architectures with respect to standard learning approaches is given by the evidence that high values of classification performance can be optimally achieved without feature selection steps that are embedded in the process, yielding more computationally efficient frameworks (for an application of deep convolutional neural networks to MRI data, see the work of Basaia et al. in [62], and for a review of deep learning methods and applications in neuroimaging data in psychiatric and neurologica disorders, see [63]). Future investigations may also take into account not only diffusion-derived features, but also additional variables, such as clinical information, morphological measures and other features related to different image processing modalities and methodologies, such as functional and anatomical magnetic resonance imaging. As a matter of fact, a diversified plethora of biological information generated by different diagnostic modalities can provide not only a holistic view of the pathological condition, but can be exploited in the pre-clinical stage for the early detection of dementia precursors in presymptomatic conditions [64–66].

Author Contributions: Conceptualization, E.L.; methodology, E.L., A.P. and R.A.; software, E.L. and A.P.; validation, E.L., A.P., D.L., R.A. and F.V.; formal analysis, E.L. and R.A.; investigation, E.L., A.P., D.L. and R.A.; resources, E.L.; data curation, E.L.; writing—original draft preparation, E.L. and R.A.; writing—review and editing, E.L., A.P., D.L., R.A. and F.V.; visualization, E.L. and R.A.; supervision, R.A. and F.V. All authors have read and agreed to the published version of the manuscript.

Funding: This research was funded by Ministero dello Sviluppo Economico (MiSE) "Grandi Progetti R&S—PON 2014/2020 Agenda Digitale e Industria sostenibile"—BigImaging Project—Grant number F/080022/01-04/X35.

Data Availability Statement: Publicly available datasets were analyzed in this study. This data can be found here: www.adni-info.org.

Acknowledgments: Data collection and sharing for this project was funded by the Alzheimer's Disease Neuroimaging Initiative (ADNI) (National Institutes of Health Grant U01 AG024904) and DOD ADNI (Department of Defense award number W81XWH-12-2-0012). ADNI is funded by the National Institute on Aging, the National Institute of Biomedical Imaging and Bioengineering, and through generous contributions from the following: AbbVie, Alzheimer's Association; Alzheimer's Drug Discovery Foundation; Araclon Biotech; BioClinica, Inc.; Biogen; Bristol-Myers Squibb Company; CereSpir, Inc.; Cogstate; Eisai Inc.; Elan Pharmaceuticals, Inc.; Eli Lilly and Company; EuroImmun; F. Hoffmann-La Roche Ltd and its affiliated company Genentech, Inc.; Fujirebio; GE Healthcare; IXICO Ltd.; Janssen Alzheimer Immunotherapy Research & Development, LLC.; Johnson and Johnson Pharmaceutical Research and Development LLC.; Lumosity; Lundbeck; Merck and Co., Inc.; Meso Scale Diagnostics, LLC.; NeuroRx Research; Neurotrack Technologies; Novartis Pharmaceuticals Corporation; Pfizer Inc.; Piramal Imaging; Servier; Takeda Pharmaceutical Company; and Transition Therapeutics. The Canadian Institutes of Health Research are providing funds to support ADNI clinical sites in Canada. Private sector contributions are facilitated by the Foundation for the National Institutes of Health (www.fnih.org). The grantee organization is the Northern California Institute for Research and Education, and the study is coordinated by the Alzheimer's Therapeutic Research Institute at the University of Southern California. ADNI data are disseminated by the Laboratory for Neuro Imaging at the University of Southern California.

Conflicts of Interest: The authors declare no conflict of interest.

References

1. Prince, M.J. *World Alzheimer Report 2015: The Global Impact of Dementia: An Analysis of Prevalence, Incidence, Cost and Trends*; Alzheimer's Disease International: London, UK, 2015.
2. Rombouts, S.A.; Barkhof, F.; Goekoop, R.; Stam, C.J.; Scheltens, P. Altered resting state networks in mild cognitive impairment and mild Alzheimer's disease: An fMRI study. *Hum. Brain Mapp.* **2005**, *26*, 231–239. [CrossRef]
3. Zhao, X.; Liu, Y.; Wang, X.; Liu, B.; Xi, Q.; Guo, Q.; Jiang, H.; Jiang, T.; Wang, P. Disrupted small-world brain networks in moderate Alzheimer's disease: A resting-state FMRI study. *PLoS ONE* **2012**, *7*, e33540. [CrossRef]
4. Lella, E.; Amoroso, N.; Lombardi, A.; Maggipinto, T.; Tangaro, S.; Bellotti, R.; Initiative, A.D.N. Communicability disruption in Alzheimer's disease connectivity networks. *J. Complex Netw.* **2019**, *7*, 83–100. [CrossRef]
5. Sidey-Gibbons, J.A.; Sidey-Gibbons, C.J. Machine learning in medicine: A practical introduction. *BMC Med. Res. Methodol.* **2019**, *19*, 64. [CrossRef] [PubMed]
6. Al-Turjman, F.; Nawaz, M.H.; Ulusar, U.D. Intelligence in the Internet of medical things era: A systematic review of current and future trends. *Comput. Commun.* **2020**, *150*, 644–660. [CrossRef]
7. Jordan, M.I.; Mitchell, T.M. Machine learning: Trends, perspectives, and prospects. *Science* **2015**, *349*, 255–260. [CrossRef]
8. Casalino, G.; Castellano, G.; Consiglio, A.; Liguori, M.; Nuzziello, N.; Primiceri, D. A Predictive Model for MicroRNA Expressions in Pediatric Multiple Sclerosis Detection. In *International Conference on Modeling Decisions for Artificial Intelligence*; Springer: Berlin/Heidelberg, Germany, 2019; pp. 177–188.
9. Angelillo, M.T.; Balducci, F.; Impedovo, D.; Pirlo, G.; Vessio, G. Attentional pattern classification for automatic dementia detection. *IEEE Access* **2019**, *7*, 57706–57716. [CrossRef]
10. Dyrba, M.; Ewers, M.; Wegrzyn, M.; Kilimann, I.; Plant, C.; Oswald, A.; Meindl, T.; Pievani, M.; Bokde, A.L.; Fellgiebel, A.; et al. Robust automated detection of microstructural white matter degeneration in Alzheimer's disease using machine learning classification of multicenter DTI data. *PLoS ONE* **2013**, *8*, e64925. [CrossRef]
11. Lella, E.; Amoroso, N.; Bellotti, R.; Diacono, D.; La Rocca, M.; Maggipinto, T.; Monaco, A.; Tangaro, S. Machine learning for the assessment of Alzheimer's disease through DTI. *SPIE Proc.* **2017**, *10396*, 1039619. Available online: https://www.spiedigitallibrary.org/conference-proceedings-of-spie/10396/2293188/Front-Matter-Volume-10396/10.1117/12.2293188.full?SSO=1 (accessed on 21 January 2021).
12. Lian, C.; Liu, M.; Zhang, J.; Shen, D. Hierarchical fully convolutional network for joint atrophy localization and Alzheimer's Disease diagnosis using structural MRI. *IEEE Trans. Pattern Anal. Mach. Intell.* **2018**, *42*, 880–893. [CrossRef]
13. Wee, C.Y.; Yap, P.T.; Li, W.; Denny, K.; Browndyke, J.N.; Potter, G.G.; Welsh-Bohmer, K.A.; Wang, L.; Shen, D. Enriched white matter connectivity networks for accurate identification of MCI patients. *Neuroimage* **2011**, *54*, 1812–1822. [CrossRef] [PubMed]
14. Rose, S.E.; Chen, F.; Chalk, J.B.; Zelaya, F.O.; Strugnell, W.E.; Benson, M.; Semple, J.; Doddrell, D.M. Loss of connectivity in Alzheimer's disease: An evaluation of white matter tract integrity with colour coded MR diffusion tensor imaging. *J. Neurol. Neurosurg. Psychiatry* **2000**, *69*, 528–530. [CrossRef] [PubMed]
15. Head, D.; Buckner, R.L.; Shimony, J.S.; Williams, L.E.; Akbudak, E.; Conturo, T.E.; McAvoy, M.; Morris, J.C.; Snyder, A.Z. Differential vulnerability of anterior white matter in nondemented aging with minimal acceleration in dementia of the Alzheimer type: Evidence from diffusion tensor imaging. *Cereb. Cortex* **2004**, *14*, 410–423. [CrossRef] [PubMed]
16. Basser, P.J.; Mattiello, J.; LeBihan, D. MR diffusion tensor spectroscopy and imaging. *Biophys. J.* **1994**, *66*, 259–267. [CrossRef]

17. Le Bihan, D.; Mangin, J.F.; Poupon, C.; Clark, C.A.; Pappata, S.; Molko, N.; Chabriat, H. Diffusion tensor imaging: Concepts and applications. *J. Magn. Reson. Imaging* **2001**, *13*, 534–546. [CrossRef] [PubMed]
18. O'Dwyer, L.; Lamberton, F.; Bokde, A.L.; Ewers, M.; Faluyi, Y.O.; Tanner, C.; Mazoyer, B.; O'Neill, D.; Bartley, M.; Collins, D.R.; et al. Using support vector machines with multiple indices of diffusion for automated classification of mild cognitive impairment. *PLoS ONE* **2012**, *7*, e32441. [CrossRef] [PubMed]
19. Mesrob, L.; Sarazin, M.; Hahn-Barma, V.; Souza, L.C.D.; Dubois, B.; Gallinari, P.; Kinkingnéhun, S. DTI and structural MRI classification in Alzheimer's disease. *Adv. Mol. Imaging* **2012**, *2*, 12–20. [CrossRef]
20. Dyrba, M.; Barkhof, F.; Fellgiebel, A.; Filippi, M.; Hausner, L.; Hauenstein, K.; Kirste, T.; Teipel, S.J. Predicting Prodromal Alzheimer's Disease in Subjects with Mild Cognitive Impairment Using Machine Learning Classification of Multimodal Multi-center Diffusion-Tensor and Magnetic Resonance Imaging Data. *J. Neuroimaging* **2015**, *25*, 738–747. [CrossRef]
21. Dyrba, M.; Grothe, M.; Kirste, T.; Teipel, S.J. Multimodal analysis of functional and structural disconnection in Alzheimer's disease using multiple kernel SVM. *Hum. Brain Mapp.* **2015**, *36*, 2118–2131. [CrossRef]
22. Lella, E.; Estrada, E. Communicability distance reveals hidden patterns of Alzheimer's disease. *Netw. Neurosci.* **2020**, *4*, 1–23. [CrossRef]
23. Rasero, J.; Alonso-Montes, C.; Diez, I.; Olabarrieta-Landa, L.; Remaki, L.; Escudero, I.; Mateos, B.; Bonifazi, P.; Fernandez, M.; Arango-Lasprilla, J.C.; et al. Group-level progressive alterations in brain connectivity patterns revealed by diffusion-tensor brain networks across severity stages in Alzheimer's disease. *Front. Aging Neurosci.* **2017**, *9*, 215. [CrossRef] [PubMed]
24. Daianu, M.; Jahanshad, N.; Nir, T.M.; Toga, A.W.; Jack, C.R., Jr.; Weiner, M.W.; Thompson, P.M. Breakdown of brain connectivity between normal aging and Alzheimer's disease: A structural k-core network analysis. *Brain Connect.* **2013**, *3*, 407–422. [CrossRef] [PubMed]
25. Ebadi, A.; Dalboni da Rocha, J.L.; Nagaraju, D.B.; Tovar-Moll, F.; Bramati, I.; Coutinho, G.; Sitaram, R.; Rashidi, P. Ensemble classification of Alzheimer's disease and mild cognitive impairment based on complex graph measures from diffusion tensor images. *Front. Neurosci.* **2017**, *11*, 56. [CrossRef] [PubMed]
26. Prasad, G.; Joshi, S.H.; Nir, T.M.; Toga, A.W.; Thompson, P.M.; Alzheimer's Disease Neuroimaging Initiative (ADNI). Brain connectivity and novel network measures for Alzheimer's disease classification. *Neurobiol. Aging* **2015**, *36*, S121–S131. [CrossRef] [PubMed]
27. Lella, E.; Lombardi, A.; Amoroso, N.; Diacono, D.; Maggipinto, T.; Monaco, A.; Bellotti, R.; Tangaro, S. Machine learning and dwi brain communicability networks for alzheimer's disease detection. *Appl. Sci.* **2020**, *10*, 934. [CrossRef]
28. Maggipinto, T.; Bellotti, R.; Amoroso, N.; Diacono, D.; Donvito, G.; Lella, E.; Monaco, A.; Scelsi, M.A.; Tangaro, S. DTI measurements for Alzheimer's classification. *Phys. Med. Biol.* **2017**, *62*, 2361. [CrossRef]
29. Dou, X.; Yao, H.; Feng, F.; Wang, P.; Zhou, B.; Jin, D.; Yang, Z.; Li, J.; Zhao, C.; Wang, L.; et al. Characterizing white matter connectivity in Alzheimer's disease and mild cognitive impairment: An automated fiber quantification analysis with two independent datasets. *Cortex* **2020**, *129*, 390–405. [CrossRef]
30. Da Rocha, J.L.D.; Bramati, I.; Coutinho, G.; Moll, F.T.; Sitaram, R. Fractional Anisotropy changes in parahippocampal cingulum due to Alzheimer's Disease. *Sci. Rep.* **2020**, *10*, 1–8.
31. Islam, J.; Zhang, Y. Brain MRI analysis for Alzheimer's disease diagnosis using an ensemble system of deep convolutional neural networks. *Brain Inform.* **2018**, *5*, 2. [CrossRef]
32. Suk, H.I.; Lee, S.W.; Shen, D.; Alzheimer's Disease Neuroimaging Initiative. Deep ensemble learning of sparse regression models for brain disease diagnosis. *Med. Image Anal.* **2017**, *37*, 101–113. [CrossRef]
33. Zheng, X.; Shi, J.; Zhang, Q.; Ying, S.; Li, Y. Improving MRI-based diagnosis of Alzheimer's disease via an ensemble privileged information learning algorithm. In Proceedings of the 2017 IEEE 14th International Symposium on Biomedical Imaging (ISBI 2017), Melbourne, Australia, 18–21 April 2017; pp. 456–459.
34. Rokach, L. Ensemble-based classifiers. *Artif. Intell. Rev.* **2010**, *33*, 1–39. [CrossRef]
35. Petersen, R.C.; Aisen, P.; Beckett, L.A.; Donohue, M.; Gamst, A.; Harvey, D.J.; Jack, C.; Jagust, W.; Shaw, L.; Toga, A.; et al. Alzheimer's disease neuroimaging initiative (ADNI): Clinical characterization. *Neurology* **2010**, *74*, 201–209. [CrossRef] [PubMed]
36. Maintz, J.A.; Viergever, M.A. A survey of medical image registration. *Med. Image Anal.* **1998**, *2*, 1–36. [CrossRef]
37. Jenkinson, M.; Beckmann, C.F.; Behrens, T.E.; Woolrich, M.W.; Smith, S.M. FSL. *Neuroimage* **2012**, *62*, 782–790. [CrossRef]
38. Smith, S.M.; Jenkinson, M.; Johansen-Berg, H.; Rueckert, D.; Nichols, T.E.; Mackay, C.E.; Watkins, K.E.; Ciccarelli, O.; Cader, M.Z.; Matthews, P.M.; et al. Tract-based spatial statistics: Voxelwise analysis of multi-subject diffusion data. *Neuroimage* **2006**, *31*, 1487–1505. [CrossRef]
39. Cortes, C.; Vapnik, V. Support-vector networks. *Mach. Learn.* **1995**, *20*, 273–297. [CrossRef]
40. Ho, T.K. The random subspace method for constructing decision forests. *IEEE Trans. Pattern Anal. Mach. Intell.* **1998**, *20*, 832–844. [CrossRef]
41. Breiman, L. Random Forests. *Mach. Learn.* **2001**, *45*, 5–32. [CrossRef]
42. Murtagh, F. Multilayer perceptrons for classification and regression. *Neurocomputing* **1991**, *2*, 183–197. [CrossRef]
43. Géron, A. *Hands-On Machine Learning with Scikit-Learn, Keras, and TensorFlow: Concepts, Tools, and Techniques to Build Intelligent Systems*; O'Reilly Media: Sebastopol, CA, USA, 2019.
44. Pedregosa, F.; Varoquaux, G.; Gramfort, A.; Michel, V.; Thirion, B.; Grisel, O.; Blondel, M.; Prettenhofer, P.; Weiss, R.; Dubourg, V.; et al. Scikit-learn: Machine Learning in Python. *J. Mach. Learn. Res.* **2011**, *12*, 2825–2830.

45. Smith, M.R.; Martinez, T.; Giraud-Carrier, C. An instance level analysis of data complexity. *Mach. Learn.* **2014**, *95*, 225–256. [CrossRef]
46. Mann, H.B.; Whitney, D.R. On a test of whether one of two random variables is stochastically larger than the other. *Ann. Math. Stat.* **1947**, *18*, 50–60. [CrossRef]
47. Hollander, M. *Nonparametric Statistical Methods*; John Wiley & Sons, Inc.: Hoboken, NJ, USA, 2013.
48. Benjamini, Y.; Hochberg, Y. Controlling the False Discovery Rate: A Practical and Powerful Approach to Multiple Testing. *J. R. Stat. Soc. Ser. B Methodol.* **1995**, *57*, 289–300. [CrossRef]
49. Wei, Q.; Dunbrack, R.L., Jr. The role of balanced training and testing data sets for binary classifiers in bioinformatics. *PLoS ONE* **2013**, *8*, e67863. [CrossRef] [PubMed]
50. Haller, S.; Nguyen, D.; Rodriguez, C.; Emch, J.; Gold, G.; Bartsch, A.; Lovblad, K.O.; Giannakopoulos, P. Individual prediction of cognitive decline in mild cognitive impairment using support vector machine-based analysis of diffusion tensor imaging data. *J. Alzheimer's Dis.* **2010**, *22*, 315–327. [CrossRef]
51. Lella, E.; Vessio, G. Ensembling complex network 'perspectives' for mild cognitive impairment detection with artificial neural networks. *Pattern Recognit. Lett.* **2020**, *136*, 168–174. [CrossRef]
52. Pierpaoli, C.; Jezzard, P.; Basser, P.J.; Barnett, A.; Di Chiro, G. Diffusion tensor MR imaging of the human brain. *Radiology* **1996**, *201*, 637–648. [CrossRef]
53. Schouten, T.M.; Koini, M.; de Vos, F.; Seiler, S.; de Rooij, M.; Lechner, A.; Schmidt, R.; van den Heuvel, M.; van der Grond, J.; Rombouts, S.A. Individual classification of Alzheimer's disease with diffusion magnetic resonance imaging. *Neuroimage* **2017**, *152*, 476–481. [CrossRef]
54. Patil, R.B.; Ramakrishnan, S. Analysis of sub-anatomic diffusion tensor imaging indices in white matter regions of Alzheimer with MMSE score. *Comput. Methods Programs Biomed.* **2014**, *117*, 13–19. [CrossRef]
55. Douaud, G.; Menke, R.A.; Gass, A.; Monsch, A.U.; Rao, A.; Whitcher, B.; Zamboni, G.; Matthews, P.M.; Sollberger, M.; Smith, S. Brain microstructure reveals early abnormalities more than two years prior to clinical progression from mild cognitive impairment to Alzheimer's disease. *J. Neurosci.* **2013**, *33*, 2147–2155. [CrossRef]
56. Nir, T.M.; Villalon-Reina, J.E.; Prasad, G.; Jahanshad, N.; Joshi, S.H.; Toga, A.W.; Bernstein, M.A.; Jack, C.R., Jr.; Weiner, M.W.; Thompson, P.M.; et al. Diffusion weighted imaging-based maximum density path analysis and classification of Alzheimer's disease. *Neurobiol. Aging* **2015**, *36*, S132–S140. [CrossRef]
57. Billeci, L.; Badolato, A.; Bachi, L.; Tonacci, A. Machine Learning for the Classification of Alzheimer's Disease and Its Prodromal Stage Using Brain Diffusion Tensor Imaging Data: A Systematic Review. *Processes* **2020**, *8*, 1071. [CrossRef]
58. Tu, M.C.; Lo, C.P.; Huang, C.F.; Hsu, Y.H.; Huang, W.H.; Deng, J.F.; Lee, Y.C. Effectiveness of diffusion tensor imaging in differentiating early-stage subcortical ischemic vascular disease, Alzheimer's disease and normal ageing. *PLoS ONE* **2017**, *12*, e0175143. [CrossRef] [PubMed]
59. Shao, J.; Myers, N.; Yang, Q.; Feng, J.; Plant, C.; Böhm, C.; Förstl, H.; Kurz, A.; Zimmer, C.; Meng, C.; et al. Prediction of Alzheimer's disease using individual structural connectivity networks. *Neurobiol. Aging* **2012**, *33*, 2756–2765. [CrossRef]
60. Graña, M.; Termenon, M.; Savio, A.; Gonzalez-Pinto, A.; Echeveste, J.; Pérez, J.; Besga, A. Computer aided diagnosis system for Alzheimer disease using brain diffusion tensor imaging features selected by Pearson's correlation. *Neurosci. Lett.* **2011**, *502*, 225–229. [CrossRef] [PubMed]
61. Parmar, C.; Grossmann, P.; Bussink, J.; Lambin, P.; Aerts, H.J. Machine learning methods for quantitative radiomic biomarkers. *Sci. Rep.* **2015**, *5*, 13087. [CrossRef]
62. Basaia, S.; Agosta, F.; Wagner, L.; Canu, E.; Magnani, G.; Santangelo, R.; Filippi, M.; Alzheimer's Disease Neuroimaging Initiative. Automated classification of Alzheimer's disease and mild cognitive impairment using a single MRI and deep neural networks. *NeuroImage Clin.* **2019**, *21*, 101645. [CrossRef]
63. Vieira, S.; Pinaya, W.H.; Mechelli, A. Using deep learning to investigate the neuroimaging correlates of psychiatric and neurological disorders: Methods and applications. *Neurosci. Biobehav. Rev.* **2017**, *74*, 58–75. [CrossRef]
64. Alberdi, A.; Aztiria, A.; Basarab, A. On the early diagnosis of Alzheimer's Disease from multimodal signals: A survey. *Artif. Intell. Med.* **2016**, *71*, 1–29. [CrossRef]
65. Chételat, G. Multimodal neuroimaging in Alzheimer's disease: Early diagnosis, physiopathological mechanisms, and impact of lifestyle. *J. Alzheimer's Dis.* **2018**, *64*, S199–S211. [CrossRef]
66. Ten Kate, M.; Redolfi, A.; Peira, E.; Bos, I.; Vos, S.J.; Vandenberghe, R.; Gabel, S.; Schaeverbeke, J.; Scheltens, P.; Blin, O.; et al. MRI predictors of amyloid pathology: Results from the EMIF-AD Multimodal Biomarker Discovery study. *Alzheimer's Res. Ther.* **2018**, *10*, 100. [CrossRef] [PubMed]

Article

Leukemia Image Segmentation Using a Hybrid Histogram-Based Soft Covering Rough K-Means Clustering Algorithm

Hannah Inbarani H. [1], Ahmad Taher Azar [2,3,*] and Jothi G [4]

1. Department of Computer Science, Periyar University, Tamil Nadu, Salem 636 011, India; hhinba@gmail.com
2. Robotics and Internet-of-Things Lab (RIOTU), Prince Sultan University, Riyadh 11586, Saudi Arabia
3. Faculty of Computers and Artificial Intelligence, Benha University, Benha 13511, Egypt
4. Department of Computer Science and Engineering, Sona College of Technology (Autonomous), Salem 636005, India; jothiys@gmail.com
* Correspondence: aazar@psu.edu.sa or ahmad.azar@fci.bu.edu.eg

Received: 1 December 2019; Accepted: 1 January 2020; Published: 19 January 2020

Abstract: Segmenting an image of a nucleus is one of the most essential tasks in a leukemia diagnostic system. Accurate and rapid segmentation methods help the physicians identify the diseases and provide better treatment at the appropriate time. Recently, hybrid clustering algorithms have started being widely used for image segmentation in medical image processing. In this article, a novel hybrid histogram-based soft covering rough k-means clustering (HSCRKM) algorithm for leukemia nucleus image segmentation is discussed. This algorithm combines the strengths of a soft covering rough set and rough k-means clustering. The histogram method was utilized to identify the number of clusters to avoid random initialization. Different types of features such as gray level co-occurrence matrix (GLCM), color, and shape-based features were extracted from the segmented image of the nucleus. Machine learning prediction algorithms were applied to classify the cancerous and non-cancerous cells. The proposed strategy is compared with an existing clustering algorithm, and the efficiency is evaluated based on the prediction metrics. The experimental results show that the HSCRKM method efficiently segments the nucleus, and it is also inferred that logistic regression and neural network perform better than other prediction algorithms.

Keywords: leukemia nucleus image; segmentation; soft covering rough set; clustering; machine learning algorithm; soft computing

---

1. Introduction

Due to the growth of advanced medical imaging modalities, it is very difficult to analyze the medical images manually. For this reason, an advanced and efficient computer-aided system is needed to diagnose the diseases. This will help the hematologist to begin the treatment at the right time and increase the patient's survival rate. Leukemia is a cancer of blood-forming tissues that affects the bone marrow. Leukemia is caused by the proliferation of abnormal white blood cells in the body. Leukemia is mostly affected by people living in developed countries and children aged 14 or under. As per the National Cancer Institute (NCI) statistics, in the United States, it is expected that there will be 62,130 persons as new cases for cancer treatment and 245,000 cases that are fatal or very serious [1]. In India, leukemia stands at ninth position among diseases (tumors) among children [2,3]. Leukemia is identified into two broad categories such as acute and chronic. Acute forms of leukemia occur when the number of immature blood cells increases, and it is the most common type of leukemia in children. Segmenting an image of a nucleus is one of the major challenging tasks in leukemia diagnosis. Recently, soft computing plays an important role in many research areas such as medical image processing, pattern recognition, big data analytics, Internet of Things (IoT) analysis, bioinformatics, and so on.

The rough set theory [4] was proposed by Pawlak in 1982. This concept is an extension of set theory for the study of intelligent systems characterized by insufficient and incomplete information. This classical rough set theory is based on equivalence relations, but it can also be extended to covering based rough sets [5–7]. In 1999, Molodtsov [8] proposed the concept of a soft set, which can be seen as a new mathematical approach to vagueness. The absence of any restrictions on the approximate description in soft set theory makes this theory very versatile and easily applicable in practice. Maji et al. [9] improved Molodtsov's idea by introducing several operations in soft set theory. In [10], the researcher investigated a soft covering-based rough set as a new kind of soft rough set. This method is a combination of a covering soft set and rough set. In [11], a covering-based rough k-means clustering approach is applied to segment the leukemia nucleus. The advantage of covering-based subsets is that they generate upper and lower approximations by using the covering feature, which brings about more roughness. Since different clusters give rise to different results, determination of the number of clusters is a difficult task in clustering-based segmentation. To overcome this limitation, the hybrid histogram-based soft covering rough k-means clustering algorithm (HSCRKM) is introduced to segment the image of the leukemia nucleus. In this algorithm, the peak values of the histogram of an image are identified and the number of clusters is initialized. This will avoid the random initialization of a number of clusters. Here, soft covering approximation space is also included. The term 'covering soft set' is more accurate than 'soft rough set.' It also combines the strengths of covering soft set theory and the rough k-means clustering algorithm to effectively segment the image of the nucleus. Soft covering rough approximation is utilized to find the lower and upper approximation values. The performance of the HSCRKM algorithm is evaluated using existing algorithms such as k-means clustering, fuzzy c-means clustering, and particle swarm optimization (PSO)-based clustering. Different types of features such as GLCM-0, GLCM-45, GLCM-90, GLCM-135, and shape color-based features are extracted from the segmented leukemia nucleus image. Nowadays, a lot of machine learning algorithms are applied to predict the degree of sickness. The state-of-art machine learning prediction algorithms such as neural networks (NN) [12], logistic regression (LR) [13], support vector machine (SVM) [14], naive Bayes (NB) [15], k-nearest neighborhood (KNN) [13], decision tree (DT) [13], and random forest (RF) [16] are applied to classify the cancerous and non-cancerous leukemia cells. The empirical results show that logistic regression and neural network efficiently predict the blast and non-blast cells when compared with other prediction algorithms.

The main objective of this research work is to develop a diagnostic approach for the identification of acute lymphoblastic leukemia blast cells using image processing and computational intelligence techniques. In experimental analysis, relevant image processing and computational intelligence techniques are applied in order to select the most suitable approach for the delineation of acute lymphoblastic leukemia cells. The following objectives have been formulated in order to predict leukemia: to apply computational intelligence-based algorithms for the segmentation of acute lymphoblastic leukemia blast cells in images and to apply machine learning algorithms to evaluate the performance of the proposed method.

The contribution of this study is summarized as follows. To find the number of clusters using the peak value of a histogram image and compute the lower and upper approximation values based on the soft covering approximation space, three clustering methods—k-means, FCM, and PSO-based clustering—are preferred for segmentation comparison. Through these methods, different kinds of features are extracted, and the efficiency of the proposed algorithm is assessed using machine learning prediction algorithms. The HSCRKM achieves the successful results i.e., above 80% when compared with the existing clustering algorithms. Therefore, it can be concluded that the HSCRKM clustering algorithm works effectively with the other clustering algorithms.

In the clustering algorithm, defining the number of clusters is a very difficult task. To overcome this limitation, the proposed algorithm identifies the peak values of the histogram of an image and initializes the number of clusters. This is one of the advantages of our proposed method, which avoids the random initialization of a number of clusters. The next advantage of the HSCRKM algorithm is that it combines the strengths of covering soft set theory and the rough k-means clustering algorithm to effectively segment the image of the nucleus. Based on a literature review, the term 'covering soft set' is more accurate than 'soft rough set', since it gives a better result than the soft rough set for several applications. In covering rough sets, the lower and upper approximation values are computed based on the soft covering approximation space.

Morphologically, a lymphoblast consists of a massive nucleus of irregular shape and size. In blood sample images, it is difficult to identify the cytoplasm, because it appears rarely and even if it does, it looks intensely colored. The nucleus and cytoplasm of lymphoblast cells reflect the morphological and functional changes. Feature extraction plays a main role in the assessment of leukemia in blood samples. After segmenting the nucleus using the proposed HSCRKM algorithm, salient features are extracted. It reduces the amount of data space and the working time of an image. In this research, different kinds of features are extracted such as gray level co-occurrence matrix (GLCM), color, and shape-based features. These were measured from every channel of the segmented nucleus image. The efficiency of the proposed algorithm is assessed using machine learning prediction algorithms. The performance of the segmentation algorithms was analyzed in the light of different machine learning (ML) prediction methods. With respect to HSCRKM clustering algorithms, most of the ML methods (except naive Bayes) achieved greater than 80% prediction accuracy compared with the existing clustering algorithms, viz., k-means clustering, fuzzy c-means clustering, and rough k-means clustering. It is inferred that the proposed clustering algorithms are more effective in segmenting the nucleus image. Due to the effective segmentation process, the extracted features have increased the prediction accuracy. To evaluate the experimental results, we have empirically set the best accuracy to be greater than 80%. The outline of the proposed system is shown in Figure 1.

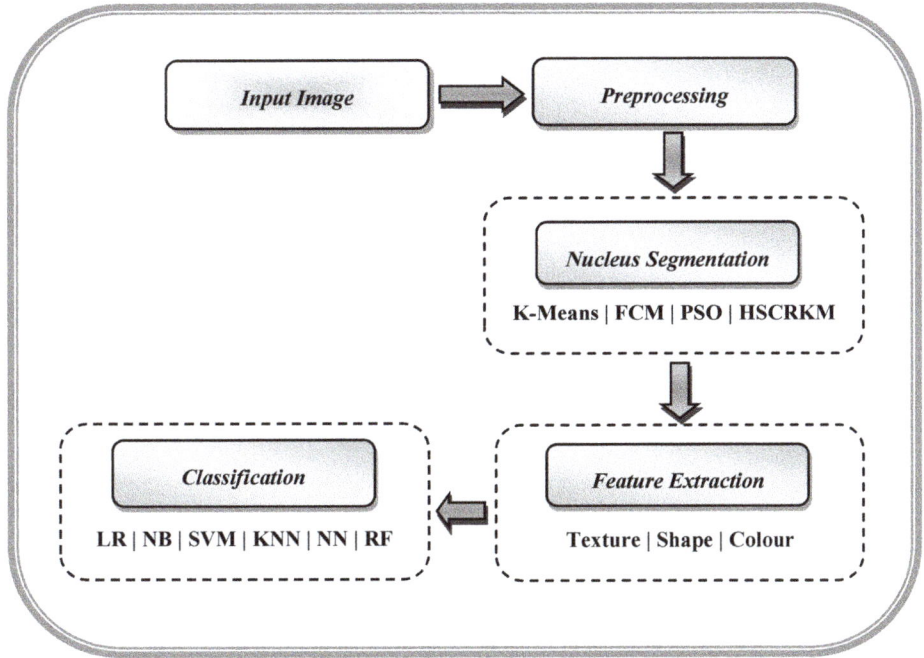

Figure 1. Outline of the proposed image segmentation process.

The rest of the research report is organized as follows. Section 2 reviews the related literature on clustering-based segmentation algorithms. Section 3 describes the methods of the proposed algorithm and its results. The empirical results are discussed in Section 4. Section 5 states the conclusion and indicates the future direction of this research.

2. Related Literature

In recent years, a lot of clustering algorithms have been developed for segmenting medical images.

Petal [17] applied k-means clustering for segmentation and the Zack algorithm for clustered white blood cells (WBCs). The features—namely, the mean, standard deviation, area, elongation, perimeter, color etc.—are extracted, and support vector machine (SVM) was used to classify the cells. The proposed algorithm effectively segmented the WBCs, which produced 93.57% accuracy. For this experiment, 27 images from the Acute Lymphoblastic Leukemia Image Database (ALL-IDB) were utilized.

Two bare-bones particle swarm optimization (BBPSO) algorithms with and without subswarms were introduced by Srisukkham et al. in 2017 [18] to diagnosis the leukemia cells. A stimulating discriminant measure (SDM)-based clustering algorithm that combined with the genetic algorithm (GA) was employed to segment the nucleus, cytoplasm, and background regions. The relevant features were extracted; then, various feature selection methods such as particle swarm optimization (PSO), cuckoo search (CS), and dragonfly algorithm (DA) were applied to select the optimal features and reduce the dimensions. An average geometric mean was computed with different sizes of training and test samples to evaluate the performance of the proposed methods. The BBPSO and binary BBPSO algorithms produced 91% to 96% of the geometric mean value.

Su [19] developed two stages of segmentation process using k-means clustering and HMRF (hidden Markov random field), which are used to group the six different types of AML cells from the bone marrow images. The segmentation algorithm achieved an accuracy of 96% to 98% (average) when compared with other existing segmentation methods.

In [20], k-means and fuzzy c-means clustering algorithms were applied to segment the brain tumor images. Various feature reduction algorithms, namely probabilistic principal component analysis (PPCA), expectation maximization-based principal component analysis (EM-PCA), the generalized Hebbian algorithm (GHA), and adaptive principal component extraction (APEX) were employed to reduce the dimensions of the feature set. The produced coefficient of variance (CV) values for k-means and Fuzzy C-mean (FCM) are 0.4582 and 0.1224, respectively.

In [21], potential field segmentation was employed to segment the MRI brain tumor images. This method achieved the standard deviation of 0.283, the average value of 0.517, and the median values of 0.644. From the experimental results, it was observed that ensemble methods generated better segmentations.

Küçükkülahlı [22] and Namburu [23] identified the number of cluster values in the clustering algorithm using the peak value of the histogram of an image. In [22], the automatic segmentation method using the histogram-based k-means clustering algorithm was developed. In [23], the soft fuzzy rough c-means clustering algorithm (SFRCM) was used to segment the MRI brain tumor images. The proposed SRFCM algorithm achieved a better Jaccard coefficient value of 0.97 for without noise and 0.79 for with 9% Gaussian noise when compared with the existing clustering algorithms namely, k-means, rough k-means (RKM), rough fuzzy c-means (RFCM), and generalized rough c-means (GFCM).

Ali [24] introduced a new clustering algorithm based on neutrosophic orthogonal matrices (CANOM) to segment the dental X-ray images. The experimental results show that the CANOM simplified silhouette width criterion (SSWC) index is 0.941 and the FCM is 0.02. CANOM is also better than Otsu and eSFCM with the values being 0.657 and 0.647, respectively. The value of CANOM is 47 times larger than that of FCM and 1.43 times larger than those of Otsu and eSFCM.

In [25], the unsupervised fuzzy c-means (FCM) clustering technique was employed for prostate cancer MRI images. The derived average dice similarity, Jaccard index, sensitivity, specificity, mean absolute difference, and Hausdorff distance is 88.68, 81.26, 90.71, 88.09, 88.09, 3.5, and 4.1 respectively.

In [26], the proposed multi-Otsu thresholding-based segmentation method can successfully segmented the CT image stacks. In addition, it sows the distribution characteristics of different components in three dimensions.

In [27], the enhanced adaptive fuzzy k-means (AFKM) algorithm was used to detect the three regions such as white matter (WM), gray matter (GM), and cerebrospinal fluid spaces (CSF) in the brain images. AFKM performed better than FCM, which produced a minimum mean square error (MSE) value of 2.2441.

In [28], the clustering method intuitionistic fuzzy c-means (IFCM) was applied for medical image segmentation. It is observed from the experimental results that the proposed method outperformed other algorithms that achieved the average quantitative index 0.95. The chronic wound region was detected using fuzzy spectral clustering in [29]. The proposed method produced 91.5% segmentation accuracy, an 86.7% Dice index, a Jaccard score of 79.0%, 87.3% sensitivity, and 95.7% specificity.

In [30], the convolutional neural networks (CNN) approach is applied to identify the subtypes of leukemia. It is observed from the experimental results that the CNN model achieves 88.25% and 81.74% accuracy for leukemia and healthy cells, respectively. From the literature review, it is inferred that the clustering-based algorithms were applied to segment the tumor region. A brief review of the literature on various clustering methods in image segmentation and their performances appears in Table 1.

Table 1. Overview of the literature on clustering algorithms.

Author	Used Methods	Objective	Type of Diseases	Imaging Modalities/Dataset Used	No. of IMAGES	Performance Metrics and Accuracy %
Patel et al., 2015 [17]	K-mean clustering Zack algorithm, Support vector machines (SVM)	The K-means clustering algorithm was used to detect the white blood cells and the Zack algorithm was applied to categorize the cells.	Leukemia	Microscopic image (ALL-IDB)	27	Classification accuracy 93.57%
Srisukkham et al., 2017 [18]	Spatial Data Mining (SDM)-based clustering, Genetic Algorithm (GA), particle swarm optimization (PSO), Bare Bones PSO (BBPSO)	This optimization method was utilized to diagnose leukemia.	Acute lymphoblastic leukemia (ALL)	Microscopic image (ALL-IDB)	180	Geometric mean 91 to 96%
Su et al., 2017 [19]	K-means, Hidden Markov random field	This algorithm segmented the nucleus from the background, extracted the features, and then classified the blast cells.	Acute myeloid leukemia	Microscopic image (AML Patient)	61	Segmentation accuracy 96 to 98% (average)
Kaya et al., 2017 [20]	K-means, fuzzy c-means	Comparative analysis of various types of PCA algorithms on MRIs for two cluster methods.	Brain tumor	MRI (Hospital)	-	Average reconstruction error rates, Euclidean distance error rate, CV of K-Means = 0.4582 FCM = 0.1224
Cabria et al., 2017 [21]	Potential field clustering	The algorithm is based on an analogy with the concept of potential field in physics and views the intensity of a pixel in an MRI as a "mass" that creates a potential field.	Brain tumor	MRI (BRATS)	30	SD = 0.283, Average = 0.517, Median = 0.644.
Küçükkülahlı et al., 2016 [22]	Histogram-based k-means clustering	This method to find the optimum cluster number based on the histogram of an image.	MATLAB media	Image Dataset	10-15	Derived metrics
Ali et al., 2017 [23]	Fuzzy clustering based on neutrosophic orthogonal matrix	This algorithm transforms image data into a neutrosophic set and computes the inner products of the cutting matrix of input. Then, pixels are segmented using the orthogonal principle to form clusters.	Dental	X-Ray (Hospital)	22	DB index Silhouette index = 0.941

Table 1. Cont.

Author	Used Methods	Objective	Type of Diseases	Imaging Modalities/Dataset Used	No. of IMAGES	Performance Metrics and Accuracy %
Rundo et al., 2018 [24]	Fuzzy c-means (FCM)	This approach automatically segments the prostate and image computes the gland volume.	Prostate cancer	MRI (Hospital)	7 (Patients)	Dice Similarity = 88.68, Jaccard index = 81.26, Sensitivity = 90.71, Specificity = 88.09, Mean Absolute Difference = 3.5, Hausdorff distance = 4.1
Zhang et al., 2017 [25]	Multi-Otsu thresholding algorithm	This segmentation method can successfully segment CT image stacks. In addition, it sows the distribution characteristics of different components in three dimensions.	Backscattered electron images	X-ray CT (Hospital)	1571 (Slice)	Derived metrics
Namburu et al., 2017 [26]	classical k-means (KM), rough k-means (RKM), rough fuzzy c-means (RFCM), and generalized rough c-means (GFCM).	In this method, soft fuzzy rough approximations are applied to obtain the rough regions of an image and compute the similarity of the clusters using soft set similarity coefficient.	Brain tumor	MRI (BRATS)	20	Jaccard's coefficient = 0.97 Accuracy
Ganesh et al., 2017 [27]	Enhanced adaptive fuzzy k-means algorithm	This approach is used to classify the three important regions in brain: namely, white matter, gray matter, and cerebrospinal fluid spaces.	Brain tumor	MRI (Brain Image)	3	MSE 2.2441
Kaur 2017 [28]	Intuitionistic fuzzy sets-based credibilistic fuzzy c-means clustering	In this method, the hesitation factor and fuzzy entropy were utilized to improve the noise sensitivity of fuzzy c-means.	Brain tumor	MRI (brainweb)	3	Quantitative index 0.95
Dhane et al., 2017 [29]	Fuzzy spectral clustering gray-based fuzzy similarity measure	This approach is adopted to compute the ulcer boundary demarcation and estimation.	Chronic wound	Digital Camera	70	Sensitivity = 87.3% Specificity = 95.7% Accuracy = 91.5% Dice index = 86.7% Jaccard score = 79.0%
Ahmed et al., 2019 [30]	Convolutional neural network (CNN)	This approach is identify the subtypes of leukemia.	Leukemia	Microscopic image (ALL-IDB) ASH Image Bank	903	Accuracy = 88.25% (Leukemia) Accuracy = 81.74% (Healthy cell)

3. Methods

3.1. Basics of Soft Covering Based Rough Set

This section describes the basic properties of soft covering-based rough approximation [11].

Definition 1. *Let $C_G = (F, A)$ be a covering soft set over U if $F(a) \neq \emptyset$, $\forall a \in A$. The pair $S = (U, C_G)$ is known as soft covering approximation space. For a set $X \subseteq U$, the soft covering lower and upper approximations are, respectively, defined as*

$$\underline{S}_*(X) = \cup_{a \in A}\{F(a) : F(a) \subseteq X\} \quad (1)$$

$$\overrightarrow{S}^*(X) = \cup\{Md_S(x) : x \in X\}. \quad (2)$$

In addition,

$$S_{pos}(X) = \underline{S}_*(X) \quad (3)$$

$$S_{neg}(X) = U - \overrightarrow{S}^*(X) \quad (4)$$

$$S_{bon}(X) = \overrightarrow{S}^*(X) - \underline{S}_*(X) \quad (5)$$

are called the soft covering positive, negative, and boundary regions of X, respectively [11].

Definition 2. *Let $S = (U, C_G)$ be a soft covering approximation space. If $\overrightarrow{S}^*(X) = \underline{S}_*(X)$, then subset $X \subseteq U$ is called soft covering. X is said to be a soft covering based rough set if $\overrightarrow{S}^*(X) \neq \underline{S}_*(X)$.*

The soft covering based rough set can be applied to image segmentation with the following considerations.

- The set of pixels in the input image is denoted as U $U = X = \{xi/xi$ is the value of the ith pixel in the image$\}$.
- Let $C_G = (F, A)$ be the covering soft set to be constructed containing the pixels belonging to clusters.
- The set of parameter A is considered as the number of clusters Cl_G $\{i = 1, 2, 3, \ldots, k\}$ to which the pixels fit.
- For example, let a set of pixels in an image be denoted as $U = \{x_1, x_2, x_3, x_4,\}$ and the parameter set A be denoted as number of clusters $\{Cl_{G1}, Cl_{G2}, Cl_{G3}\}$ to which the pixels belong. The distance between each pixel and the centroids are calculated. Based on the minimum distance, the pixels are grouped to the clusters. Assume that the input pixels are grouped in one cluster or more than one clusters as follows.

$$F(Cl_{G1}) = \{x_2, x_3, x_4\}$$
$$F(Cl_{G2}) = \{x_1, x_4,\}$$
$$F(Cl_{G3}) = \{x_1, x_3\}$$

Let (F, A) be represented as $(F, A) = \{F(Cl_G) \mid Cl_G \in A\}$. The soft covering based rough set representation of the above example is given by

$$(F, A) = \left\{ \begin{array}{l} Cl_{G1} = \{x_2, x_3, x_4\} \\ Cl_{G2} = \{x_1, x_4,\} \\ Cl_{G3} = \{x_1, x_3\} \end{array} \right\}.$$

A tabular presentation of soft sets appears in Table 2. If $x_i \in F(Cl_{Gi})$, then the value is one; else, it is zero.

Table 2. Soft covering-based rough set representation of an image.

U	Cl_{G1}	Cl_{G2}	Cl_{G3}
x_1	0	1	1
x_2	1	0	0
x_3	1	0	1
x_4	1	1	0

3.2. The Proposed Histogram-Based Soft Covering Rough K-Means Clustering

The proposed histogram-based soft covering rough k-means clustering is summarized in Algorithm 1. The combination of the covering soft set and rough set gives rise to a new kind of soft rough sets. Based on the covering soft sets, soft covering rough approximation was proposed by Yüksel et al. in 2014 [11,31], which is more accurate than the soft rough set. Here, we establish a rough k-means clustering using soft covering-based rough approximation to segment the image of the leukemia nucleus. Let $\underline{S}_*(X)$, $\overrightarrow{S}^*(X)$ be denoted as soft covering lower and upper approximation, and for $\underline{S}_*(X) \in \overrightarrow{S}^*(X)$ i.e., in soft covering-based rough k-means clustering, the lower approximation is a subset of the upper approximation. The pixel data $X_n = (x_1, x_2, \ldots \ldots .x_n)$ of the lower approximation surely belong to the cluster; in this way, they can not have a place with some other cluster. The pixel data $X_n = (x_1, x_2, \ldots \ldots .x_n)$ in an upper approximation may belong to the cluster. Since their participation is dubious, they should be an individual set from an upper approximation of at least another cluster. The distance between the pixel data X_n and the mean sm_k is defined as [32]

$$d(X_n, sm_k) = \|X_n - sm_k\|. \tag{6}$$

The cluster center sm_k i.e., the mean, is computed using the following equation:

$$sm_k = \begin{cases} w_{low} \sum_{X_n \in \underline{S}_*} \frac{X_n}{|\underline{S}_{*k}|} + w_{upp} \sum_{X_n \in \overrightarrow{S}^*} \frac{X_n}{|\overrightarrow{S}^*_k|} & \text{for } \underline{S}_* \neq \phi \\ \sum_{X_n \in \overrightarrow{S}^*} \frac{X_n}{|\overrightarrow{S}^*_k|} & \text{otherwise,} \end{cases} \tag{7}$$

where $|\underline{S}_{*k}|$ indicates the numbers of pixels in the lower approximation of the cluster k and $|\overrightarrow{S}^*_k|$ is the number of pixels in the upper approximation of the cluster k. The weight parameters w_{low} and w_{upp} stress the significance of the lower and upper approximation of the cluster.

Explanation: In this algorithm, identify the peak value of a histogram image and use it to define the number of clusters k. Initially, assign each pixel $X_n = (x_1, x_2, \ldots \ldots .x_n)$ to exactly one lower approximation. Here, soft covering-based rough approximation is applied instead of rough approximation. Determine the new means sm_k using Equation (7). Assign each pixel data to its closest mean using Equation (6). Compute the distance between each pixel X_n with centroid sm_k i.e., $d(X_n, sm_k)$. For each pixel, compute the relative distance (RD). If it is greater than the threshold, then the pixel is put into the upper approximation of the cluster k; otherwise, put it into the lower approximation of the cluster h. This algorithm is continued until all the data objects close to the cluster remain unchanged. Finally, the clustered image is labeled by the cluster index, and the segmented image of the nucleus is extracted.

Algorithm 1 : Based Soft Covering Rough K − Means Clustering Algorithm

Input : $Img\,(X_n)$, k, w_{low}, w_{upp}, δ
Output : Segmented Nucleus Image (Seg_{neu})
Initialization :

$$X_n = (x_1, x_2, \ldots \ldots .x_n) \,//\, n = \text{no. of pixels in an image}$$

$K = \text{hist}(Img(X_n))$ No. of Clusters found using the peak value of a histogram image
$w_{low} = $ Lower Approximation Weight
$w_{upp} = $ Upper Approximation Weight
$\delta = $ Threshold Value
Randomly assign each pixel into exactly one lower approximation.
Procedure :
Step1 : Randomly assign each pixel's data to the soft covering approximations
Step2 : Compute cluster centers sm_k using Equation (7)
Step3 : Assign the pixels to the approximations.
The pixel data X_n determine its closest mean sm_h.
$$sd_{n,h}^{min} = d(X_n, sm_h) = \min_{k=1,2,\ldots K} d(X_n, sm_k)$$
Assign X_n to the upper approximation of the cluster h : $X_n \in \vec{S}_h$.
Step4 : The relative distance is defined as
$$RD = d(X_n, sm_k) - d(X_n, sm_h)$$
$ST = \{t : RD \leq \delta \cup h \neq k\}$.
If $ST \neq \phi$ then $X_n \epsilon \vec{S}_t$ $\forall t \in T$.
Else, $X_n \epsilon \underline{S}_{*h}$.
Step5 : Check the convergence of the algorithm; if not, make it converge, and then continue
with Step 1.
Step6 : Lable the image by cluster index and extract the leukemia nucleus (Seg_{neu}).

3.3. Performance Assessment for Segmentation Algorithms

After preprocessing, a novel HSCRKM algorithm is applied for leukemia nucleus image segmentation. The peak values of histogram are identified, and these values will automatically be assigned the number of clusters (K). In each iteration, the k value will change. The range of weight of the lower and boundary region in rough k-means algorithms is (0.0 <= w_{low}, w_{bon} <= 1.0). The relative threshold in the HSCRKM algorithm is defined as δ <= 1.0. The parameters' values are assigned as $w_{low} = 0.7$, $w_{bon} = 0.3$, and $\delta = 0.5$. These values give possible stable results in rough k-means [30]. Figure 2 illustrates the segmentation results produced by the proposed HSCRKM algorithm.

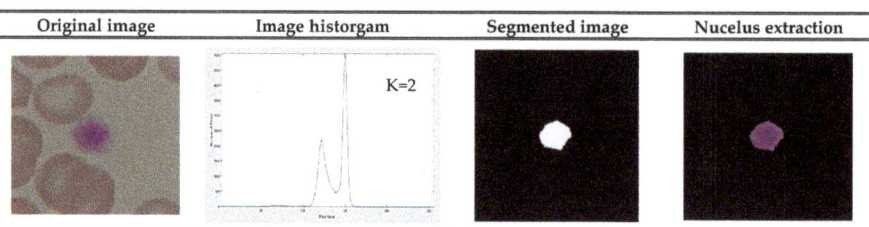

Figure 2. *Cont.*

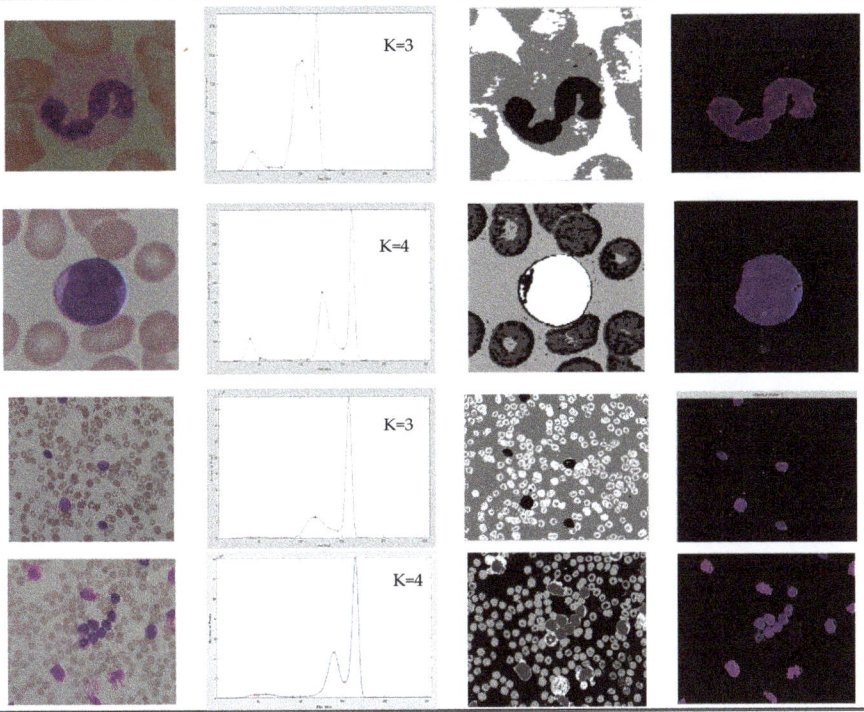

Figure 2. Segmentation results produced by the proposed histogram-based soft covering rough k-means clustering (HSCRKM) algorithm.

In Figure 2, the first column displays the original image, the second column shows the histogram of an image that helps find the number of clusters (K), the third column displays the clustered image, and the last column displays the extracted nucleus. It is observed that if the k value is at its minimum, we get a better segmentation result. This helps reduce the processing time. The parameters utilized in the clustering algorithms are presented in Figure 3.

K-Means Clustering	• K=3, Max Iteration = 500
FCM Clustering	• K=3, v=0.000001, m=2
PSO-based Clustering	• K= 3
HSCRKM Clustering	• $K = Peak\ value\ of\ Histogram\ image$, • $w_{low} = 0.7, w_{bon} = 0.3, and\ \delta = 0.5$

Figure 3. Parameters utilized in clustering algorithms.

Figure 4 shows the sample output of leukemia image segmentation using existing clustering algorithms such as k-means clustering, FCM clustering, and PSO-based clustering algorithms. Here, the number of clusters k is assigned as three using the elbow method.

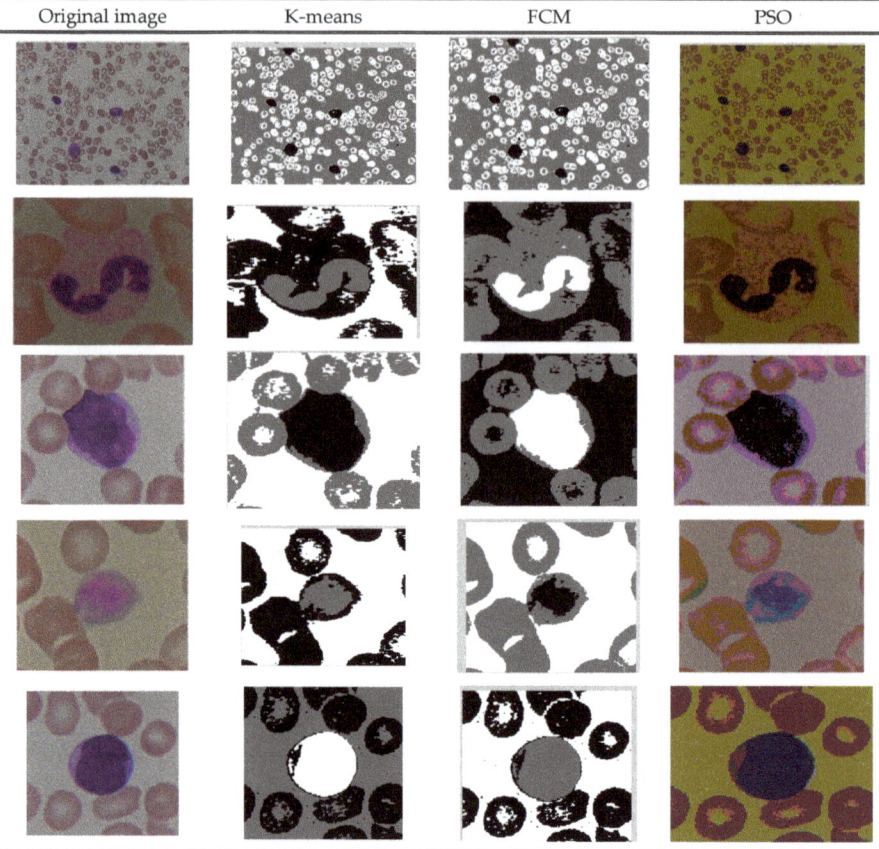

Figure 4. Segmentation results by k-means, FCM, and particle swarm optimization (PSO) algorithms.

4. Results and Discussion

4.1. Dataset

The Acute Lymphoblastic Leukemia Image Database (ALL-IDB) datasets were used for this experiment. These data were downloaded from the website www.dti.unimi.it/fscotti/all/ [33–36]. There were 368 images—175 benign and 193 malignant—taken for this experimental analysis. Digital microscopes are not suitable, since they are usually designed to work in the RGB color space. In the preprocessing step, all the RGB input images are converted into a LAB color space.

4.2. Feature Extraction

The segmented image data were too large, and it was very difficult to process them. Feature extraction is a technique to extract the relevant informative data of a segmented image. This will reduce the processing speed, time, and dimensionality of an image. In this research, 21 shape and color-based features—namely, the area, perimeter, roundness, elongation, form_factor, length_to_diameter_ratio, compactness, discrete_fourier_transform, mean_of_harra_coefficient, h_coefficient, v_coefficient, variance_of_harra_coefficient, h_coefficient, v_coefficient, mean_colour_intensity for red, green, and blue, hue, saturation, value component, and class attribute—were extracted [37]. Twenty-three texture-based features—namely, angular_second_moment, entropy, dissimilarity, contrast, inverse_difference, correlation, homogeneity, autocorrelation, cluster_shade, cluster_prominence, maximum_probability, sum_of_squares, sum_average, sum_variance, sum_entropy, difference_variance, difference_entropy, information_measures_correlation1, information_measures_correlation2, maximal_correlation_ coefficient, inverse_difference_normalized, inverse_difference_moment_normalized, and class attribute were extracted. These features are derived from the gray level co-occurrence matrix (GLCM) in directions 0°, 45°, 90°, and 135° [38,39]. From the literature review, we found that these features are widely used for leukemia image analysis.

4.3. Performance Assessments of Segmentation Algorithms

The empirical results are interpreted in two ways. First, we analyze the efficiency of various clustering-based segmentation algorithms through state-of-the-art machine learning algorithms. Secondly, we compare the machine learning methods using some evaluation measures such as receiver operating characteristic (ROC) curve analysis and kappa statistics. The extracted feature set was fed into the machine learning (ML) prediction algorithms to classify the segments indicating the tumor and non-tumor leukemia in the image. In this experiment, there were seven ML algorithms—namely, logistic regression (LR), naive Bayes (NB), support vector machine (SVM), k-nearest neighborhood (KNN), neural network (NN), random forest (RF), and decision tree (DT)—were used to evaluate the performance of the clustering algorithms.

The performance of the machine learning prediction algorithm was analyzed using various evaluation metrics such as accuracy (A), precision (P), recall (R), F1 measure, area under the ROC Curve (AUC), mean absolute error (MAE), and coefficient of determination (R^2) [40,41]. It is noted that the prediction value of R^2 lies between 0 and 1 for no-fit and perfect fit, respectively.

The classification results of k-means clustering, FCM clustering, PSO-based clustering, and the proposed HSCRKM clustering algorithms are presented in Tables 3–6, respectively. The performance of the segmentation algorithms was analyzed through different machine learning prediction methods. The experimental results show that the proposed method HSCRKM clustering algorithm performs better than the existing algorithms. On a closer look at the overall performance of the proposed method, it is believed that logistic regression and neural network perform well when compared to other prediction algorithms and also produce the highest classification accuracy i.e., 93%. It is also observed that the naive Bayes method produces the lowest classification accuracy rate i.e., 58%.

Table 3 presents the performance analysis of k-means clustering. The LR, NN, and RF algorithms produce the highest classification accuracy of 79%. The NB algorithm gives the minimum accuracy of 65%. KNN and DT produce 72% accuracy and SVM produces 74% accuracy. The overall performance of k-means clustering was 69%, which is computed by the average accuracy of all the datasets with all the ML algorithms.

Table 5 presents the performance analysis of FCM clustering. The LR, DT, and RF algorithms achieve the maximum accuracy value of 88%. Obviously, it gives the lowest mean absolute error (MAE) value. Similar to k-means clustering, the NB algorithm gives the lowest accuracy value of 81% when compared to other algorithms. The SVM and NN give the accuracy of 83% and 84%, respectively. The overall accuracy of FCM clustering is 77%.

Table 3. Performance analysis of k-means clustering. A: accuracy, AUC: area under the receiver operating characteristic curve, DT: decision tree, KNN: k-nearest neighborhood, LR: logistic regression, MAE: mean absolute error, NB: naive Bayes, NN: neural network, P: precision, R: recall, RF: random forest.

ML Algorithms	Dataset	P	R	F1	AUC	MAE	R^2	A
LR	GLCM-0	81.00	77.00	78.00	0.821	0.134	0.195	76.74
	GLCM045	79.00	79.00	78.00	0.660	0.087	0.076	**79.07**
	GLCM-90	60.00	66.00	68.00	0.706	0.112	0.097	65.17
	GLCM-135	70.00	66.00	67.00	0.805	0.128	0.159	67.44
	SC	76.00	74.00	75.00	0.805	0.115	0.152	74.42
NB	GLCM-0	61.00	60.00	61.00	0.738	0.082	0.193	60.47
	GLCM045	62.00	61.00	58.00	0.880	0.093	0.068	60.60
	GLCM-90	54.00	51.00	50.00	0.799	0.128	0.162	51.16
	GLCM-135	60.00	56.00	57.00	0.710	0.088	0.132	55.81
	SC	68.00	65.00	65.00	0.618	0.110	0.047	**65.11**
SVM	GLCM-0	77.00	74.00	71.00	0.805	0.073	0.106	**74.41**
	GLCM045	80.00	72.00	72.00	0.871	0.113	0.323	72.09
	GLCM-90	82.00	70.00	73.00	0.792	0.032	0.143	69.77
	GLCM-135	65.00	65.00	65.00	0.750	0.130	0.372	65.11
	SC	73.00	70.00	67.00	0.692	0.113	0.090	69.78
KNN	GLCM-0	71.00	72.00	72.00	0.928	0.119	0.083	**72.09**
	GLCM045	71.00	67.00	39.00	0.819	0.062	0.169	67.44
	GLCM-90	69.00	67.00	67.00	0.817	0.138	0.162	67.44
	GLCM-135	63.00	63.00	63.00	0.787	0.135	0.162	62.79
	SC	67.00	67.00	67.00	0.839	0.112	0.135	67.44
NN	GLCM-0	79.00	79.00	76.00	0.821	0.077	0.274	**79.06**
	GLCM045	77.00	77.00	77.00	0.806	0.139	0.348	76.74
	GLCM-90	66.00	67.00	69.00	0.859	0.094	0.079	66.66
	GLCM-135	72.00	70.00	71.00	0.817	0.105	0.052	69.69
	SC	65.00	65.00	64.00	0.853	0.116	0.090	65.11
RF	GLCM-0	74.00	72.00	72.00	0.777	0.158	0.288	72.09
	GLCM045	70.00	70.00	69.00	0.761	0.127	0.275	69.77
	GLCM-90	69.00	65.00	65.00	0.798	0.106	0.182	65.11
	GLCM-135	79.00	79.00	79.00	0.805	0.126	0.186	**79.06**
	SC	67.00	67.00	67.00	0.472	0.131	0.342	67.42
DT	GLCM-0	66.00	70.00	66.00	0.865	0.073	0.192	69.76
	GLCM045	80.00	79.00	76.00	0.549	0.093	0.101	79.06
	GLCM-90	71.00	70.00	67.00	0.664	0.118	0.250	69.79
	GLCM-135	72.00	72.00	71.00	0.852	0.118	0.250	**72.09**
	SC	72.00	70.00	71.00	0.817	0.105	0.052	69.69
Average Overall Accuracy								**69%**

Table 4. Performance analysis of FCM clustering.

ML Algorithms	Dataset	P	R	F1	AUC	MAE	R^2	A
LR	GLCM-0	79.00	79.00	76.00	0.802	0.089	0.098	79.06
	GLCM045	89.00	88.00	89.00	0.950	0.080	0.401	**88.37**
	GLCM-90	71.00	72.00	71.00	0.816	0.105	0.185	72.09
	GLCM-135	88.00	86.00	82.00	0.792	0.058	0.156	86.04
	SC	81.00	77.00	78.00	0.821	0.134	0.195	76.74
NB	GLCM-0	75.00	60.00	62.00	0.767	0.076	0.135	60.64
	GLCM045	60.00	60.00	60.00	0.716	0.113	0.143	60.45
	GLCM-90	63.00	63.00	63.00	0.787	0.135	0.162	62.79
	GLCM-135	67.00	67.00	67.00	0.926	0.112	0.135	67.44
	SC	84.00	81.00	81.00	0.825	0.145	0.132	**81.39**

Table 4. Cont.

ML Algorithms	Dataset	P	R	F1	AUC	MAE	R^2	A
SVM	GLCM-0	77.00	74.00	71.00	0.805	0.073	0.106	74.41
	GLCM045	73.00	72.00	72.00	0.655	0.195	0.269	72.09
	GLCM-90	75.00	74.00	73.00	0.822	0.176	0.265	74.41
	GLCM-135	72.00	72.00	72.00	0.766	0.128	0.161	72.09
	SC	83.00	84.00	83.00	0.849	0.053	0.167	**83.72**
KNN	GLCM-0	79.00	79.00	79.00	0.821	0.077	0.274	79.06
	GLCM045	76.00	74.00	74.00	0.812	0.151	0.048	74.41
	GLCM-90	83.00	83.00	84.00	0.893	0.122	0.368	83.72
	GLCM-135	85.00	84.00	85.00	0.866	0.098	0.312	**85.31**
	SC	79.00	80.00	79.00	0.910	0.079	0.171	79.07
NN	GLCM-0	84.00	84.00	84.00	0.745	0.125	0.349	83.72
	GLCM045	87.00	85.00	82.00	0.773	0.148	0.238	**84.84**
	GLCM-90	76.00	74.00	75.00	0.805	0.115	0.152	74.42
	GLCM-135	79.00	79.00	79.00	0.805	0.126	0.186	79.07
	SC	80.00	77.00	77.00	0.771	0.101	0.156	77.18
RF	GLCM-0	77.00	77.00	75.00	0.785	0.080	0.186	76.74
	GLCM045	81.00	86.00	71.00	0.852	0.158	0.437	68.76
	GLCM-90	80.00	77.00	77.00	0.839	0.155	0.248	76.74
	GLCM-135	88.00	88.00	88.00	0.899	0.073	0.114	**88.37**
	SC	86.00	79.00	78.00	0.795	0.086	0.090	79.06
DT	GLCM-0	84.00	83.00	83.00	0.929	0.159	0.265	82.75
	GLCM045	88.00	88.00	88.00	0.953	0.050	0.138	**88.37**
	GLCM-90	81.00	81.00	81.00	0.793	0.115	0.049	81.39
	GLCM-135	87.00	86.00	86.00	0.938	0.064	0.053	86.04
	SC	85.00	81.00	76.00	0.813	0.131	0.095	81.39
	Average Overall Accuracy							77%

Table 5 shows the efficiency of the algorithm for PSO-based clustering. In this table, it is noted that the NN method attains 90% accuracy. The LR, SVM, KNN, and RF methods give above 80% of the classification accuracy. The NB algorithm again provides the minimum accuracy of 67%. The overall classification accuracy of PSO-based clustering is 78%.

Table 5. Performance analysis of PSO-based clustering.

ML Algorithms	Dataset	P	R	F1	AUC	MAE	R^2	A
LR	GLCM-0	86.00	81.00	82.00	0.717	0.141	0.279	81.39
	GLCM045	88.00	86.00	85.00	0.741	0.150	0.060	**86.04**
	GLCM-90	84.00	79.00	76.00	0.739	0.143	0.095	79.06
	GLCM-135	90.00	86.00	86.00	0.963	0.065	0.093	**86.04**
	SC	86.00	81.00	82.00	0.793	0.092	0.334	81.39
NB	GLCM-0	69.00	67.00	68.00	0.833	0.082	0.098	**67.44**
	GLCM045	60.00	64.00	66.00	0.713	0.118	0.129	63.63
	GLCM-90	56.00	61.00	58.00	0.880	0.093	0.068	60.61
	GLCM-135	64.00	64.00	65.00	0.764	0.012	0.165	63.63
	SC	61.00	62.00	62.00	0.876	0.118	0.148	62.69
SVM	GLCM-0	84.00	79.00	76.00	0.739	0.143	0.095	79.07
	GLCM045	79.00	79.00	78.00	0.827	0.085	0.142	79.06
	GLCM-90	71.00	72.00	71.00	0.816	0.105	0.185	72.09
	GLCM-135	76.00	77.00	72.00	0.807	0.086	0.192	76.74
	SC	81.00	81.00	79.00	0.801	0.120	0.167	**81.39**

Table 5. Cont.

ML Algorithms	Dataset	P	R	F1	AUC	MAE	R^2	A
KNN	GLCM-0	82.00	79.00	80.00	0.811	0.123	0.017	79.06
	GLCM045	71.00	73.00	71.00	0.864	0.082	0.108	72.72
	GLCM-90	70.00	67.00	68.00	0.816	0.141	0.526	67.44
	GLCM-135	75.00	74.00	73.00	0.822	0.176	0.265	74.41
	SC	82.00	81.00	81.00	0.788	0.118	0.147	**80.66**
NN	GLCM-0	62.00	76.00	68.00	0.726	0.075	0.448	75.44
	GLCM045	61.00	73.00	66.00	0.848	0.123	0.261	72.12
	GLCM-90	88.00	84.00	83.00	0.849	0.053	0.167	83.72
	GLCM-135	91.00	91.00	91.00	0.929	0.062	0.210	**90.67**
	SC	86.00	86.00	86.00	0.950	0.070	0.070	86.12
RF	GLCM-0	84.00	81.00	81.00	0.825	0.145	0.135	**81.39**
	GLCM045	74.00	79.00	74.00	0.885	0.114	0.264	78.77
	GLCM-90	79.00	70.00	79.00	0.747	0.139	0.102	79.65
	GLCM-135	78.00	78.00	77.00	0.917	0.082	0.538	77.47
	SC	81.00	81.00	81.00	0.841	0.097	0.056	**81.39**
DT	GLCM-0	87.00	84.00	80.00	0.717	0.115	0.207	83.72
	GLCM045	89.00	88.00	89.00	0.929	0.081	0.229	**88.37**
	GLCM-90	87.00	85.00	82.00	0.662	0.086	0.125	84.84
	GLCM-135	82.00	82.00	82.00	0.950	0.102	0.214	81.82
	SC	90.00	88.00	88.00	0.926	0.103	0.221	88.37
Average Overall Accuracy								**78%**

The performance analysis of the HSCRKM algorithm is shown in Table 6. The LR, NN, and DT algorithms achieve 93% classification accuracy. NB, KNN, and RF give accuracy values of 84%, 85%, and 86%, respectively. It is also interesting to note that the SVM gives the minimum accuracy, i.e., 84%. The overall accuracy of the HSCRKM algorithm is 82%. The proposed method leads the accuracy of 13% for k-means clustering, 5% for FCM, and 4% for PSO-based clustering. It means that the accurate segmentation produces the best performance. The experimental results show that the HSCRKM algorithm accurately segments the nucleus. From the literature review report, the various authors produce above 90% accuracy. However, they are using a very small number of images for the experiments. In this research, around 350 images are used to evaluate the performance of the proposed HSCRKM algorithm.

Table 6. Performance analysis of the HSCRKM algorithm.

ML Algorithms	Dataset	P	R	F1	AUC	MAE	R^2	A
LR	GLCM-0	84.00	84.00	85.00	0.848	0.017	0.214	84.72
	GLCM045	93.00	93.00	93.00	0.944	0.072	0.584	**93.02**
	GLCM-90	87.00	86.00	86.00	0.825	0.032	0.219	87.65
	GLCM-135	89.00	88.00	88.00	0.899	0.112	0.427	88.37
	SC	86.00	85.00	85.00	0.965	0.047	0.138	85.65
NB	GLCM-0	70.00	70.00	70.00	0.848	0.190	0.133	69.76
	GLCM045	67.00	65.00	65.00	0.782	0.128	0.171	65.11
	GLCM-90	67.00	65.00	65.00	0.782	0.128	0.171	65.11
	GLCM-135	61.00	58.00	56.00	0.750	0.152	0.131	58.13
	SC	84.00	84.00	85.00	0.848	0.017	0.214	**84.72**
SVM	GLCM-0	84.00	81.00	81.00	0.760	0.140	0.206	81.39
	GLCM045	84.00	81.00	81.00	0.760	0.140	0.206	81.36
	GLCM-90	79.00	79.00	79.00	0.768	0.321	0.341	79.06
	GLCM-135	80.00	74.00	73.00	0.780	0.132	0.122	74.41
	SC	86.00	84.00	84.00	0.967	0.089	0.312	**83.92**

Table 6. *Cont.*

ML Algorithms	Dataset	P	R	F1	AUC	MAE	R^2	A
KNN	GLCM-0	86.00	84.00	84.00	0.967	0.072	0.309	83.92
	GLCM045	82.00	81.00	81.00	0.952	0.097	0.291	81.39
	GLCM-90	75.00	72.00	71.00	0.727	0.127	0.102	72.09
	GLCM-135	77.00	77.00	76.00	0.911	0.101	0.151	76.74
	SC	86.00	85.00	85.00	0965	0.047	0.138	**85.65**
NN	GLCM-0	86.00	86.00	86.00	0.982	0.070	0.135	86.04
	GLCM045	91.00	91.00	90.00	0.950	0.054	0.274	90.69
	GLCM-90	84.00	84.00	85.00	0.848	0.017	0.138	84.72
	GLCM-135	93.00	93.00	93.00	0.939	0.074	0.526	**93.02**
	SC	86.00	87.00	86.00	0.965	0.047	0.138	85.65
RF	GLCM-0	82.00	81.00	81.00	0.860	0.174	0.331	81.39
	GLCM045	86.00	85.00	85.00	0.965	0.047	0.138	85.65
	GLCM-90	82.00	81.00	81.00	0.890	0.441	0.321	81.39
	GLCM-135	84.00	84.00	85.00	0.848	0.017	0.214	84.72
	SC	86.00	87.00	86.00	0.913	0.144	0.225	**86.05**
DT	GLCM-0	84.00	84.00	85.00	0.848	0.017	0.214	84.72
	GLCM045	93.00	93.00	93.00	0.944	0.072	0.584	**93.02**
	GLCM-90	86.00	84.00	84.00	0.967	0.072	0.309	83.72
	GLCM-135	89.00	88.00	88.00	0.899	0.112	0.427	88.72
	SC	91.00	91.00	90.00	0.930	0.072	0.297	90.69
Average Overall Accuracy								**82%**

Figure 5 shows the overall prediction accuracy for various machine learning algorithms. With respect to k-means clustering, all the machine learning algorithms produce the lowest prediction accuracy i.e., below 80%. It is noted that with respect to PSO and FCM, some of the ML methods (i.e., logistic regression, random forest, and decision tree) attain above 80% prediction accuracy. With respect to the HSCRKM clustering algorithm, most of the ML methods (except naive Bayes) achieve above 80% prediction accuracy. It can also be inferred that the proposed HSCRKM clustering algorithm efficiently segment the nucleus, and the extracted features (based on the segments) probably increase the prediction accuracy. To interpret the experimental results, we are manually preserving the best accuracy range as above 80%.

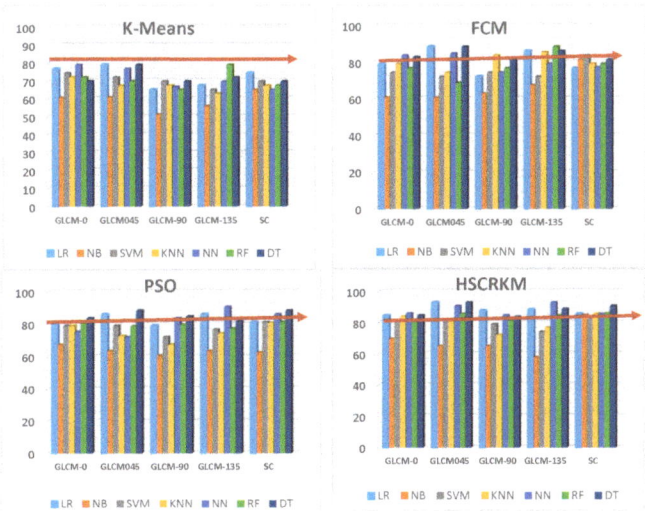

Figure 5. Overall prediction accuracy.

4.4. Performance Assessments of Machine Learning Algorithms

4.4.1. Kappa Statistics

Figure 6 shows a comparison of the performances for various prediction algorithms and the proposed HSCRKM algorithm in terms of Cohen's kappa value [42], which is a statistical measure used to evaluate the inter-rater reliability of the classifier. The reliability rate lies on a 0 to 1 scale, where "1" means perfect agreement and less than "1" means less than perfect agreement. With respect to the shape and color-based feature dataset, the proposed algorithm produces a substantial agreement range [43] (i.e., 0.61 to 0.80) amidst all the existing prediction algorithms taken up for study. Compared with other machine learning algorithms, neural networks have the capability to learn and model nonlinear and complex relationships. It also has the ability to perceive all possible interactions between predictor variables and the availability of multiple training algorithms. From the figure, it is noted that the neural network algorithm produces the highest kappa value (i.e., 0.67 to 0.85), which means perfect agreement for prediction. It also produces the highest classification accuracy when compared with other machine learning algorithms.

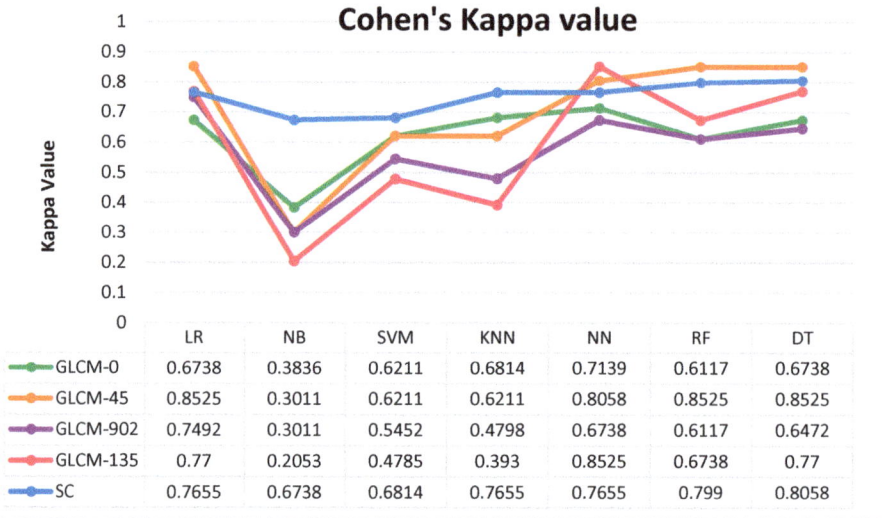

Figure 6. Kappa value for HSCRKM clustering.

4.4.2. ROC Curve Analysis

Receiver operating characteristic (ROC) curve analysis is a widely used validation method to evaluate the diagnostic ability of the various prediction algorithms [44]. It can be generated by plotting the cumulative distribution function of the true positive rate versus the false positive rate. If the ROC curve of the prediction algorithm appears in the top left corner, then the algorithm accurately predicts disease. If it is closer to the diagonal line, then the performance of the prediction algorithm is less accurate. Figure 7 depicts the ROC curve analysis for the proposed algorithm HSCRKM. The ROC curve is generated for all the extracted datasets, namely GLCM_0, GLCM_45, GLCM_90, GLCM_135, and Shape_Colour. From Figure 6, we inferred that the shape and color-based feature datasets produce the highest accuracy values when compared to another dataset. It is noted that decision tree, random forest, and SVM attain similar prediction accuracy. So, the curves appear in the same orientation. It is also noted that the neural network (NN) and logistic regression (LR) algorithms performed better than the other machine learning algorithms. Those algorithms curve lines almost appeared in the top left corner of the graph. The naive Bayes algorithm curve line is executed near the diagonal line. So, this method probably attains minimum accuracy compared to the other ML algorithms.

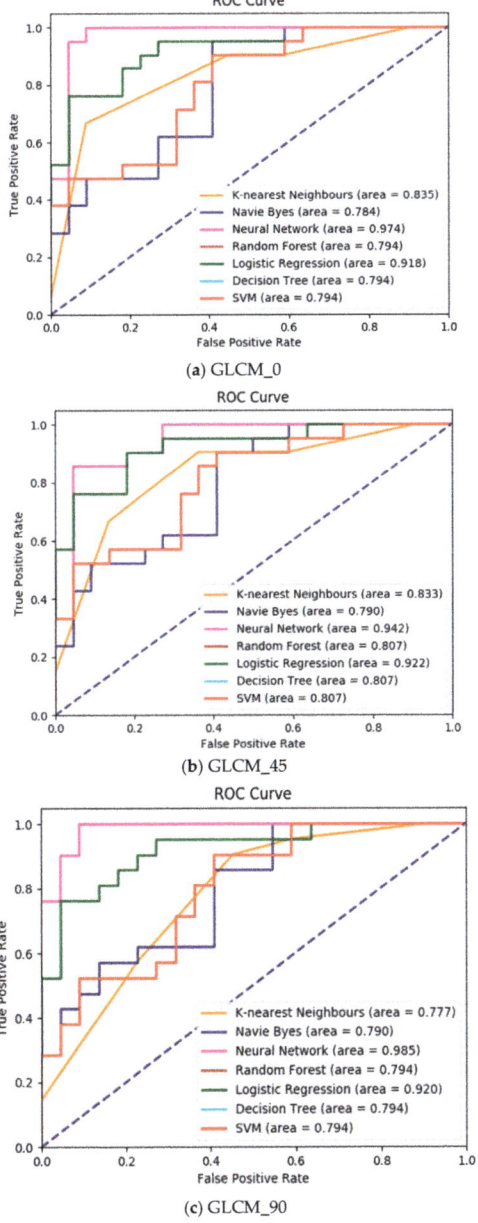

(a) GLCM_0

(b) GLCM_45

(c) GLCM_90

Figure 7. *Cont.*

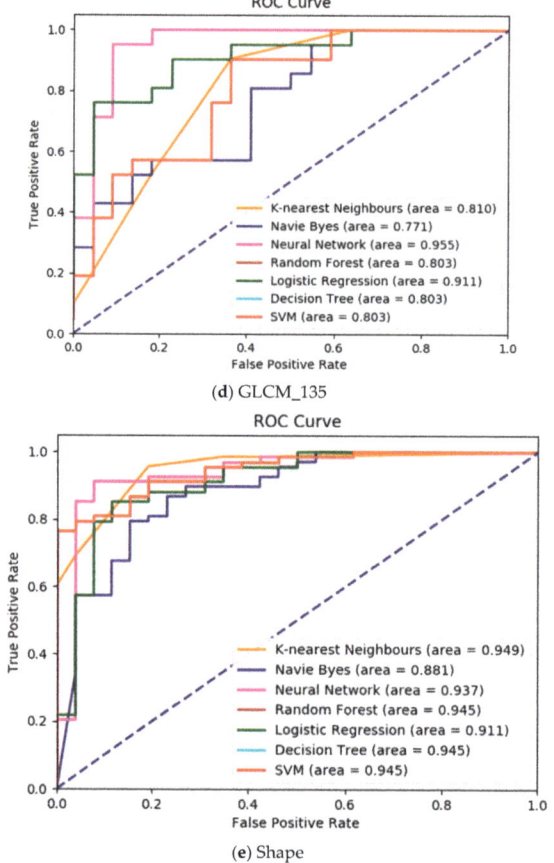

(d) GLCM_135

(e) Shape

Figure 7. ROC curve analysis for HSCRKM clustering.

5. Conclusions and Future Work

Clustering is an unsupervised classification method that is widely employed for image segmentation. Throughout the present research, a hybrid histogram-based soft covering rough k-means clustering algorithm is proposed to segment the image of the leukemia nucleus. In this method, the histogram is used to initialize the number of clusters. The main advantage of this method is that it applies the soft covering rough approximation instead of rough approximation. It is a new kind of soft rough set that efficiently deals with uncertainties. The results are interpreted in the following two ways. (1) The efficiency of the proposed technique is compared with the popular and frequently used clustering algorithms such as k-means clustering, FCM, and PSO-based clustering. (2) The state-of-the-art prediction techniques in machine learning (ML) were compared using evolution metrics.

From the experimental results, it is inferred that the HSCRKM clustering algorithm and all of the ML methods (except for naive Bayes) achieve above 80% prediction accuracy. It is also noted that logistic regression and neural network provide on average above 90% accuracy, which performs better than other prediction methods. The limitation of this method is that when we go for multiple color images such as satellite images, agricultural images, photographs etc., the number of peak values in the histogram is increased, and consequently the processing time is also increased. This method is more suitable for the segmentation of medical images and the extraction of specific portions with high clarity (for deep study). In the future, bio-inspired algorithms could be used to optimize the number of clusters.

Author Contributions: Conceptualization, J.G., A.T.A., and H.I.H.; methodology, J.G., A.T.A.; software, J.G.; validation, J.G., A.T.A., and H.I.H.; formal analysis, A.T.A. and H.I.H.; investigation, H.I.H.; resources, H.I.H.; data curation, J.G.; writing—original draft preparation, J.G., A.T.A., and H.I.H.; writing—review and editing, A.T.A. and H.I.H.; visualization, J.G.; funding acquisition, A.T.A. All authors have read and agreed to the published version of the manuscript.

Funding: This research is funded by Prince Sultan University, Riyadh, Saudi Arabia.

Acknowledgments: The authors would like to thank Prince Sultan University, Riyadh, Saudi Arabia for supporting and funding this work. Special acknowledgment to Robotics and Internet-of-Things Lab (RIOTU) at Prince Sultan University, Riyadh, SA. In addition, the authors wish to acknowledge the editor and anonymous reviewers for their insightful comments, which have improved the quality of this publication.

Conflicts of Interest: The authors declare no conflict of interest.

References

1. Surveillance, Epidemiology, and End Results (SEER). Cancer Stat Facts: Leukemia. Available online: https://seer.cancer.gov/statfacts/html/leuks.html (accessed on 3 January 2020).
2. Arora, R.S.; Arora, B. Acute leukemia in children: A review of the current Indian data. *South Asian J. Cancer* **2016**, *5*, 155. [CrossRef] [PubMed]
3. National Centre for Disease Informatics and Research. Available online: http://ncdirindia.org/ (accessed on 3 January 2020).
4. Pawlak, Z. Rough sets. *Int. J. Comput. Inf. Sci.* **1982**, *11*, 341–356. [CrossRef]
5. Zhu, W.; Wang, F. On three types of covering-based rough sets. *IEEE Trans. Knowl. Data Eng.* **2007**, *19*, 1131–1143. [CrossRef]
6. Zhu, W. Topological approaches to covering rough sets. *Inf. Sci.* **2007**, *177*, 1499–1508. [CrossRef]
7. Kumar, S.S.; Inbarani, H.H.; Azar, A.T.; Polat, K. Covering-based rough set classification system. *Neural Comput. Appl.* **2017**, *28*, 2879–2888. [CrossRef]
8. Molodtsov, D. Soft set theory—first results. *Comput. Math. Appl.* **1999**, *37*, 19–31. [CrossRef]
9. Maji, P.K.; Biswas, R.; Roy, A. Softset theory. *Comput. Math. Appl.* **2003**, *45*, 555–562. [CrossRef]
10. Yüksel, Ş.; Güzel Ergül, Z.; Tozlu, N. Soft covering based rough sets and their application. *Sci. World J.* **2014**. [CrossRef]
11. Jothi, G.; Hannah Inbarani, H. Leukemia Nucleus Image Segmentation Using Covering-Based Rough K-Means Clustering Algorithm. In Proceedings of the International Conference on Intelligent Computing Systems, Tamilnadu, India, 15–16 December 2017; pp. 373–385.
12. Zhang, G.P. Neural networks for classification: A survey. *IEEE Trans. Syst. Man Cybern. Part C* **2000**, *30*, 451–462. [CrossRef]
13. Mitchell, T.M. *Machine Learning*; McGraw Hill: Burr Ridge, IL, USA, 1997; Volume 45, pp. 870–877.
14. Cortes, C.; Vapnik, V. Support-vector networks. *Mach. Learn.* **1995**, *20*, 273–297. [CrossRef]
15. Friedman, N.; Geiger, D.; Goldszmidt, M. Bayesian network classifiers. *Mach. Learn.* **1997**, *29*, 131–163. [CrossRef]
16. Liaw, A.; Matthew, W. Classification and regression by random Forest. *R News* **2002**, *2*, 18–22.
17. Patel, N.; Mishra, A. Automated Leukaemia Detection Using Microscopic Images. *Procedia Comput. Sci.* **2015**, *58*, 635–642. [CrossRef]
18. Srisukkham, W.; Zhang, L.; Neoh, S.C.; Todryk, S.; Lim, C.P. Intelligent leukaemia diagnosis with bare-bones PSO based feature optimization. *Appl. Soft Comput.* **2017**, *56*, 405–419. [CrossRef]
19. Su, J.; Liu, S.; Song, J. A segmentation method based on HMRF for the aided diagnosis of acute myeloid leukemia. *Comput. Methods Programs Biomed.* **2017**, *152*, 115–123. [CrossRef] [PubMed]
20. Kaya, I.E.; Pehlivanlı, A.Ç.; Sekizkardeş, E.G.; Ibrikci, T. PCA based clustering for brain tumor segmentation of T1w MRI images. *Comput. Methods Programs Biomed.* **2017**, *140*, 19–28. [CrossRef]
21. Cabria, I.; Gondra, I. MRI segmentation fusion for brain tumor detection. *Inf. Fusion* **2017**, *36*, 1–9. [CrossRef]
22. Küçükkülahlı, E.; Erdoğmuş, P.; Polat, K. Histogram-based automatic segmentation of images. *Neural Comput. Appl.* **2016**, *27*, 1445–1450. [CrossRef]

23. Namburu, A.; kumar Samay, S.; Edara, S.R. Soft fuzzy rough set-based MR brain image segmentation. *Appl. Soft Comput.* **2017**, *54*, 456–466. [CrossRef]
24. Ali, M.; Khan, M.; Tung, N.T. Segmentation of Dental X-ray Images in Medical Imaging using Neutrosophic Orthogonal Matrices. *Expert Syst. Appl.* **2018**, *91*, 434–441. [CrossRef]
25. Rundo, L.; Militello, C.; Russo, G.; D'Urso, D.; Valastro, L.M.; Garufi, A.; Gilardi, M.C. Fully Automatic Multispectral MR Image Segmentation of Prostate Gland Based on the Fuzzy C-Means Clustering Algorithm. In *Multidisciplinary Approaches to Neural Computing. Smart Innovation, Systems and Technologies*; Esposito, A., Faudez-Zanuy, M., Eds.; Springer: Cham, Switzerland, 2017; Volume 69, pp. 23–37.
26. Zhang, P.; Lu, S.; Li, J.; Zhang, P.; Xie, L.; Xue, H.; Zhang, J. Multi-component segmentation of X-ray computed tomography (CT) image using multi-Otsu thresholding algorithm and scanning electron microscopy. *Energy Explor. Exploit.* **2017**, *35*, 281–294. [CrossRef]
27. Ganesh, M.; Naresh, M.; Arvind, C. MRI Brain Image Segmentation Using Enhanced Adaptive Fuzzy K-Means Algorithm. *Intell. Autom. Soft Comput.* **2017**, *23*, 325–330. [CrossRef]
28. Kaur, P. Intuitionistic fuzzy sets based credibilistic fuzzy C-means clustering for medical image segmentation. *Int. J. Inf. Technol.* **2017**. [CrossRef]
29. Dhane, D.M.; Maity, M.; Mungle, T.; Bar, C.; Achar, A.; Kolekar, M.; Chakraborty, C. Fuzzy spectral clustering for automated delineation of chronic wound region using digital images. *Comput. Biol. Med.* **2017**, *89*, 551–560.
30. Ahmed, N.; Yigit, A.; Isik, Z.; Alpkocak, A. Identification of Leukemia Subtypes from Microscopic Images Using Convolutional Neural Network. *Diagnostics* **2019**, *9*, 104. [CrossRef]
31. Yüksel, Ş.; Tozlu, N.; Dizman, T.H. An application of multicriteria group decision making by soft covering based rough sets. *Filomat* **2015**, *29*, 209–219. [CrossRef]
32. Peters, G. Some refinements of rough k-means clustering. *Pattern Recognit.* **2006**, *39*, 1481–1491. [CrossRef]
33. Labati, R.D.; Piuri, V.; Scotti, F. ALL-IDB: The Acute Lymphoblastic Leukemia Image Database for Image Processing. In Proceedings of the IEEE International Conference on Image Processing (ICIP), Brussels, Belgium, 11–14 September 2011.
34. Scotti, F. Robust Segmentation and Measurements Techniques of White Cells in Blood Microscope Images. In Proceedings of the IEEE Instrumentation and Measurement Technology Conference, Sorrento, Italy, 24–27 April 2006; pp. 43–48.
35. Scotti, F. Automatic morphological analysis for acute leukemia identification in peripheral blood microscope images. In Proceedings of the IEEE International Conference on Computational Intelligence for Measurement Systems and Applications, Giardini Naxos, Italy, 20–22 July 2005; pp. 96–101.
36. Piuri, V.; Scotti, F. Morphological classification of blood leucocytes by microscope images. In Proceedings of the IEEE International Conference on Computational Intelligence for Measurement Systems and Applications, Boston, MA, USA, 14–16 July 2004; pp. 103–108.
37. Jothi, G.; Inbarani, H.H. Hybrid Tolerance Rough Set–Firefly based supervised feature selection for MRI brain tumor image classification. *Appl. Soft Comput.* **2016**, *46*, 639–651.
38. Jothi, G.; Inbarani, H.H.; Azar, A.T. Hybrid Tolerance Rough Set: PSO Based Supervised Feature Selection for Digital Mammogram Images. *Int. J. Fuzzy Syst. Appl.* **2013**, *3*, 15–30. [CrossRef]
39. Jothi, G.; Inbarani, H.H. Soft set based feature selection approach for lung cancer images. *arXiv* **2012**, arXiv:1212.5391.
40. Inbarani, H.H.; Azar, A.T.; Jothi, G. Supervised hybrid feature selection based on PSO and rough sets for medical diagnosis. *Comput. Methods Programs Biomed.* **2014**, *113*, 175–185. [CrossRef] [PubMed]
41. Ganesan, J.; Inbarani, H.H.; Azar, A.T.; Polat, K. Tolerance rough set firefly-based quick reduct. *Neural Comput. Appl.* **2017**, *28*, 2995–3008. [CrossRef]
42. Landis, J.R.; Koch, G.G. The measurement of observer agreement for categorical data. *Biometrics* **1977**, *33*, 159–174. [CrossRef] [PubMed]
43. Viera, A.J.; Garrett, J.M. Understanding interobserver agreement: The kappa statistic. *Fam. Med.* **2005**, *37*, 360–363.
44. Fawcett, T. An introduction to ROC analysis. *Pattern Recognit. Lett.* **2006**, *27*, 861–874. [CrossRef]

© 2020 by the authors. Licensee MDPI, Basel, Switzerland. This article is an open access article distributed under the terms and conditions of the Creative Commons Attribution (CC BY) license (http://creativecommons.org/licenses/by/4.0/).

Article

Blended Multi-Modal Deep ConvNet Features for Diabetic Retinopathy Severity Prediction

Jyostna Devi Bodapati [1], Veeranjaneyulu Naralasetti [2], Shaik Nagur Shareef [1], Saqib Hakak [3], Muhammad Bilal [4], Praveen Kumar Reddy Maddikunta [5] and Ohyun Jo [6,*]

- [1] Department of CSE, Vignan's Foundation for Science Technology and Research, Guntur 522213, India; jyostna.bodapati82@gmail.com (J.D.B.); shaiknagurshareef6@gmail.com (S.N.S.)
- [2] Department of IT, Vignan's Foundation for Science Technology and Research, Guntur 522213, India; veeru2006n@gmail.com
- [3] Faculty of Computer Science, University of Northern British Columbia, Prince George, BC V2N 4Z9, Canada; saqib.hakak@unbc.ca
- [4] Department of Computer and Electronics Systems Engineering, Hankuk University of Foreign Studies, Yongin-si 17035, Korea; m.bilal@ieee.org
- [5] School of Information Technology and Engineering, The Vellore Institute of Technology (VIT), Vellore 632014, India; praveenkumarreddy@vit.ac.in
- [6] Department of Computer Science, College of Electrical and Computer Engineering, Chungbuk National University, Cheongju 28644, Korea
- * Correspondence: ohyunjo@chungbuk.ac.kr

Received: 3 May 2020; Accepted: 28 May 2020; Published: 30 May 2020

Abstract: Diabetic Retinopathy (DR) is one of the major causes of visual impairment and blindness across the world. It is usually found in patients who suffer from diabetes for a long period. The major focus of this work is to derive optimal representation of retinal images that further helps to improve the performance of DR recognition models. To extract optimal representation, features extracted from multiple pre-trained ConvNet models are blended using proposed multi-modal fusion module. These final representations are used to train a Deep Neural Network (DNN) used for DR identification and severity level prediction. As each ConvNet extracts different features, fusing them using 1D pooling and cross pooling leads to better representation than using features extracted from a single ConvNet. Experimental studies on benchmark Kaggle APTOS 2019 contest dataset reveals that the model trained on proposed blended feature representations is superior to the existing methods. In addition, we notice that cross average pooling based fusion of features from Xception and VGG16 is the most appropriate for DR recognition. With the proposed model, we achieve an accuracy of 97.41%, and a kappa statistic of 94.82 for DR identification and an accuracy of 81.7% and a kappa statistic of 71.1% for severity level prediction. Another interesting observation is that DNN with dropout at input layer converges more quickly when trained using blended features, compared to the same model trained using uni-modal deep features.

Keywords: diabetic retinopathy (DR); pre-trained deep ConvNet; uni-modal deep features; multi-modal deep features; transfer learning; 1D pooling; cross pooling

1. Introduction

Diabetic Retinopathy (DR) is an adverse effect of Diabetes Mellitus (DM) [1] that leads to permanent blindness in humans. It is usually caused by the damage to blood vessels that provide nourishment to light-sensitive tissue called the retina. As per statistics [2], DR is the fifth leading cause for blindness across the globe. According to the World Health Organization (WHO), in 2013, around 382 million people were suffering from DR, and this number may rise to 592 million by 2025. It is possible to save many people from going blind if DR is identified in the early stages. Small lesions are formed in the eyes of DR-affected people and the type of lesions formed decides the level of severity of DR. Figure 1a shows types of lesions that include Micro Aneurysms (MA), exudates, hemorrhages, cotton wool spots, and improperly grown blood vessels on the retina.

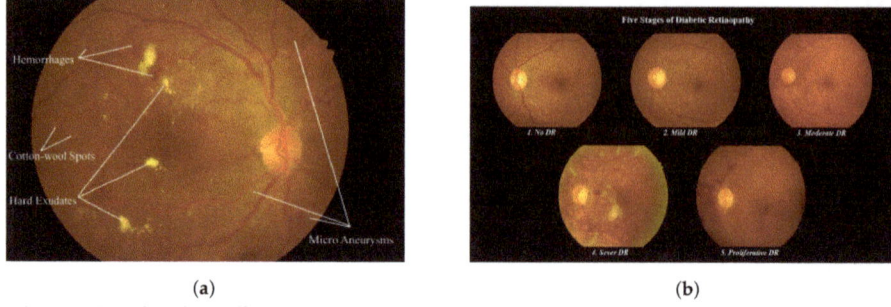

Figure 1. Samples of DR-affected fundus images: (**a**) types of lesions formed; and (**b**) levels of severity.

DR can be categorized into five different stages [3]: no DR (Class 0), mild DR (Class 1), moderate DR (Class 2), severe DR (Class 3), and proliferative DR (Class 4). Sample retinal images with different severity levels of DR are shown in Figure 1b. Mild DR is the early stage during which the formation of Micro Aneurysms (MA) can be observed. As the disease progresses to moderate stage, swelling of blood vessels can be found, which leads to blurred vision. During the later non-proliferative DR (NPDR) stage, abnormal growth of blood vessels can be noticed. This stage is severe due to the blockage of a large number of blood vessels. Proliferative DR (PDR) is the advanced stage of DR; during this stage, retinal detachment along with large retinal break can be observed that leads to complete vision loss [4].

In traditional DR diagnosis approaches, manual grading of the retinal scan is required to identify the presence or absence of retinopathy. If DR is confirmed as positive, further diagnosis is recommended to identify severity level of the disease. This kind of diagnosis is quite expensive and time consuming as it demands human expertise. If DR identification is automated, then diagnosis of the disease becomes affordable to many people. In the recent past, several machine learning tools have been introduced to address this problem.

Early approaches to DR identification, where the presence or absence of DR is revealed, focuses on spotting the Hard Exudates (HEs). A dynamic threshold based Support Vector Machine (SVM) is used to segment HE in the retinal images [5]. Fuzzy C-means is used to detect HE and SVM is used to identify severity level of the disease to make the system more sophisticated [6]. SVM-based classifiers are adapted to find cotton wool spots in the retinal images.

With the introduction of deep learning, the focus of researchers has shifted from spotting HEs to MAs. A two-step CNN has been introduced to segment MAs in the given retinal scans [7]. Another CNN architecture that is trained using selective sampling approach is proposed to detect hemorrhages [8]. A max-out activation is introduced to improve the performance of a DNN model, for which DR is used as an application to find MA [9]. Recently, a bounding box based approach has been introduced to identify the region of interest in the retinal images [10]. Although many methods are available in the literature, they are either sub-optimal or complex. Hence, there is a need for a solution that is simple and robust.

The objective of this work is to design a simple and robust deep learning-based approach to recognize DR from the given retinal images. The major focus of this work is to obtain a better feature representation of the retinal images, which ultimately leads to a better model. To accomplish this, we propose uni- and multi-modal approaches. Initially, for the given retinal images, deep features are extracted from different pre-trained ConvNets such as VGG16, NASNet, Xception, and Inception ResNetV2. In the uni-modal approach, features extracted from a single pre-trained ConvNet gives the final feature representation. In the multi-modal approach, our idea is to blend the deep features extracted from multiple ConvNets to get the final feature representation. We propose different pooling-based approaches to blend multiple deep features. To check the efficiency of our feature representation, a Deep Neural Network (DNN) architecture is proposed for identification of DR (Task 1) and to recognize severity level of DR (Task 2). We observe that, in the multi-modal approach, blending deep features from Xception and Inception ResNet V2 outperforms others in both tasks. Another interesting observation is that there is a drop in the number of false positives, which is most desirable. Experimental studies on the benchmark APTOS 2019 dataset revealed that our blended feature representations trained using DNN model give superior performance compared to the existing methods.

The following are the major contributions of the proposed work:

- Effectiveness of the uni-modal feature representation is verified.
- A blended multi-modal feature representation approach is introduced
- Different pool-based approaches are proposed to blend deep features.
- A DNN architecture with dropout at the input layer is proposed to test the efficiency of the proposed uni-modal and blended multi-modal feature representations.
- APTOS 2019 benchmark dataset was used to compare the performance of the proposed approach with existing models.

2. Related Work

Recently, machine learning models are very popular to solve various problems such as image classification [11], text processing [12], real-time fault diagnosis [13], and healthcare tasks [14,15]. It is very common to use ML algorithms to address disease prediction [16–18].

In this section, we report various conventional models available in the literature for the task of DR recognition. In [19], an easy to remember scientific approach is introduced for DR severity identification. In [20], the authors presented a hybrid classifier by using both GMM and SVM as an ensemble model to improve the accuracy of the model. The same approach has been modified by augmenting the feature set with shape, intensity, and statistics of the affected region [21]. A random forest-based approach is proposed in [22,23] and segmentation-based approaches are proposed in [24]. In [25], a genetic algorithm-based feature extraction method is introduced. Different shallow classifiers such as GMM, KNN, SVM, and AdaBoost have been analyzed [26] to differentiate lesions from non-lesions. A hybrid feature extraction based approach is used in [27].

In the next few lines, deep learning models available in the literature for the task of DR severity identification are introduced. A large dataset consisting of 1,28,175 retinal images is used and trained using deep CNN. In [28], data augmentation method is used to generate the data on CNN architecture. Fuzzy models are used in [29]; a hybrid model that is designed based on fuzzy logic, Hough Transform, and numerous extraction methods are implemented as part of their system. A combination of fuzzy C-means and deep CNN architectures are used in [30]. A Siamese convolutional neural network is used in [31] to detect diabetic retinopathy.

With the introduction of deep learning models, focus has shifted to deep feature-based models. In [32], used features extracted from different layers of pre-trained ConvNets such as VGG19 and further applied PCA and SVD on those features for dimension reduction [33] to avoid overfitting. In the case of former models, the model is not robust, and, in the latter case, the models are robust, but large datasets are needed to train them. A PCA based fire-fly model [34] along with deep neural network is used for DR detection in [35], and the UCI repository is used for the experiments.

The performance of any ML algorithm is subject to the features extracted from the given data. Conventional ML models need a separate algorithm (GIST, HOG, and SIFT) for feature learning and give a global or local representation of the images and the features. Features extracted in this process are known as handcrafted features. Until the entry of deep learning models, these handcrafted features were dominant and being widely used for feature extraction.

Deep ConvNets for Feature Extraction and Transfer Learning

Deep learning models [36–38] learn the essential characteristics of the input images. This exceptional capability of the deep models make them representation models, as they can represent the data efficiently and reduce the use of the additional feature extraction phase where features are handcrafted. Deeper layers of the CNN models can represent the entire given input more efficiently than the early layers.

The downside of the deep learning models is that they need enormous amounts of data for training, which is usually scarce for most real-time applications. This problem can be addressed by the introduction of transfer learning, where the knowledge gained by a deep learning model can be transferred to other models. To achieve this, deep pre-trained CNN models such as VGG16 and ResNet152 are available for transfer learning. Pre-trained models are the models that are trained on large amounts of data, and the weights updated during the training of the complex model can be applied to similar kinds of tasks.

There are different types of pre-trained models which are trained on large scale datasets, such as ImageNet that consists of more than a million images. Popular pre-trained deep CNN models such as VGG16, VGG19, ResNet152, InceptionV3, Xception, NASNet, Inception ResNet V2 and DarkNet are briefly described below:

- **Visual Geometric Group (VGG 16):** VGG16 is a deep ConvNet trained on 14 million images belonging to 1000 different classes and topped the leader board in ILSVR (ImageNet) challenge. In this architecture, 2×2 filters are used with stride 1 for convolution operation, and 2×2 filters with stride two and the same padding are used for max-pooling operation across the network. At the end of architecture, two fully connected dense layers of 4096 neurons are connected followed by soft-max layer.
- **Neural Architecture Search Network (NASNet):** This is a special kind of deep CNN which searches for a better architectural building block on small datasets such as CIFAR10 and transfers it to larger datasets such as ImageNet. It has a better regularization mechanism called scheduled drop path, which significantly improves generalization.
- **Xception:** Xception is another deep ConvNet architecture that supports depth-wise separable convolution operations and outperformed ResNet and InceptionV3 in the ILSVR challenge.
- **Inception ResNetV2:** This is popularly known as InceptionV4, as it combines two different architectures: InceptionV3 and ResNet152. It has both inception and residual connections, which boost the performance of the model.

Deep neural networks give excellent performance only when trained with extensive data. If the data used to train are not sufficient, then the DNN models tend to overfit. Deep, convolutional neural networks are introduced in [39] for the task of scalable image recognition. Xception, a deep CNN, is developed using depth-wise separable convolutions to improve the performance [40]. A flexible architecture is defined in [41], which can search for a better convolutional cell with better regularization mechanism. All these models are trained on ImageNet Dataset for ILSVR challenge.

Our objective is to create a robust and efficient model to recognize DR with limited datasets and with limited computational resources. To achieve our objective of creating a robust model with small datasets, we seek the help of transfer learning and use various pre-trained ConvNets to extract deep features. We use the knowledge of these models to extract the most prominent features of color fundus images. A deep neural network with dropout introduced at early layers is trained to detect and classify the severity levels of diabetic retinopathy. As we introduced dropout at the input layer, deep neural network is immune to overfitting.

3. Proposed Methodology

In this work, our objective is to develop a robust and efficient model to automate DR diagnosis. We focus on the extraction of deep features that are most descriptive and discriminate, which ultimately improves the performance of DR recognition. To get an optimal representation, features are extracted from multiple pre-trained CNN architectures and are blended using pooling-based approaches. These final representations are used to train a deep neural network with a dropout at the input layer. The proposed model has three different modules: feature extraction, model training, and evaluation module.

3.1. Feature Extraction

Performance of any machine learning model is highly influenced by the feature representations and the same is applicable to models used for DR recognition. With this motivation, we propose two different approaches (uni-modal and multi-modal) to extract optimal features from the given retinal images.

In the proposed work, initial representations of the retinal images are obtained from the pre-trained VGG16, NASNet, Xception Net, and Inception ResNetV2. As each of the pre-trained models expects input images of varying sizes, the given retinal images are reshaped according to the input dimensions accepted by these models. For example, when VGG16 is used, images are reshaped to $224 \times 224 \times 3$. These reshaped retinal images are fed to the pre-trained models after removing the soft-max layer and freezing the rest of the layers. Activation outputs from the penultimate layers form the basis for the proposed feature extraction module. For each retinal image, deep features are extracted from the pre-trained ConvNets and the details are as follows:

- Each of the first (fc1) and second (fc2) fully connected layers of VGG16 produces a feature vector of 4096 dimensions.
- The final global average pooling layer of NASNet, Xception, and InceptionResNetV2 gives feature vectors of size 4032, 2048, and 1536, respectively.

Figure 2 gives the architectural details of the pre-trained VGG16, NASNet, Xception, and InceptionResNetV2 and pointers are marked at the feature extraction layers. These features form the input to the proposed uni-modal and blended multi-modal approaches to obtain the optimal feature representations of the retinal images.

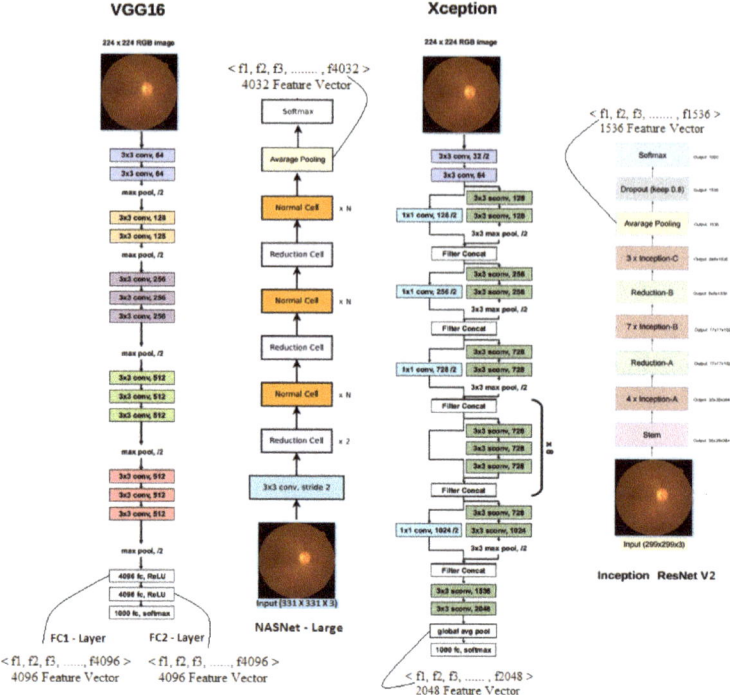

Figure 2. Architectures of various pre-trained models along with an indication of layers from which features are extracted.

3.2. Uni-Modal Deep Feature Extraction

In this approach, deep features are extracted from the final layers of one of the pre-trained ConvNets (VGG16, NASNet, Xception, or ResNet V2) to get the global representation of the retinal images. These deep features are fed to classification models for DR identification and recognition. We propose to use DNN architecture with a dropout at the input layer for DR identification and classification. Figure 3 gives the details of different stages involved in DR recognition process that uses uni-modal deep ConvNet features.

Figure 3. Stages involved in uni-modal deep feature based DR recognition.

3.3. Blended (Multi-Modal) Deep Feature Extraction

Unlike uni-modal approaches, multi-modal approaches use deep features extracted from multiple ConvNets and are blended using fusion techniques. The features obtained from different pre-trained models provide a different representation of the retinal images as they follow different architectures and are trained on different datasets. A stronger representation can be obtained by blending features from multiple ConvNets, as features of one ConvNet complement the features from other ConvNets involved in the process.

We propose various pooling approaches to fuse the deep features extracted from multiple pre-trained ConvNets. The final blended deep features provide better descriptive and discriminate representation of the retinal images. These blended features are fed to the classification models for DR identification or severity recognition. Figure 4 gives the details of different stages involved in DR recognition process that uses blended multi-modal deep ConvNet features. The proposed blended multi-modal feature extraction module uses features from both the fully connected layers of VGG16 (fc1 and fc2) and global average poling layer of Xception as input. The rationale behind choosing features of VGG16 and Xception over the others is two fold. In VGG16, each feature map of the final convolution block learns the presence of different lesions from the retinal images. Xception Net learns correlations across the 2D space; as a result, each feature map provides the comprehensive representation of the entire retinal scan. Figure 5 visualizes the feature maps obtained from the final convolution blocks of VGG16 and Xception models when a retinal image is passed to these models.

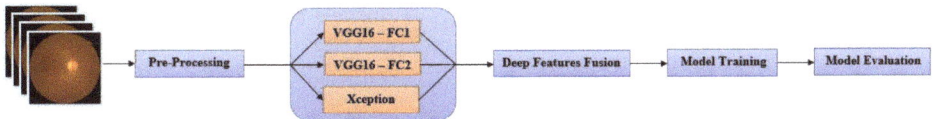

Figure 4. Stages involved in blended deep feature based DR recognition.

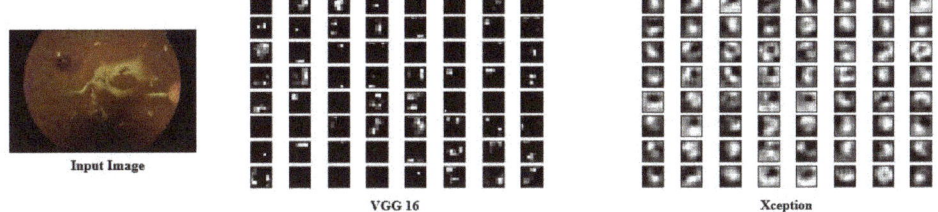

Figure 5. Visualization of the feature maps of the final convolution blocks of VGG16 and Xception models on passing retinal image as input.

Approaches to Blend Deep Features from Multiple ConvNets

In this work, two different pooling-based approaches (1D pooling and cross pooling) are proposed to fuse multi-modal deep features that are extracted from VGG16 (fc1 and fc2) and Xception. 1D pooling is used to select prominent local features from each region of VGG16, whereas cross pooling allows aggregating the prominent features obtained by 1D pooling with global representation of Xception.

1D pooling-based fusion takes one feature vector U as input and produces another feature vector $\hat{U}$, where $U \in R^{d1}$, $\hat{U} \in R^{d2}$, and $d_2 \leq d_1$. $\hat{U}$ is a reduced representation of U, where $U = \{u_1, u_2...u_{d1}\}$ and $\hat{U} = \{\hat{u}_1, \hat{u}_2...\hat{u}_{d2}\}$. Each feature element $\hat{u}_i$, of the output vector $\hat{U}$, is computed using one of the following three approaches:

$$\text{1D Max pooling:} \hat{u}_i = max(u_{i*2}, u_{i*2+1}) \; \forall i \in \{1, 2...d_2\} \quad (1)$$

$$\text{1D Min pooling:} \; \hat{u}_i = min(u_{i*2}, u_{i*2+1}); \; \forall i \in \{1, 2...d_2\} \quad (2)$$

$$\text{1D Average pooling:} \; \hat{u}_i = mean(u_{i*2}, u_{i*2+1}); \forall i \in \{1, 2...d_2\} \quad (3)$$

$$\text{1D Sum pooling:} \hat{u}_i = u_{i*2} + u_{i*2+1}; \forall i \in \{1, 2...d_2\} \quad (4)$$

In cross pooling-based feature fusion, two different feature vectors X and Y are passed as input and another feature vector Z is produced, where $X, Y, Z \in R^d$. Each feature element z_i, of the output vector Z, is computed using one of the following three approaches:

$$\text{Cross Max pooling:} \; z_i = max(x_i, y_i) \quad \forall i \in \{1, 2...d\} \quad (5)$$

$$\text{Cross Min pooling:} z_i = min(x_i, y_i) \quad \forall i \in \{1, 2...d\} \tag{6}$$

$$\text{Cross Average pooling:} z_i = mean(x_i, y_{i+1}) \forall i \in \{1, 2...d\} \tag{7}$$

$$\text{Cross Sum pooling:} \quad y_i = x_i + y_i \quad \forall i \in \{1, 2...d\} \tag{8}$$

1D pooling is applied independently on features extracted from fc1 and fc2 layers of VGG16. Then, the cross pooling approach is applied on the resultant pooled features. This feature vector is merged with the features extracted from the Xception using cross pooling. Fusion module produces deep blended features, which are used to train the proposed DNN model. Figure 6 shows the proposed architecture of the deep feature fusion approach used to blend features from different ConvNets. As the final feature vector is a blended version of the local and global representations of the retinal images, it provides strong features. Algorithm 1 gives the sequence of steps involved in the blended multi-modal feature fusion-based DR recognition.

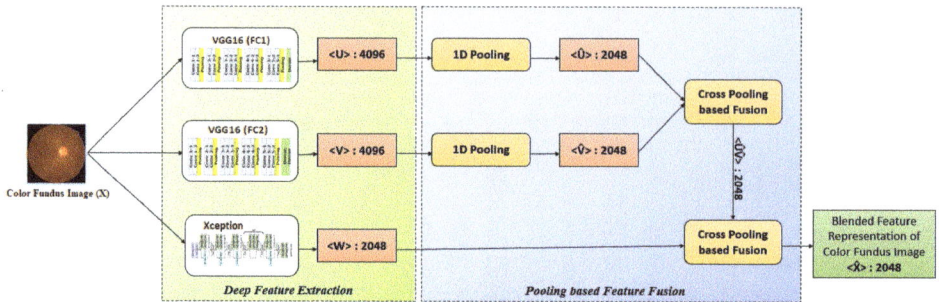

Figure 6. Approaches for fusion of features extracted from Deep ConvNets.

Algorithm 1: Blended multi-modal deep feature fusion based DR recognition task.

Input: Let D^{Tr} and D^{Tst} be the train and test datasets of fundus images, respectively, where $D^{Tr} = \{(x_i, y_i)\}_{i=1}^{N_{Tr}}$ and $D^{Tst} = \{(x_i)\}_{i=1}^{N_{Tst}}$. x_i represents ith color fundus image in the dataset and y_i is the severity level of DR associated with x_i. In the case of DR identification task, $y_i \in \{0, 1\}$, whereas, in the case of DR severity classification, task $y_i \in \{0, 1, 2, 3\}$.

Output: y_i for each $x_i \in D^{Tst}$

Step 1: Preprocess each image x_i in the dataset.

Step 2: Feature Extraction

For each preprocessed image x_i three different features (V_i, U_i, W_i) are extracted.

$V_i \leftarrow$ Features extracted from fc1 layer of VGG16
$U_i \leftarrow$ Features extracted from fc2 layer of VGG16
$W_i \leftarrow$ Features extracted from global avg pool layer of Xception

Where $V_i \in d1, U - i \in d2$ and $W_i \in d3$

Step 3: Deep feature fusion

Apply feature feature fusion on the deep features extracted from each image

$\hat{V}_i \leftarrow max(V_{i*2}, V_{i*2+1}); \quad \forall i \in \{1, 2...d_1\}$ (1D max pooling)
$\hat{U}_i \leftarrow max(U_{i*2}, U_{i*2+1}); \quad \forall i \in \{1, 2...d_2\}$ (1D max pooling)
$\hat{UV}_i \leftarrow \frac{(\hat{V}_i + \hat{U}_i)}{2}; \quad \forall i \in \{1, 2...d_2\}$ (Average Cross pooling)
$\hat{x}_i \leftarrow \frac{(\hat{UV}_i + W_i)}{2}; \quad \forall i \in \{1, 2...d_3\}$ (Average Cross pooling)

$\hat{x}_i$: blended feature vector corresponding to x_i

Step 4: Model Training

Training dataset is prepared using the blended features $D^{Tr} = \{(\hat{x}_i, y_i)\}_{i=1}^{N_{Tr}}$
Train a deep neural network (DNN) using D^{Tr}

Step 5: Model evaluation

Test dataset is prepared using the blended features $D^{Tst} = \{(\hat{x}_i)\}_{i=1}^{N_{Tst}}$
Evaluate the performance of D^{Tst} using the DNN trained in **Step 4**

3.4. Model Training and Evaluation

During this phase, we trained the ML model with deep blended pre-trained features. We preferred to use Deep Neural Network (DNN) model for training. For DR identification task, as it is a simple binary classification task, a DNN with two hidden layers with 256 and 128 units, respectively, with ReLU activation was used.

For DR severity classification task, a DNN with three hidden layers with 512, 256, and 128 units, respectively, using ReLU activation was used. For both the DNNs with the input layer, we applied 0.2 dropout to avoid the model from overfitting. This helped the model to become robust. Figure 7 represents the architecture of proposed approach for model training and evaluation.

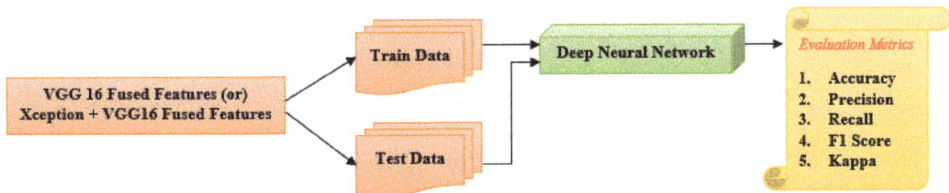

Figure 7. Training and Evaluation of DNN model for identification and recognition of DR.

4. Experimental Results

In this section, we provide details of experimental studies that were carried out to understand the efficiency of the proposed blended multi-modal deep features representation.

4.1. Dataset Summary

For the experimental studies, the APTOS 2019 kaggle benchmark dataset available as part of the blindness detection challenge was used [42]. This is a large dataset of retinal images taken using fundus photography under a variety of imaging conditions. The images are graded manually on a scale of 0 to 4 (0, no DR; 1, mild; 2, moderate; 3, severe; and 4, proliferative DR) to indicate different severity levels.

Table 1 gives the number of retinal images available in the dataset under each level of severity. We can observe that the dataset has an imbalance with more normal images and very few images in Class 3. In all experiments, 80% of the data were used for training and the remaining 20% were used for validation.

Table 1. Dataset summary of APTOS 2019 dataset.

Severity Level	# Samples
Class 0 (Normal)	1805
Class 1 (Mild Stage)	370
Class 2 (Moderate Stage)	999
Class 3 (Severe Stage)	193
Class 4 (Proliferative Stage)	295
Total	3662

4.2. Performance Measures

For the evaluation of the proposed model, we report different measures: accuracy, precision, recall, and F1 score. In addition, we used an additional metric called lappa statistic to compare an observed accuracy with an expected accuracy. Kappa Statistic is calculated as

$$\text{Kappa Score} = \frac{(\text{Observed Accuracy} - \text{Expected Accuracy})}{(1 - \text{Expected Accuracy})}$$

Observed accuracy is defined as the number of samples that are correctly classified. Expected accuracy is defined as the accuracy that a classifier would be expected to achieve, which is directly related to the number of examples of each class, along with the number of examples that the predicted value satisfied with the correct label.

4.3. DR Identification and Severity Level Prediction

The experiments carried out in this work were divided into two different tasks. In Task 1, presence or absence of DR was identified, whereas, in Task 2, the severity level was predicted for the given retinal image.

4.3.1. Task 1—DR Identification

In this task, given the DR image of a diabetic patient, we need to check whether the person is affected by retinopathy or not. DR identification is a binary classification task, thus binary cross entropy loss was used to measure the loss, and Adam optimizer was used to optimize the objective function. The dataset contains images belonging to five different classes, as shown in Table 1, and is not suitable for binary classification task. Merging all the DR-affected images into a single class gives 1857 positively labeled images and the remaining 1805 normal images are labeled as negative.

4.3.2. Task 2—Severity Level Prediction

The objective of Task 1 is to identify the presence or absence of DR, given a retinal image. While treating the DR-affected patients, mere identification of DR would not be sufficient and understanding the level of severity would be helpful for better treatment. Hence, we treat severity level identification as a separate task that categorizes the given retinal image into one of the five severity levels. Categorical cross entropy loss was used to represent loss and Adam optimizer was used to optimize the objective function.

4.4. Experimental Studies to Show the Representative Nature of Uni-Modal Features for Task 1

This experiment was carried out to understand how efficiently retinal images are represented using uni-modal features that are directly obtained from single pre-trained ConvNet. Models such as VGG16, Xception, NASNET, and ResNetV2 were considered to extract uni-modal features. For classification, models such as Naïve Bayes classifier, logistic regression, decision tree, k-Nearest Neighborhood (KNN) classifier, Multi Layered Perceptron (MLP), Support Vector Machine (SVM), and Deep Neural Network (DNN) were used.

Tables 2 and 3 show the performance of DR identification task using different ML models when the retinal images are represented with the features extracted from the first fully connected layer (fc2) of VGG16 and Xception, respectively. Based on these results, we concluded that DNN outperforms the rest of the ML models irrespective of the models. Hence, we decided to use DNN model alone in the rest of the experiments.

Table 2. Performance of ML algorithms on Task 1 using features from fc2 layer of VGG16.

Model	Accuracy	Precision	Recall	F1 Score	Kappa Statistic
Logistic Regression	97.13	97	97	97	94.27
KNN	95.36	96	95	95	90.73
Naive Bayes	77.08	82	77	76	54.45
Decision Tree	91.27	91	91	91	82.52
MLP	96.45	97	96	96	92.91
SVM (linear)	96.58	97	97	97	93.17
SVM (RBF)	96.86	97	97	97	93.73
DNN	97.32	98	98	98	94.63

Table 3. Performance of ML algorithms on Task 1 using features from Xception.

Model	Accuracy	Precision	Recall	F1 Score	Kappa Statistic
Logistic Regression	96.45	96	96	96	93
KNN	95.5	96	95	95	91
Naive Bayes	82.95	84	83	83	65.9
Decision Tree	87.59	88	88	88	75.17
MLP	96	96	96	96	91.89
SVM (linear)	96.18	96	96	96	92.36
SVM (RBF)	97.4	97	97	97	94.82
DNN	97.41	97	97	97	94.82

Table 4 shows the representative power of uni-modal features that are extracted from different pre-trained models. It is clear from the results that the performance of the DNN model varies depending on the uni-modal features used. This experiment gives a clue that each pre-trained model extracts a different set of features from retinal images. The features extracted from Xception yield better performance in terms of accuracy for the diabetic retinopathy identification task. A nominal difference in terms of accuracy and kappa score can be observed between the models trained using different uni-modal features.

Table 4. Task 1 performance using DNN trained on different uni-modal features.

Model	Accuracy	Precision	Recall	F1 Score	Kappa Statistic
VGG16-fc1	97.27	97	98	97	95.12
VGG16-fc2	97.32	98	98	98	94.63
NASNet	97.14	97	97	97	94.27
Xception	97.41	97	97	97	94.82
Inception ResNetV2	97.34	97	97	97	94.54

To better understand the representative nature of different uni-modal features, loss and number of epochs taken to converge by the DNN models are reported in Table 5. We can observe that the model trained using VGG16-Fc1 reaches minimum loss compared to the rest of the models. In terms of convergence, Xception takes only 16 epochs, whereas the Inception ResNetV2 outperforms the other models.

Table 5. Task 1: Comparison of DNN model (trained on uni-modal features) in terms of loss and number of epochs when trained on different uni-modal features.

Model	# Epochs	Loss	Accuracy
VGG16-fc1	65	0.0024	97.27
VGG16-fc2	67	0.0139	97.32
NASNet	37	0.0310	97.14
Xception	16	0.0213	97.41
Inception ResNet V2	19	0.0815	97.34

To summarize the experiments on DR identification task, features extracted from Xception, VGG16-fc2, and Inception ResnetV2 yields the same accuracy with nominal differences. However, models trained on the VGG16-fc1 features give better kappa scores compared to others. We can also observe that models trained on the VGG16-fc2 features give better performance in terms of precision, recall, and F1 scores. Regardless of the type of uni-modal features used, DNN consistently outperforms the rest of the models, especially in terms of kappa scores. The reason for the superior performance of the models trained using VGG16 and Xception features is that these models are good at extracting the lesion information that is useful to discriminate the DR-affected images from those that are not affected.

4.5. Experimental Studies to Show the Representative Nature of Uni-Modal Features for Task 2

We ran a set of experiments to understand the nature of uni-modal features for severity prediction of DR. Task 2 is more challenging compared to Task 1 as it involves multiple classes. DNN model with dropout at the input layer was used with different uni-modal features.

Based on the results reported in Table 6, we can observe the same trend that was observed in Task 1. The scores obtained for Task 2 show the complexity of severity prediction. The model trained on VGG-16+fc1 features shows superior performance to rest of the models. The same can be observed in terms of all the metrics.

Table 6. Task 2 performance using DNN trained on different uni-modal features.

Type of Uni-Modal Features	Accuracy	Precision	Recall	F1 Score	Kappa Statistic
VGG16-fc1	80.06	80	81	80	70.02
VGG16-fc2	79.81	79	80	79	68.88
NASNET	76.4	75	76	75	63.87
Xception	78.99	78	79	78	67.67
Inception ResNetV2	79.73	78	78	78	67.67

In Table 7, it is clear that, among all the pre-trained features, VGG16-fc1 yields superior performance with minimum loss. However, Xception converges in fewer epochs compared to other models.

Table 7. Task 2: Comparison of DNN model (trained on uni-modal features) in terms of loss and number of epochs when trained on different uni-modal features.

Model	# Epochs	Loss	Accuracy
VGG16-fc1	76	0.3623	80.06
VGG16-fc2	79	0.3986	79.81
NASNet	37	0.5612	76.39
Xception	23	0.4175	78.99
Inception ResNet V2	89	0.382	79.73

4.6. Performance Evaluation of the Proposed Blended Multi-Modal Features

A clue from the experiments on uni-modal features is that different uni-modal features extract different sets of features from the retinal images. If we can use multiple deep features extracted from different models, they complement each other and help to improve the scores. To benefit from more than one set of uni-modal features, we propose a blended multi-modal feature representation. This section is dedicated to show the representative power of the proposed feature representation with an application to DR identification and severity level prediction.

In addition, we applied the proposed pooling methods to blend the features from multiple pre-trained models. Initially, we blended features from the first and second fully connected layers of VGG16. Then, we extended this to the fusion of three different features from fc1 and fc2 layers of VGG16 and Xception.

4.6.1. Blended Multi-Modal Deep Features for Task 1

We experimented on the effect of blending deep features extracted from multiple pre-trained models on DR identification task. In addition, we verified the proposed maximum, sum, and average pooling approaches to blend multiple deep features.

In Table 8, we can observe that average pooling based fusion works better for DR Detection compared to other models. Using average fusion the models trained on multi-modal features leads to superior performance in terms of accuracy and kappa static. In addition, the model converges more quickly, in less than 50 epochs, and attains minimum loss. The accuracy obtained by model trained using multi-modal features is significantly better compared with to those trained on uni-modal features.

Table 8. DNN with blended multi-modal features with different fusions for Task 1.

Modalities	Pooling	Accuracy	Kappa Statistic	Epochs	Loss
VGG16-fc1 and VGG16-fc2	Max-pooling	96.12	91.89	68	0.0352
	Avg-pooling	97.39	94.61	51	0.0293
	Sum-pooling	95.5	91	64	0.0419
VGG16-fc1, VGG16-fc2 and Xception	Max-pooling	96.85	92.6	69	0.0314
	Avg-pooling	97.92	94.93	43	0.0201
	Sum-pooling	96.1	92.31	56	0.0396

4.6.2. Blended Multi-Modal Deep Features for Task 2

From the previous experiments, we understand that the models trained on multi-modal features give better performance compared to those trained on uni-modal features in the context of DR identification which is simple binary task. To understand that the proposed blended performs efficiently for more complex multi-class classification task, we applied the proposed feature representation for the severity prediction task shown in Table 9.

Table 9. DNN with blended multi-modal features with different fusions for Task 2.

Modalities	Pooling	Accuracy	Kappa Statistic	Epochs	Loss
VGG16-fc1 and VGG16-fc2	Maximum	78.06	66.87	72	0.4176
	Average	80.34	69.21	62	0.2987
	Sum	76.8	65.64	68	0.5693
VGG16-fc1, VGG16-fc2 and Xception	Maximum	79.25	67.29	74	0.3986
	Average	80.96	70.9	54	0.2619
	Sum	77.12	66.42	61	0.4782

In Table 10, we can see that average pooling based fusion of multiple deep features works better for diabetic severity prediction. Compared to the blended features from VGG16-fc1 and VGG16-fc2, the blended features from VGG16-fc1, VGG16-fc2, and Xception gives better representation. For severity prediction as well, the model that uses average pooling approach for fusion converges more quickly with better accuracy and kappa score when compared with the other approaches for fusion.

4.7. Comparison of Proposed Blended Feature Extraction with Existing Methods

In this experiment, we showed the effectiveness of the proposed DNN with dropout at the input layer trained using the proposed blended multi-modal deep feature representation and with the existing models in the literature for DR prediction. We compared the proposed model with the performances of the models used in [43,44]. In Table 10, we can see that the proposed method gives an accuracy of 80.96%, which is significantly better than existing models in the literature. When compared to the existing models, the proposed DNN model is simple with only three hidden layers with 512, 256 and 128 units each hidden layer. The confusion matrix in Figure 8 shows the mis-classifications produced by the proposed model when applied for DR severity prediction task. In the figure, we can see that most of the proliferate DR type images are predicted as moderate.

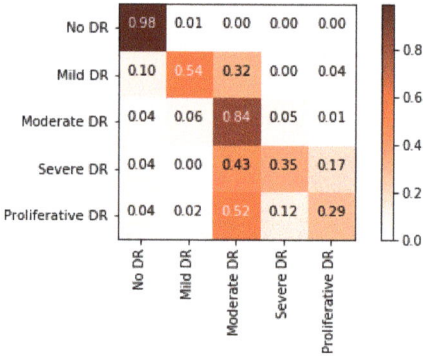

Figure 8. Confusion matrix for the severity prediction task.

As the final feature vector is a blended version of the local and global representations of the retinal images the final representation provides strong features. The reason for improvement in the performance of the proposed model is that each feature map of the final convolution block of VGG16 learns the presence of different lesions from the retinal images and Xception Net comprehensive representation of the entire retinal scan. When we combine the deep features from VGG16 and Xception gives a compact representation that gives the wholistic representation of DR images.

Table 10. Comparison of Proposed method using with existing methods.

Model	Accuracy
DR detection using Deep Learning [43]	57.2%
DR Classification Using Xception [44]	79.59
DR Classification Using InceptionV3 [44]	78.72
DR Classification Using MobileNet [44]	79.01
DR Classification Using ResNet50 [44]	74.64
Blended features + DNN (proposed)	80.96

5. Conclusions

The major objective of this work is to acquire a compact and comprehensive representation of retinal images as the feature representations extracted from retinal images significantly influence the performance of DR prediction. Initially, we extract features from deep pre-trained VGG16-fc1, CGG16-fc2 and Xception models. VGG16 model learns the lesions and Xception learns the global representation of the images. Then, the features from multiple ConvNets are blended to get final prominent representation of color fundus images. The final representation is obtained by pooling the representations from VGG16 and Xception features. A DNN model was trained using these blended features for the task of diabetic retinopathy severity level prediction. The proposed DNN model with dropout at the input avoids overfitting and converges more quickly. Our experiments on benchmark APTOS 2019 dataset showed the superiority of the proposed model when compared to the existing models. Among the proposed pooling approaches, average pooling used to fuse the features extracted from the penultimate layers of multiple pre-trained ConvNets gives better performance with minimum loss in fewer epochs compared to others.

Author Contributions: Conceptualization, J.D.B.; methodology, S.N.S.; software, S.H.; validation, M.B., P.K.R.M. and O.J.; formal analysis, O.J.; investigation, P.K.R.M.; resources, J.D.B.; writing—original draft preparation, J.D.B. and V.N.; writing—review and editing, V.N.; visualization, S.N.S.; supervision, M.B.; project administration, S.H.; funding acquisition, O.J. All authors have read and agreed to the published version of the manuscript.

Funding: This work was supported by the National Research Foundation of Korea (NRF) grant funded by the Korea government (MSIT) under Grant NRF-2018R1C1B5045013.

Conflicts of Interest: The authors declare no conflict of interest.

References

1. Cheung, N.; Rogers, S.L.; Donaghue, K.C.; Jenkins, A.J.; Tikellis, G.; Wong, T.Y. Retinal arteriolar dilation predicts retinopathy in adolescents with type 1 diabetes. *Diabetes Care* **2008**, *31*, 1842–1846. [CrossRef] [PubMed]
2. Flaxman, S.; Bourne, R.; Resnikoff, S.; Ackland, P.; Braithwaite, T.; Cicinelli, M.; Das, A.; Jonas, J.; Keeffe, J.; Kempen, J.; et al. Global causes of blindness and distance vision impairment 1990-2020: A systematic review and meta-analysis. *Lancet Glob. Health* **2017**, *5*, e1221–e1234. [CrossRef]
3. Gulshan, V.; Peng, L.; Coram, M.; Stumpe, M.C.; Wu, D.; Narayanaswamy, A.; Venugopalan, S.; Widner, K.; Madams, T.; Cuadros, J.; et al. Development and validation of a deep learning algorithm for detection of diabetic retinopathy in retinal fundus photographs. *JAMA* **2016**, *316*, 2402–2410. [CrossRef] [PubMed]
4. Williams, R.; Airey, M.; Baxter, H.; Forrester, J.M.; Kennedy-Martin, T.; Girach, A. Epidemiology of diabetic retinopathy and macular oedema: A systematic review. *Eye* **2004**, *18*, 963–983. [CrossRef] [PubMed]
5. Long, S.; Huang, X.; Chen, Z.; Pardhan, S.; Zheng, D. Automatic detection of hard exudates in color retinal images using dynamic threshold and SVM classification: Algorithm development and evaluation. *BioMed Res. Int.* **2019**, *2019*, 3926930. [CrossRef]
6. Haloi, M.; Dandapat, S.; Sinha, R. A Gaussian scale space approach for exudates detection, classification and severity prediction. *arXiv* **2015**, arXiv:1505.00737.
7. Noushin, E.; Pourreza, M.; Masoudi, K.; Ghiasi Shirazi, E. Microaneurysm detection in fundus images using a two step convolution neural network. *Biomed. Eng. Online* **2019**, *18*, 67.

8. Grinsven, M.; Ginneken, B.; Hoyng, C.; Theelen, T.; Sanchez, C. Fast convolution neural network training using selective data sampling. *IEEE Trans. Med. Imaging* **2016**, *35*, 1273–1284. [CrossRef]
9. Haloi, M. Improved microaneurysm detection using deep neural networks. *arXiv* **2015**, arXiv:1505.04424.
10. Srivastava, R.; Duan, L.; Wong, D.W.; Liu, J.; Wong, T.Y. Detecting retinal microaneurysms and hemorrhages with robustness to the presence of blood vessels. *Comput. Methods Programs Biomed.* **2017**, *138*, 83–91. [CrossRef]
11. Bodapati, J.D.; Veeranjaneyulu, N. Feature Extraction and Classification Using Deep Convolutional Neural Networks. *J. Cyber Secur. Mobil.* **2019**, *8*, 261–276. [CrossRef]
12. Bodapati, J.D.; Veeranjaneyulu, N.; Shaik, S. Sentiment Analysis from Movie Reviews Using LSTMs. *Ingénierie des Systèmes d'Information* **2019**, *24*, 125–129. [CrossRef]
13. Zhuo, P.; Zhu, Y.; Wu, W.; Shu, J.; Xia, T. Real-Time Fault Diagnosis for Gas Turbine Blade Based on Output-Hidden Feedback Elman Neural Network. *J. Shanghai Jiaotong Univ. (Sci.)* **2018**, *23*, 95–102. [CrossRef]
14. Xia, T.; Song, Y.; Zheng, Y.; Pan, E.; Xi, L. An ensemble framework based on convolutional bi-directional LSTM with multiple time windows for remaining useful life estimation. *Comput. Ind.* **2020**, *115*, 103182. [CrossRef]
15. Moreira, M.W.; Rodrigues, J.J.; Korotaev, V.; Al-Muhtadi, J.; Kumar, N. A comprehensive review on smart decision support systems for health care. *IEEE Syst. J.* **2019**, *13*, 3536–3545. [CrossRef]
16. Gadekallu, T.R.; Khare, N.; Bhattacharya, S.; Singh, S.; Maddikunta, P.K.R.; Srivastava, G. Deep neural networks to predict diabetic retinopathy. *J. Ambient Intell. Humaniz. Comput.* **2020**. [CrossRef]
17. Patel, H.; Singh Rajput, D.; Thippa Reddy, G.; Iwendi, C.; Kashif Bashir, A.; Jo, O. A review on classification of imbalanced data for wireless sensor networks. *Int. J. Distrib. Sens. Netw.* **2020**, *16*, 1550147720916404. [CrossRef]
18. Reddy, G.T.; Reddy, M.P.K.; Lakshmanna, K.; Rajput, D.S.; Kaluri, R.; Srivastava, G. Hybrid genetic algorithm and a fuzzy logic classifier for heart disease diagnosis. *Evol. Intell.* **2019**, *13*, 185–196. [CrossRef]
19. Wu, L.; Fernandez-Loaiza, P.; Sauma, J.; Hernandez-Bogantes, E.; Masis, M. Classification of diabetic retinopathy and diabetic macular edema. *World J. Diabetes* **2013**, *4*, 290. [CrossRef]
20. Akram, M.U.; Khalid, S.; Khan, S.A. Identification and classification of microaneurysms for early detection of diabetic retinopathy. *Pattern Recognit.* **2013**, *46*, 107–116. [CrossRef]
21. Akram, M.U.; Khalid, S.; Tariq, A.; Khan, S.A.; Azam, F. Detection and classification of retinal lesions for grading of diabetic retinopathy. *Comput. Biol. Med.* **2014**, *45*, 161–171. [CrossRef] [PubMed]
22. Casanova, R.; Saldana, S.; Chew, E.Y.; Danis, R.P.; Greven, C.M.; Ambrosius, W.T. Application of random forests methods to diabetic retinopathy classification analyses. *PLoS ONE* **2014**, *9*, e98587. [CrossRef] [PubMed]
23. Verma, K.; Deep, P.; Ramakrishnan, A. Detection and classification of diabetic retinopathy using retinal images. In Proceedings of the 2011 Annual IEEE India Conference, Hyderabad, India, 16–18 December 2011; pp. 1–6.
24. Welikala, R.; Dehmeshki, J.; Hoppe, A.; Tah, V.; Mann, S.; Williamson, T.H.; Barman, S. Automated detection of proliferative diabetic retinopathy using a modified line operator and dual classification. *Comput. Methods Programs Biomed.* **2014**, *114*, 247–261. [CrossRef] [PubMed]
25. Welikala, R.A.; Fraz, M.M.; Dehmeshki, J.; Hoppe, A.; Tah, V.; Mann, S.; Williamson, T.H.; Barman, S.A. Genetic algorithm based feature selection combined with dual classification for the automated detection of proliferative diabetic retinopathy. *Comput. Med. Imaging Graph.* **2015**, *43*, 64–77. [CrossRef]
26. Roychowdhury, S.; Koozekanani, D.D.; Parhi, K.K. DREAM: Diabetic retinopathy analysis using machine learning. *IEEE J. Biomed. Health Inform.* **2013**, *18*, 1717–1728. [CrossRef]
27. Mookiah, M.R.K.; Acharya, U.R.; Martis, R.J.; Chua, C.K.; Lim, C.M.; Ng, E.; Laude, A. Evolutionary algorithm based classifier parameter tuning for automatic diabetic retinopathy grading: A hybrid feature extraction approach. *Knowl. Based Syst.* **2013**, *39*, 9–22. [CrossRef]
28. Porter, L.F.; Saptarshi, N.; Fang, Y.; Rathi, S.; Den Hollander, A.I.; De Jong, E.K.; Clark, S.J.; Bishop, P.N.; Olsen, T.W.; Liloglou, T.; et al. Whole-genome methylation profiling of the retinal pigment epithelium of individuals with age-related macular degeneration reveals differential methylation of the SKI, GTF2H4, and TNXB genes. *Clin. Epigenet.* **2019**, *11*, 6. [CrossRef]
29. Rahim, S.S.; Jayne, C.; Palade, V.; Shuttleworth, J. Automatic detection of microaneurysms in colour fundus images for diabetic retinopathy screening. *Neural Comput. Appl.* **2016**, *27*, 1149–1164. [CrossRef]

30. Dutta, S.; Manideep, B.; Basha, S.M.; Caytiles, R.D.; Iyengar, N. Classification of diabetic retinopathy images by using deep learning models. *Int. J. Grid Distrib. Comput.* **2018**, *11*, 89–106. [CrossRef]
31. Zeng, X.; Chen, H.; Luo, Y.; Ye, W. Automated diabetic retinopathy detection based on binocular Siamese-like convolutional neural network. *IEEE Access* **2019**, *7*, 30744–30753. [CrossRef]
32. Mateen, M.; Wen, J.; Song, S.; Huang, Z. Fundus image classification using VGG-19 architecture with PCA and SVD. *Symmetry* **2019**, *11*, 1. [CrossRef]
33. Reddy, G.T.; Reddy, M.P.K.; Lakshmanna, K.; Kaluri, R.; Rajput, D.S.; Srivastava, G.; Baker, T. Analysis of Dimensionality Reduction Techniques on Big Data. *IEEE Access* **2020**, *8*, 54776–54788. [CrossRef]
34. Bhattacharya, S.; Kaluri, R.; Singh, S.; Alazab, M.; Tariq, U. A Novel PCA-Firefly based XGBoost classification model for Intrusion Detection in Networks using GPU. *Electronics* **2020**, *9*, 219. [CrossRef]
35. Gadekallu, T.R.; Khare, N.; Bhattacharya, S.; Singh, S.; Reddy Maddikunta, P.K.; Ra, I.H.; Alazab, M. Early Detection of Diabetic Retinopathy Using PCA-Firefly Based Deep Learning Model. *Electronics* **2020**, *9*, 274. [CrossRef]
36. Jindal, A.; Aujla, G.S.; Kumar, N.; Prodan, R.; Obaidat, M.S. DRUMS: Demand response management in a smart city using deep learning and SVR. In Proceedings of the 2018 IEEE Global Communications Conference (GLOBECOM), Abu Dhabi, UAE, 9–13 December 2018; pp. 1–6.
37. Vinayakumar, R.; Alazab, M.; Srinivasan, S.; Pham, Q.V.; Padannayil, S.K.; Simran, K. A Visualized Botnet Detection System based Deep Learning for the Internet of Things Networks of Smart Cities. *IEEE Trans. Ind. Appl.* **2020**. [CrossRef]
38. Alazab, M.; Khan, S.; Krishnan, S.S.R.; Pham, Q.V.; Reddy, M.P.K.; Gadekallu, T.R. A Multidirectional LSTM Model for Predicting the Stability of a Smart Grid. *IEEE Access* **2020**, *8*, 85454–85463. [CrossRef]
39. Simonyan, K.; Zisserman, A. Very deep convolutional networks for large-scale image recognition. *arXiv* **2014**, arXiv:1409.1556.
40. Chollet, F. Xception: Deep learning with depthwise separable convolutions. In Proceedings of the 2017 IEEE Conference on Computer Vision and Pattern Recognition (CVPR), Honolulu, HI, USA, 21–26 July 2017; pp. 1251–1258.
41. Zoph, B.; Vasudevan, V.; Shlens, J.; Le, Q.V. Learning transferable architectures for scalable image recognition. In Proceedings of the 2018 IEEE/CVF Conference on Computer Vision and Pattern Recognition, Salt Lake City, UT, USA, 18–23 June 2018; pp. 8697–8710.
42. APTOS 2019. Available online: https://www.kaggle.com/c/aptos2019-blindness-detection (accessed on 30 December 2019).
43. Gargeya, R.; Leng, T. Automated identification of diabetic retinopathy using deep learning. *Ophthalmology* **2017**, *124*, 962–969. [CrossRef]
44. Kassani, S.H.; Kassani, P.H.; Khazaeinezhad, R.; Wesolowski, M.J.; Schneider, K.A.; Deters, R. Diabetic Retinopathy Classification Using a Modified Xception Architecture. In Proceedings of the 2019 IEEE International Symposium on Signal Processing and Information Technology (ISSPIT), Ajman, UAE, 10–12 December 2019; pp. 1–6.

© 2020 by the authors. Licensee MDPI, Basel, Switzerland. This article is an open access article distributed under the terms and conditions of the Creative Commons Attribution (CC BY) license (http://creativecommons.org/licenses/by/4.0/).

Article

Integrating Enhanced Sparse Autoencoder-Based Artificial Neural Network Technique and Softmax Regression for Medical Diagnosis

Sarah A. Ebiaredoh-Mienye, Ebenezer Esenogho * and Theo G. Swart

Center for Telecommunication, Department of Electrical and Electronic Engineering Science, University of Johannesburg, Johannesburg 2006, South Africa; snabofa@yahoo.com (S.A.E.-M.); ebenic4real@gmail.com (T.G.S.)
* Correspondence: ebenezere@uj.ac.za

Received: 28 September 2020; Accepted: 2 November 2020; Published: 20 November 2020

Abstract: In recent times, several machine learning models have been built to aid in the prediction of diverse diseases and to minimize diagnostic errors made by clinicians. However, since most medical datasets seem to be imbalanced, conventional machine learning algorithms tend to underperform when trained with such data, especially in the prediction of the minority class. To address this challenge and proffer a robust model for the prediction of diseases, this paper introduces an approach that comprises of feature learning and classification stages that integrate an enhanced sparse autoencoder (SAE) and Softmax regression, respectively. In the SAE network, sparsity is achieved by penalizing the weights of the network, unlike conventional SAEs that penalize the activations within the hidden layers. For the classification task, the Softmax classifier is further optimized to achieve excellent performance. Hence, the proposed approach has the advantage of effective feature learning and robust classification performance. When employed for the prediction of three diseases, the proposed method obtained test accuracies of 98%, 97%, and 91% for chronic kidney disease, cervical cancer, and heart disease, respectively, which shows superior performance compared to other machine learning algorithms. The proposed approach also achieves comparable performance with other methods available in the recent literature.

Keywords: sparse autoencoder; unsupervised learning; Softmax regression; medical diagnosis; machine learning; artificial neural network; e-health

1. Introduction

Medical diagnosis is the process of deducing the disease affecting an individual [1]. This is usually done by clinicians, who analyze the patient's medical record, conduct laboratory tests, and physical examinations, etc. Accurate diagnosis is essential and quite challenging, as certain diseases have similar symptoms. A good diagnosis should meet some requirements: it should be accurate, communicated, and timely. Misdiagnosis occurs regularly and can be life-threatening; in fact, over 12 million people get misdiagnosed every year in the United States alone [2]. Machine learning (ML) is progressively being applied in medical diagnosis and has achieved significant success so far.

In contrast to the shortfall of clinicians in most countries and expensive manual diagnosis, ML-based diagnosis can significantly improve the healthcare system and reduce misdiagnosis caused by clinicians, which can be due to stress, fatigue, and inexperience, etc. Machine learning models can also ensure that patient data are examined in more detail and results are obtained quickly [3]. Hence, several researchers and industry experts have developed numerous medical diagnosis models using machine learning [4]. However, some factors are hindering the growth of ML in the medical domain, i.e., the imbalanced nature of medical data and the high cost of labeling data. Imbalanced data are a classification problem in which the number of instances per class is not uniformly distributed. Recently, unsupervised feature learning methods have received massive attention since they do not entirely rely on labeled data [5], and are suitable for training models when the data are imbalanced.

There are various methods used to achieve feature learning, including supervised learning techniques such as dictionary learning and multilayer perceptron (MLP), and unsupervised learning techniques which include independent component analysis, matrix factorization, clustering, unsupervised dictionary learning, and autoencoders. An autoencoder is a neural network used for unsupervised feature learning. It is composed of input, hidden, and output layers [6]. The basic architecture of a three-layer autoencoder (AE) is shown in Figure 1. When given an input data, autoencoders (AEs) are helpful to automatically discover the features that lead to optimal classification [7]. There are diverse forms of autoencoders, including variational and regularized autoencoders. The regularized autoencoders have been mostly used in solving problems where optimal feature learning is needed for subsequent classification, which is the focus of this research. Examples of regularized autoencoders include denoising, contractive, and sparse autoencoders. We aim to implement a sparse autoencoder (SAE) to learn representations more efficiently from raw data in order to ease the classification process and ultimately, improve the prediction performance of the classifier.

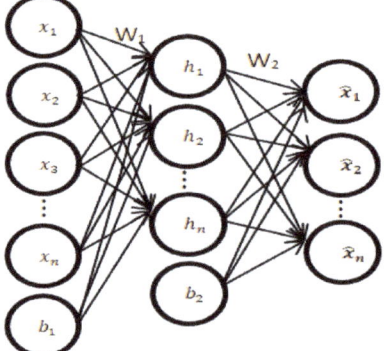

Figure 1. The structure of an autoencoder.

Usually, the sparsity penalty in the sparse autoencoder network is achieved using either of these two methods: L1 regularization or Kullback–Leibler (KL) divergence. It is noteworthy that the SAE does not regularize the weights of the network; rather, the regularization is imposed on the activations. Consequently, suboptimal performances are obtained with this type of structure where the sparsity makes it challenging for the network to approximate a near-zero cost function [8]. Therefore, in this paper, we integrate an improved SAE and a Softmax classifier for application in medical diagnosis. The SAE imposes regularization on the weights, instead of the activations as in conventional SAE, and the Softmax classifier is used for performing the classification task.

To demonstrate the effectiveness of the approach, three publicly available medical datasets are used, i.e., the chronic kidney disease (CKD) dataset [9], cervical cancer risk factors dataset [10], and Framingham heart study dataset [11]. We also aim to use diverse performance evaluation metrics to assess the performance of the proposed method and compare it with some techniques available in the recent literature and other machine learning algorithms such as logistic regression (LR), classification and regression tree (CART), support vector machine (SVM), k-nearest neighbor (KNN), linear discriminant analysis (LDA), and conventional Softmax classifier. The rest of the paper is structured as follows: Section 2 reviews some related works, while Section 3 introduces the methodology and provides a detail background of the methods applied. The results are tabulated and discussed in Section 4, while Section 5 concludes the paper.

2. Related Works

This section discusses some recent applications of machine learning in medical diagnosis. Glaucoma is a vision condition that develops gradually and can lead to permanent vision loss. This condition destroys the optic nerve, the health of which is essential for good vision and is usually caused by too much pressure inside one or both eyes. There are diverse forms of glaucoma, and they have no warning signs; hence, early detection is difficult yet crucial. Recently, a method was developed for the early detection of glaucoma using a two-layer sparse autoencoder [7]. The SAE was trained using 1426 fundus images to identify salient features from the data and differentiate a normal eye from an affected eye. The structure of the network comprises of two cascaded autoencoders and a Softmax layer. The autoencoder network performed unsupervised feature learning, while the Softmax was trained in a supervised fashion. The proposed method obtained excellent performance with an F-measure of 0.95.

In another research, a two-stage approach was proposed for the prediction of heart disease using a sparse autoencoder and artificial neural network (ANN) [12]. Unsupervised feature learning was performed with the help of the sparse autoencoder, which was optimized using the adaptive moment estimation (Adam) algorithm, whereas the ANN was used as the classifier. The method achieved an accuracy of 90% on the Framingham heart disease dataset and 98% on the cervical cancer risk factors dataset, which outperformed some ML algorithms. In a similar research, Verma et al. [13] proposed a hybrid technique for the classification of heart disease, where optimal features were selected via the particle swarm optimization (PSO) search technique and k-means clustering. Several supervised learning methods, including decision tree, MLP, and Softmax regression, were then utilized for the classification task. The method was tested using a dataset containing 335 cases and 26 attributes, and the experimental results revealed that the hybrid model enhanced the accuracy of the various classifiers, with the Softmax regression model obtaining the best performance with 88.4% accuracy.

Tama et al. [14] implemented an ensemble learning method for the diagnosis of heart disease. The ensemble method was developed via a stacked structure, whereby the base learners were also ensembles. The base learners include gradient boosting, random forest (RF), and extreme gradient boosting (XGBoost). Additionally, feature ranking and selection were conducted using correlation-based feature selection and PSO, respectively. When tested on different heart disease datasets, the proposed method outperformed the conventional ensemble methods. Furthermore, Ahishakiye et al. [15] developed an ensemble learning classifier to detect cervical cancer risk. The model comprised of CART, KNN, SVM, and naïve Bayes (NB) as base learners, and the ensemble model achieved an accuracy of 87%.

The application of sparse autoencoders in the medical domain has been widely studied, especially for disease prediction [12]. Furthermore, sparse autoencoders have been utilized for classifying Parkinson's disease (PD). Recently, Xiong and Lu [16] proposed an approach which involved a feature extraction step using a sparse autoencoder, to classify PD efficiently. Prior to the feature extraction, the data were preprocessed and an appropriate input subset was selected from the vocal features via the adaptive grey wolf optimization method. After feature extraction by the SAE, six ML classifiers were then applied to perform the classification task, and the experimental results signaled improved performance compared to other related works.

From the above-related works, we observed that most of the studies have some limitations: firstly, most of the authors utilized a single medical dataset to validate the performance of their models and not many studies experimented on more than two different diseases. By training and testing the model on two or more datasets, appropriate and more reliable conclusions can be drawn, and this can further validate the generalization ability of the ML method. Secondly, some recent research works have implemented sparse autoencoders for feature learning; however, most of these methods achieved sparsity by regularizing the activations [17], which is the norm. However, in this paper, sparsity is achieved via weight regularization. Additionally, poor generalization of ML algorithms resulting from imbalanced datasets, which is common in medical data, can be easily addressed using an effective feature learning method such as this.

3. Methodology

The sparse autoencoder (SAE) is an unsupervised learning method which is used to automatically learn features from unlabeled data [14]. In this type of autoencoder, the training criterion involves a sparsity penalty. Generally, the loss function of an SAE is constructed by penalizing activations within the hidden layers. For any particular sample, the network is encouraged to learn an encoding by activating only a small number of nodes. By introducing sparsity constraints on the network, such as limiting the number of hidden units, the algorithm can learn better relationships from the data [18]. An autoencoder consists of two functions: an encoder and decoder function. The encoder maps the d-dimensional input data to obtain a hidden representation. In contrast, the decoder maps the hidden representation back to a d-dimensional vector that is as close as possible to the encoder input [12,19]. Assuming m denotes the input features and n represents the neurons of the hidden layer, the encoding and decoding process can be represented with the following equations:

$$a^1 = \begin{bmatrix} a_1^1 \\ \vdots \\ a_n^1 \end{bmatrix} = \begin{bmatrix} w_{1,1}^1 & w_{1,2}^1 & \cdots & w_{1,m}^1 \\ \vdots & \vdots & \ddots & \vdots \\ w_{n,1}^1 & w_{n,2}^1 & \cdots & w_{n,m}^1 \end{bmatrix} \begin{bmatrix} x_1 \\ x_2 \\ \vdots \\ x_m \end{bmatrix} + \begin{bmatrix} b_1^1 \\ \vdots \\ b_n^1 \end{bmatrix}, \qquad (1)$$

$$a^2 = \begin{bmatrix} a_1^2 \\ a_2^2 \\ \vdots \\ a_m^2 \end{bmatrix} = \begin{bmatrix} w_{1,1}^2 & \cdots & w_{1,n}^2 \\ \vdots & \ddots & \vdots \\ w_{m,1}^2 & \cdots & w_{m,n}^2 \end{bmatrix} \begin{bmatrix} a_1^1 \\ \vdots \\ a_n^1 \end{bmatrix} + \begin{bmatrix} b_1^2 \\ \vdots \\ b_m^2 \end{bmatrix}, \qquad (2)$$

where $w^1 \in R^{n,m}$ and $w^2 \in R^{m,n}$ represent the weight matrices of the hidden layer and output layer, respectively; $b^1 \in R^{n,1}$ and $b^2 \in R^{m,1}$ denotes the bias matrices of the hidden layer and output layer, respectively; the vector $a^1 \in R^{n,1}$ denotes the inputs of the output layer; the vector $a^2 \in R^{m,1}$ represents the output of the sparse autoencoder, which is fed into the Softmax classifier for classification. The mean squared error function E_{MSE} is used as the reconstruction error function between the input x_i and reconstructed input a_i^2. Additionally, we introduce a regularization function $\Omega_{sparsity}$ to the error function in order to achieve sparsity by penalizing the weights $w^1 \in R^{n,m}$ and $w^2 \in R^{m,n}$. Therefore, the cost function E_{SAE} of the sparse autoencoder can be represented as:

$$E_{SAE} = E_{MSE} + \Omega_{sparsity}, \qquad (3)$$

The mean squared error function and the regularization function can be expressed as:

$$E_{MSE} = \frac{1}{m} \sum_{i=1}^{m} \left(x_i - a_i^2\right)^2, \qquad (4)$$

$$\Omega_{sparsity} = \frac{1}{m} \sum_{i=1}^{m} \left((x_i + 10) \log \frac{x_i + 10}{a_i^2 + 10} + (10 - x_i) \log \frac{10 - x_i}{10 - a_i^2} \right), \qquad (5)$$

Once the data have been transmitted from input to output of the sparse autoencoder, the next stage involves evaluating the cost function and fine-tuning the model parameters for optimal performance. Meanwhile, the cost function E_{SAE} does not explicitly relate the weights and bias of the network; hence, it is necessary to define a sensitivity measure to sensitize the changes in E_{SAE} and transmit the changes backwards via the backpropagation learning method [8]. To achieve this, and iteratively optimize the loss function, stochastic gradient descent is employed. The stochastic gradient descent to update the bias and weights of the output layer can be written as:

$$b^2 = b^2 - \eta^2 \frac{\partial E_{SAE}}{\partial b^2}, \tag{6}$$

$$w^2 = w^2 - \eta^2 \frac{\partial E_{SAE}}{\partial w^2}, \tag{7}$$

where η^2 represents the learning rate in relation to the output layer. The derivative of the loss function E_{SAE} measures the sensitivity to change of the function value with respect to a change in its input value. Furthermore, the gradient indicates the extent to which the input parameter needs to change to minimize the loss function. Meanwhile, the gradients are computed using the chain rule. Therefore, (6) and (7) can be rewritten as:

$$b^2 = b^2 - \eta^2 \frac{\partial E_{SAE}}{\partial a^2} \times \frac{\partial a^2}{\partial b^2}, \tag{8}$$

$$w^2 = w^2 - \eta^2 \frac{\partial E_{SAE}}{\partial a^2} \times \frac{\partial a^2}{\partial w^2}, \tag{9}$$

The sensitivity at the output layer of the SAE is represented and defined as $S^2 = \frac{\partial E_{SAE}}{\partial a^2}$. Therefore, (8) and (9) can be rewritten as:

$$b^2 = b^2 - \eta^2 s^2, \tag{10}$$

$$w^2 = w^2 - \eta^2 s^2 (a^1)^T, \tag{11}$$

where

$$S^2 = \begin{bmatrix} s_1^2 \\ s_2^2 \\ \vdots \\ s_m^2 \end{bmatrix} = \begin{bmatrix} \frac{-(x_1+10)}{\log(10)(a_1^2+10)} + \frac{(10-x_1)}{\log(10)(10-a_1^2)} - (x_1 - a_1^2) \\ \frac{-(x_2+10)}{\log(10)(a_2^2+10)} + \frac{(10-x_2)}{\log(10)(10-a_2^2)} - (x_2 - a_2^2) \\ \vdots \\ \frac{-(x_m+10)}{\log(10)(a_m^2+10)} + \frac{(10-x_m)}{\log(10)(10-a_m^2)} - (x_m - a_m^2) \end{bmatrix}, \tag{12}$$

Using the same method for computing S^2, the sensitivities can be transmitted back to the hidden layer

$$b^1 = b^1 - \eta^1 s^1, \tag{13}$$

$$w^1 = w^1 - \eta^1 s^1 (x)^T, \tag{14}$$

where η^1 denotes the learning rate with respect to the hidden layer, whereas s^1 is defined as:

$$s^1 = \begin{bmatrix} s_1^1 \\ \vdots \\ s_n^1 \end{bmatrix} = \begin{bmatrix} s_1^2 w_{1,1}^2 + s_2^2 w_{2,1}^2 + \cdots + s_m^2 w_{m,1}^2 \\ \vdots \\ s_1^2 w_{1,n}^2 + s_2^2 w_{2,n}^2 + \cdots + s_m^2 w_{m,n}^2 \end{bmatrix}, \tag{15}$$

Furthermore, the Softmax classifier is employed for the classification task. The learned features from the proposed SAE are used to train the classifier. Though, Softmax regression, otherwise called multinomial logistic regression (MLR), is a generalization of logistic regression that can be utilized for multi-class classification [20]. However, in the literature, the Softmax classifier has been applied for several binary classification tasks and has obtained excellent performance [21]. The Softmax function provides a method to interpret the outputs as probabilities and is expressed as:

$$f(x_i) = \frac{e^{x_i}}{\sum_{j=1}^{k} e^{x_j}} \quad (i = 1, 2, \ldots, N), \tag{16}$$

where $x_1, x_2, \ldots, x_N$ represent the input values and the output $f(x_i)$ is the probability that the sample belongs to the ith label [22]. For N input samples, the error at the Softmax layer is measured using the cross-entropy loss function:

$$L(w) = \frac{1}{N}\sum_{n=1}^{N} H(p_n, q_n) = -\frac{1}{N}\sum_{n=1}^{N}[y_n \log \hat{y}_n + (1 - y_n)\log(1 - \hat{y}_n)], \quad (17)$$

where the true probability p_n is the actual label and q_n is the predicted value. $H(p_n, q_n)$ is a measure of the dissimilarity between p_n and q_n. Furthermore, neural networks can easily become stuck in local minima, whereby the algorithm assumes it has reached the global minima, thereby resulting in non-optimal performance. To prevent the local minima problem and further enhance classifier performance, the mini-batch gradient descent with momentum is applied to optimize the cross-entropy loss of the Softmax classifier. This optimization algorithm splits the training data into small batches which are then used to compute the model error and update the model parameters [23]. The momentum [24] ensures better convergence is obtained.

The flowchart to visualize the proposed methodology is shown in Figure 2. The initial dataset is preprocessed; then, it is divided into training and testing sets. The training set is utilized for training the sparse autoencoder in an unsupervised manner. Meanwhile, the testing set is transformed and inputted into the trained model to obtain the low-dimensional representation dataset. The low-dimensional training set is used to train the Softmax classifier, and its performance is tested using the low-dimensional test set. Hence, there is no possible data leakage since the classifier sees only the low-dimensional training set.

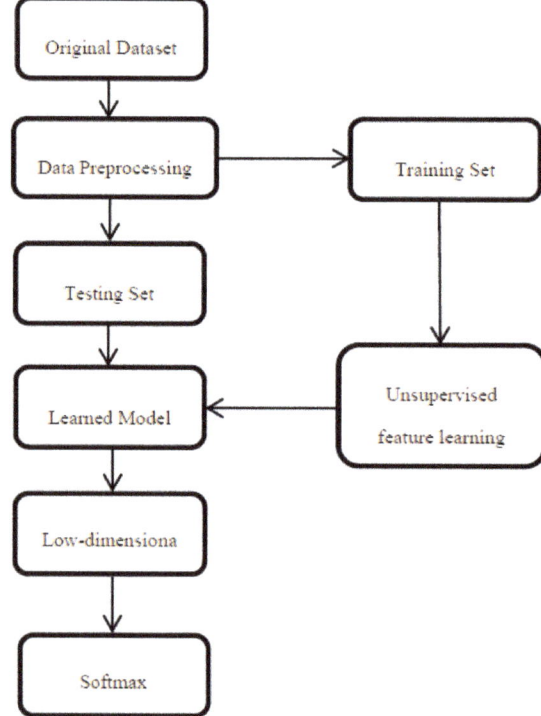

Figure 2. Flowchart of the methodology.

4. Results and Discussion

The proposed method is applied for the prediction of three diseases in order to show its performance in diverse medical diagnosis situations. The datasets include the Framingham heart study [11], which was obtained from the Kaggle website, and it contains 4238 samples and 16 features. The second dataset is the cervical cancer risk factors dataset [10], which was obtained from the University of California, Irvine (UCI) ML repository, and it contains 858 instances and 36 attributes. Thirdly, the CKD dataset [9] was also obtained from the UCI ML repository, and it contains 400 samples and 25 features. We used mean imputation to handle missing variables in the datasets.

The training parameters of the SAE include: $\eta^1 = 0.01$, $\eta^2 = 0.1$, $n = 25$, and number of epochs = 200. The hyperparameters of the Softmax classifier include learning rate = 0.01, number of samples in mini batches = 32, momentum value = 0.9, and number of epochs = 200. These parameters were obtained from the literature [12,23], as they have led to optimal performance in diverse neural network applications.

The effectiveness of the proposed method is evaluated using the following performance metrics: accuracy, precision, recall, and F1 score. Accuracy is the ratio of the correctly classified instances to the total number of instances in the test set, and precision measures the fraction of correctly predicted instances among the ones predicted to have the disease, i.e., positive [25]. Meanwhile, recall measures the proportion of sick people that are predicted correctly, and F1 score is a measure of the balance between precision and recall [26]. The following equations are used to determine these metrics:

$$Classification\ accuracy = \frac{TP + TN}{TP + TN + FP + FN}, \tag{18}$$

$$Precision = \frac{TP}{TP + FP}, \tag{19}$$

$$Recall = \frac{TP}{TP + FN}, \tag{20}$$

$$F1\ score = \frac{2 * Precision * Recall}{Precision + Recall} = \frac{2TP}{2TP + FP + FN}, \tag{21}$$

where

- True positive (*TP*): Sick people correctly predicted as sick.
- False-positive (*FP*): Healthy people wrongly predicted as sick.
- True negative (*TN*): Healthy people rightly predicted as healthy.
- False-negative (*FN*): Sick people wrongly predicted as healthy.

To demonstrate the efficacy of the proposed method, it is benchmarked with other algorithms, such as LR, CART, SVM, KNN, LDA, and conventional Softmax regression. In order to show the improved performance of the proposed method, no parameter tuning was performed on these algorithms; hence, their default parameter values in scikit-learn were used, which are adequate for most machine learning problems. The K-fold cross-validation technique was used to evaluate all the models. Tables 1–3 show the experimental results when the proposed method is tested on the Framingham heart study, cervical cancer risk factors, and CKD datasets, respectively. Meanwhile, Figures 3–5 show the receiver operating characteristic (ROC) curves comparing the performance of the conventional Softmax classifier and the proposed approach for the various disease prediction models. The ROC curve illustrates the diagnostic ability of binary classifiers, and it is obtained by plotting the true positive rate (TPR) against the false positive rate (FPR).

Table 1. Performance of the proposed method and other classifiers on the Framingham dataset.

Algorithm	Accuracy (%)	Precision (%)	Recall (%)	F1 Score (%)
LR	83	84	86	84
CART	75	74	75	74
SVM	82	78	82	80
KNN	81	75	81	77
LDA	83	81	83	82
Softmax classifier	86	84	88	86
Proposed SAE + Softmax	91	93	90	92

Table 2. Performance of the proposed method and other classifiers on the cervical cancer dataset.

Algorithm	Accuracy (%)	Precision (%)	Recall (%)	F1 Score (%)
LR	94	96	91	93
CART	90	93	96	94
SVM	94	90	93	91
KNN	93	98	95	96
LDA	95	93	91	92
Softmax classifier	94	97	91	94
Proposed SAE + Softmax	97	98	95	97

Table 3. Performance of the proposed method and other classifiers on the chronic kidney disease (CKD) dataset.

Algorithm	Accuracy (%)	Precision (%)	Recall (%)	F1 Score (%)
LR	98	93	97	95
CART	95	97	95	96
SVM	96	94	96	95
KNN	94	93	89	91
LDA	96	97	93	95
Softmax classifier	96	95	97	96
Proposed SAE + Softmax	98	97	97	97

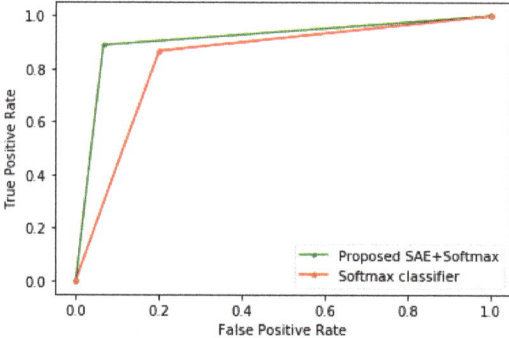

Figure 3. Receiver operating characteristic (ROC) curve of the heart disease model.

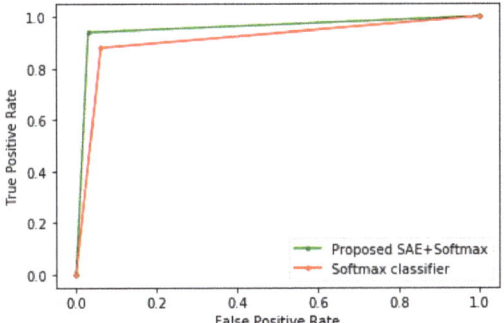

Figure 4. ROC curve of the cervical cancer model.

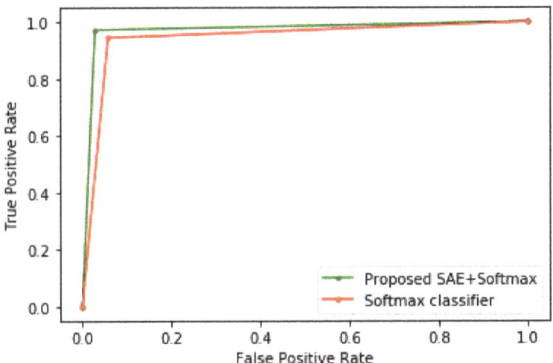

Figure 5. ROC curve of the CKD model.

From the experimental results, it can be seen that the sparse autoencoder improves the performance of the Softmax classifier, which is further validated by the ROC curves of the various models. The proposed method also performed better than the other machine learning algorithms. Furthermore, the misclassifications obtained by the model in the various disease predictions are also considered. For the prediction of heart disease, the proposed method recorded an FPR of 7% and a false-negative rate (FNR) of 10%. In addition, the model specificity, which is the true negative rate (TNR), is 93%, and the TPR is 90%. For the cervical cancer dataset, the following were obtained: FPR = 3%, FNR = 5%, TNR = 97%, and TPR = 95%. For the CKD prediction: FPR = 0, FNR = 3%, TNR = 100%, and TPR = 97%.

Additionally, to further validate the performance of the proposed method, we compare it with some models for heart disease prediction available in the recent literature, including a feature selection method using PSO and Softmax regression [13], a two-tier ensemble method with PSO-based feature selection [14], an ensemble classifier comprising of the following base learners: NB, Bayes Net (BN), RF, and MLP [27], a hybrid method of NB and LR [28], and a hybrid RF with a linear model (HRFLM) [29]. The other techniques include a combination of LR and Lasso regression [30], an intelligent heart disease detection method based on NB and advanced encryption standard (AES) [31], a combination of ANN and Fuzzy analytic hierarchy method (Fuzzy-AHP) [32], and a sparse autoencoder feature learning method combined ANN classifier [12]. This comparison is tabulated in Table 4. Meanwhile, in order to give a fair comparison, only the accuracies of the various techniques were considered because some authors did not report the values for other performance metrics.

Table 4. Comparison of the proposed method with the recent literature that used the heart disease dataset.

Algorithm	Method	Accuracy (%)
Verma et al. [13]	PSO and Softmax regression	88.4
Tama et al. [14]	Ensemble and PSO	85.71
Latha and Jeeva [27]	An Ensemble of NB, BN, RF, and MLP	85.48
Amin et al. [28]	A hybrid NB and LR	87.4
Mohan et al. [29]	HRFLM	88.4
Haq et al. [30]	LASSO-LR Model	89
Repaka et al. [31]	NB-AES	89.77
Samuel et al. [32]	ANN-Fuzzy-AHP	91
Mienye et al. [12]	SAE+ANN	90
Our approach	Improved SAE + Softmax	91

In Table 5, we compare the proposed approach with some recent scholarly works that used the cervical cancer dataset, including principal component analysis (PCA)-based SVM [33], a research work where the dataset was preprocessed and classified using numerous algorithms, in which LR and SVM had the best accuracy [34], a C5.0 decision tree [35]. The other methods include a multistage classification process which combined isolation forest (iForest), synthetic minority over-sampling technique (SMOTE), and RF [36], a sparse autoencoder feature learning method combined ANN classifier [12], and a feature selection method combined with C5.0 and RF [37].

Table 5. Comparison of the proposed method with the recent literature that used the cervical cancer dataset.

Algorithm	Method	Accuracy (%)
Wu and Zhou [33]	SVM-PCA	94.03
Abdullah et al. [34]	SVM	93.4884
	LR	93.4884
Chang et al. [35]	C5.0	96
Ijaz et al. [36]	iForest+SMOTE+RF	98.925
Mienye et al. [12]	SAE+ANN	98
Nithya and Ilango [37]	C5.0	97
	RF	96.9
Our approach	Improved SAE + Softmax	97

In Table 6, we compare the proposed method with other recent CKD prediction research works, including an optimized XGBoost method [38], a probabilistic neural network (PNN) [39], and a method using adaptive boosting (AdaBoost) [40]. The other research works include a hybrid classifier of NB and decision tree (NBTree) [41], XGBoost [42], and a 7-7-1 MLP neural network [43].

Table 6. Comparison of the proposed method with the recent literature that used the cervical CKD dataset.

Algorithm	Method	Accuracy (%)
Ogunleye and Qing-Guo [38]	Optimized XGBoost	100
Rady and Anwar [39]	PNN	96.7
Gupta et al. [40]	AdaBoost	88.66
Khan et al. [33]	NBTree	98.75
Raju et al. [42]	XGBoost	99.29
Aljaaf et al. [43]	MLP	98.1
Our approach	Improved SAE + Softmax	98

From the tabulated comparisons, the proposed sparse autoencoder with Softmax regression obtained comparable performance with the state-of-the-art methods in various disease predictions. Additionally, the experimental results show an improved performance obtained due to efficient feature representation by the sparse autoencoder. This further demonstrates the importance of training classifiers with relevant data, since they can significantly affect the performance of the prediction model. Lastly, this research also showed that excellent classification performance could be obtained not only by performing hyperparameter tuning of algorithms but also by employing appropriate feature learning techniques.

5. Conclusions

In this paper, we developed an approach for improved prediction of diseases based on an enhanced sparse autoencoder and Softmax regression. Usually, autoencoders achieve sparsity by penalizing the activations within the hidden layers, but in the proposed method, the weights were penalized instead. This is necessary because by penalizing the activations, it makes approximating near-zero loss function challenging for the network. The proposed method was tested on three different diseases, including heart disease, cervical cancer, and chronic kidney disease, and it achieved accuracies of 91%, 97%, and 98%, respectively, which outperformed conventional Softmax regression and other algorithms. By experimenting with different datasets, we aimed to demonstrate the effectiveness of the method in diverse conditions. We also conducted a comparative study with some prediction models available in the recent literature, and the proposed approach obtained comparable performance in terms of accuracy. Thus, it can be concluded that the proposed approach is a promising method for the detection of diseases and can be further developed into a clinical decision support system to assist health professionals as in [44]. Meanwhile, future research will apply the method studied in this paper for the prediction of more diseases, and also employ other performance metrics such as training time, classification time, computational speed, and other metrics, which could be beneficial for the performance evaluation of the model.

Author Contributions: Conceptualization, S.A.E.-M.; methodology, S.A.E.-M., E.E., T.G.S.; software, S.A.E.-M., E.E.; validation, S.A.E.-M., E.E.; formal analysis, S.A.E.-M., E.E., T.G.S.; investigation, S.A.E.-M., E.E., T.G.S.; resources, E.E., T.G.S.; data curation, E.E., T.G.S.; writing—original draft preparation, S.A.E.-M., E.E.; writing—review and editing, E.E., T.G.S.; visualization, E.E., T.G.S.; supervision, E.E., T.G.S.; project administration, E.E., T.G.S.; funding acquisition, E.E., T.G.S. All authors have read and agreed to the published version of the manuscript.

Funding: This research received no external funding but will be funded by Research Center funds.

Acknowledgments: This work is supported by the Center of Telecommunications, University of Johannesburg, South Africa.

Conflicts of Interest: The authors declare no conflict of interest.

References

1. Stanley, D.E.; Campos, D.G. The Logic of Medical Diagnosis. *Perspect. Biol. Med.* **2013**, *56*, 300–315. [CrossRef] [PubMed]
2. Epstein, H.M. The Most Important Medical Issue Ever: And Why You Need to Know More About It. Society to Improve Diagnosis in Medicine. 2019. Available online: https://www.improvediagnosis.org/dxiq-column/most-important-medical-issue-ever/ (accessed on 30 August 2020).
3. Liu, N.; Li, X.; Qi, E.; Xu, M.; Li, L.; Gao, B. A novel Ensemble Learning Paradigm for Medical Diagnosis with Imbalanced Data. *IEEE Access* **2020**, *8*, 171263–171280. [CrossRef]
4. Ma, Z.; Ma, J.; Miao, Y.; Liu, X.; Choo, K.K.R.; Yang, R.; Wang, X. Lightweight Privacy-preserving Medical Diagnosis in Edge Computing. *IEEE Trans. Serv. Comput.* **2020**, 1. [CrossRef]
5. Li, X.; Jia, M.; Islam, M.T.; Yu, L.; Xing, L. Self-supervised Feature Learning via Exploiting Multi-modal Data for Retinal Disease Diagnosis. *IEEE Trans. Med. Imaging* **2020**, 1. [CrossRef] [PubMed]
6. Chen, Z.; Guo, R.; Lin, Z.; Peng, T.; Peng, X. A data-driven health monitoring method using multi-objective optimization and stacked autoencoder based health indicator. *IEEE Trans. Ind. Inform.* **2020**, 1. [CrossRef]
7. Raghavendra, U.; Gudigar, A.; Bhandary, S.V.; Rao, T.N.; Ciaccio, E.J.; Acharya, U.R. A Two Layer Sparse Autoencoder for Glaucoma Identification with Fundus Images. *J. Med. Syst.* **2019**, *43*, 299. [CrossRef]

8. Musafer, H.; Abuzneid, A.; Faezipour, M.; Mahmood, A. An Enhanced Design of Sparse Autoencoder for Latent Features Extraction Based on Trigonometric Simplexes for Network Intrusion Detection Systems. *Electronics* **2020**, *9*, 259. [CrossRef]
9. Rubini, L.J.; Eswaran, P. UCI Machine Learning Repository: Chronic_Kidney_Disease Data Set. 2015. Available online: https://archive.ics.uci.edu/ml/datasets/chronic_kidney_disease (accessed on 26 June 2020).
10. UCI Machine Learning Repository: Cervical cancer (Risk Factors) Data Set. Available online: https://archive.ics.uci.edu/ml/datasets/Cervical+cancer+%28Risk+Factors%29 (accessed on 27 January 2020).
11. Framingham Heart Study Dataset. Available online: https://kaggle.com/amanajmera1/framingham-heart-study-dataset (accessed on 24 January 2020).
12. Mienye, I.D.; Sun, Y.; Wang, Z. Improved sparse autoencoder based artificial neural network approach for prediction of heart disease. *Inform. Med. Unlocked* **2020**, *18*, 100307. [CrossRef]
13. Verma, L.; Srivastava, S.; Negi, P.C. A Hybrid Data Mining Model to Predict Coronary Artery Disease Cases Using Non-Invasive Clinical Data. *J. Med. Syst.* **2016**, *40*, 178. [CrossRef]
14. Tama, B.A.; Im, S.; Lee, S. Improving an Intelligent Detection System for Coronary Heart Disease Using a Two-Tier Classifier Ensemble. *BioMed. Res. Int.* **2020**. Available online: https://www.hindawi.com/journals/bmri/2020/9816142/ (accessed on 28 August 2020). [CrossRef]
15. Ahishakiye, E.; Wario, R.; Mwangi, W.; Taremwa, D. Prediction of Cervical Cancer Basing on Risk Factors using Ensemble Learning. In Proceedings of the 2020 IST-Africa Conference (IST-Africa), Kampala, Uganda, 6–8 May 2020; pp. 1–12.
16. Xiong, Y.; Lu, Y. Deep Feature Extraction from the Vocal Vectors Using Sparse Autoencoders for Parkinson's Classification. *IEEE Access* **2020**, *8*, 27821–27830. [CrossRef]
17. Daoud, M.; Mayo, M.; Cunningham, S.J. RBFA: Radial Basis Function Autoencoders. In Proceedings of the 2019 IEEE Congress on Evolutionary Computation (CEC), Wellington, New Zealand, 10–13 June 2019; pp. 2966–2973. [CrossRef]
18. Ng, A. Sparse Autoencoder. 2011. Available online: https://web.stanford.edu/class/cs294a/sparseAutoencoder.pdf (accessed on 6 June 2020).
19. İrsoy, O.; Alpaydın, E. Unsupervised feature extraction with autoencoder trees. *Neurocomputing* **2017**, *258*, 63–73. [CrossRef]
20. Kayabol, K. Approximate Sparse Multinomial Logistic Regression for Classification. *IEEE Trans. Pattern Anal. Mach. Intell.* **2020**, *42*, 490–493. [CrossRef]
21. Herrera, J.L.L.; Figueroa, H.V.R.; Ramírez, E.J.R. Deep fraud. A fraud intention recognition framework in public transport context using a deep-learning approach. In Proceedings of the 2018 International Conference on Electronics, Communications and Computers (CONIELECOMP), Cholula Puebla, Mexico, 21–23 February 2018; pp. 118–125. [CrossRef]
22. Wang, M.; Lu, S.; Zhu, D.; Lin, J.; Wang, Z. A High-Speed and Low-Complexity Architecture for Softmax Function in Deep Learning. In Proceedings of the 2018 IEEE Asia Pacific Conference on Circuits and Systems (APCCAS), Chengdu, China, 26–28 October 2018; pp. 223–226. [CrossRef]
23. Ruder, S. An overview of gradient descent optimization algorithms. *arXiv* **2017**, arXiv:1609.04747.
24. Qian, N. On the momentum term in gradient descent learning algorithms. *Neural Netw.* **1999**, *12*, 145–151. [CrossRef]
25. Mienye, I.D.; Sun, Y.; Wang, Z. An improved ensemble learning approach for the prediction of heart disease risk. *Inform. Med. Unlocked* **2020**, *20*, 100402. [CrossRef]
26. Abdulhammed, R.; Musafer, H.; Alessa, A.; Faezipour, M.; Abuzneid, A. Features Dimensionality Reduction Approaches for Machine Learning Based Network Intrusion Detection. *Electronics* **2019**, *8*, 322. [CrossRef]
27. Latha, C.B.C.; Jeeva, S.C. Improving the accuracy of prediction of heart disease risk based on ensemble classification techniques. *Inform. Med. Unlocked* **2019**, *16*, 100203. [CrossRef]
28. Amin, M.S.; Chiam, Y.K.; Varathan, K.D. Identification of significant features and data mining techniques in predicting heart disease. *Telemat. Inform.* **2019**, *36*, 82–93. [CrossRef]
29. Mohan, S.; Thirumalai, C.; Srivastava, G. Effective Heart Disease Prediction Using Hybrid Machine Learning Techniques. *IEEE Access* **2019**, *7*, 81542–81554. [CrossRef]
30. Haq, A.U.; Li, J.P.; Memon, M.H.; Nazir, S.; Sun, R. A Hybrid Intelligent System Framework for the Prediction of Heart Disease Using Machine Learning Algorithms. *Mob. Inf. Syst.* **2018**, *2018*, 3860146. [CrossRef]

31. Repaka, A.N.; Ravikanti, S.D.; Franklin, R.G. Design and Implementing Heart Disease Prediction Using Naives Bayesian. In Proceedings of the 2019 3rd International Conference on Trends in Electronics and Informatics (ICOEI), Tirunelveli, India, 23–25 April 2019; pp. 292–297. [CrossRef]
32. Samuel, O.W.; Asogbon, G.M.; Sangaiah, A.K.; Fang, P.; Li, G. An integrated decision support system based on ANN and Fuzzy_AHP for heart failure risk prediction. *Expert Syst. Appl.* **2017**, *68*, 163–172. [CrossRef]
33. Wu, W.; Zhou, H. Data-Driven Diagnosis of Cervical Cancer with Support Vector Machine-Based Approaches. *IEEE Access* **2017**, *5*, 25189–25195. [CrossRef]
34. Abdullah, F.B.; Momo, N.S. Comparative analysis on Prediction Models with various Data Preprocessings in the Prognosis of Cervical Cancer. In Proceedings of the 2019 10th International Conference on Computing, Communication and Networking Technologies (ICCCNT), Kanpur, India, 6–8 July 2019; pp. 1–6. [CrossRef]
35. Chang, C.-C.; Cheng, S.-L.; Lu, C.-J.; Liao, K.-H. Prediction of Recurrence in Patients with Cervical Cancer Using MARS and Classification. *Int. J. Mach. Learn. Comput.* **2013**, *3*, 75–78. [CrossRef]
36. Ijaz, M.F.; Attique, M.; Son, Y. Data-Driven Cervical Cancer Prediction Model with Outlier Detection and Over-Sampling Methods. *Sensors* **2020**, *20*, 2809. [CrossRef]
37. Nithya, B.; Ilango, V. Evaluation of machine learning based optimized feature selection approaches and classification methods for cervical cancer prediction. *SN Appl. Sci.* **2019**, *1*, 641. [CrossRef]
38. Ogunleye, A.A.; Qing-Guo, W. XGBoost Model for Chronic Kidney Disease Diagnosis. *IEEE/ACM Trans. Comput. Biol. Bioinform.* **2019**, 1. [CrossRef]
39. Rady, E.-H.A.; Anwar, A.S. Prediction of kidney disease stages using data mining algorithms. *Inform. Med. Unlocked* **2019**, *15*, 100178. [CrossRef]
40. Gupta, D.; Khare, S.; Aggarwal, A. A method to predict diagnostic codes for chronic diseases using machine learning techniques. In Proceedings of the 2016 International Conference on Computing, Communication and Automation (ICCCA), Greater Noida, India, 29–30 April 2016; pp. 281–287. [CrossRef]
41. Khan, B.; Naseem, R.; Muhammad, F.; Abbas, G.; Kim, S. An Empirical Evaluation of Machine Learning Techniques for Chronic Kidney Disease Prophecy. *IEEE Access* **2020**, *8*, 55012–55022. [CrossRef]
42. Raju, N.V.G.; Lakshmi, K.P.; Praharshitha, K.G.; Likhitha, C. Prediction of chronic kidney disease (CKD) using Data Science. In Proceedings of the 2019 International Conference on Intelligent Computing and Control Systems (ICCS), Madurai, India, 15–17 May 2019; pp. 642–647. [CrossRef]
43. Aljaaf, A.J.; Al-Jumeily, D.; Haglan, H.M.; Alloghani, M.; Baker, T.; Hussain, A.J.; Mustafina, J. Early Prediction of Chronic Kidney Disease Using Machine Learning Supported by Predictive Analytics. In Proceedings of the 2018 IEEE Congress on Evolutionary Computation (CEC), Rio de Janeiro, Brazil, 8–13 July 2018; pp. 1–9. [CrossRef]
44. Ebiaredoh-Mienye, S.A.; Esenogho, E.; Swart, T.G. Artificial Neural Network Technique for Improving Prediction of Credit Card Default: A Stacked Sparse Autoencoder Approach. *Int. J. Electr. Comput. Eng. (IJECE)* **2020**. [CrossRef]

Publisher's Note: MDPI stays neutral with regard to jurisdictional claims in published maps and institutional affiliations.

© 2020 by the authors. Licensee MDPI, Basel, Switzerland. This article is an open access article distributed under the terms and conditions of the Creative Commons Attribution (CC BY) license (http://creativecommons.org/licenses/by/4.0/).

Article

Two-Stage Monitoring of Patients in Intensive Care Unit for Sepsis Prediction Using Non-Overfitted Machine Learning Models

Vytautas Abromavičius , Darius Plonis *, Deividas Tarasevičius and Artūras Serackis

Department of Electronic Systems, Vilnius Gediminas Technical University, Naugarduko str. 41, 03227 Vilnius, Lithuania; vgtu@vgtu.lt or vytautas.abromavicius@vgtu.lt (V.A.); deividas.tarasevicius@vgtu.lt (D.T.); arturas.serackis@vgtu.lt (A.S.)
* Correspondence: darius.plonis@vgtu.lt

Received: 5 June 2020; Accepted: 9 July 2020; Published: 12 July 2020

Abstract: The presented research faces the problem of early detection of sepsis for patients in the Intensive Care Unit. The PhysioNet/Computing in Cardiology Challenge 2019 facilitated the development of automated, open-source algorithms for the early detection of sepsis from clinical data. A labeled clinical records dataset for training and verification of the algorithms was provided by the challenge organizers. However, a relatively small number of records with sepsis, supported by Sepsis-3 clinical criteria, led to highly unbalanced dataset (only 2% records with sepsis label). A high number of unbalanced data records is a great challenge for machine learning model training and is not suitable for training classical classifiers. To address these issues, a method taking into the account the amount of time the patients spent in the intensive care unit (ICU) was proposed. The proposed method uses two separate ensemble models, one trained on patient records under 56 h in the ICU, and another for patients who stayed longer than 56 h. A solution including feature selection and weighting based training on imbalanced data was proposed in this paper. In addition, several performance metrics were investigated. Results show, that for successful prediction, a particular model having few or more predictors based on the length of stay in the Intensive Care Unit should be applied.

Keywords: early detection; sepsis; evaluation metrics; machine learning; medical informatics; feature extraction; physionet challenge

---

1. Introduction

Sepsis is a syndrome of physiological, pathological, and biochemical abnormalities induced by infection [1]. The conservative estimates indicate that sepsis is a leading cause of mortality and critical illness worldwide [2,3]. World Health Organization concerned that sepsis continues to cause approximately six million deaths worldwide every year, most of which are preventable [4]. In their study, the Department of Health in Ireland reported that survival from sepsis-induced hypotension is over 75% if it is recognized promptly, but that every delay by an hour causes that figure to fall by over 7%, implying that the mortality increases by about 30%.

In this paper, we present our solution for the early detection of sepsis by joining the PhysioNet/Computing in Cardiology Challenge 2019 [5]. Here, a detailed explanation of the Challenge data, participant evaluation metrics, and primary results are provided, and therefore, we will not explain it in this paper. However, a few important findings we should share in this paper in order to better explain the motivation to construct our algorithm in a particular way.

According to the requirements of the Challenge, our open-source algorithm works on clinical data provided on a real-time basis by giving a positive or negative prediction of sepsis for every single hour.

The algorithm predicts sepsis development for the patient using a pre-trained mathematical model. Therefore, not only the appropriate model should be used but also the training should be performed in the right way.

Data used in the competition was collected from intensive care unit (ICU) patients in three separate hospital systems. However, data from two hospital systems only were publicly available for training (40,336 patients in total). Another set of records (24,819 patients in total), obtained from all three different hospital systems was hidden and used for official scoring only by challenges organizers. Such separation of the data prevented participants from over-fitting their models. Taking into account that the trained model may learn not only dependencies in the clinical records but also hospital system-related behavior, for our approach, we have tested different data selection strategies for training. Models trained on hospital system A data we tested on data from hospital system B and vice versa.

The most challenging issue in the available data records was a high number of unbalanced records. Only 2932 septic patients were included in the dataset, together with 37,404 non-septic patients. From the perspective of mathematical model training, the data balance is much worse. Since the sepsis prediction had to be made on an hourly basis, 6 h in advance to the onset time of sepsis, specified according to Sepsis-3 clinical criteria, a number of non-sepsis examples we also took from the septic patient early records. After such reorganization of training data, only 2% from 1,484,384 [1,424,171] events (16,933 from 752,946 [739,663] in set A and 10,557 from 73,438 [684,508] in set B) had to be classified as an early prediction of sepsis.

The imbalance of the data can be treated in different ways. Nemati et al. successfully used random subsampling to train deep cancer subtype classifier [6]. Vicar et al. used special cost function—Generalized Dice Loss [7]. Sweetly et al. created 54 datasets using the same sepsis data and different non-sepsis data records [8]. He et al. have applied a random subsampling to this Challenge data [9]. Although the rank of their solution was quite high in the Challenge, the model was highly overfitted on hospital systems A and B when comparing to the model performance on hidden hospital system C data. An interesting approach was proposed by Li et al., where they decided to divide data into three stages (1–9, 10–49 and above 50 h stay in ICU) [10].

Dealing with missing values is another decision to be taken and it also may have an influence to the selected model training and overall performance. Forward-fill method [8,11–15]. Singh at al. found in their study, that mean imputation model gave worst results [16]. Other authors successfully used mean calculation over whole dataset [15,17].

Our proposed algorithm was scored on a censored data set, dedicated for scoring and using utility function that rewards early predictions and penalizes late predictions as well as false alarms.

2. Materials and Methods

In this section, we address the challenges regarding the problem of early sepsis detection and propose a methodology to overcome them. A labeled clinical records dataset for training and verification of the algorithms was provided by the PhysioNet/Computing in Cardiology Challenge 2019 organizers [5].

2.1. The Data

Data contained records of 40,336 ICU patients with up to 40 clinical variables divided into two datasets, based on hospital systems A and B. For each patient, the data were recorded at every hour during the stay in ICU. The records were labeled (on an hourly basis) according to Sepsis-3 clinical criteria. A total of 1,407,716 h of data was collected and labeled. Data labels included vital signs, laboratory values, and demographic values of the patients. Eight vital signs were a heart rate (HR), pulse oximetry (O2sat), temperature (Temp), systolic blood pressure (SBP), mean arterial pressure (MAP), diastolic blood pressure (DBP), respiration rate (Resp) and end-tidal carbon dioxide (EtCO2). A total of 26 laboratory values were included in the dataset. Demographic values include age, gender, hospital identifiers, the time between hospital and ICU admission (Hosp), and ICU length of stay (ICULOS). Data were labeled as positive 12 h before and 3 h after the onset time of sepsis. Positive labels of sepsis were found in 2932 of the 40,336 records, which is 7.27% of the data. Labels consisting of positive (sepsis) labels were found in 27,916 rows, which is only 1.98% of all data.

Investigation of the data showed large numbers of missing values. The percentage of missing rows of vital signs is shown in Figure 1. Missing values of vital signs make about 10% of the data, with the exception of Temp (66% missing data) and EtCO2 (100% and 92% missing data, for dataset A and dataset B, respectively). Therefore, EtCO2 was not used as a feature for the model. The percentage of missing rows of laboratory measurements is shown in Figure 2. Missing data of laboratory values makes from 78% to 100% for all values. We did not use laboratory values to develop our model.

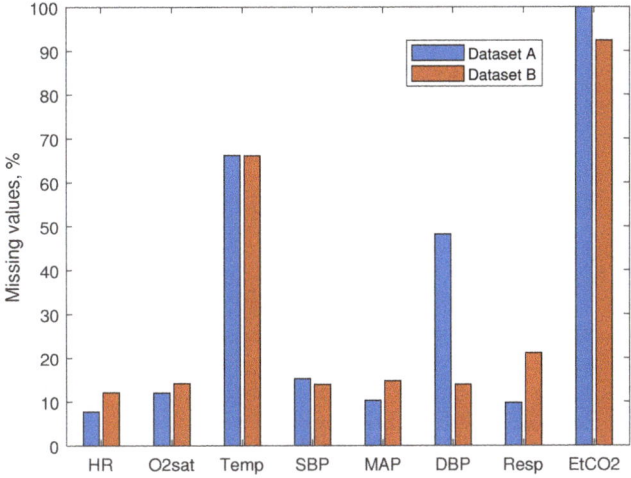

Figure 1. Missing vital values in the data.

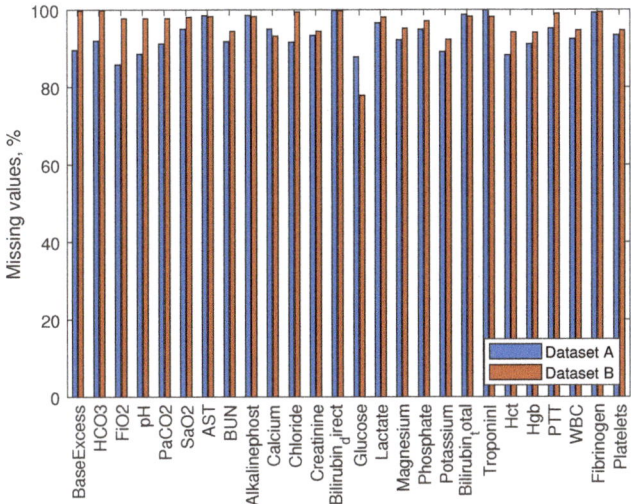

Figure 2. Missing laboratory values in the data.

Average values of vitals are shown in Table 1. Measured SBP, MAP and DBP values are higher in dataset B. Also, the measured HR is slightly lower in dataset B. Having two datasets collected in separate hospitals allowed us to develop models that are robust to measurement errors rising from the specificity of electronic medical record systems. Thus, the nature of data increases the difficulty of predicting sepsis. During the development of the model, we had to take into account the high unbalance of positive and negative cases, large amounts of missing values, and the fact that data was recorded using two different measurement systems.

Table 1. Average values of vitals and their standard error.

Measures	Dataset A	Dataset B
HR	84.6 ± 0.100	83.1 ± 0.106
O2sat	97.2 ± 0.016	97.1 ± 0.014
Temp	36.9 ± 0.004	36.8 ± 0.004
SBP	120.3 ± 0.115	126.4 ± 0.132
MAP	78.5 ± 0.076	86.7 ± 0.091
DBP	60.2 ± 0.070	66.6 ± 0.076
Resp	18.6 ± 0.026	18.5 ± 0.022
EtCO2	NaN	33.1 ± 0.072

2.2. Feature Extraction

A solution proposed in this paper to the early sepsis prediction problem employs information of the ICU length of stay, hospitalization time, age, and seven vital signs—HR, O2sat, Temp, SBP, MAP, DBP, and Resp. We did not use EtCO2 for feature extraction due to a large number of missing values.

We have calculated the mean, standard deviation, and the max-min difference for the vital sign data. We took those values from the whole duration of the record. Additionally, we have considered some other measures for our approach, such as kurtosis, entropy, and the standard error. However, after further analysis, we decided to discard these features. Kurtosis can only be calculated for four or more variables, not including the missing values. Additionally, kurtosis is not a representative statistic estimate for sample sizes less than 200 [18]. The entropy value is proportional to the sample size. In the problem we have investigated in this paper, the sample size changes each hour of the patient stay and can be reduced with missing values for some patients [19]. Therefore, in this case, the entropy just represents a number of samples used for its calculation. Thus, it is unlikely that entropy can carry useful information for the model training. The standard error is calculated by a division by the sample size, and it is inversely proportional to the sample size. Therefore, results can lead to a reduction of standard error for larger data sample sizes, which in its order increases unwanted load model training [20].

After our theoretical investigation, we have calculated 21 features for each hour. Missing values of the data were removed when calculating features. In some cases, features could not be calculated due to a small set of available data (e.g., during the first few hours of ICU stay, or due to a large number of missing values). In such cases, we set the value of the feature to '−1'. Finally, we have assembled a feature set of 24 features for model training: 21 calculated featured from vital signs and three demographic values (Hosp, age, ICULOS). Obtained data had different measurement units, measurement errors, and scales. Therefore, we have applied data standardization to have zero mean and standard deviation '1'. The sample mean and sample standard deviation were used the same for each patient, obtained from all sample data of both datasets containing 40,336 patients in total.

2.3. Data Balancing

The data from the experiment were strongly unbalanced, as discussed in Section 2.1. The balancing of the data can be performed using various oversampling or subsampling techniques that change the data in the dataset before the model is trained. In our investigation, we followed the alternative approach by setting different weights for the individual data points according to their class.

During our investigation of possible data balancing approaches, we surveyed various sampling methods, also used in the Challenge by other authors. The challengers applied undersampling, subsampling methods and some oversampling. The immensity of the imbalance problem is very great; the ratio of the labels is 1:50. Additionally, clinical data is very contextual. Oversampling methods haven't shown good results in the Challenge. Undersampling methods possibly removed valuable information of non-septic patients. Most of the subsampling methods overtrained showed high Utility scores on known datasets and poor scores on hidden datasets. The variability of the clinical (ICU) data is very high. Non-septic cases have various other conditions and unknown prescribed medications. We think that adjustment of classification cost is a more robust and effective way to address this issue of data imbalance. The highest rank in the 2019 Challenge was received by a solution, where the classification cost was calculated using Utility function value differences between correct and incorrect classification [13]. In our solution, we used simple weighting and investigated the behavior of the model training with differently selected weighs.

We have weighed the positive and negative predictions in accordance with the duration before or after the onset time of sepsis. Positive values, with various weights, make only 1.98% of the data. For this reason, the investigated models were trained with uneven classification costs. We have addressed the data balance issue by utilizing and modifying the classification cost function:

$$loss = -\sum_{i=1}^{N} c_i |t_i - y_i|, \qquad (1)$$

where N is the number of observations, t_i is the target output for observation i, y_i is the predicted value for observation i, and c_i is the classification cost for the observation i.

To investigate the influence of the selected weight on the model's behavior during training, we trained our models using different classification costs. A misclassified non-septic observations were weighted by 1 (c_1), and a misclassified septic observation weighted selecting different c_2 (1, 10, 20, 30, 100). Classification cost was selected based on the amount of "unbalance". As it was expected, since the positive values make only 1.98% of the data, the most effective value should be found when the classification cost c_2 is between 20 and 30. Models with c_2 parameter lower than 20 tend to predict most of the data as non-septic, while models with higher c_2 tend to predict all data as septic.

2.4. Model Training

In our investigation, we have used models based on Decision trees, naive Gaussian Bayes, Support Vector Machines (SVM), and Ensemble learners. All models were trained using stratified 5-fold cross validation. Decision trees based models were important in this stage of the problem solution. The Decision tree models give insights about the relevance of selected features. However, they tend to overfit the data [21]. Less over-fitting can be expected when using Ensemble learner models [22]. We have trained the ensemble learning-based models using hyperparameter optimization among Bag, GentleBoost, LogitBoost, AdaBoost, and RUSBoost methods. Hyperparameter tuning was performed for the number of decision tree splits, number of learners used in the model, learning rate, number of features in the ensemble. The number of decision tree splits search scaled in the range from 1 to 500. Many branches tend to overfit the data, while simpler trees can be more robust, which is especially important for the clinical data. The number of learners used in the search was from 10 to 100. A high number of learners can produce higher accuracy but can be time-consuming to train. We changed the learning rate in the ranged from 0.0001 to 1, and the number of features in ensemble hyperparameter tuning scaled from 1 to 24.

Gaussian naive Bayes based models are known for their simplicity, high bias, and low overfit. Typically good results using Naive Bayes are achieved using low variance data. These models are not recommended for high variance data [23]. Models trained using SVM tends to overfit data less. However, they are not very successful in problems with a high number of missing values in data [24].

We have trained each model separately using features estimated on an hourly basis in random order. In order to avoid over-fitting and increase robustness, we have trained the models on records taken from a single hospital system (dataset A) and tested on records from another hospital (dataset B, hidden during the training). We trained models on the dataset A using 5-fold cross-validation. Using our selected approach, only half of the available data was used for training. However, as it was shown in the results of the challenge [5], proposed solutions to the problem performed well on known datasets, even if scoring was done on a hidden part of the same set, and performed marginally worse on new hospital system C, hidden from challenge contestants. Additionally, the advantage of this approach to train and evaluate models is supported by Biglarbeigi [25].

Based on the results of the trained models and insights into the data, we proposed a method that takes into account the amount of time the patients have already spent in the ICU. The first model used AdaBoost ensemble method with a decision tree to evaluate features of patients extracted during the first 56 h (11,146 sepsis labels and 654,866 non-sepsis labels; it makes approximate imbalance ratio of 1:59). The second model is applied for patients with ICULOS time greater than 56 (5990 sepsis labels and 118,213 non-sepsis labels; it makes an approximate imbalance ratio of 1:20). The second model was developed using the discriminant subspace-based ensemble method. The method generates decision trees using pseudorandomly selected feature components. Decisions of the trees are then combined by averaging the estimates. As this method is based on decision trees, it is fast to train and easy to interpret [26]. Both models were using features described in Section 2.2. Additionally, our proposed model was trained on both datasets, 75% of the data used for training. This allowed us to investigate how much model overtrains on known hospital systems.

2.5. Model Scoring

Models, proposed in this paper for Sepsis prediction, were evaluated using several different metrics. Traditional scoring metrics, such as the area under the receiver operating characteristics (AUROC), the area under the precision-recall curve (AUPRC), accuracy, F-measure, and Matthews correlation coefficient (MCC) were used. Additionally, investigated models were scored using a specific scoring function developed by the authors of the dataset, called Utility score. Performance of the investigated models was based on the Utility score metric. Additionally, using different scoring metrics allowed us a better comparison of investigated models. AUPRC is recommended for imbalanced data over the AUROC measure [27,28]. F-measure is a harmonic mean of precision and recall [29]. Lately, MCC measure was shown to be more advantageous over F-measure in the binary classification of imbalanced data [30].

The utility score metric was proposed by the authors of the dataset for the 2019 physionet Challenge [5]. This metric was recently proposed. The utility score metric reward algorithms that facilitate early sepsis detection and treatment. Additionally, it addresses the problem of infrequent events and sequential prediction tasks. It is designed to capture the clinical utility of early sepsis detection by weighting early and late predictions. Moreover, decision threshold metrics (AUROC and AUPRC) have problems evaluating unbalanced datasets. Additionally, other challengers evaluated their models using the Utility score, therefore, it is easier to compare the results. However, the experimental results showed that Utility score correlates with two traditional metrics F-measure and MCC.

Utility score—a specifically designed scoring function rewards algorithms for early predictions and penalizes them for late or missed predictions and false alarms. Scoring was conducted by predicting each hourly label for each patient. Each positive label had a defined score depending on correct prediction time to sepsis. Scoring function awarded models for correct prediction at most 12 h before and 3 h after the onset time of sepsis. Scoring function penalized models who predicted septic state 12 h before onset time of sepsis and slightly penalized models with false-positive predictions.

True negative predictions were not penalized or rewarded by the function. Best Utility score the most optimal model could achieve would be 1. Thus, a better model would have higher Utility score. A more detailed scoring description can be found in the original paper. The utility score was a reference metric. Using it, we evaluated the performance of our investigated models. AUROC, AUPRC, accuracy, F-measure, and MCC scores were used to gain insight into the models (e.g., if they correlate with any other parameter of the experiment, such as classification cost, feature reduction, model configuration, or Utility score).

Our investigated and proposed models were compared with five challengers who received the highest Utility score on hidden test C. Additionally, a result of three baseline models was generated. Baseline models were scored using all positive, all negative and random performance to clearly show the unbalance of the data and the difficulty of the challenge.

3. Results

As it was noted in Section 2.4, decision trees, naive Gaussian Bayes, SVM and ensemble learners were investigated in our experiment. Various parameters of the models were adjusted. Additionally, the effect of classification cost and feature reduction was investigated. The performance of developed models was evaluated using Utility score as a reference metric. To complement, several other metrics, such as AUROC, AUPRC, accuracy, F-measure, and MCC were calculated to compare investigated models. Models were trained using dataset A, and scored using dataset B. Results of the experiment are given in Table 2. Models, based on decision trees, are labeled from 1 to 14. Models, based on the Naive Bayes algorithm, are labeled from 21 to 25. SVM based models are labeled from 31 to 34. Models from 41 to 44 were using an optimizable ensemble method for searching the best model for the problem.

The random guess of the sepsis with an accuracy of 50% showed −0.529 Utility score and 0.125 AUROC. By labeling all cases as positive, the Utility score was reduced to −1.059 and AUROC was 0, F-measure—0.029. Labeling all cases as negative increased the Utility score to 0, AUROC was 0.5 and F-measure—0. AUROC was generally expected to be equal or above 0.5 when the dataset is balanced. In Table 2, the third row indicates the AUROC value of a random performance, having an accuracy of 50%). The AUROC value in such a case is 0.125 (for balanced datasets it would be 0.5). It is a direct insight into the importance of the problem.

Based on the results of the Physionet challenge 2019 on the hidden dataset, several of the highest Utility scores were from 0.017 to 0.193. The highest Utility score (0.193) was achieved by Hong et al. using deep recurrent reinforcement learners [31]. Murugesan et al. applied XGBoost algorithm and achieved 0.182 Utility score on hidden test set [32]. Our proposed method was developed based on the results of further described investigations and results. The proposed method predicted 3753 true positive, 707,606 true negative, 7027 false positive and 43,309 false negative observations of dataset B. The precision of the method was 34.82%, recall—7.98%. Our proposed method achieved 0.306 AUROC, 0.009 AUPROC, 0.934 accuracy, 0.129 F-measure, 0.142 MCC and 0.245 Utility scores. Additionally, this model was trained on both datasets (70% of the data used for training) achieved 0.276 Utility score.

Decision trees are fast to train and to evaluate. We started our investigation using these models. The baseline score of Model1, with default parameters, gave a Utility score of 0.01. Secondly, a feature reduction using principal component analysis (PCA) was applied. Six features to explain 95% variance was kept. Model2 gave Utility score of 0.004. For Model3, increasing feature set to 14 (out of 24) increased Utility score to 0.0124. Forth model used 14 features and a modified classification cost ratio of 1:10. Model4 obtained Utility score of 0.1236. Further increasing classification (Model5) ratio to 1:100 Utility score decreased to −0.296. Using all available features in the set (24 features) Utility score was slightly improved to −0.242, for Model6. Using 24 features and classification cost 1:10 obtained Utility score was 0.184 for Model7. For Model8 we modified classification cost to 1:20, obtained Utility score was 0.22. Further increasing classification cost to 1:30 (Model9) decreased Utility score to 0.216.

Model10, having a modified classification cost of 1:20, and a reduced feature set to 20 got Utility score decreased to 0.157. Next, we limited the tree split criterion to 50. Model11 achieved Utility score of 0.232. Higher Utility score was achieved by reducing split criterion to 4, it was 0.233 (Model12). Reducing split criterion to 2 for Model13 got a similar Utility score of 0.233. Model14, with a further reduced split criterion to 1, achieved the highest Utility score of 0.242. Only 1 tree branch was used for this model. A feature that was used for this model was ICULOS. Features used for Model12 and Model14 also included ICULOS, and also mean SBP and Resp.

Models labeled from 21 to 25 were based on the Naive Bayes algorithm. Model21 without feature reduction and using classification cost 1:20 achieved Utility score of 0.1334. For Model23, using PCA, the number of features was reduced to 14, achieved Utility score was 0.129. Further reducing the number of features to 6 (95% explained variance using PCA) improved Utility score to 0.150, as shown in Table 2 Model24 row. Adjusting the classification cost led to a reduced score—Model22 and Model25 used a reduced feature set and a modified classification cost of 1:10 and 1:30; they yielded Utility scores of 0.097 and 0.143, respectively. SVM models were computed using the Gaussian kernel function. Results of the SVM models are shown in Table 2, under Model31 to Model34. Model31, using a classification cost ratio of 1:20 and 24 features for training, achieved a 0.151 Utility score. Model32, using 6 features to explain 95% variance, achieved a 0.144 Utility score. Model33 and Model34, using classification costs 1:30 and 1:10, respectively, achieved 0.1294 and 0.1302 Utility scores.

Models labeled from 41 to 44 were trained using ensemble methods, searching between Bag, GentleBoost, LogitBoost, AdaBoost, and RUSBoost methods and other hyperparameters. The classification cost for all investigated models were set to 1:20. Model41 using a full feature set achieved Utility score of 0.082. Reducing the tree split criterion to 10 (Model42) gave an improved Utility score of—0.124. Ensemble model (Model43) using bagged decision trees, having 29 learners, 4 splits and using 24 features achieved a Utility score of 0.173, further reducing split criterion to 1 did not improve the Utility score—0.173. Using principal component analysis (95%) reduced the Utility score to 0.008 (Model44).

High AUROC, AUPRC and accuracy scores using decision tree models were achieved when classification cost was 1:1, for example, 0.492, 0.497, 0.491 AUROC score for Model1, Model2, Model3, respectively. Model12 and Model14 with high Utility scores gave low AUROC (0.313 and 0.309, respectively), AUPRC (0.009, both) and accuracy (0.931 and 0.937, respectively) scores.

High AUROC, AUPRC, and accuracy scores using ensemble learners were achieved using Model41: 0.413, 0.012, and 0.955, respectively. However, this ensemble model achieved low Utility (0.082). In the same manner, low AUROC (0.347), AUPRC (0.01), and accuracy (0.939) scores, and the highest Utility score (0.173) was achieved using Model43. Other investigated models performed similarly, high AUROC, AUPRC and accuracy, and low Utility score; or low AUROC, AUPRC and accuracy, and higher Utility score was observed in all investigated models, namely decision trees, SVM, naive Bayes, and ensemble-based models.

Highest F-measure and MCC scores using decision tree models were achieved for models that showed the highest Utility scores. F-measure score of Model14 was 0.133 (Utility—0.242), score of Model11 was 0.131 (Utility—0.232). MCC score of Model14 was 0.143; the score of Model11 was 0.14. Lowest F-measure and MCC scores were achieved using Model2: F-measure—0.011, MCC—0.018. However, the lowest Utility score (-0.296) using decision tree models was achieved using Model5. F-measure score of Model5 was 0.04, MCC—0.057.

Naive Gaussian Bayes models achieved lowest F-measure (0.062) and MCC (0.085) scores when Model22 (Utility score—0.097) was scored, highest F-measure (0.099) and MCC (0.122) scores using Model24 (Utility score—0.15).

Model32 trained using SVM achieved F-measure (0.108) and MCC (0.104) score, and scored 0.144 using Utility performance metric. However, Model31's Utility score (0.1515) was slightly higher, while F-measure (0.099) and MCC (0.1) score lower. Low F-measure (0.081) and MCC (0.087) scores also showed low Utility scores—0.129, for Model33.

Comparably low F-measure (0.025) and MCC (0.02) scores using ensemble learners were achieved using Model44 (Utility score—0.008). Model43 with a high Utility score (0.173) demonstrated a high F-measure (0.115) and MCC (0.113) scores.

Table 2. Results of the investigated models, baseline scores, and five highest Utility scores on hidden test set from the challenge. Our Investigated models labeled from 1 to 14 were based on decision trees. Models labeled from 21 to 25 were based on naive Bayes algorithm. SVM based models were labeled from 31 to 34. Models labeled from 41 to 44 were using ensemble methods with hyperparameter search. Best performing models, having the highest Utility score, were highlighted.

Model	AUROC	AUPRC	Accuracy	F-Measure	MCC	Utility
All positive	0.000	0.000	0.014	0.029	0.000	−1.059
All negative	0.500	0.014	0.986	0.000	0.000	0.000
Random performance	0.125	0.007	0.500	0.027	0.000	−0.529
Hong et al. [31]	0.060	0.003	0.937	0.094	N/A	0.193
Murugesan et al. [32]	0.256	0.006	0.962	0.113	N/A	0.182
Narayanaswamy et al. [33]	0.701	0.069	0.881	0.059	N/A	0.062
Alfaras et al. [34]	0.702	0.078	0.877	0.058	N/A	0.055
Deogire [35]	0.586	0.016	0.984	0.048	N/A	0.017
Proposed method	**0.307**	**0.009**	**0.934**	**0.130**	**0.143**	**0.245**
when trained on both datasets	0.291	0.009	0.934	0.140	0.158	0.276
Model1	0.492	0.014	0.984	0.024	0.028	0.010
Model2	**0.497**	**0.014**	**0.985**	0.011	0.018	0.004
Model3	0.491	0.014	0.984	0.028	0.033	0.012
Model4	0.379	0.011	0.945	0.095	0.090	0.124
Model5	0.058	0.003	0.486	0.040	0.057	−0.296
Model6	0.097	0.005	0.562	0.040	0.051	−0.242
Model7	0.357	0.011	0.950	0.126	0.125	0.184
Model8	0.314	0.010	0.930	0.118	0.129	0.220
Model9	0.278	0.009	0.901	0.100	0.119	0.216
Model10	0.321	0.010	0.914	0.091	0.098	0.157
Model11	0.321	0.010	0.940	0.131	0.140	0.232
Model12	0.309	0.009	0.931	0.124	0.136	0.233
Model13	0.309	0.009	0.931	0.124	0.136	0.233
Model14	0.313	0.009	0.937	**0.133**	**0.143**	**0.242**
Model21	0.226	0.008	0.828	0.070	0.092	0.133
Model22	**0.241**	**0.009**	**0.874**	0.062	0.085	0.097
Model23	0.23	0.008	0.831	0.069	0.090	0.129
Model24	0.201	0.006	0.785	**0.099**	**0.122**	**0.150**
Model25	0.202	0.006	0.790	0.092	0.118	0.143
Model31	0.353	0.011	0.935	0.099	0.100	**0.151**
Model32	0.375	0.011	0.949	0.108	0.104	0.144
Model33	0.320	0.010	0.904	0.081	0.087	0.129
Model34	**0.392**	**0.012**	**0.956**	**0.109**	**0.101**	0.130
Model41	0.413	0.012	0.955	0.084	0.072	0.082
Model42	0.358	0.011	0.937	0.100	0.099	0.124
Model43	0.347	0.010	0.939	**0.115**	**0.113**	**0.173**
Model44	**0.489**	**0.014**	**0.981**	0.025	0.020	0.008

4. Discussion

The highest Utility score was achieved using our proposed method, which divided patients based on their length of stay and then the appropriate model was applied. Additionally, decision trees with a low number of nodes achieved high Utility scores when ICU length of stay was included as a branch of decision tree. Therefore, we believe that future models should be developed based on ICU-stay time. For example, one model predicting recently hospitalized ICU patients, another would be used if a patient's ICU length of stay reaches a certain length of time. Also, this approach can be implemented using three or more temporal divisions. This finding of our investigation is supported by Lauritsen [36], Vincent [37] and Shimabukuro [38] papers. Each intervention, vital measurement, intravenous therapy, and duration of stay in general increases a chance of infection—a direct cause of sepsis.

Regarding the dataset, other papers tackled this problem and proposed methods, which were trained on both datasets, and officially scored on hidden set C. Dataset C is not available anymore. Therefore, one must find other means to compare the results with the challenge score. Most of the challengers performed well on known hospital systems, obtaining Utility scores of about 0.4. However, Utility scores for the hidden hospital systems were low [5]. One author suggested evaluating the proposed methodology using one dataset and testing it on another [25]. Our achieved Utility score was for the known dataset, but the hidden percentage of data was 0.276 when trained on 75% of the records. This shows that our proposed model is robust to overtrain.

We assume that the Utility score can be improved a little by finding better value for classification cost, where a true positive prediction reward would be multiplied somewhere between 20 and 30. However, this would fit the data and would not solve the general problem of the Challenge. Therefore, we recommend using an arbitrary value between 20 and 30 to increases the robustness of the system.

MCC and F-measure scores gave similar results, which increases and decreases with the Utility score. However, the bounds of MCC are from -1 to 1, while the F-measure is from 0 to 1. The bounds of the Utility score are from -2 to 1. We support the idea of using the Utility score as a metric for this dataset. Moreover, we showed that the MCC and F-measure are effective metrics for this problem, while other traditional metrics AUROC, AURRC and Accuracy are misleading for a highly unbalanced dataset. Additionally, due to the nature of the Utility score, results can be difficult to interpret, as Roussel et al. pointed out in their work [39].

Investigated decision trees achieved Utility score of 0.242, AUROC score of 0.313, and MCC score of 0.143 on hidden set. Models with such results are far from applicable to the clinical setting. Additionally, our investigation showed that increasing AUROC and accuracy usually leads to decreased Utility, F-measure, and MCC scores. Moreover, accuracy is high for all investigated models. Accuracy can be miss-leading when interpreting models, results for this kind of highly unbalanced data, and a large number of negatives [22]. When developing methods for this kind of problem, one needs to be careful; the accuracy of 98.2% can be achieved just by guessing all rows as negative. We showed that balancing data reduces AUROC, accuracy scores and improves F-measure, MCC, and Utility scores.

There are many models to experiment with, for example, k-Nearest Neighbor (kNN) and Long Short-Term Memory (LSTM) models were not tested in our work. LSTM models are more difficult to configure to use them effectively. Additionally, LSTM tends to overfit the data. Moreover, even if one successfully tackles the overfitting problem, there is still another downside, which is more important in the current state of the early sepsis prediction problem. The developed model may be hard to interpret and would not reveal much insight into data [40]. The clustering of unbalanced data (including Sepsis-related records) may give promising results for sepsis prediction. However, kNN overfits data with large variances [41]. On the other hand, a trained kNN model having 1000 or 2000 clusters to represent the data can be expected to be robust. In general, we believe results using these models can be promising, and we encourage future works exploring LSTM and kNN model capabilities.

It is notable that investigated models do not differ significantly in Utility score if a number of features is reduced. This shows that some features are not useful for the model. On the other hand, our proposed features were relatively simple. We believe that more advanced features are needed to solve the early detection of the sepsis problem. Using advanced features should improve the score. However, feature engineering is a difficult, time-consuming process, which also requires understanding the nature of the data. In this paper, we provide many insights into the nature of the data, different scoring metrics, advantages of various models, and feature combinations.

We believe that the results of our investigation presented in this paper will benefit the fundamental need of early sepsis prediction and will answer some basic questions about the limits of early detection. Our results should benefit the search for advanced combinations of features, ease the use of machine learning tools. With meaningful insights peer researchers can apply advanced feature engineering techniques and develop more sophisticated and robust models in order to reach reliable results. Reaching better results is available through the use of combined models and handcrafted features [42], thus, further contributing to this field. The main challenges of this problem, as we revealed, are—the highly unbalanced dataset, the high number of missing data, simple features calculated using vitals does not have enough predictive power, proposed solutions are prone to overtrain. Adjusting the classification cost function helps to address the latter problem. In addition, the insights and conclusions of our experiment may benefit not only machine learning specialists, researchers, but also ICU personnel and scientists in the medical field.

5. Conclusions

In this study, we provide a comparison of several alternative methods for early sepsis prediction. The performance of the investigated models was based on the Utility score metric. Our selected models and insights show how to deal with unbalanced data and with a large number of missing values.

The results, obtained during an experimental investigation, are based on publicly available data containing 40,336 records with 1,407,716 of rows and 40 dimensions. Results showed:

1. Our proposed method, using two separate ensemble models, based on length of stay in the ICU, performed better than other tested models when using vital and demographic data to calculate simple features.
2. Adjusting classification cost function improves the Utility score of the tested models. Best results, on the investigated dataset, were achieved when the reward of true positive prediction was increased 20 times.
3. Feature ranking, using PCA, applied for our proposed features does not always improve Utility score. Utility score changes, when reducing the number of features based on the investigated model. In some models, such as Naive Gaussian, reducing the number of features improved the Utility score.
4. Performance metrics AUROC, AUPRC, and accuracy are not suitable for this highly unbalanced dataset. Additionally, these metrics do not reflect the Utility score. These metrics can be high for models with low Utility scores. Dealing with the early sepsis prediction problem, one should not apply these performance metrics. On the contrary, F-measure and MCC performance metrics reflect the Utility score.
5. High Utility score was obtained using decision tree models limited to 50 and fewer splits. All investigated decision trees chose ICULOS—ICU length of stay, as an important feature. Additionally, reducing the number of tree splits up to 4, and 1 further increased the Utility score. Utility score of 0.242 was achieved using only ICULOS as a single feature for the decision tree model.

Author Contributions: Conceptualization and methodology, all authors; validation, V.A. and D.T.; Analysis, A.S. and V.A.; writing—original draft preparation, A.S. and V.A.; project administration, A.S.; supervision, D.P.; writing—review and editing, all authors. All authors have read and agreed to the published version of the manuscript.

Funding: This research received no external funding.

Conflicts of Interest: The authors declare no conflict of interest.

References

1. Singer, M.; Deutschman, C.S.; Seymour, C.W.; Shankar-Hari, M.; Annane, D.; Bauer, M.; Bellomo, R.; Bernard, G.R.; Chiche, J.D.; Coopersmith, C.M.; et al. The third international consensus definitions for sepsis and septic shock (sepsis-3). *JAMA* **2008**, *10*, 142–149. [CrossRef]
2. Vincent, J.L.; Marshall, J.C.; Ñamendys-Silva, S.A.; François, B.; Martin-Loeches, I.; Lipman, J.; Reinhart, K.; Antonelli, M.; Pickkers, P.; Njimi, H.; et al. Assessment of the worldwide burden of critical illness: The intensive care over nations (icon) audit. *Lancet Respir. Med.* **2014**, *2*, 380–386. [CrossRef]
3. Fleischmann, C.; Scherag, A.; Adhikari, N.K.; Hartog, C.S.; Tsaganos, T.; Schlattmann, P.; Angus, D.C.; Reinhart, K. Assessment of global incidence and mortality of hospital-treated sepsis. current estimates and limitations. *Am. J. Respir. Crit. Care Med.* **2016**, *193*, 259–272. [CrossRef]
4. Reinhart, K.; Daniels, R.; Kissoon, N.; Machado, F.R.; Schachter, R.D.; Finfer, S. Recognizing sepsis as a global health priority—A who resolution. *N. Engl. J. Med.* **2017**, *377*, 414–417. [CrossRef]
5. Reyna, M.A.; Josef, C.S.; Jeter, R.; Shashikumar, S.P.; Westover, M.B.; Nemati, S.; Clifford, G.D.; Sharma, A. Early prediction of sepsis from clinical data: The PhysioNet/Computing in Cardiology Challenge 2019. *Crit. Care Med.* **2020**, *48*, 210–217. [CrossRef]
6. Nemati, S.; Holder, A.; Razmi, F.; Stanley, M.D.; Clifford, G.D.; Buchman, T.G. An Interpretable Machine Learning Model for Accurate Prediction of Sepsis in the ICU. *Crit. Care Med.* **2018**, *46*, 547–553. [CrossRef] [PubMed]
7. Vicar, T.; Hejc, J.; Novotna, P.; Ronzhina, M.; Smisek, R. Sepsis Detection in Sparse Clinical Data Using Long Short-Term Memory Network with Dice Loss. In Proceedings of the 2019 Computing in Cardiology (CinC), Singapore, 8–11 September 2019.
8. Sweely, B.; Park, A.; Winter, L.; Liu, L.; Zhao, X. Time-Padded Random Forest Ensemble to Capture Changes in Physiology Leading to Sepsis Development. In Proceedings of the 2019 Computing in Cardiology (CinC), Singapore, 8–11 September 2019.
9. He, Z.; Chen, X.; Fang, Z.; Yi, W.; Wang, C.; Jiang, L.; Pan, Y. Early Sepsis Prediction Using Ensemble Learning with Features Extracted from LSTM Recurrent Neural Network. In Proceedings of the 2019 Computing in Cardiology (CinC), Singapore, 8–11 September 2019.
10. Li, X.; Kang, Y.; Jia, X.; Wang, J.; Xie, G. TASP: A Time-Phased Model for Sepsis Prediction. In Proceedings of the 2019 Computing in Cardiology (CinC), Singapore, 8–11 September 2019.
11. Nejedly, P.; Plesinger, F.; Viscor, I.; Halamek, J.; Jurak, P. Prediction of Sepsis Using LSTM with Hyperparameter Optimization with a Genetic Algorithm. In Proceedings of the 2019 Computing in Cardiology (CinC), Singapore, 8–11 September 2019.
12. Yang, M.; Wang, X.; Gao, H.; Li, Y.; Liu, X.; Li, J.; Liu, C. Early Prediction of Sepsis Using Multi-Feature Fusion Based XGBoost Learning and Bayesian Optimization. In Proceedings of the 2019 Computing in Cardiology (CinC), Singapore, 8–11 September 2019.
13. Morrill, J.; Kormilitzin, A.; Nevado-Holgado, A.; Swaminathan, S.; Howison, S.; Lyons, T. The Signature-Based Model for Early Detection of Sepsis from Electronic Health Records in the Intensive Care Unit. In Proceedings of the 2019 Computing in Cardiology (CinC), Singapore, 8–11 September 2019.
14. Anda Du, J.; Sadr, N.; de Chazal, P. Automated Prediction of Sepsis Onset Using Gradient Boosted Decision Trees. In Proceedings of the 2019 Computing in Cardiology (CinC), Singapore, 8–11 September 2019.
15. Hammoud, I.; Ramakrishnan, I.; Henry, M. Early Prediction of Sepsis Using Gradient Boosting Decision Trees with Optimal Sample Weighting. In Proceedings of the 2019 Computing in Cardiology (CinC), Singapore, 8–11 September 2019.
16. Singh, J.; Oshiro, K.; Krishnan, R.; Sato, M.; Ohkuma, T.; Kato, N. Utilizing Informative Missingness for Early Prediction of Sepsis. In Proceedings of the 2019 Computing in Cardiology (CinC), Singapore, 8–11 September 2019.
17. Tran, L.; Shahabi, C.; Nguyen, M. Representation Learning for Early Sepsis Prediction. In Proceedings of the 2019 Computing in Cardiology (CinC), Singapore, 8–11 September 2019.

18. DeCarlo, L.T. On the meaning and use of kurtosis. *Psychol. Methods* **1997**, *2*, 292. [CrossRef]
19. Dehmer, M. Information processing in complex networks: Graph entropy and information functionals. *Appl. Math. Comput.* **2008**, *201*, 82–94. [CrossRef]
20. Hamaker, E.L.; Ryan, O. A squared standard error is not a measure of individual differences. *Proc. Natl. Acad. Sci. USA* **2019**, *116*, 6544–6545. [CrossRef]
21. Tanha, J.; van Someren, M.; Afsarmanesh, H. Semi-supervised self-training for decision tree classifiers. *Int. J. Mach. Learn. Cybern.* **2017**, *8*, 355–370. [CrossRef]
22. Hu, B.; Wang, J.; Zhu, Y.; Yang, T. Dynamic Deep Forest: An Ensemble Classification Method for Network Intrusion Detection. *Electronics* **2019**, *8*, 968. [CrossRef]
23. Chen, Y.; Lu, L.; Yu, X.; Li, X. Adaptive Method for Packet Loss Types in IoT: An Naive Bayes Distinguisher. *Electronics* **2019**, *8*, 134. [CrossRef]
24. Gu, B.; Quan, X.; Gu, Y.; Sheng, V.S.; Zheng, G.S. Chunk incremental learning for cost-sensitive hinge loss support vector machine. *Pattern Recognit.* **2018**, *83*, 196–208. [CrossRef]
25. Biglarbeigi, P.; McLaughlin, D.; Rjoob, K.; Abdullah, A.; McCallan, N.; Jasinska-Piadlo, A.; Bond, R.; Finlay, D.; Ng, K.Y.; Kennedy, A.; et al. Early Prediction of Sepsis Considering Early Warning Scoring Systems. In Proceedings of the 2019 Computing in Cardiology (CinC), Singapore, 8–11 September 2019.
26. Ho, T.K. The random subspace method for constructing decision forests. *IEEE Trans. Pattern Anal. Mach. Intell.* **1998**, *20*, 832–844.
27. Boyd, K.; Eng, K.H.; Page, C.D. Area under the precision-recall curve: Point estimates and confidence intervals. In *Joint European Conference on Machine Learning and Knowledge Discovery in Databases*; Springer: Berlin/Heidelberg, Germany, 2013.
28. Saito, T.; Rehmsmeier, M. The precision-recall plot is more informative than the ROC plot when evaluating binary classifiers on imbalanced datasets. *PLoS ONE* **2015**, *10*, e0118432. [CrossRef] [PubMed]
29. Rousseau, R. The F-measure for research priority. *J. Data Inf. Sci.* **2018**, *3*, 1–18. [CrossRef]
30. Chicco, D.; Jurman, G. The advantages of the Matthews correlation coefficient (MCC) over F1 score and accuracy in binary classification evaluation. *BMC Genom.* **2020**, *21*, 6. [CrossRef]
31. Hong, S.; Shang, J.; Wu, M.; Zhou, Y.; Sun, Y.; Chou, Y.H.; Song, M.; Li, H. Early Sepsis Prediction with Deep Recurrent Reinforcement Learning. *Physionet Chall.* **2019**. Available online: https://docs.google.com/spreadsheets/d/1PPQY0SdguwCx_CxbR1BYlkh0dwpINlhEFxejc10xwgM/edit?fbclid=IwAR3psdL1QQ_PxlukPT89fE-v0ZVFgLdax11mrAeQwkdCO9WXeEKFfn8ek2o#gid=0 (accessed on 5 May 2020).
32. Murugesan, I.; Murugesan, K.; Balasubramanian, L.; Arumugam, M. Interpretation of Artificial Intelligence Algorithms in the Prediction of Sepsis. In Proceedings of the 2019 Computing in Cardiology (CinC), Singapore, 8–11 September 2019.
33. Narayanaswamy, L.; Garg, D.; Narra, B.; Narayanswamy, R. Machine Learning Algorithmic and System Level Considerations for Early Prediction of Sepsis. In Proceedings of the 2019 Computing in Cardiology (CinC), Singapore, 8–11 September 2019.
34. Alfaras, M.; Varandas, R.; Gamboa, H. Ring-Topology Echo State Networks for ICU Sepsis Classification. In Proceedings of the 2019 Computing in Cardiology (CinC), Singapore, 8–11 September 2019.
35. Deogire, A. A Low Dimensional Algorithm for Detection of Sepsis From Electronic Medical Record Data. In Proceedings of the 2019 Computing in Cardiology (CinC), Singapore, 8–11 September 2019.
36. Lauritsen, S.M.; Kalør, M.E.; Kongsgaard, E.L.; Lauritsen, K.M.; Jørgensen, M.J.; Lange, J.; Thiesson, B. Early detection of sepsis utilizing deep learning on electronic health record event sequences. *Early Detect. Sepsis Util. Deep Learn. Electron. Health Rec. Event Seq.* **2020**, *104*, 101820. [CrossRef]
37. Vincent, J.L. The clinical challenge of sepsis identification and monitoring. *PLoS Med.* **2016**, *13*, e1002022. [CrossRef]
38. Shimabukuro, D.W.; Barton, C.W.; Feldman, M.D.; Mataraso, S.J.; Das, R. Effect of a machine learning-based severe sepsis prediction algorithm on patient survival and hospital length of stay: A randomised clinical trial. *BMJ Open Respir. Res.* **2017**, *4*, e000234. [CrossRef] [PubMed]
39. Roussel, B.; Behar, J.; Oster, J. A Recurrent Neural Network for the Prediction of Vital Sign Evolution and Sepsis in ICU. In Proceedings of the 2019 Computing in Cardiology (CinC), Singapore, 8–11 September 2019.
40. Wan, R.; Mei, S.; Wang, J.; Liu, M.; Yang, F. Multivariate temporal convolutional network: A deep neural networks approach for multivariate time series forecasting. *Electronics* **2019**, *8*, 876. [CrossRef]

41. Mullick, S.S.; Datta, S.; Das, S. Daptive Learning-Based *k*-Nearest Neighbor Classifiers With Resilience to Class Imbalance. *IEEE Trans. Neural Networks Learn. Syst.* **2018**, *29*, 5713–5725.
42. Sawada, Y.; Sato, Y.; Nakada, T.; Yamaguchi, S.; Ujimoto, K.; Hayashi, N. Improvement in Classification Performance Based on Target Vector Modification for All-Transfer Deep Learning. *Appl. Sci.* **2019**, *9*, 128. [CrossRef]

© 2020 by the authors. Licensee MDPI, Basel, Switzerland. This article is an open access article distributed under the terms and conditions of the Creative Commons Attribution (CC BY) license (http://creativecommons.org/licenses/by/4.0/).

Article

Searching for Premature Ventricular Contraction from Electrocardiogram by Using One-Dimensional Convolutional Neural Network

Junsheng Yu [1], Xiangqing Wang [1,*], Xiaodong Chen [2] and Jinglin Guo [1]

[1] School of Electronic Engineering, Beijing University of Posts and Telecommunications, Beijing 100876, China; jsyu@bupt.edu.cn (J.Y.); jinglinguo@126.com (J.G.)
[2] Queen Mary University of London, London E1 4NS, UK; xiaodong.chen@qmul.ac.uk
* Correspondence: wangxiangqing@bupt.edu.cn

Received: 21 September 2020; Accepted: 27 October 2020; Published: 28 October 2020

Abstract: Premature ventricular contraction (PVC) is a common cardiac arrhythmia that can occur in ordinary healthy people and various heart disease patients. Clinically, cardiologists usually use a long-term electrocardiogram (ECG) as a medium to detect PVC. However, it is time-consuming and labor-intensive for cardiologists to analyze the long-term ECG accurately. To this end, this paper suggests a simple but effective approach to search for PVC from the long-term ECG. The recommended method first extracts each heartbeat from the long-term ECG by applying a fixed time window. Subsequently, the model based on the one-dimensional convolutional neural network (CNN) tags these heartbeats without any preprocessing, such as denoise. Unlike previous PVC detection methods that use hand-crafted features, the proposed plan rationally and automatically extracts features and identify PVC with supervised learning. The proposed PVC detection algorithm acquires 99.64% accuracy, 96.97% sensitivity, and 99.84% specificity for the MIT-BIH arrhythmia database. Besides, when the number of samples in the training set is 3.3 times that of the test set, the proposed method does not misjudge any heartbeat from the test set. The simulation results show that it is reliable to use one-dimensional CNN for PVC recognition. More importantly, the overall system does not rely on complex and cumbersome preprocessing.

Keywords: electrocardiogram; deep learning; convolutional neural network; Premature ventricular contraction

1. Introduction

The heart is a vital organ of the human body and has four chambers: right atrium, right ventricle, left atrium, left ventricle. These four chambers cooperate in providing power for blood flow in the blood vessel. First, the oxygen-poor blood flows through the right atrium and right ventricle in turn, and finally reaches the lungs. Then the oxygen-poor blood absorbs oxygen from the air in the alveoli. With the left atrium and left ventricle's work, the rest organ and tissue will receive the oxygenated blood. The most intuitive feeling of this process is the heartbeat. Every heartbeat moves blood forward through the arteries. Heart rhythm, which is the heartbeat pattern, is a critical clinical indicator to assess whether the heart is working correctly. Healthy heart rhythm is orderly and uniform. Abnormal heart rhythm, also called arrhythmia, is usually closely related to cardiovascular disease (CVD). According to the World Health Organization (WHO), CVD is widespread globally. Taking America and China as examples, ten people die every 6 min in America from CVD, and nearly 20.7% of China residents suffer from CVD [1].

Although there are many origins of the arrhythmia, premature ventricular contraction (PVC) caused by an ectopic cardiac pacemaker located in the ventricle is the most common cause. Moreover,

PVC is also related to multiple conditions, such as myocardial infarction (MI), left ventricular dysfunction (LVD) [2,3]. Electrocardiogram (ECG), which can record the heart's electrical signals, is a non-invasive and effective visualization tool widely used by cardiologists [4]. A normal heartbeat generates four entities with different shapes in ECG—a P wave, a QRS complex, a T wave, and a U wave, as shown in Figure 1.

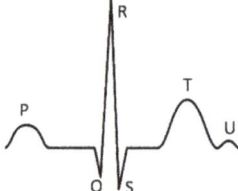

Figure 1. There is a normal heartbeat in electrocardiogram (ECG). The atria's depolarization caused the P wave; the ventricles' depolarization caused the QRS complex; the repolarization of the ventricles caused the T wave; the repolarization of the Purkinje fibers caused the U wave.

It is worth mentioning that the long-term ECG is more clinically significant for the diagnosis of PVC. However, it is time-consuming and arduous for cardiologists to analyze many long-term ECGs. Therefore, accurate and automatic searching for PVC from the long-term ECG is crucial for improving cardiology workflow efficiency.

In recent years, many researchers have developed various algorithms to search for PVC from ECG, as summarized in Table 1. Most of the algorithms manually extract morphological-based features. Manikandan et al. designed a set of temporal characteristics and proposed a decision-rule-based detection algorithm. The suggested method achieved an average sensitivity of 89.69% and specificity of 99.63% based on the MIT-BIH arrhythmia database [5]. Jun et al. extracted six features from the ECG signal and developed a classification algorithm on TensorFlow [6], an open-source machine learning platform. This algorithm used an optimized deep neural network (DNN) whose input is the six features, as the classifier. These six characteristics are R-peak amplitude, R-R interval time, QRS duration time, ventricular activation time, Q-peak, and S-peak amplitude. The experimental results based on the MIT-BIH arrhythmia database achieved 99.41% accuracy [7].

Hadia et al. not only summarized a feature extraction procedure based on the Principal Component Analysis (PCA) and waveform estimation but also combined the extracted features and k-nearest neighbor (KNN) algorithm. The classification sensitivity of this model is 93.45% [8]. Atanasoski et al. presented an unsupervised clustering method based on the R-R intervals and morphological rule. This algorithm does not rely on pre-existing labels and has an excellent overall accuracy above 99.5% and specificity above 99.6% [9]. Junior et al. developed a system based on threshold adaptive algorithm and wavelet transform for PVC detection. The result validated on the MIT-BIH arrhythmia database reported that Daubechies 2 wavelet mother is more indicated compared with Coiflets and Symlets [10]. Oliveira et al. proposed a simplified set of features extracted from geometric figures constructed over QRS complexes and selected the most suitable classifiers based on the analytic hierarchy process (AHP). The results of this method indicated that the artificial immune system (AIS) classifier with the geometrical features is the best suggestion for PVC recognition [11].

Considering that labeled ECG data is rare and precious, Lynggaarda suggested a multivariate statistical classifier that used robust designed features and a regularization mechanism. Even though this classifier's input is a very sparse amount of expert annotated ECG data, this model's average accuracy, specificity, and sensitivity are above 96% by using the MIT-BIH arrhythmia database [12]. Sokolova et al. recommended a set of weighted shape parameters from the different QRS shape metrics and designed a two-stage PVC detection rule. All these shape parameters are in the time and frequency domains. It is worth noting that this method achieved good results on the multi-lead ECG database: the St. Petersburg INCART 12-lead Arrhythmia Database [13]. Rizal and Wijayanto proposed a simple and low computation method. This method only used six characteristics obtained by the multi-order Rényi entropy and chose the support vector machine (SVM) with six kernels to detect PVC. The simulation results obtained 95.8% accuracy [14]. Chen et al. designed an algorithm to distinguish the QRS complex's peak points and proposed a PVC identification system based on the back-propagation neural network (BPNN). The system's input is a set of features obtained from the QRS complex peak points. The simulation result's average accuracy attains 97.46% on the China Physiological Signal Challenge 2018 (CPSC2018) Database [15].

Mazidi et al. evaluated three sets of ECG features and two classifiers on the field programable gate arrays (FPGAs). These three groups of characteristics come from time-domain based on the reconfiguration Pan–Tompkins algorithm, frequency-domain based on the Haar wavelet algorithm, and time-domain combination of frequency-domain based on the above two. The two classifiers are the SVM and the Naive Bayes [16]. Besides, Mazidi et al. introduced six robust features extracted by morphological assessment, polynomial curve fitting, discrete wavelet transform, and nonlinear analysis. Moreover, this literature used an SVM with a linear kernel to recognize PVC. This algorithm acquires the overall accuracy of 99.78%, with a sensitivity of 99.91% and 99.37% specificity for the MIT-BIH arrhythmia database [17]. Allami applied an artificial neural network (ANN) to classify the features extracted through morphological and statistical methods. The proposed method resulted in a sensitivity and accuracy of 98.7% and 98.6%, respectively, on the MIT-BIH arrhythmia database. Additionally, this method is computationally simple and suitable for real-time patient monitoring. [18]. Chen et al. extracted three features and provided these to a classifier based on the perceptron model. The three characteristics are the ratio of the QRS areas, the previous R-R interval, and the last R-R interval ratio to the next RR-interval. The experiments applied to the MIT-BIH arrhythmia database achieved high accuracy with a sensitivity of 98.7%. Moreover, this method's logic resources and power consumption are low, so it is suited for wearable monitoring [19]. Jeon et al. designed a model based on the error backpropagation algorithm and used four characteristics to detect PVC. These features are R-R interval, Q-S interval, Q-R amplitude, and R-S amplitude. The proposed approach's overall accuracy was above 90%, with testing on the MIT-BIH arrhythmia database [20].

With the popularity of deep learning and outstanding performance in other fields, researchers use deep learning to monitor PVC. Many experts used deep learning to detect PVC. Zhou et al. developed a reliable ECG analysis program to detect PVC. This system consists of two parts: data preprocessing and a recurrent neural network (RNN) with long short-term memory (LSTM). The accuracy of this method based on the MIT-BIH arrhythmia database is 96–99% since the RNN is good at processing time-series signals [21]. Zhao et al. combined the Modified Frequency Slice Wavelet Transform (MFSWT) and CNN, which has 25 layers, to search for PVC from 12-lead ECG data provided by the CPSC2018 Database. The MFSWT can transform one-dimensional time-series signals into two-dimensional time-frequency images as the input of the CNN. The test results of this method achieved a high accuracy of 97.89% [22].

Li et al. used three types of wavelets to convert single-channel ECG signals to wavelet power spectrums and constructed a CNN consisting of three convolutional layers, two max-pooling layers, and a rectified linear unit layer, a fully connected layer. These three wavelets are Morlet wavelet, Paul wavelet, and Gaussian derivative. The CNN receives and processes the transformed wavelet power spectrums, then labels it. It is commendable that the generalization ability of this method is excellent. The validation results on the American Heart Association (AHA) database achieved an overall F1 score of 84.96% and an accuracy of 97.36% with the training data from the MIT-BIH arrhythmia database [23]. Gordon and Williams developed a PVC detection algorithm based on autoencoder and random forest classifier. The proposed autoencoder consists of two parts. The first part is an encoder with two convolutional layers used for encoding the ECG to a latent space representation, which is low-dimensional and effective. The second part is a decoder with transposed convolutional layers for decoding the latent space representation to recover the ECG. The random forest classifier composed of 10 decision trees takes the latent space representation as input and annotate it. This algorithm achieved an overall accuracy above 97% on the MIT-BIH arrhythmia database [24].

Rahhal et al. report a model based on the Stacked Denoising Autoencoders (SDAs) networks and DNN to search PVC from the multi-lead ECG signals. The SDAs networks have the function of extracting features. The DNN classifies the ECG according to the obtained features. In the experiments with St. Petersburg INCART 12-lead Arrhythmia Database, the results are 98.6% and 91.4% respectively for accuracy and sensitivity [25]. Hoang et al. proposed a PVC detection algorithm for the multi-leads ECG and deployed it on wearable devices. The algorithm includes the Wavelet fusion method, Tucker-decomposition, and CNN, which has six layers: two convolutional layers, two max-pooling layers, a fully connected layer, and a dropout layer. Although this algorithm's accuracy is 90.84% on the 12 lead ECG St. Petersburg Arrhythmias Database, the proposed method is scalable to analyze 3-Lead to 16-Lead ECG systems [26]. Liu et al. applied deep learning to develop models that can search PVC from children's ECG. The children's ECG used in the experiment are JPEG images from the hospital. This study's experimental results show that the Inception-V3 with waveform images and one-dimensional CNN with time-series data extracted from waveform images can detect PVC in children [27].

According to Table 1, various algorithms for detecting PVC in recent years, we can quickly obtain the following conclusions. First, the amount of morphological-based literature is more than Deep Learning. Secondly, relevant researchers prefer these three classifiers: DNN, SVM, and Pattern matching. Third, the R-R interval is recognized by most research as a useful feature, but the other features do not seem to be unanimously recognized by most research. Finally, the model's performance based on morphology is slightly better than that of Deep Learning, thanks to the expertise of the person who designed the feature.

Although the morphological-based methods have achieved good results, they still have some limitations. First of all, these methods rely heavily on professional knowledge about ECG and signal processing to design the rules for extracting features. Second, these features extracted manually are biased and varies from person to person. Finally, most morphological-based methods are also limited by each wave's positioning algorithm in a heartbeat. For example, the inaccurate positioning of Q wave and S wave will directly affect the performance of detecting PVC, in literature 20.

Fortunately, some methods based on deep learning mostly avoid these limitations. The approach based on deep learning has the following three characteristics: first, it can automatically extract features, such as by convolution kernels; second, it can continuously optimize and select features during the training process to make the features non-redundant, such as by max-pooling; third, it can directly analyze the preprocessed heartbeats.

However, these existing methods based on the Deep Learning require preprocessing of the original ECG or the cooperation of other classifiers. The method proposed in the literature [21] has many preprocessing steps, such as resampling, denoising, signature detection, normalize. The studies [22,23,26] performed wavelet transform on the ECG to obtain 2-D time-frequency images. Moreover, the research [24,25] used the features extracted by a trained autoencoder to recognize PVC. There is no doubt that the above methods are computationally intensive.

Furthermore, identifying PVC is very complicated because the PVC waveform is quite uncertain, even for the same patient. Figure 2 shows some PVC waveforms from the same person. Therefore, achieving a real-time classifier with high accuracy and sensitivity is a challenging problem to address.

Table 1. Various algorithms for detecting premature ventricular contraction (PVC) in recent years.

Reference	Features	Classifier	Accuracy	Sensitivity	Specificity
[5]	Temporal characteristics.	Pattern matching	-	89.69%	99.63%
[7]	R-peak amplitude, R-R interval time, QRS duration time, ventricular activation time, Q-peak amplitude, S-peak amplitude.	DNN	99.41%	-	-
[8]	Principal Component Analysis and Waveform estimation.	KNN	-	93.45%	93.14%
[9]	R-R intervals, cross-correlation coefficient.	Pattern matching	99.5%	94.7%	99.6%
[10]	Energy wavelet coefficients.	Adaptive thresholding	-	99.18%	99.94%
[11]	Geometrical features.	AIS	98.04%	91.08%	98.65%
[12]	Maximal signal value in the P-Q interval; the area between the signal in the P-Q interval and zero, etc.	Multivariate statistical classier	-	96%	99%
[13]	Weighted six different QRS shape parameters.	Pattern matching	-	82.7%	98.82%
[14]	Six characteristics based on the Multiorder Rényi Entropy.	SVM	95.8%	-	-
[15]	Amplitude of R peaks; R-R interval; R-R interval ratio, etc.	DNN	97.46%	-	-
[16]	three groups of characteristics come from time-frequency domain.	SVM	99%	98.4%	99.8%
[17]	Six features extracted by several methodologies.	SVM	99.78%	99.91%	99.37%
[18]	Three morphological features and seven statistical features.	DNN	98.6%	98.7%	-
[19]	the ratio of the QRS areas; the previous R-R interval; the last R-R interval ratio to the next R-R interval.	a single neuron perceptron	98.8%	98.7%	98.9%

Table 1. Cont.

Reference	Features	Classifier	Accuracy	Sensitivity	Specificity
[20]	R-R interval; Q-S interval; Q-R amplitude; R-S amplitude.	DNN	Above 90%	-	-
[21]	Learned features automatically.	RNN	96–99%	99–100%	94–96%
[22]	Learned features automatically from time-frequency images	2D CNN	97.89%	98.58%	97.17%
[23]	Learned features automatically from wavelet power spectrums	2D CNN	97.96%	82.60%	99.11%
[24]	Learned features automatically by convolutional autoencoder	RF	98.55%	91.41%	99.06%
[25]	Learned features automatically by the stacked denoising autoencoders networks	DNN	98.6%	91.4%	93.9%
[26]	Learned features automatically by the Wavelet fusion method, Tucker-decomposition	2D CNN	90.84%	78.6%	99.86%
[27]	Learned features automatically from waveform images	2D CNN	88.5%	-	-

Abbreviations: deep neural network (DNN), K-nearest neighbor (KNN), artificial immune system (AIS), support vector machine (SVM), recurrent neural network (RNN), convolutional neural network (CNN), random forest (RF). Besides, "-" means that relevant information is not mentioned in the literature.

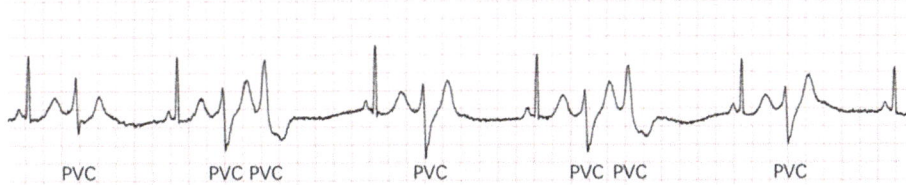

Figure 2. There are some PVC waveforms from the same person. The waveforms of these PVCs in the picture are different, especially the second and third.

In summary, considering the limitations of manually extracted features and the advantage that deep learning can automatically extract features, this study proposed a method based on one-dimensional CNN. This method can autonomously learn features from the labeled ECG data with supervised learning to avoid the manually extracted features' bias. Secondly, this method does not rely on professional knowledge that is used to design features. Third, this method does not have to preprocessing steps such as denoising and can directly process and analyze heartbeats, which will improve the efficiency of searching for PVC from ECG. Notably, the MIT-BIH arrhythmia database [28,29] will assess the validity of our proposed method. The following is the arrangement of the remainder: Section 2 describes the dataset, proposed framework, and evaluation measures; Section 3 presents and discusses the results; finally, Section 4 gives the conclusion and directions.

2. Materials and Methods

2.1. Materials

The MIT-BIH arrhythmia database is the first generally available benchmark database for the evaluation of arrhythmia detectors. The database contains 48 long-term Holter recordings obtained from 25 men subjects and 22 women subjects. Each of the 48 records numbered from 100 to 234 inclusive with some numbers missing, is slightly over half an hour-long and has two leads (the upper signal and lower signal). The upper signal in most records is a modified limb lead II (MLII), but the lower signal is occasionally V1, V2, V4, or V5. It is worth noting that recordings 201 and 202 came from the same male subject and the rest records are from a different subject. Furthermore, all records in this database are annotated by two or more cardiologists independently. Detailed annotations and a large number of records have made most researchers admire this database.

To effectively use this database, the Association for the Advancement of Medical Instrumentation (AAMI) recommends that records 102, 104, 107, and 217 are discarded because of the pacemaker or presenting complete heart block. Besides, this study designed three schemes to divide the remaining ECG records for evaluating the proposed method's effectiveness. Table 2. Splitting data into training and test sets. and Figure 3 showed the grouping schemes. It is worth mentioning that blind cross-validation cannot reasonably evaluate the performance of the model and comes with risks associated with label leakage.

Taking Scheme 1 in Table 2, splitting data into training and test sets, and Figure 3, splitting data into training and test sets, the information in Figure 3 is the same as in Table 2. As an example: the "DS1" and "DS2" represent the training set and the test set. The "101" represents the records number in the MIT-BIH arrhythmia database. The "N" and "V" respectively represent the number of the regular beat and PVC in the dataset. The "Ratio" means the ratio of the samples' number in the training set and the test set, such as (35640 + 2851)/(33868 + 2548) = 0.9778. Notably, most researchers adopt Scheme 1, which AAMI suggested and can also guarantee a reasonable comparison between our proposed method and other studies. Scheme 2 and Scheme 3 can evaluate the proposed method's performance in the situation that the number of samples in the training set is higher than the test set.

Table 2. Splitting data into training and test sets.

Scheme	Dataset	Records	N	V	Ratio
Scheme 1	Training set (DS1)	101, 106, 108, 109, 112, 114, 115, 116, 118, 119, 122, 124, 201, 203, 205, 207, 208, 209, 215, 220, 223, 230	35,640	2851	0.9778
	Test set (DS2)	100, 103, 105, 111, 113, 117, 121, 123, 200, 202, 210, 212, 213, 214, 219, 221, 222, 228, 231, 232, 233, 234	33,868	2548	
Scheme 2	Training set (DS3)	100, 103, 105, 106, 108, 109, 111, 113, 114, 116, 118, 119, 121, 123, 124, 200, 201, 202, 203, 205, 207, 208, 209, 210, 212, 213, 214, 215, 219, 222, 223, 228, 230, 231, 232, 234	53,279	4277	3.3172
	Test set (DS4)	101, 112, 115, 117, 122, 220, 221, 233	16,229	1122	
Scheme 3	Training set (DS5)	100, 101, 103, 105, 106, 108, 109, 111, 112, 113, 114, 115, 117, 118, 119, 121, 122, 123, 124, 200, 201, 202, 203, 207, 208, 209, 210, 212, 213, 214, 215, 219, 220, 222, 223, 228, 230, 231, 232, 233, 234	62,706	4862	9.2067
	Test set (DS6)	116, 205, 221	6802	537	

In this table, the 'Scheme' represents the name of the scheme for splitting data; the 'Dataset' represents the name of the training set or test set; the 'Records' represents ECG recordings in each 'Dataset'; the 'N' and 'V' respectively represent the number of the regular heartbeat and PVC in each 'Dataset'; the 'Ratio' means the ratio of the samples' number in the training set and the test set of each scheme.

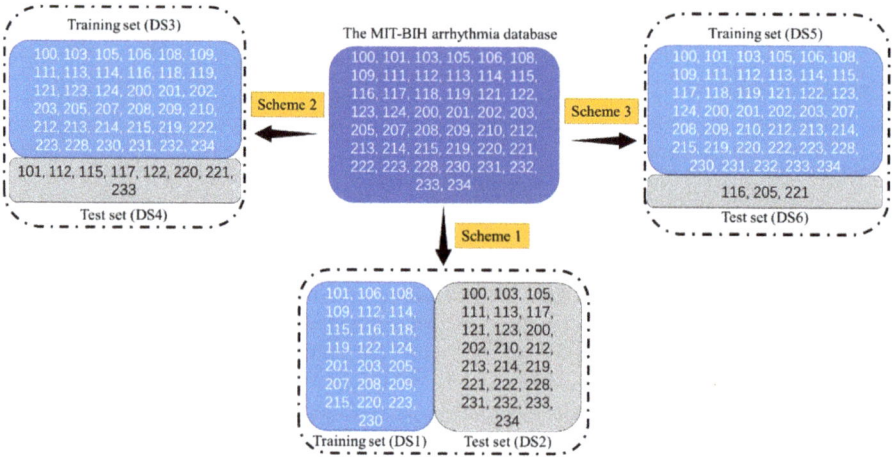

Figure 3. Splitting data into training and test sets. The information in this figure is the same as in Table 2. Splitting data into training and test sets.

2.2. Methodology

Figure 4 shows a block diagram of the proposed study, with a view showing the proposed method's flow. Initially, this research divided each ECG signal from the modified limb lead II (MLII) into separate heartbeats according to a fixed time window and an R peak detection algorithm. The duration of each heartbeat composed of 433 sampling points is 1.2 s. Then the proposed model based on the one-dimensional CNN takes these heartbeats as input to search PVC.

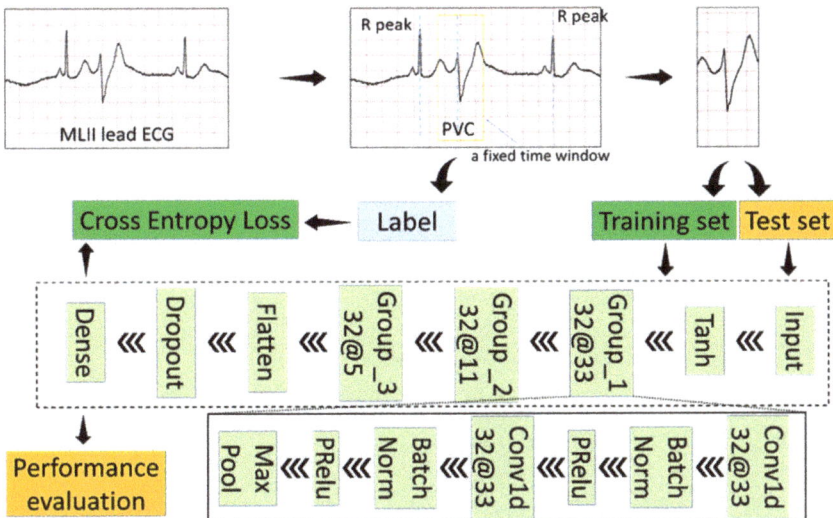

Figure 4. Block diagram of the proposed study.

2.2.1. Generate Input Data

Since the MIT-BIH arrhythmia database provides detailed annotations, including R-peak locations and rhythms' label, input data is the raw signal directly corresponding to each heartbeat without any preprocessing. We use a fixed-size window to extract the heartbeat from the MLII ECG lead since each heartbeat's dimension must be the same as the proposed classification model's input dimension. The window's size is 433, and the window's center is the location of R-peak. Because R-peak detection algorithms [30–33], such as Pan–Tompkins algorithm, can accurately find the R-peak point. We use the R-peak location in the database directly without developing a novel method to detect R-peak location.

2.2.2. Classifier Structure

First, the proposed model uses the Tanh function to transform the input data. The Tanh function can normalize the input data between −1 and 1, which is conducive to the training of the model. Equation (1) is the definition of the Tanh function.

$$\text{Tanh}(x) = \frac{Sinh(x)}{Cosh(x)} = \frac{e^x - e^{-x}}{e^x + e^{-x}} \tag{1}$$

Secondly, the proposed model has three convolutional groups, as shown in Figure 4. Each convolutional group contains five layers. A one-dimensional convolutional layer is a powerful tool that results in a feature map representing a detected feature's positions and intensity in an input. Convolution is a simple operation:

(1) Flip the convolution kernel;
(2) Move the convolution kernel one data point at a time along the input vector;
(3) Calculate the dot product of two corresponding points at each position;
(4) The generated sequence is the convolution of the convolution kernel with the input vector.

For example, specifying the input vector and the convolution kernel are discrete sequences, then the definition of convolution is as follows.

$$y_j = \sum_{i=-\infty}^{\infty} x_i \times h_{j-i} \tag{2}$$

The batch normalization layer allows the neural network to complete training faster and more stably by normalizing the feature map and does the following during training time [34]:

(1) Compute the mean and variance of the layer's input;

$$\text{Batch mean} \quad \mu_B = \frac{1}{m}\sum_{i=1}^{m} x_i \qquad (3)$$

$$\text{Batch variance} \quad \sigma_B^2 = \frac{1}{m}\sum_{i=1}^{m}(x_i - \mu_B)^2 \qquad (4)$$

(2) Normalize the layer's input using the mean and variance;

$$\overline{x_i} = \frac{x_i - \mu_B}{\sqrt{\sigma_B^2 + \epsilon}} \qquad (5)$$

(3) Obtain the output with scaling and shifting;

$$y_i = \gamma \overline{x_i} + \beta \qquad (6)$$

Notice that m is the number of samples per batch, ϵ is a small constant for numerical stability. Additionally, γ and β are learnable parameters.

The Parametric Rectified Linear Unit (PReLU) is an excellent activation function and has become the default activation function for many neural networks [35]. Although PReLU will introduce slope parameters, the increase in training costs is negligible. The mathematical definition of PReLU is as follows.

$$f(y_i) = \max(0, y_i) + a_i \times \min(0, y_i) \qquad (7)$$

The max-pooling layer can reduce the computational cost and effectively cope with the over-fitting phenomenon by down-sampling and summarizing in the feature map. Additionally, the max-pooling layer provides fundamental translation invariance.

Take 'Group_1 32@33' in the Figure 4 block diagram of the proposed study as an example to comprehend the convolution group. 'Group _1' is the convolution group's name; '32@33' represents the number and size of the one-dimensional convolutional layer's convolution kernels in the convolution group.

The proposed model also includes the Flatten layer, the Dropout layer, and the Dense layer. The Flatten layer collapses the spatial dimensions to make the multidimensional input one-dimensional. The Dropout layer refers to ignoring some neurons during a forward or backward pass to prevent over-fitting [34]. The Dense layer is a basic neural network layer and functions as a 'classifier.'

Tables 3 and 4 give the necessary parameters and the dimensional change of the proposed model's input data. The random seed in this study is 0, which can ensure that the experimental results are reproducible. Dropout in Table 3 refers to the probability of an element to be zeroed.

Table 3. Parameters of the proposed model.

Parameter Type	The Proposed Model
Batch size	512
Loss function	cross-entropy
Optimizer	Adam
Regularization rate	1
Epoch	100
Random seed	0
Dropout	0.7

Table 4. The dimensional change of the input data in the proposed model.

Layer Name	Input Shape	Out Shape
Input	None	(1, 433)
Tanh	(1, 433)	(1, 433)
Group_1	(1, 433)	(32, 216)
Group_2	(32, 216)	(32, 108)
Group_3	(32, 108)	(32, 54)
Flatten	(32, 54)	(1728)
Dropout	(1728)	(1728)
Dense	(1728)	(2)

'Batch size' refers to the number of training examples utilized in one iteration; 'Loss function' represents the category of loss function; 'Optimizer' represents how to change the parameters of the model; 'Regularization rate' means the regularization coefficient; 'Epoch' means the number of times each sample participated in training; 'Random seed' is a number used to initialize a pseudorandom number generator; 'Dropout' refers to the probability of an element to be zeroed.

2.3. Evaluation Measures

We chose five metrics, which have also been used in the literature [11], to measure the recognition performance of our proposed method: Accuracy (ACC), Sensitivity (Se), Specificity (Sp), Positive prediction (P_+), Negative prediction (P_-). The confusion matrix is the basis of these five metrics which can be expressed as Equation (8). Where TN, FN, TP, and FP respectively represent true negatives, false negatives, true positives, false positives. In this work, negative samples are those belonging to the regular class labeled 'N.' Additionally, this study also used the Youden's index to evaluate classification performance.

$$\text{Confusion Matrix} = \begin{bmatrix} TN & FP \\ FN & TP \end{bmatrix} \tag{8}$$

$$\text{Accuracy Acc} = \frac{TP + TN}{TP + TN + FN + FP} \tag{9}$$

$$\text{Sensitivity Se} = \frac{TP}{TP + FN} \tag{10}$$

$$\text{Specificity Sp} = \frac{TN}{TN + FP} \tag{11}$$

$$\text{Positive prediction } P_+ = \frac{TP}{TP + FP} \tag{12}$$

$$\text{Negative prediction } P_- = \frac{TN}{TN + FN} \tag{13}$$

$$J = Se + Sp - 1 \tag{14}$$

3. Results and Discussion

The size and number of kernels, number of layers, and batch size are the essential hyper-parameters in CNN. The kernels are the convolutional filters. In a convolution, the filters slide over all the points of the signal taking their dot product, which can extract some features from the input data. To quickly abstract the useful features, it is necessary to choose the size and number of kernels. The number of layers has a significant influence on the performance of CNN. Generally speaking, CNN's ability to detect PVC and the numbers of layers are positive correlations. However, more layers mean longer training time and more learnable parameters, which is very likely to cause overfitting. The batch size is the number of signals used to train a single forward and backward pass. The larger batch size can speed up the training and verification of the CNN but does not usually achieve high accuracy.

In this section, this study performed experiments on three different schemes, according to Table 2. Before anything else, we assessed the impact of varying size and number of kernels on recognizing PVC with CNN. Secondly, we evaluated the performance of CNN with a different number of layers on distinguishing PVC and regular rhythm. Immediately afterward, we tested the batch size's effect in detecting PVC. To improve the performance of the proposed model, we tried two activation functions (Sigmoid, Tanh) to normalize the input data. The data for training and verifying the above four experiments are all from Scheme 1. Finally, we checked the capabilities of the adjusted CNN to detect PVC with Scheme 2 and Scheme 3. Ubuntu 16.04.6 LTS operating system with an Nvidia GeForce RTX 2070 GPU, 32GB RAM, and Python programming language are the basis for the simulation process.

3.1. Experiment 1: Assess the Impact of Varying Size and Number of Kernels

The kernel size is usually related to the receptive field (RF), the size of the region in the input that generates the feature. In many outstanding image classification or detection algorithms, the kernel size is usually 3×3, 5×5, or 7×7 and decreases gradually. In this experiment, we tried multiple combinations of the size and number of kernels. The data for training and verifying are both from Scheme 1. Besides, the experimental environment is also the same. The strategy for adjusting the learning rate is multiplying the learning rate by 0.1 when the network reaches the 20th and 80th epoch. Moreover, Table 5 shows specific details and results. Figure 5 displays the receiver operating characteristic (ROC) curve about this experiment.

Table 5. The details and results of the varying size and number of kernels.

Group_1	Group_2	Group_3	Acc (%)	Se (%)	Sp (%)	P+ (%)	P− (%)	J (%)	Time [1]
32@43	32@11	32@5	99.47	96.35	99.71	96.12	99.73	96.06	9.68
32@33	32@11	32@5	**99.64**	96.98	**99.84**	**97.86**	99.77	96.82	9.30
32@23	32@11	32@5	99.54	**97.25**	99.72	96.27	**99.79**	**96.97**	8.82
32@33	32@7	32@5	99.62	96.94	99.82	97.63	99.77	96.76	9.15
32@11	32@7	32@5	99.54	**97.25**	99.71	96.16	**99.79**	96.96	8.20
32@7	32@5	32@3	99.37	94.31	99.75	96.66	99.57	94.06	**7.80**
64@33	64@11	64@5	99.52	96.74	99.73	96.48	99.75	96.47	14.92
16@33	16@11	16@5	99.57	96.31	99.82	97.57	99.72	96.13	7.88

[1] 'Time' refers to the duration of the training, in minutes.

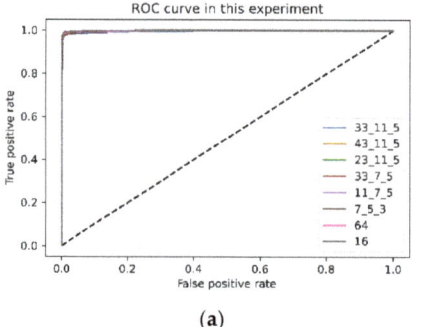 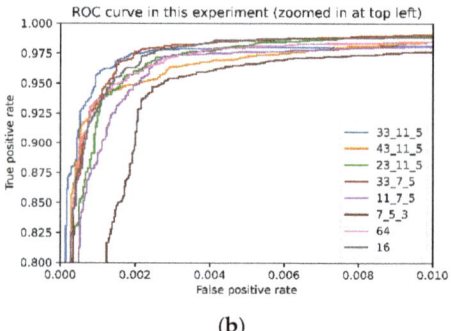

(a) (b)

Figure 5. Receiver operating characteristic (ROC) curve about this experiment: (a) original ROC curve; (b) zoomed ROC curve.

It is not difficult to find from Table 5 that although these results are not much different, the larger-sized convolution kernel's performance is slightly better in the first convolution group.

The convolution kernel size is different; the receptive field of the convolution kernel is also other. For the data used in this experiment, a larger size convolution kernel is more suitable for this task than a smaller size convolution kernel.

On the other hand, when the number of convolution kernels in each layer is 64 or 16, the model's performance has declined somewhat. The reason for this experimental phenomenon is that the number of convolution kernels is positively correlated with the learnable parameters in the model. The fewer the number of convolution kernels, the fewer the model's learnable parameters, which leads to the model not being able to extract features effectively. Also known as the underfitting state.

Furthermore, the number of convolution kernels also has a positive correlation with the time spent training the model. Especially when the number of convolution kernels in each layer is 64, the time spent training the model is nearly 15 min. Considering the accuracy, sensitivity, and Youden's index, the better combinations are the second to the fifth set of records in Table 5.

Moreover, from the ROC curves Figure 5, we can quickly know that the better combinations are the second combination in this experiment. Coincidentally, the receptive field of the convolution kernel is about 0.1 s of ECG signal when the kernel size is 33 because the sampling rate of the ECG is 360, and the QRS complexes of PVC are unusually long (typically >120 ms). In future work, we will study whether there is a relationship between the kernel size and the QRS duration of PVC.

3.2. Experiment 2: The Performance of CNN with a Different Number of Layers

With the popularity of CNN, the number of convolutional layers in each network is continually increasing, such as AlexNet (5), VGGNet16(13), ResNet50(49). The emergence of batch normalization and residual structure solves the vanishing gradient problem that makes the previous CNN challenging. Considering the marginal effects and the efficiency of the proposed model, we performed three tests. Figure 6 illustrates the basic structure of the model used in the three experiments. The configuration in this experiment is the same as the previous experiment. Moreover, Table 6 gives the results.

Table 6. The details and results of the varying size and number of kernels.

Structure	Acc (%)	Se (%)	Sp (%)	P_+ (%)	P_- (%)	J (%)	Time 1 (m) [1]
a	99.54	96.39	99.78	97.04	99.73	96.17	5.17
b	**99.64**	**96.98**	**99.84**	**97.86**	**99.77**	**96.82**	9.30
c	99.46	94.90	99.81	97.34	99.62	94.71	13.58

[1] 'Time 1' refers to the duration of the training.

The experimental records in Table 6 illustrate that the number of convolutional layers is not as significant as possible, which is the same as the existing prior knowledge. For example, the network with the first structure requires shorter training time than the third structure and better in some index, such as accuracy.

Besides, the number of layers is usually an essential factor that affects the complexity of the model. High-complexity models may have over-fitting problems during the training process, while low-complexity models may have under-fitting questions. Those models with too high or too low complexity have difficulty and time-consuming training. Therefore, choosing a moderately complex model can speed up the training process and make training easier.

To balance the model's efficiency and effectiveness, we choose the second structure described in Figure 6 to build the model according to the experimental results in Table 6.

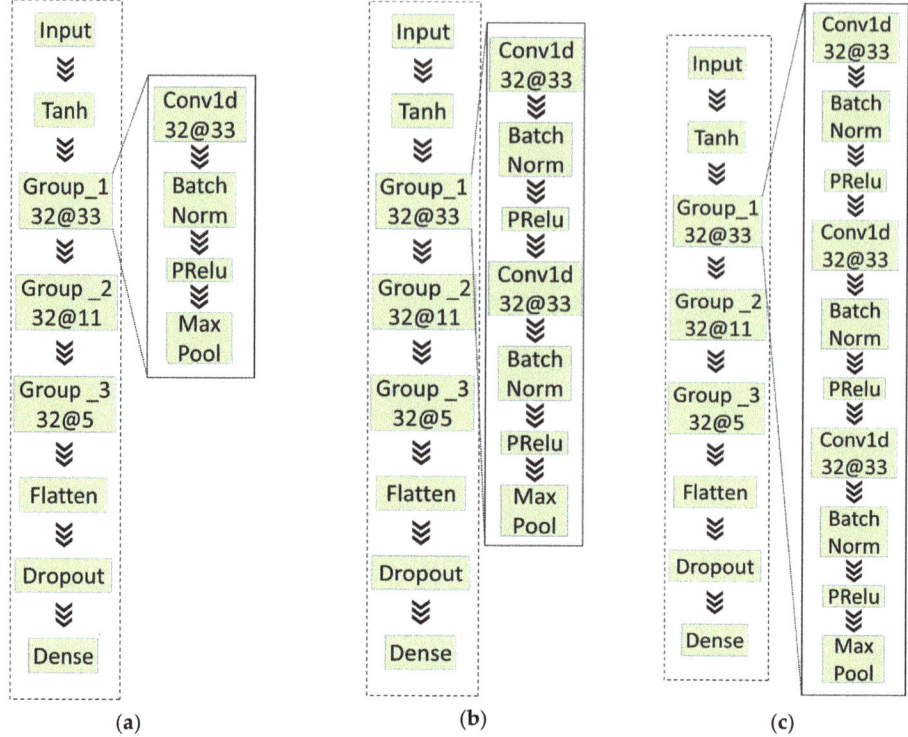

Figure 6. The basic structure of the models in experiment 2: (**a**) A convolutional layer in each convolutional; (**b**) two convolutional layers in each convolutional; (**c**) three convolutional layers in each convolutional.

3.3. Experiment 3: Test the Batch Size's Effect on Detecting PVC

Batch size is a very critical parameter and affects the performance of the neural networks. Too large or too small batch size is not appropriate. The larger batch size can reduce the training time and improve the stability of the structure. However, the smaller batch size can enhance the generalization ability of the model. To balance the generalization ability of the model and training time, we tested a series of batch sizes. Table 7 shows the results of this experiment.

Table 7. Test the batch size's effect in detecting PVC.

Batch Size	Acc (%)	Se (%)	Sp (%)	P_+ (%)	P_- (%)	J (%)	Time (m)[1]
64	99.46	95.02	99.79	97.15	99.63	94.81	22.17
128	99.43	94.82	99.78	96.95	99.61	94.60	13.63
512	**99.64**	**96.98**	**99.84**	**97.86**	**99.77**	**96.82**	9.30
1024	99.51	95.45	99.81	97.47	99.66	95.26	8.8
2048	99.47	94.86	99.82	97.54	99.61	94.68	**8.68**

[1] 'Time 1' refers to the duration of the training.

According to the experimental results in Table 7, we can find this rule that the relationship between training time and batch size is negatively correlated. Further, as the batch size keeps getting bigger, the training time is decreasing more and more slowly. Considering the training time, accuracy, and other indicators, we set the batch size in subsequent experiments to 512. After deploying the trained model, increasing the batch size can predict multiple heartbeats at the same time within the allowable range of video memory. This characteristic can significantly improve the efficiency of PVC detection in practical applications.

3.4. Experiment 4: Test the Activation Functions (Sigmoid, Tanh) Used to Normalize the Input Data

Considering the waveform of the ECG, normalizing the input data can improve the performance of the proposed model. Because the amplitude of the R wave is several times that of the other waves, we adopted the Sigmoid and Tanh function to normalize the input data. The Tanh function can normalize the input data between −1 and 1. The Sigmoid function can normalize the input data between 0 and 1. The difference is that the overall slope of Tanh is greater. Table 8 shows the results of this experiment.

Table 8. Test the activation functions.

Activation Function	Acc (%)	Se (%)	Sp (%)	P_+ (%)	P_- (%)	J (%)
None	99.56	96.74	99.77	96.97	99.75	96.51
Sigmoid	99.56	96.15	99.82	97.57	99.71	95.97
Tanh	**99.64**	**96.98**	**99.84**	**97.86**	**99.77**	**96.82**

The waveform of the ECG is very special. The amplitude of QRS complexes usually is much higher than the remaining wave. As shown in Figure 7, the points on the unnormalized waveform are mostly near the straight line with y = −1.0, and only a few moments deviate seriously. To solve this problem, we tried two activation functions (Tanh and Sigmoid) to normalize the input ECG. Figure 7 shows the normalized waveform of the ECG. The experimental results in Table 8 show that the suitable activation functions (Tanh) used to normalize the input ECG can slightly improve the model's performance. Nevertheless, inappropriate activation functions (Sigmoid) have a negative impact. The advantage of the Tanh function is that the value range of the normalized data is between −1 and 1, and the average is 0, unlike sigmoid, which is 0.5.

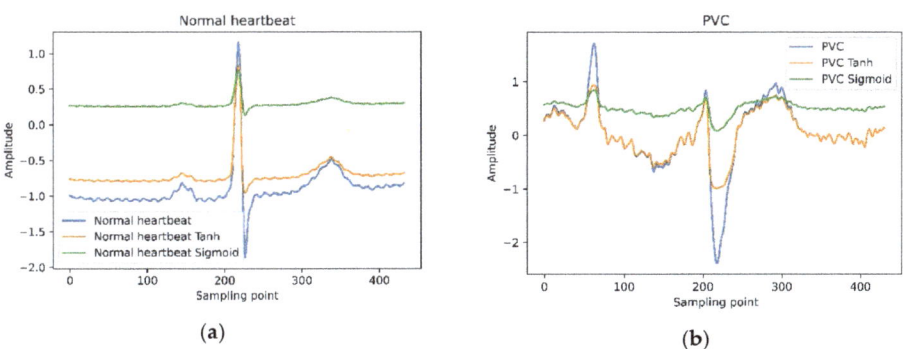

Figure 7. Tanh and Sigmoid normalize the waveform of a normal heartbeat and PVC.

3.5. Experiment 5: Employ CNN to Identify PVC with Scheme 2 and Scheme 3

As we all know, it is a common practice to distribute training and test sets in the proportion of 9:1 or 4:1 in deep learning. This experiment re-divides the data set according to Scheme 2 and Scheme 3, described in Table 2. After obtaining the training set and test set, this experiment employs the proposed model. Figure 8 shows the confusion matrix of each scheme. Table 9 shows the results of this experiment and comparisons with the consequence of Scheme 1 and previous studies.

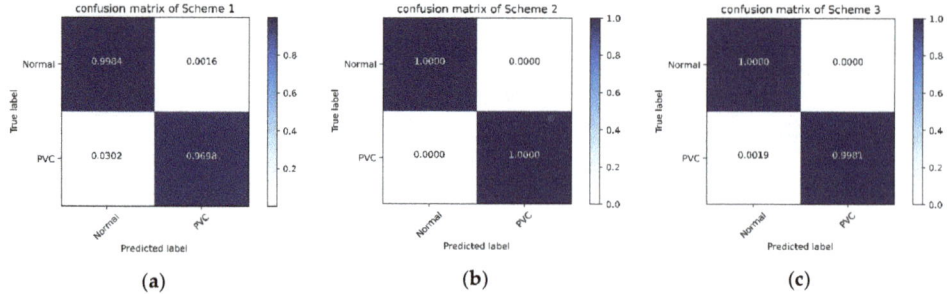

Figure 8. The confusion matrix of each scheme: (**a**) confusion matrix of Scheme 1; (**b**) confusion matrix of Scheme 2; (**c**) confusion matrix of Scheme 3.

Table 9. Employ the proposed model with Scheme 2 and Scheme 3.

Method	Acc (%)	Se (%)	Sp (%)	P+ (%)	P− (%)	J (%)
Scheme 1 [1]	99.64	96.98	99.84	97.86	99.77	96.82
Scheme 2 [1]	**100.00**	**100.00**	**100.00**	**100.00**	**100.00**	**100.00**
Scheme 3 [1]	99.99	99.81	100.00	100.00	99.99	99.81
Atanasoski et al. [9]	99.5%	94.7%	99.6%	-	-	94.8
Oliveira et al. [11]	98.04	91.08	98.65	85.68	99.21	89.73
Lynggaard [12]	-	96.00	99.00	93.00	99.00	95.00
Sokolova et al. [13]	-	82.70	98.82	82.97	-	81.52
Mazidi et al. [17]	99.78	99.91	99.37	-	-	99.5
Li et al. [23]	97.96	82.60	99.11	87.42	-	81.71
Gordon et al. [24]	97.61	77.81	99.02	-	-	76.83
Rahhal et al. [25]	98.6	91.4	93.9	-	-	86.7

[1] The performance of the proposed method in each Scheme.

The above experiments 1–4 confirmed the architecture and parameters of our proposed model. In Experiment 5, to evaluate the proposed model's performance in this situation: the number of samples in the training set is more than the test set. We employed the proposed model with Scheme 2 and 3. According to Table 9 and Figure 8, the proposed model's performance is unexpected, and the indicators are full marks with Scheme 2. The convolutional neural network is a class of deep learning technology. In deep learning, the number of samples used to train is generally more than that used for testing. In this case, the performance of the proposed method is remarkable.

Compared with the literature 9, 11, 12, and 13, the performance of the proposed method in Scheme 1 is better in all indicators. Additionally, the proposed method does not rely on professional knowledge to manually extract features. Next, the proposed method can directly predict the heartbeats' category in the MIT-BIH arrhythmia database without denoising.

For literature 17, the performance of the proposed method in Scheme 1 is bleak in all indicators. The literature 17 is based on a patient-independent separation approach to divide the training set and test set. This separation approach follows a principle that the same subject's heartbeats cannot appear in both training and test sets. The experiment in literature 17 considered 10% of heartbeat in the MIT-BIH arrhythmia database for training and 90% as the test set, similar to Scheme 3. The proposed method's performance in Scheme 3 is almost close to full marks and is better than literature 17.

Compared with the literature 23, 24, and 25, the proposed method's results are better. In the proposed plan, the process of extracting features and recognizing heartbeats are performed simultaneously. Finally, the proposed model can directly identify heartbeats in the MIT-BIH arrhythmia database. On the contrary, literature 23 used wavelet function to transform the heartbeat before training the model; before training the classifier model, literature 24 and 25 must first train the feature extraction network. In summary, our method has reached the most advanced level compared with other studies.

4. Conclusions

In this study, we successfully apply a model based on the one-dimensional convolutional neural network to recognize PVC and worked highly efficiently by using the raw ECG data without complex signal preprocessing such as denoising. The experimental results show that the classification effect achieved by the proposed method is significantly better than the morphological-based method and other methods. Additionally, according to Table 9, applying more ECG data can improve the performance of the proposed method. However, the annotated ECG data is hard to come by. In future works, we plan to use the generative adversarial networks (GAN) to deal with insufficient data. Next, we hope to tap the potential of our approach to classify many different types of heartbeats simultaneously. Lastly, we plan to deploy our proposed method on cloud servers or wearables to help doctors and patients in developing countries or remote regions.

Author Contributions: Conceptualization, X.C.; data curation, X.W. and J.G.; formal analysis, X.W.; methodology, J.Y., X.C. and J.G.; project administration, X.C.; resources, J.Y.; software, J.G.; visualization, J.G.; writing—original draft, X.W.; writing—review and editing, J.Y. and X.C. All authors have read and agreed to the published version of the manuscript.

Funding: This research received no external funding.

Conflicts of Interest: The authors declare no conflict of interest.

References

1. Zhang, Y.; Cong, H.; Man, C.; Su, Y.; Sun, H.; Yang, H.; Guo, Z. Risk factors for cardiovascular disease from a population-based screening study in Tianjin, China: A cohort study of 36,215 residents. *Ann. Transl. Med.* **2020**, *8*, 444. [CrossRef]
2. Gerstenfeld, E.P.; De Marco, T. Premature ventricular contractions. *Circulation* **2019**, *140*, 624–626. [CrossRef] [PubMed]
3. Park, K.M.; Im, S.I.; Chun, K.J.; Hwang, J.K.; Park, S.J.; Kim, J.S.; On, Y.K. Asymptomatic ventricular premature depolarizations are not necessarily benign. *EP Eur.* **2015**, *18*, 881–887. [CrossRef] [PubMed]
4. Zipes, D.P.; Libby, P.; Bonow, R.O.; Mann, D.L.; Tomaselli, G.F. *Braunwald's Heart Disease E-Book: A Textbook of Cardiovascular Medicine*; Elsevier Health Sciences: Philadelphia, PA, USA, 2018.
5. Manikandan, M.S.; Ramkumar, B.; Choudhary, T.; Deshpande, P.S. Robust detection of premature ventricular contractions using sparse signal decomposition and temporal features. *Health Technol. Lett.* **2015**, *2*, 141–148. [CrossRef] [PubMed]
6. Abadi, M.; Barham, P.; Chen, J.; Chen, Z.; Davis, A.; Dean, J.; Devin, M.; Ghemawat, S.; Irving, G.; Isard, M. Tensorflow: A system for large-scale machine learning. *arXiv* **2016**, arXiv:1605.08695.
7. Jun, T.J.; Park, H.J.; Minh, N.H.; Kim, D.; Kim, Y. Premature ventricular contraction beat detection with deep neural networks. In Proceedings of the 15th IEEE International Conference on Machine Learning and Applications (ICMLA), Anaheim, CA, USA, 18–20 December 2016; pp. 859–864. [CrossRef]
8. Hadia, R.; Guldenring, D.; Finlay, D.D.; Kennedy, A.; Janjua, G.; Bond, R.; McLaughlin, J. Morphology-based detection of premature ventricular contractions. In *2017 Computing in Cardiology (CinC)*; IEEE: Rennes, France, 2017; pp. 1–4. [CrossRef]
9. Atanasoski, V.; Ivanovic, M.D.; Marinkovic, M.; Gligoric, G.; Bojovic, B.; Shvilkin, A.V.; Petrovic, J. Unsupervised classification of premature ventricular contractions based on R-R interval and heartbeat morphology. In Proceedings of the 14th Symposium on Neural Networks and Applications (NEUREL), Belgrade, Serbia, 20–21 November 2018; pp. 1–6. [CrossRef]
10. Junior, E.A.; Valentim, R.A.D.M.; Brandão, G.B. Real-time premature ventricular contractions detection based on Redundant Discrete Wavelet Transform. *Res. Biomed. Eng.* **2018**, *34*, 187–197. [CrossRef]
11. De Oliveira, B.R.; De Abreu, C.C.E.; Duarte, M.A.Q.; Filho, J.V. Geometrical features for premature ventricular contraction recognition with analytic hierarchy process based machine learning algorithms selection. *Comput. Methods Programs Biomed.* **2019**, *169*, 59–69. [CrossRef]
12. Lynggaard, P. Detecting premature ventricular contraction by using regulated discriminant analysis with very sparse training data. *Appl. Artif. Intell.* **2018**, *33*, 229–248. [CrossRef]

13. Sokolova, A.; Markelov, O.; Bogachev, M.; Uljanitski, Y. Multi-parametric algorithm for premature ventricular contractions detection and counting. *AIP Conf. Proc.* **2019**, *2140*, 020074. [CrossRef]
14. Rizal, A.; Wijayanto, I. Classification of Premature Ventricular Contraction based on ECG Signal using Multiorder Rényi Entropy. In Proceedings of the 2019 International Conference of Artificial Intelligence and Information Technology (ICAIIT), Yogyakarta, Indonesia, 13–15 March 2019; pp. 225–229. [CrossRef]
15. Chen, H.; Bai, J.; Mao, L.; Wei, J.; Song, J.; Zhang, R. Automatic Identification of Premature Ventricular Contraction Using ECGs. In Proceedings of the 2019 International Conference on Health Information Science (HIS), Xi'an, China, 18–20 October 2019; pp. 143–155. [CrossRef]
16. Mazidi, M.H.; Eshghi, M.; Raoufy, M.R. FPGA implementation of wearable ECG system for detection premature ventricular contraction. *Int. J. COMADEM* **2019**, *22*, 51–59.
17. Mazidi, M.H.; Eshghi, M.; Raoufy, M.R. Detection of premature ventricular contraction (PVC) using linear and nonlinear techniques: An experimental study. *Clust. Comput.* **2019**, *23*, 759–774. [CrossRef]
18. Allami, R. Premature ventricular contraction analysis for real-time patient monitoring. *Biomed. Signal. Process. Control.* **2019**, *47*, 358–365. [CrossRef]
19. Chen, Z.; Xu, H.; Luo, J.; Zhu, T.; Meng, J. Low-power perceptron model based ECG processor for premature ventricular contraction detection. *Microprocess. Microsyst.* **2018**, *59*, 29–36. [CrossRef]
20. Jeon, E.; Jung, B.K.; Nam, Y.; Lee, H. Classification of premature ventricular contraction using error back-propagation. *KSII Trans. Internet Inf. Syst.* **2018**, *12*, 988–1001. [CrossRef]
21. Zhou, X.; Zhu, X.; Nakamura, K.; Mahito, N.P. Premature ventricular contraction detection from ambulatory ECG using recurrent neural networks. In Proceedings of the 40th Annual International Conference of the IEEE Engineering in Medicine and Biology Society (EMBC), Honolulu, HI, USA, 18–21 July 2018; pp. 2551–2554. [CrossRef]
22. Zhao, Z.; Wang, X.; Cai, Z.; Li, J.; Liu, C.P. PVC Recognition for wearable ECGs using modified frequency slice wavelet transform and convolutional neural network. In Proceedings of the 2019 Computing in Cardiology (CinC), Biopolis, Singapore, 8–11 September 2019; pp. 1–4. [CrossRef]
23. Li, Q.; Liu, C.; Li, Q.; Shashikumar, S.P.; Nemati, S.; Shen, Z.; Clifford, G.D. Ventricular ectopic beat detection using a wavelet transform and a convolutional neural network. *Physiol. Meas.* **2019**, *40*, 055002. [CrossRef] [PubMed]
24. Gordon, M.G.; Williams, C.M. PVC detection using a convolutional autoencoder and random forest classifier. In Proceedings of the Pacific Symposium on Biocomputing 2019, Kohala Coast, HI, USA, 3–7 January 2019; pp. 42–53. [CrossRef]
25. Rahhal, M.M.A.; Ajlan, N.A.; Bazi, Y.; Hichri, H.A.; Rabczuk, T. Automatic premature ventricular contractions detection for multi-lead electrocardiogram signal. In Proceedings of the IEEE International Conference on Electro/Information Technology (EIT), Rochester, MI, USA, 3–5 May 2018; pp. 169–173. [CrossRef]
26. Hoang, T.; Fahier, N.; Fang, W.C. Multi-leads ECG premature ventricular contraction detection using tensor decomposition and convolutional neural network. In Proceedings of the BioCAS 2019—Biomedical Circuits and Systems Conference, Nara, Japan, 17–19 October 2019; pp. 1–4. [CrossRef]
27. Liu, Y.; Huang, Y.; Wang, J.; Liu, L.; Luo, J. Detecting premature ventricular contraction in children with deep learning. *J. Shanghai Jiaotong Univ.* **2018**, *23*, 66–73. [CrossRef]
28. Moody, G.; Mark, R. The impact of the MIT-BIH arrhythmia database. *IEEE Eng. Med. Biol. Mag.* **2001**, *20*, 45–50. [CrossRef] [PubMed]
29. Goldberger, A.L.; Amaral, L.A.N.; Glass, L.; Hausdorff, J.M.; Ivanov, P.C.; Mark, R.G.; Mietus, J.E.; Moody, G.B.; Peng, C.K.; Stanley, H.E. PhysioBank, PhysioToolkit, and PhysioNet: Components of a new research resource for complex physiologic signals. *Circulation* **2000**, *101*, e215–e220. [CrossRef]
30. Pan, J.; Tompkins, W. A Real-Time QRS Detection Algorithm. *IEEE Trans. Bio-Med. Eng.* **1985**, *32*, 230–236. [CrossRef]
31. Lin, C.C.; Chang, H.Y.; Huang, Y.H.; Yeh, C.Y. A novel wavelet-based algorithm for detection of QRS complex. *Appl. Sci.* **2019**, *9*, 2142. [CrossRef]
32. Chen, C.L.; Chuang, C.T. A QRS detection and R point recognition method for wearable single-lead ECG devices. *Sensors* **2017**, *17*, 1969. [CrossRef] [PubMed]
33. Chen, A.; Zhang, Y.; Zhang, M.; Liu, W.; Chang, S.; Wang, H.; He, J.; Huang, Q. A real time QRS detection algorithm based on ET and PD controlled threshold strategy. *Sensors* **2020**, *20*, 4003. [CrossRef] [PubMed]

34. Garbin, C.; Zhu, X.; Marques, O. Dropout vs. batch normalization: An empirical study of their impact to deep learning. *Multimedia Tools Appl.* **2020**, *79*, 12777–12815. [CrossRef]
35. He, K.; Zhang, X.; Ren, S.; Sun, J. Delving Deep into Rectifiers: Surpassing Human-Level Performance on ImageNet Classification. In Proceedings of the 2015 IEEE International Conference on Computer Vision (ICCV), Santiago, Chile, 7–13 December 2015; pp. 1026–1034. [CrossRef]

Publisher's Note: MDPI stays neutral with regard to jurisdictional claims in published maps and institutional affiliations.

© 2020 by the authors. Licensee MDPI, Basel, Switzerland. This article is an open access article distributed under the terms and conditions of the Creative Commons Attribution (CC BY) license (http://creativecommons.org/licenses/by/4.0/).

Article

Realizing an Integrated Multistage Support Vector Machine Model for Augmented Recognition of Unipolar Depression

Kathiravan Srinivasan [1], Nivedhitha Mahendran [1], Durai Raj Vincent [1], Chuan-Yu Chang [2,*] and Shabbir Syed-Abdul [3,4,*]

1. School of Information Technology and Engineering, Vellore Institute of Technology (VIT), Vellore 632 014, India; kathiravan.srinivasan@vit.ac.in (K.S.); nivedhitha.m2019@vitstudent.ac.in (N.M.); pmvincent@vit.ac.in (D.R.V.)
2. Department of Computer Science and Information Engineering, National Yunlin University of Science and Technology, Yunlin 64002, Taiwan
3. International Center for Health Information Technology (ICHIT), Taipei Medical University, Taipei 110, Taiwan
4. Graduate Institute of Biomedical Informatics, Taipei Medical University, Taipei 110, Taiwan
* Correspondence: chuanyu@yuntech.edu.tw (C.-Y.C.); drshabbir@tmu.edu.tw (S.S.-A.)

Received: 11 March 2020; Accepted: 13 April 2020; Published: 15 April 2020

Abstract: Unipolar depression (UD), also referred to as clinical depression, appears to be a widespread mental disorder around the world. Further, this is a vital state related to a person's health that influences his/her daily routine. Besides, this state also influences the person's frame of mind, behavior, and several body functionalities like sleep, appetite, and also it can cause a scenario where a person could harm himself/herself or others. In several cases, it becomes an arduous task to detect UD, since, it is a state of comorbidity. For that reason, this research proposes a more convenient approach for the physicians to detect the state of clinical depression at an initial phase using an integrated multistage support vector machine model. Initially, the dataset is preprocessed using multiple imputation by chained equations (MICE) technique. Then, for selecting the appropriate features, the support vector machine-based recursive feature elimination (SVM RFE) is deployed. Subsequently, the integrated multistage support vector machine classifier is built by employing the bagging random sampling technique. Finally, the experimental outcomes indicate that the proposed integrated multistage support vector machine model surpasses methods such as logistic regression, multilayer perceptron, random forest, and bagging SVM (majority voting), in terms of overall performance.

Keywords: multistage support vector machine model; multiple imputation by chained equations; SVM-based recursive feature elimination; unipolar depression

1. Introduction

In recent years, depression seems to be a very prevalent disorder around the globe, having a presence among approximately 264 million individuals. Psychiatrists usually claim that this disorder is unique, and it is unlike mood swings or ephemeral emotions and their reactions. Usually, when such a depressive condition is prevalent for a long duration among individuals, it might be a somber state of health. Additionally, the causes and effects of such cases are severe, and it critically rescinds the day to day functioning of individuals. In the worst scenario, it might stimulate suicidal tendencies in an individual.

In the millennial (born 1981–1996) era, depression is found to be on the rise; the reason is not apparent. Research shows that depression is greater among the younger Millennials, which results in many risk factors such as substance abuse and behavioral failures [1]. It is found that the depression symptoms have gone to 15 percent from 9 percent between 2005 and 2015, which is very shocking [1]. The three main parts of the brain that are affected by depression are the hypothalamus, the prefrontal cortex, and the amygdala. Some of the common reasons for being depressed are hormonal imbalance, stress, or genetic [2]. The symptoms of depression involve prolonged feelings of regret, sadness and hopelessness, irregular appetite, weight gain or weight loss, and many others. These days, more than the physical health issues, mental health issues are increasing exponentially [3]. It seems like almost everyone is affected by stress, anxiety, and depression [4].

More than physical health, mental health is essential, as it would directly affect physical health too. It will be easier if we have proper techniques to identify mental health as well [5]. There are few significant issues in diagnosing and treating the individual affected with unipolar depression such as, it is not easy for a depressed individual to seek expert help due to motivation and cost, and in some cases, the individual fails to take the mental health seriously [6].

In order to treat the depressed individuals better, we have proposed a machine learning classification algorithm, integrated multistage support vector machine model. It is an ensemble-based classification algorithm, where the support vector machine (SVM) classifiers are integrated with the help of the SVR-based weighted voting method to produce the outcome. Machine learning techniques are the best in identifying the patterns in the dataset and predict the outcome. We gathered data with the help of a questionnaire and preprocessed it to handle the missing values. The preprocessed data is then processed with a feature selection technique to select the relevant features.

The key contributions of this work include the following:

- The multiple imputation by chained equations (MICE) method is deployed for preprocessing and cleaning the gathered dataset
- The feature selection process is accomplished by employing the support vector machine-based recursive feature elimination (SVM RFE).
- The UD classification is performed using the proposed integrated multistage support vector machine classifier, which is built by employing the bagging random sampling approach.

The significant motivation of this research is to devise a random sampling-based integrated multistage SVM model for classifying the unipolar depression dataset, and we also attempt to enhance the overall performance of the proposed model. The rest of this research work is organized as follows. Section 2 elucidates the methodology formulation process and provides a detailed outlook into the individual modules of the proposed integrated multistage SVM model. Section 3 focuses on the experimental results. Section 4 provides information regarding the conclusion and future work.

2. Materials and Methods

2.1. Utilized Dataset

The dataset we used in this study was collected from various individuals with an average age of 30. We framed a questionnaire based on the "Hamilton Depression Rating Scale" [7] and prepared a self-rating report. The dataset collected had 3040 samples with 22 features, including the target variable. The features are the demographic attributes and symptom scores. For processing, we split the dataset into training and testing sets (75-25 rule). The model was trained with the training set then tested with the test set and evaluated with specific performance metrics. Essential features are portrayed in Table 1.

Table 1. The portrayal of essential features.

Features	Description
Age	Average Age 30.
Gender	Male/Female.
Sleep Quotient	Time taken to fall asleep.
Early Wake-Up	The irregular waking uptime.
Sleeping excessively	Irregular sleep hours.
Gloomy	Prolonged feelings of sadness, sometimes in the day or all the time.
Exasperation	Prolonged feelings of irritation, sometimes in the day or all the time.
Apprehensive or Nervous	Prolonged feelings of anxiousness or tension, sometimes in the day or all the time.
Response of the Individual to Preferred Happenings	Reactions, mood-wise to the events happening in life.
Relation between an Individual's Mood and Time	Moods at different time of the day.
Mood Quality	If the individual is sad, is it because of something happened or sad for no reason.
Reduced Desire for food	Not eating enough food.
Augmented Desire for food	Eating more than enough food.
Weight Reduction	Losing more weight in two weeks without any reason.
Weight Increase	Gaining weight at a specific time.
Ability to make Decisions/Attentiveness	Failure in making decisions and losing focus.
Future Perspective	Positive and Negative thoughts about the future.
Suicidal Contemplations	Attempting to harm oneself.
Happiness Quotient	Feeling good or extremely annoyed with pleasure and enjoyment in life.
Fidgety	Constant pacing and difficulty in concentrating.
Physical Indications	Sweating, increased heartbeat, blurred vision, shivering, chest pain or none at all.
Paranoid Signs	Constant panic attacks or none at all.
Result	Depressed or Not Depressed.

2.2. Data Cleaning and Preprocessing

The data cleaning and preprocessing were performed by utilizing the multivariate imputation by chained equations (MICE) [8]. MICE is a flexible, advanced method in handling the missing values [9]. This technique handles the missing values by imputing multiple values [10]. The primary assumption in MICE is that the imputation variables were from the observed values, not from the unobserved values [11]. The process of chained equations involves various steps as follows,

Step 1: For every missing value in the dataset, the mean imputation technique was performed. These mean imputations were considered as placeholders.

Step 2: The mean imputation placeholder for any one of the variables say "var" was set back to null.

Step 3: In Step 2, the values that were observed for the "var" variable, which was made null, were regressed with other variables present in the imputation model and might or might not have all the variables from the dataset. In simpler terms, in this regression model, "var" was considered to be the dependent variable, and the other variables were considered to be independent.

Step 4: The variable "var", which was made as null, was now replaced with the actual imputations or predictions from the regression model. In the later stages, when "var" was used as an independent variable for other variables in the regression model, the observed values, as well as the imputed values, were used.

Step 5: For every missing value in the dataset, steps 2–4 were repeated to impute values. This process was continued to one iteration or one cycle. At the end of the first cycle, all the missing values would have been handled and imputed with the predictions from the regression model that can be seen in the observed data.

Step 6: Steps 2–4 were repeated for several cycles; the iterations depend on one's requirement. The imputation values would be updated at the end of each cycle. The final imputation values were retained at the end, which formed an imputed dataset. The most common number of cycles used was ten.

2.3. Selection of Features

In the dataset we collected the Hamilton Depression Rating Scale based self-rating report, there were about 22 features, including the target variable with 3040 samples. In the dataset, we found that there were features that interacted with each other. The features that were dependent on each other directly affected the accuracy of the model. In order to reduce the interaction between the features and remove the irrelevant or redundant variables, we implemented a wrapper based feature selection algorithm, support vector machine-based recursive feature elimination (SVM RFE).

Using this approach, nine features were selected. Alternatively, it has to be witnessed that choosing extra features will not assure higher accuracy levels in classification scenarios. Table 2 demonstrates the selected features and their indices for UD classification.

Table 2. Selected features and their indices for unipolar depression (UD) classification.

Selected Features	Index
Gloomy	1
Exasperation	2
Apprehensive or Nervous	3
Response of the Individual to Preferred Happenings	4
Relation between an Individual's Mood and Time	5
Suicidal Contemplations	6
Happiness Quotient	7
Physical Indications	8
Paranoid Signs	9

2.4. Machine Learning Approaches Considered

2.4.1. Logistic Regression Approach

Logistic regression (LR) is a statistical approach, borrowed by machine learning in predictive analysis. This approach is mainly used when the dependent or the target variable is categorical. In logistic regression, the dependent variable must be dichotomous (i.e., Binary, Yes or No) [12]. The main assumptions made in logistic regression are that there are no outliers in the data, and that there is no multicollinearity between the predictor variables. Logistic regression is an extension of linear regression when the target variable seems to be categorical [13]. In this work, the penalized logistic regression uses a Glmnet in RStudio for predicting the unipolar depression. Table 3 presents the parameter settings for the logistic regression approach. Logistic regression is calculated through the probability of event occurrence with the help of the following the logistic function.

$$logit(p) = log\left(\frac{p(z=1)}{1-(p=1)}\right) = \alpha_0 + \alpha_1 y_{j2} + \cdots \alpha_x y_{jn} \quad (1)$$

where, p is the probability of event occurrence, for $j = 1, \ldots, n$.

Table 3. Logistic regression approach—parameter settings.

Parameters	Settings
fdev	0.00001
devmax	0.999
eps	0.000001
big	9.9×10^{35}
mnlam	5
pmin	0.00001
exmx	250
prec	0.0000000001
mxit	100
factory	FALSE

2.4.2. Multilayer Perceptron Approach

Usually, when there is an increase in the complexity of the problem, the complexity of the theoretical understanding of the problem also upsurges. In that case, traditional statistical approaches are sought after. Currently, the studies show that neural networks, multilayered perceptron (MLP) in particular, seem to be replacing traditional statistical approaches. Multilayered perceptron does not make any prior assumptions about the data distribution, unlike the statistical models, and it can model even a highly non-linear function to accuracy by training it with new unseen data [14]. Multilayered perceptron is a model with interconnected nodes or neurons, which are connected by connection links with weights and the output signals [14]. We implemented the MLP in RStudio by deploying the RSNNS package. Table 4 shows the parameter settings for the multilayer perceptron approach. The input and the output signals are connected with the help of these neurons and connection links. The net input is calculated by,

$$PA = \sum_{k=1}^{n} Wt_k I_k + b \qquad (2)$$

where,

PA—preactivation function or Net input;
Wt_k—the weight associated with the connection link;
I_k—inputs ($I_1, I_2, \ldots, I_n$);
B—bias.

Based on the error rate at every iteration, the weights of the neurons can be adjusted. The perceptron weight adjustment is calculated by,

$$\Delta Wt = L \times P \times I \qquad (3)$$

where

ΔWt—change in weights of the neurons;
L—learning rate;
P—predicted or desired output.

Table 4. Multilayer perceptron approach—parameter settings.

Parameters	Settings
Max. output unit error	0.2
Learning function	Rprop Backprop
Modification	None
Print covariance and error	No
Cache the unit activations	No
Prune new hidden unit	No
Min. covariance change	0.040
Candidate patience	25
Max. no. of covariance updates	200
Activation function	LogSym
Error change	0.010
Output patience	50
Max. no. of epochs	200

2.4.3. Random Forest Approach

In this work, we utilized the tuneRanger package in RStudio for the quick deployment of the random forests. Table 5 presents the hyperparameter settings of the random forest (RF) approach in this work. Random forest is an ensemble approach; it uses a recursive partitioning method to produce numerous trees, which are then aggregated to get the results [15–17]. Every tree in the random forest was constructed independently with the help of bootstraps of the training data. In random forest, each tree was constructed using two-thirds of the training data and the remaining one-third was used for testing the tree. The error rate of the forest depends on the strength of the individual trees and the correlation between each tree. The main advantage of using random forest is that there is no need to use any cross-validation methods, as the random forest approach itself has a built-in method called the out-of-bag errors to determine the test set errors in an unbiased manner. When compared with decision tree, random forest seems to have better accuracy and was less dependent on the training set and more tolerant to noise.

Table 5. Random forest approach—hyperparameter settings.

Hyperparameter	Settings
mtry	3
sample size	3040
replacement	TRUE
node size	1
number of trees	1000
splitting rule	random

2.4.4. SVM Classifier

Support vector machine (SVM) is a machine learning algorithm that can be modeled for both regression and classification problems but it is majorly used for classification of a binary class problem [18,19]. In this work, we utilized the e1071package in RStudio for the deployment of the SVM classifier. Table 6 illustrates the hyperparameter settings for the SVM classifier in this work.

Table 6. Support vector machine (SVM) classifier—hyperparameter settings.

Hyperparameter	Settings
Kernel	RBF
Problem type	Classification
$\log_2 C$	−5, 15, 2
$\log_2 \gamma$	3, −15, −2

When a labeled training data is given as an input, the model gives an optimal hyperplane as an output, which categorizes the samples. It is easy to maintain a linear hyperplane between two classes. However, when there is no precise classification between the vector points, manual separation is not possible [20]. For such situations, SVM has a strategy called the kernel. Kernel techniques convert a non-separable space to a separable space, which is called kernels used in non-linear separation models. Some of the commonly used kernel techniques are Gaussian kernel, Polynomial kernel, and many more [21,22].

2.5. Integrated MultiStage Support Vector Machine Classification Model

The proposed integrated multistage support vector machine classification model comprises of two segments: the first one being the design of the SVM classifier, and the second is the UD feature selecting and ranking.

2.5.1. Design of Integrated Multistage Support Vector Machine Classifier

In the proposed model, we were combining the individual SVM classifiers into a stronger and accurate model to improve the robustness and the generality of the SVM classifier. The deployment of this integration model depends on two factors: (i) the efficient way to build the member classifiers, aligning with the integration technique, and (ii) how to make all the member classifiers fuse to end up with a robust classifier. Therefore, to form a group of member classifiers, a random sampling method based on bagging is applied repeatedly [23]. For every individual SVM classification member classifier, around 75% from the original data sample is selected randomly for the training set, and the rest of the samples are used as a test or validation set to evaluate the performance of the model. A grid search utilizing the factor ranges C = {1, 2, 3, 4, 5, ..., 30} and γ = {0.1, 0.2, 03, 0.4, 0.5, ..., 5} is accomplished, for determining the optimimum values of C and γ. Later, without considering the optimal number of members in an integrated classifier, in this study, we implemented 10 different SVM classifiers with data from 10 random samplings and validated using the 10-fold cross-validation. This technique uses SVM RFE as the base learner. Thus, we constructed an SVM classifier with ten members in this study. In the SVM RFE, the features will be selected by the member classes based on their rankings in the support vector ratio-based ranking criteria. As the member classifiers are built with different random samples, they tend to have behaviors different from each other, and also, they will have different classification outcomes for the same data. As the final step, to integrate all the decisions by the individual classifiers to form ensemble SVM classifiers, the SVR-based weighted voting technique is implemented. The overall design of the proposed method is shown in Figure 1. Once the integrated classifier is built, it can be used for any classification tasks, as shown in Figure 1. In Figure 1, we can see that, once the member classifier was trained, the rest of the samples, which was 25% from the training set, was used as a temporary validation set for evaluating the performance of the model. In order to maintain the diversity of the classifiers and the simplicity of the integrated model, we used m = 10 member classifiers in this study.

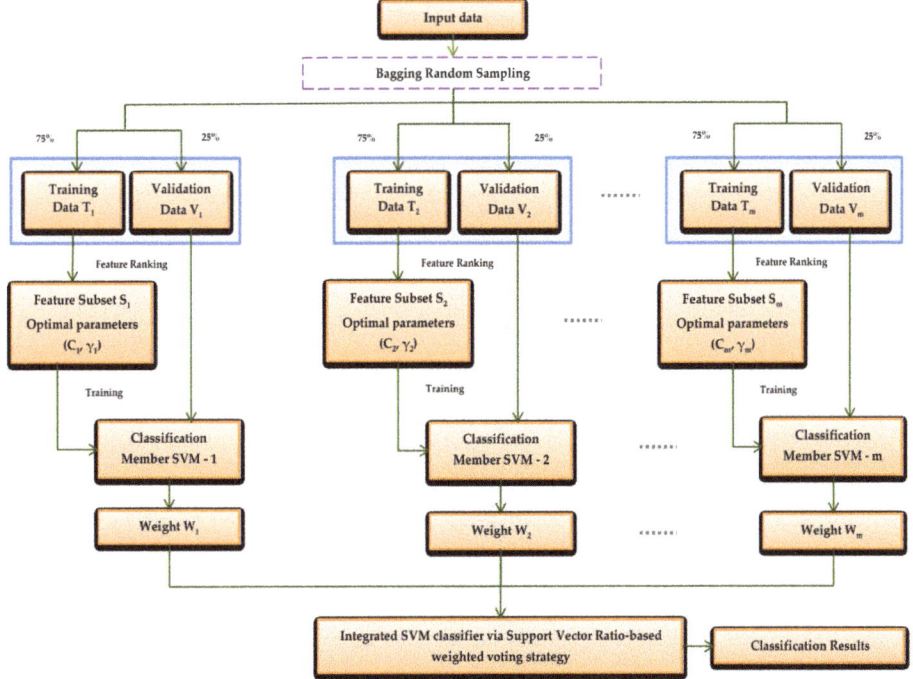

Figure 1. Proposed support vector ratio-based integrated multistage support vector machine classification model—architectural framework.

2.5.2. Ranking and Selection of Features

The essential step in implementing the integrated multistage SVM classification model is selecting the feature subset, which eventually enhances the performance of the member classifiers. Figure 2 represents the flow diagram of the support vector ratio-based support vector machine recursive feature ranking—the irrelevant variables and the variables that interact with each other usually slow down the overall performance of the model concerning computation and storage, during training or prediction. Sometimes, the irrelevant features can make drastic effects on the learning phase of the model. To improve the performance of the SVM classifier, we implemented an effective feature ranking and feature selection method to remove the irrelevant features from the 22 available features in the dataset, which can be seen in Table 1. The commonly used feature selection algorithms come under two categories, the filter methods and wrapper methods [24]. As simple as the filter methods look, they are not considered most of the time because they do not take into account the interaction between the features, which reduces the optimality of the feature subset, though they are computationally effective. On the other hand, wrapper methods evaluate the features jointly and iteratively, which results in effective capturing of interaction between the features [25].

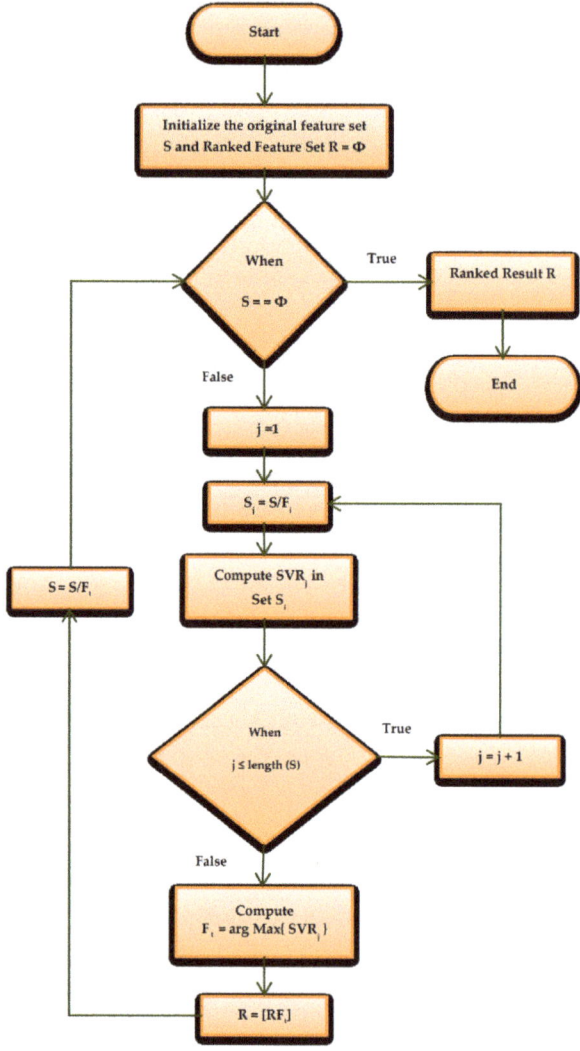

Figure 2. Support vector ratio-based support vector machine recursive feature ranking—flow diagram.

Due to the above-mentioned advantage, we used a wrapper method for feature selection in constructing the ensemble-based SVM classifier. Among all the existing wrapper-based feature selection methods, SVM RFE is considered as the most effective [26]. In this study, we implemented RFE as a part of the RBF SVM classification with the help of the support vector rate (SVR) metric for ranking all the 22 features shown in Table 1. The SVR is given by,

$$Support\ Vector\ Ratio = \frac{The\ number\ of\ support\ vectors}{the\ number\ of\ total\ training\ samples} \times 100\% \qquad (4)$$

The features are the support vectors in SVM; it is known that some of the support vectors help in minimizing the computational load of SVM and also improve its efficiency during the training. The ranking process is illustrated in Figure 2. The algorithm for the ranking process is as follows,

Step 1: Initialize the feature set, define S with all the 22 features from the dataset.

Step 2: Assume the ranked feature set as R.

Step 3: Eliminate one feature from the set and train the SVM model with 21 features. The classifier is initialized with empirical parameters, in order to calculate the SVR, which allows us to find out the contribution of the removed feature.

Step 4: Repeat step 3 for all the 22 features in the dataset. The feature with higher SVR after removal is placed in the ranked set R. It implies that the feature is not a support vector and is far away from the hyperplane.

3. Results and Discussion

The collected dataset had 3040 samples with 22 features, including the outcome variable. We preprocessed the dataset for removing the missing values using the MICE technique. Once the missing values were handled, we applied a wrapper-based feature selection technique, SVM RFE, to eliminate the less relevant and low performing features from the set. The algorithm removed the features in iteration and ranked them based on the SVR score. From the total 22 features, the algorithm selected nine features as the most important ones. These nine features did not depend on each other and also there was no interaction among them. The dataset was then divided into training and testing sets, where the model was trained with a training set and evaluated with the testing set. The composition was 75-25 for the training and testing dataset, respectively, with 10-fold cross-validation. In the numerical implementation, we implemented the proposed method with 10-member SVM classifiers and then integrated them with the help of the SVR-based weighted voting technique, as explained in the previous section.

To evaluate the proposed model, we have used the confusion matrix [27]. The confusion matrix was used to validate the performance of the model, which was tested with test data and whose true values were known. The technical terms involved in the confusion matrix are the true positive TP (model prediction—positive, actual outcome—positive), true negative TN (model prediction—negative, actual outcome—negative), false positive FP (model prediction—positive, actual outcome—negative), and false negative FN (model predicted—negative, actual outcome—positive). From the confusion matrix, different performance metrics can be calculated, such as accuracy, specificity, precision, sensitivity, and FMeasure [27]. The respective formulas for the metrics can be seen in Table 7. The results are tabulated in Table 8; the proposed model was compared with other methods such as logistic regression (LR), multilayer perceptron (MLP), random forest (RF), and bagging SVM (majority voting). Figure 3 represents the confusion matrix for LR, MLP, RF, and bagging SVM (majority voting), the proposed model, respectively. A comparison of evaluation metrics of the proposed model with other approaches is illustrated in Figure 4. It can be witnessed that the proposed model surpasses all other compared approaches in terms of performance and superior accuracy. The receiver operating characteristic (ROC) curve for the LR, MLP, RF, bagging SVM (majority voting), and the proposed model is depicted in Figure 5, Figure 6, Figure 7, Figure 8, and Figure 9, respectively. Stability comparison between the integrated SVM classifier and the member classifiers is shown in Figure 10.

Figure 3. Confusion matrix: (**a**) Logistic regression (LR), (**b**) multilayer perceptron (MLP), (**c**) Random Forest (RF), (**d**) bagging SVM (majority voting), and the (**e**) proposed model.

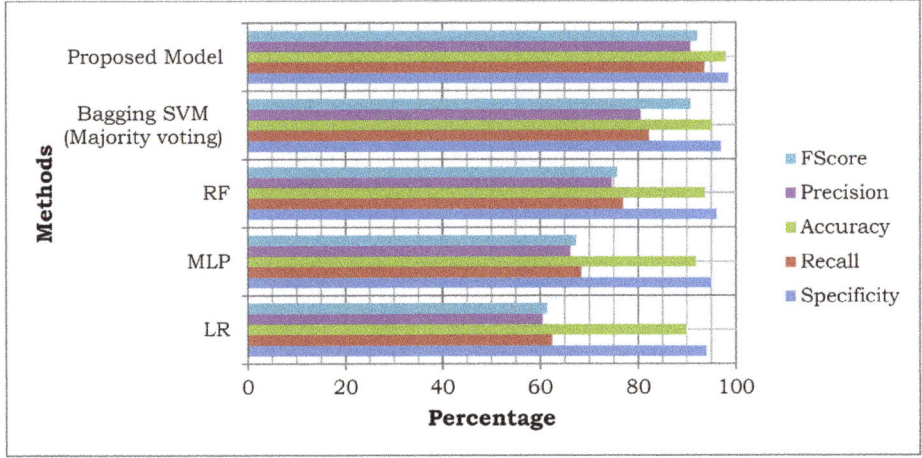

Figure 4. Comparison of evaluation metrics of the proposed model with other approaches.

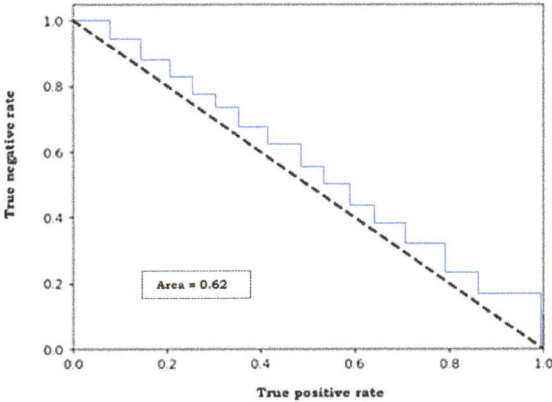

Figure 5. Receiver operating characteristic (ROC) curve for logistic regression.

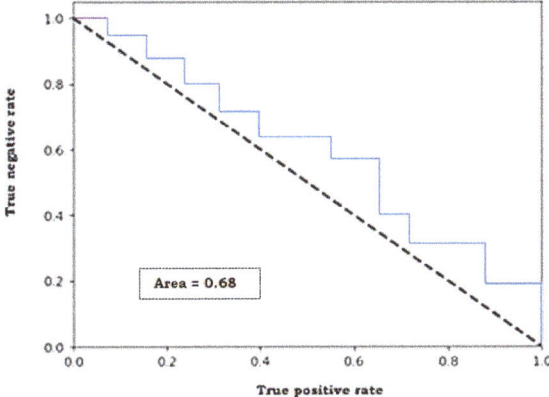

Figure 6. Receiver operating characteristic curve for multilayer perceptron.

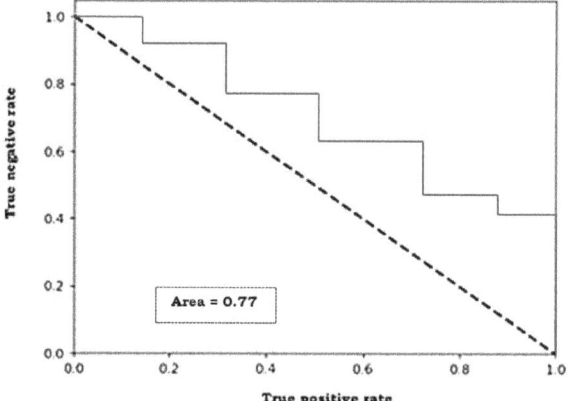

Figure 7. Receiver operating characteristic curve for random forest.

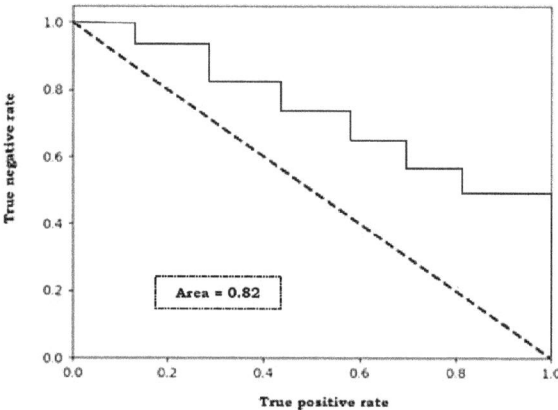

Figure 8. Receiver operating characteristic curve for bagging SVM (majority voting).

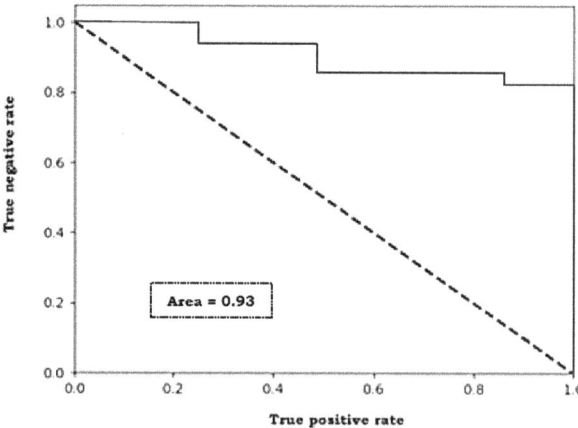

Figure 9. Receiver operating characteristic curve for the proposed model.

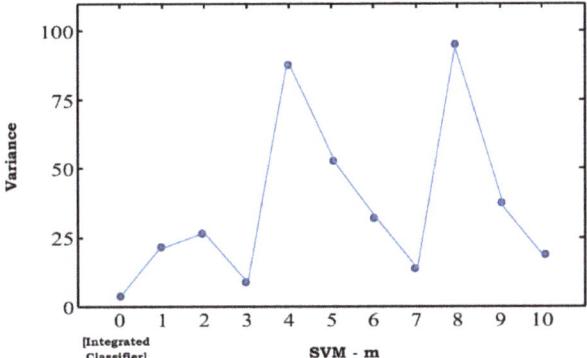

Figure 10. Stability comparison between the integrated SVM classifier and the member classifiers.

Table 7. Confusion matrix related metrics.

Confusion Matrix	Formula
Specificity	TN/TN + FP
Recall	TP/TP + FN
Accuracy	TN + TP/TP + FP + TN + FN
Precision	TP/TP + FP
FScore	2 × (Precision × Recall)/(Recall + Precision)

Table 8. Comparison of evaluation metrics of the proposed model with other approaches.

Evaluation Metric	LR (%)	MLP (%)	RF (%)	Bagging SVM (Majority Voting)	Proposed Model (%)
Specificity	94.12	95.20	96.23	97.13	98.64
Recall	62.5	68.47	77.08	82.29	93.75
Accuracy	90.13	91.97	93.81	95.26	98.02
Precision	60.6	66.31	74.74	80.61	90.91
FScore	61.53	67.37	75.89	81.44	92.31

4. Conclusions

In this study, we proposed an effective ensemble-based classification model, integrated multistage support vector machine classification model for enhancing the predicting accuracy of UD. As the first step, we cleaned the data with MICE for handling the missing values. Then we implemented SVM RFE, a wrapper-based feature selection technique in order to reduce the feature dimension and select the necessary features, which are not dependent on each other, which eventually improves the accuracy of the model. The initial number of features in the original dataset was 22 on which the feature selection technique was applied. We used a 75-25 composition for training and testing datasets. The results proved that the proposed methodology had improved the prediction accuracy of UD when compared with other classification models. It could be observed that the proposed model was better than all other compared approaches in terms of performance and also offered greater accuracy.

Author Contributions: Conceptualization, K.S., N.M. and D.R.V.; Methodology, K.S. and N.M.; Software, K.S.; Validation, C.-Y.C. and S.S.-A.; Formal Analysis, K.S.; Investigation, K.S.; Resources, C.-Y.C. and S.S.-A.; Data Curation, N.M. and D.R.V.; Writing—Original Draft Preparation, K.S.; Writing—Review & Editing, K.S., N.M., C.-Y.C., and S.S.-A; Visualization, K.S.; Supervision, C.-Y.C.; Project Administration, C.-Y.C. and S.S.-A.; Funding Acquisition, C.-Y.C. and S.S.-A. All authors have read and agreed to the published version of the manuscript.

Funding: This work was financially supported by the "Intelligent Recognition Industry Service Center" from The Featured Areas Research Center Program within the framework of the Higher Education Sprout Project by the Ministry of Education (MOE) in Taiwan and The APC was funded by Ministry of Education (MOE) in Taiwan.

This work was partly supported by Ministry of Science and Technology (MOST), Taiwan (106-2923-E-038-001-MY2, 107-2923-E-038-001 -MY2, 106-2221-E-038-005, 108-2221-E-038-013); Taipei Medical University (106-3805-004-111, 106-3805-018-110, 108-3805-009-110); Wanfang hospital (106TMU-WFH-01-4).

Conflicts of Interest: The authors declare no conflict of interest.

References

1. Patalay, P.; Gage, S.H. Changes in millennial adolescent mental health and health-related behaviours over 10 years: A population cohort comparison study. *Int. J. Epidemiol.* **2019**, *48*, 1650–1664. [CrossRef] [PubMed]
2. McElroy, E.; Fearon, P.; Belsky, J.; Fonagy, P.; Patalay, P. Networks of Depression and Anxiety Symptoms Across Development. *J. Am. Acad. Child Adolesc. Psychiatry* **2018**, *57*, 964–973. [CrossRef] [PubMed]
3. Fried, E.I.; Nesse, R.M.; Zivin, K.; Guille, C.; Sen, S. Depression is more than the sum score of its parts: Individual DSM symptoms have different risk factors. *Psychol. Med.* **2013**, *44*, 2067–2076. [CrossRef]
4. Fried, E.I.; Nesse, R.M. Depression is not a consistent syndrome: An investigation of unique symptom patterns in the STAR*D study. *J. Affect. Disord.* **2014**, *172*, 96–102. [CrossRef]
5. Klakk, H.; Kristensen, P.L.; Andersen, L.B.; Froberg, K.; Møller, N.C.; Grøntved, A. Symptoms of depression in young adulthood is associated with unfavorable clinical- and behavioral cardiovascular disease risk factors. *Prev. Med. Rep.* **2018**, *11*, 209–215. [CrossRef] [PubMed]
6. Papakostas, G.I.; Petersen, T.; Mahal, Y.; Mischoulon, D.; Nierenberg, A.A.; Fava, M. Quality of life assessments in major depressive disorder: A review of the literature. *Gen. Hosp. Psychiatry* **2004**, *26*, 13–17. [CrossRef] [PubMed]
7. Hamilton, M. A Rating Scale For Depression. *J. Neurol. Neurosurg. Psychiatry* **1960**, *23*, 56–62. [CrossRef] [PubMed]
8. Azur, M.; Stuart, E.; Frangakis, C.; Leaf, P.J. Multiple imputation by chained equations: What is it and how does it work? *Int. J. Methods Psychiatr. Res.* **2011**, *20*, 40–49. [CrossRef]
9. Raghunathan, T.W.; Lepkowksi, J.M.; Van Hoewyk, J.; Solenbeger, P. A multivariate technique for multiply imputing missing values using a sequence of regression models. *Surv. Methodol.* **2001**, *27*, 85–95.
10. Van Buuren, S. Multiple imputation of discrete and continuous data by fully conditional specification. *Stat. Methods Med. Res.* **2007**, *16*, 219–242. [CrossRef]
11. Schafer, J.L.; Graham, J.W. Missing data: Our view of the state of the art. *Psychol. Methods* **2002**, *7*, 147–177. [CrossRef] [PubMed]
12. Peduzzi, P.; Concato, J.; Kemper, E.; Holford, T.R.; Feinstein, A.R. A simulation study of the number of events per variable in logistic regression analysis. *J. Clin. Epidemiol.* **1996**, *49*, 1373–1379. [CrossRef]
13. Press, S.J.; Wilson, S. Choosing between logistic regression and discriminant analysis. *J. Am. Stat. Assoc.* **1978**, *73*, 699–705. [CrossRef]
14. Gardner, M.; Dorling, S. Artificial neural networks (the multilayer perceptron)—A review of applications in the atmospheric sciences. *Atmos. Environ.* **1998**, *32*, 2627–2636. [CrossRef]
15. Breiman, L. Random Forests. *Mach. Learn.* **2011**, *45*, 5–32. [CrossRef]
16. Kandaswamy, K.K.; Chou, K.-C.; Martinetz, T.; Möller, S.; Suganthan, P.N.; Sridharan, S.; Pugalenthi, G. AFP-Pred: A random forest approach for predicting antifreeze proteins from sequence-derived properties. *J. Theor. Boil.* **2011**, *270*, 56–62. [CrossRef]
17. Zhou, Q.; Zhou, H.; Zhou, Q.; Yang, F.; Luo, L. Structure damage detection based on random forest recursive feature elimination. *Mech. Syst. Signal Process.* **2014**, *46*, 82–90. [CrossRef]
18. Hamed, T.; Dara, R.; Kremer, S.C. An Accurate, Fast Embedded Feature Selection for SVMs. In Proceedings of the 2014 13th International Conference on Machine Learning and Applications, Detroit, MI, USA, 3–5 December 2014; pp. 135–140.
19. Cortes, C.; Vapnik, V. Support-Vector Networks. *Mach. Learn.* **1995**, *20*, 273–297. [CrossRef]
20. Jarrett, K.; Kavukcuoglu, K.; Ranzato, M.A.; LeCun, Y. What is the best multi-stage architecture for object recognition? In Proceedings of the 2009 IEEE 12th International Conference on Computer Vision, Kyoto, Japan, September 27–October 4 2009; pp. 2146–2153.
21. Chang, C.-Y.; Srinivasan, K.; Chen, M.-C.; Chen, S.-J. SVM-Enabled Intelligent Genetic Algorithmic Model for Realizing Efficient Universal Feature Selection in Breast Cyst Image Acquired via Ultrasound Sensing Systems. *Sensors* **2020**, *20*, 432. [CrossRef]

22. Guyon, I.; Weston, J.; Barnhill, S.; Vapnik, V. Gene Selection for Cancer Classification using Support Vector Machines. *Mach. Learn.* **2002**, *46*, 389–422. [CrossRef]
23. Breiman, L. Bagging Predictors. *Mach. Learn.* **1996**, *24*, 123–140. [CrossRef]
24. Tuia, D.; Pacifici, F.; Kanevski, M.; Emery, W.J. Classification of Very High Spatial Resolution Imagery Using Mathematical Morphology and Support Vector Machines. *IEEE Trans. Geosci. Remote. Sens.* **2009**, *47*, 3866–3879. [CrossRef]
25. Ataş, M.; Yardimci, Y.; Temizel, A. A new approach to aflatoxin detection in chili pepper by machine vision. *Comput. Electron. Agric.* **2012**, *87*, 129–141. [CrossRef]
26. Wang, R.; Li, R.; Lei, Y.; Zhu, Q. Tuning to optimize SVM approach for assisting ovarian cancer diagnosis with photoacoustic imaging. *Bio-Med. Mater. Eng.* **2015**, *26*, S975–S981. [CrossRef] [PubMed]
27. Sokolova, M.; Lapalme, G. A systematic analysis of performance measures for classification tasks. *Inf. Process. Manag.* **2009**, *45*, 427–437. [CrossRef]

© 2020 by the authors. Licensee MDPI, Basel, Switzerland. This article is an open access article distributed under the terms and conditions of the Creative Commons Attribution (CC BY) license (http://creativecommons.org/licenses/by/4.0/).

MDPI
St. Alban-Anlage 66
4052 Basel
Switzerland
Tel. +41 61 683 77 34
Fax +41 61 302 89 18
www.mdpi.com

Electronics Editorial Office
E-mail: electronics@mdpi.com
www.mdpi.com/journal/electronics

www.ingramcontent.com/pod-product-compliance
Lightning Source LLC
LaVergne TN
LVHW070410100526
838202LV00014B/1427